STALIN'S ROMEO SPY

STALIN'S ROMEO SPY

THE REMARKABLE RISE AND FALL OF THE KGB'S MOST DARING OPERATIVE

THE TRUE LIFE OF DMITRI BYSTROLYOTOV

EMIL DRAITSER

Foreword by Gary Kern

DUCKWORTH OVERLOOK

First published in the UK in 2011 by
Duckworth Overlook
90-93 Cowcross Street, London EC1M 6BF
Tel: 020 7490 7300
Fax: 020 7490 0080
info@duckworth-publishers.co.uk
www.ducknet.co.uk

Published in the USA in 2010 by
Northwestern University Press.

Parts of this book previously appeared, in somewhat
diff erent form, in the *Journal of Intelligence History* 6:2
(Winter 2006–7) and Gulag Studies 1 (2008).

A catalogue record for this book is available
from the British Library

ISBN 978 0 7156 4085 2

Printed in Great Britain by the
MPG Books Group

To Jola,
whose patience and moral support
endured through years of this author's obsession
with a stranger's life

Do you want to write your testimony in ink or in your own blood? The choice is yours.

—KGB INTERROGATOR TO
DMITRI BYSTROLYOTOV

Truth is stranger than fiction, but it is because fiction is obliged to stick to possibilities; truth isn't.

—MARK TWAIN

He who controls the present, controls the past. He who controls the past, controls the future.

—GEORGE ORWELL

Contents

Gallery follows page 166.

FOREWORD

Gary Kern

Writers don't always choose their subjects; sometimes their subjects choose them. An idea comes to mind and takes hold of the imagination; the writer walks around talking to others and answering questions but thinking about the idea. He begins to imagine the way it could go, how it might develop. He might consider that he doesn't have time for it, and so he writes it down in his notebook in order to put it off. But one way or another it comes back. Did he choose it, or did it choose him? He begins to wonder. Ultimately he decides to go with it. He understands: it has grabbed him.

At other times it's not an idea, but an experience or a person. The writer finds that some other person is interesting, that his story is worth telling, and just like the idea, so the image of this person begins to work on him. When he learns that this person has died and that his story has not been told or, even worse, has been told wrongly, then from out of nowhere he feels a responsibility. He can tell the true story, he can save the other's soul, not in the religious sense, but in the sense of preserving something of his spirit, something of his suffering. And so he embarks on a research project to recover all the facts and figures about his subject, to piece together his broken and scattered biography, to look into his motives, and to try to understand his mind. Years go by. What is he doing? Working like a slave for his subject, a dead man, trying to bring him back to life, to consign his deeds to posterity. It's the same as with the idea: his hero has chosen him.

In his prologue to this fascinating book, Emil Draitser describes the time and place it happened: Moscow, September 11, 1973. He didn't realize its significance at the time but didn't forget the incident either. The man was curious, impressive, singular even, a former intelligence officer who had spent long years in the Gulag, but Draitser had pressing matters to attend to, such as getting out of the Soviet Union, establishing himself in a new country, making his career as a writer in a new language, surviving, and paying the bills. All the while he was developing the abilities that would enable him to take on the monumental task, in 2003, of recovering the biography of the man he had met, Dmitri Bystrolyotov. And it was good that he was delayed thirty years, because it was necessary for the Soviet Union to crumble, for archives to open, and for previously unpublished materials to come out, including the voluminous memoirs of Bystrolyotov himself. So many new materials were published in the 1990s, not only on Bystrolyotov, but on Soviet espionage in general, that only a native Russian like Draitser could have assimilated them in the six years he spent on the project. For a non-native it could easily have taken ten years or more.

But Draitser didn't stop with what was available. As he relates in the prologue, he flew to Moscow, Prague, and London and collected a body of publications, manuscripts, and documents such as no one else possesses, save the Russian State Security—the KGB. Also, he sought out and interviewed a relative of Bystrolyotov who himself had already collected and preserved rare materials and who kindly furnished him copies. By the end of his project, he had become—like every biographer—the one man in the world who could tell the complete story of his hero.

His quest perhaps would have seemed a private mania had the name Bystrolyotov not meanwhile emerged from obscurity and revealed its legendary status. Bystrolyotov was one of the "Great Illegals," the first generation of Soviet spies who operated underground throughout Europe with the flair and success that earned them such a striking title. Even among them, he was outstanding, both for his feats of espionage in Europe, Africa, and America, and for his personal traits. He was a "Romeo spy," handsome and dashing, with slick dark hair, a moustache, and a Greek or Hungarian name, who seduced secretaries and other women with access to government secrets; he recruited agents under a "false flag," encouraging them to think that they were helping Japan or Germany when actually they were helping the Soviet Union. He destroyed people's careers and lives wherever he went. His manipulation of a London code clerk and his wife was particularly sordid, and the end was messy. Yet, like some others of his clan, he was a sensitive and troubled man, with artistic and literary talents, humane aspirations, and selfless dedication to the Communist ideal.

He was, in short, a monster—a cheat, seducer, and destroyer of other people's lives for the glory of the Soviet state and the good of all mankind. The biographer of such a figure is confronted by more than one task. First, of course, he must establish the basic facts in the life and career of a spy, a man whose person and profession are clandestine and deceptive by nature. Even in his own writings, the spy may spin the story, not only minimizing his unheroic deeds or failing to recall entire episodes, but also embellishing his exploits. His idea of the truth is not the same as that of his biographer. Further, Bystrolyotov lived and died in the Soviet period, so everything he wrote and hoped to get published had to keep the censor in mind. Draitser, sifting through all these problems and gleaning the basic facts, has also to account for his hero's actions—for the fact that he became a monster. And here he is obliged to engage in psychoanalysis, finding a cold mother, who gave birth to an illegitimate son only as a form of feminist protest and then left the boy to suffer years of agonizing loneliness; the wounded boy becomes a Romeo spy but has a pathological relationship with his wife, a beautiful woman who conceals her sexual proclivities. Draitser has also to explain the historical and social context in which the spy operated: the Stalin period, the purges, the omnipresence of the Secret Police, the Leader, the Doctrine. He knows the period well, having spent his childhood and teenage years under Stalin. Naturally, he has to accomplish all these tasks not one after the other, but simultaneously.

Bystrolyotov the Great Illegal did not enjoy a long career and retire with a comfortable pension. His reward for selfless sacrifice was the same that many other intelligence men received in the years of the Stalin purges: arrest on false charges, torture at the hands of the KGB, and a twenty-year sentence in the Gulag. Unlike most others, he survived his term and recorded his life inside the camps. Thus his story continues beyond the espionage phase and joins the literature of the Gulag.

This in turn leads to a spiritual transformation, a redemption of sorts that produces the stately man who sought out the young Draitser. Bystrolyotov knew that this young journalist was a Jew, which automatically meant that he would know about persecution. The older Draitser, the biographer, therefore proceeds with great sensitivity to follow the changes in his subject, to show what must have gone through his mind: his persistence in believing in the doctrine and the cause, even while being wronged by the state; his recognition of his own guilt before others; his questioning of the results of his work and the work of others like him; his reassessment of the great cause; and his ultimate realization that the Soviet system was no better than Nazism. Describing this process, Draitser conveys Bystrolyotov's indomitable spirit, which carries him through periods of great mental stress to write memoirs and other literary works, to paint landscapes, and to assume a serene transcendence. It is a slow transformation, from monster to hero.

Deep in his work, Draitser was astonished to discover that new versions of Bystrolyotov's life and career were being produced in Russia. In articles, books, and three documentary films, Bystrolyotov was presented as heroic and patriotic; basic facts were cut from his biography, personal relationships were changed, and cloak-and-dagger scenes were invented. The mustachioed Romeo spy had become the latest icon in the State Security's ongoing series of public relations programs. Looked at another way, the beaten and imprisoned "traitor" had become, in Draitser's words, a "poster boy" for the FSB. And so a new task arose before the biographer: clear away the propaganda.

Without invention, without embellishment, the life of Dmitri Bystrolyotov, as Draitser tells it, is one of the most sensational in the pantheon of desperate lives lived by Stalin's illegals. By turns routine, thrilling, conventional, extraordinary, disquieting, disgusting, pathetic, and inspiring, it stirs emotions of both revulsion and respect, even as it adds a new and instructive chapter to a bleak and terrifying period of history. In this case, the hero chose his biographer well: no one but Draitser could have written this book.

ACKNOWLEDGMENTS

It is customary for an author to begin his acknowledgments with the phrase "This book would never have been written if not for the help of many people," which is true of any book project. It is even more so when it comes to one as intricate and complex as the biography of a spy, whose job description calls for aptitude in duplicity and the ability to leave as few tracks as possible. But regarding my colleague—scholar, writer, and publisher Dr. Gary Kern—the word "help" is grossly inadequate to describe his contribution to this project. To begin with, if not for a fateful conversation with him, described in the prologue, the bug of historical research into the life of a man whom I had met three decades earlier would have had very little chance to bite me. Before that day, my scholarly interests lay in areas that had nothing to do with the history of Soviet espionage and Gulag studies. In addition, Gary's own scholarship offered the highest standard of meticulous research and superb writing, a hard act to follow. His many useful suggestions on how to go about my work significantly shortened the time spent on this project—for this alone I express my deep gratitude. Gary's spirit of generosity is, by far, among the highest and rarest I have ever encountered.

I would also like to thank Sergei Sergeyevich Milashov, Bystrolyotov's stepgrandson, who gave me unlimited access to my subject's invaluable personal archive. I greatly benefited from his noble intention to finally make public the true life of the man whom he had always admired so much and who strongly influenced him as he was growing up.

I am also indebted to my friend and colleague Dr. Vadim Birstein, whose vast knowledge of minute details of both Soviet secret police operations and the Soviet labor camp system elucidated for me many circumstances of Bystrolyotov's life, to which my subject only alluded in his writing.

I also highly appreciate the help of Czech scholar Dr. Anastasia Koprivova. Besides expertly navigating me through the catalogue maze of the Czech State Archives as I searched for material related to Bystrolyotov and the Soviet Trade Mission in Prague, she also brought to my attention her own research on the lives of the Russian immigrant community in Czechoslovakia of the 1920s and translated a few archival documents from Czech into Russian.

I am also indebted to Loic Damilaville, for helping me to track down the whereabouts of documents related to Bystrolyotov's French agent, and Dr. Peter Huber, who generously shared with me some of his findings in the French National Archives pertaining to Bystrolyotov's assistants in many of his operations, Joseph Leppin and Erica Weinstein. I also appreciate the help of my electronic correspondents, Edward Kershaw of Great Britain, who provided me with information on the background of Lucy and Ernest Oldham, and Nick Crittenden, who filled me in on additional Italian sources related to Bystrolyotov's activities.

I would like to thank Norman Clarius of the Hunter College Interloan Department, Paul Johnson, manager of the Image Library of the British National Archives, and alas, nameless, the employees of the State Archive of the Russian Federation (GARF) and Centre des Archives Diplomatiques de Nantes. I also appreciate the help Isabelle de Rezende of the University of Michigan gave me in fine-tuning some cultural notions in my African chapter.

I would also like to express my appreciation for the benefit I received from the questions and encouragement of many participants in the annual meeting of the European Studies Conference at the University of Nebraska at Omaha, especially Dr. Raymond W. Leonard of Central Missouri State University, and the conference organizer, my friend and colleague Dr. Tatyana Novikova. To get to the bottom of such a complex personality as Dmitri Bystrolyotov was not an easy task. To that extent, I solicited help from some of my professional friends, including psychiatrist K. P. S. ("Bob") Kamath, M.D., and psychoanalyst Harvey Mindess, Ph.D. However, any mistakes I have made in trying to decipher the motives for Bystrolyotov's behavior are mine only.

My friend of many years, Dr. Anthony Saidy, one of the most enthusiastic supporters of this project for the duration of my work, not only provided feedback but also advised me regarding the medical aspects of Bystrolyotov's life, whether it concerned assessment of his medical training, his medical practice in the camps, or his own health-related problems. Here again, I am solely responsible for any mistakes concerning these aspects of the book.

As my work progressed, my friends Selim Karady, Martin Weiss, and Dr. Jolanta Kunicka read several chapters of the manuscript and gave valuable suggestions. I also owe a great deal to my former dissertation adviser and friend, Professor Michael Henry Heim of UCLA, for his constant moral support during what has been the most challenging undertaking of my writing career. I also enjoyed the moral support of my friend and colleague Dr. Susan Weissman, whose own work inspired me along the way.

My friend writer Bill Bly read a few chapters of my manuscript-in-progress and helped to fine-tune my command of idiomatic English. In this respect, I greatly benefited from Therese Malhame's thorough and expert work on the whole manuscript before it went into production. I deeply appreciate the extra efforts of Anne Gendler, managing editor of Northwestern University Press, not only for her diligent reading of my work but also for bringing to my attention those episodes of Bystrolyotov's messy life that needed additional elucidation for the reader.

And last (but by no means least), I express deep appreciation to my brother Vladimir, whose expert knowledge of computer hardware and software applications saved me during sporadic panic attacks when the data mined with tremendous expenditure of time and energy suddenly seemed to disappear before my eyes.

Reproduction of artwork and photographs from Bystrolyotov's personal archive, as well as permission to quote from his and Milashov's writings are courtesy of Sergei Milashov (the copyright holder on all of Dmitri Bystrolyotov's writings and custodian of his estate).

Notes on Sources, Transliterations, and Translation

Although, to this day, only part of Bystrolyotov's file in the KGB archives is officially declassified, most of its content is known from the writings of former KGB officers who had access to his file—Vassili Mitrokhin, Evgeni Primakov, and Oleg Tsarev. (I, too, was able to secure a copy of a substantial portion of this file.) I also consulted documents concerning Bystrolyotov's life and activities held in the Russian, British, French, Czech, and American archives.

Additional sources come from notes that I took during my meeting with Bystrolyotov in 1973 and transcripts of a series of in-depth audio taped interviews with Bystrolyotov's stepgrandson, Sergei Milashov, who maintained a close relationship with him for nearly twenty years, the last years of Bystrolyotov's life. I was given unrestricted access to Bystrolyotov's personal archive—his employment documents, letters to Soviet authorities, and personal correspondence.

I made judicial use of information contained in Bystrolyotov's writings. In that respect, the reader should be aware that my subject's thoughts and feelings at crucial moments in his life, including occasional dialogues, are reconstructed from the galleys of his unpublished memoirs in three volumes titled "Pir bessmertnykh" ("The Feast of the Immortals"). (This should not be confused with the excerpts from this work published in Moscow in one volume under the same name by Granitsa, 1993.) At the time of this writing, two copies of "Pir bessmertnykh" are available to the public, one at the U.S. Library of Congress and the other at the National Library of Russia (formerly "Saltykov-Shchedrin Library") in St. Petersburg. The details of some of Bystrolyotov's operations are culled from the typescript pages of his unpublished screenplay titled "Shchedrye serdtsem" ("Generous Hearts"), a copy of which is also held at the National Library of Russia in St. Petersburg; his two published novels, *Para*

Bellum (*Prepare for War*) and *V staroi Afrike* (*In Old Africa*); and other sources.

I transliterated Russian words according to the Library of Congress system for the Cyrillic alphabet. However, for some personal names and geographical locations, I retain their traditional rendering in British and American literature. All translations of excerpts from Bystrolyotov's writings, as well as of other Russian and French texts, are my own.

Abbreviations and Terms

Abwehr The military intelligence service of Nazi Germany

Center The headquarters for the Soviet security apparatus located on Lubyanka Square in Moscow; also called the Lubyanka

Cheka A vernacular version of VChK, an acronym for the All-Russia's Extraordinary Commission for Combating Counterrevolution and Sabotage (1917–22)

Comintern Communist International (1919–43)

FSB Federal Security Service of the Russian Federation (1991–present), the KGB successor

Gestapo Secret State Police of Nazi Germany

Gulag Abbreviation for Chief Directorate of Labor Camps; also, the system of Soviet labor camps

INO Foreign Intelligence Department of Soviet Security Services

KGB Soviet Committee for State Security (1954–91)

MGB Soviet Ministry of State Security (1946–53)

MI5 British Security Service responsible for security and counterintelligence on British territory, a counterpart to the American FBI

NKVD People's Commissariat for Internal Affairs (1922–23, 1934–43), the OGPU successor

OGPU Joint State Political Directorate (1923–34), the Cheka successor

Politburo   Political Bureau, the inner ruling body of the Central Committee of the Communist Party of the Soviet Union

Pravda   *The Truth,* the central newspaper of the Communist Party of the USSR

rezident   Soviet spymaster residing in a foreign country; a legal *rezident* operated under his own name and usually had a cover position with a Soviet institution abroad; an illegal *rezident* operated under an assumed identity

rezindentura   The spy station of the *rezident;* also, the area of his operation

Romeo spy   A spy who uses his sex appeal to recruit an agent through seduction

RSFSR   Russian Socialist Federative Soviet Republic, became part of the USSR on Dec. 30, 1922 (renamed Russian Soviet Federative Socialist Republic in 1937)

"source"   A person who is recruited to supply a spy with secret information

SS   *Schutzstaffel,* elite Nazi police force

SVR   Russian Foreign Intelligence Service, part of FSB (1991–present)

USSR   Union of Soviet Socialist Republics, the Soviet Union (1922–91)

Wehrmacht   The armed forces of Nazi Germany

STALIN'S ROMEO SPY

| Tea with a Master Spy

The most daring Russian spy ever to operate in the West . . . He stole British secrets for the Soviets years before Kim Philby . . . A doctor of medicine and doctor of law who learned from American gangsters how to shoot through his coat pocket . . . A "sexspionage" ace, an aristocrat by upbringing, an illegitimate offspring of Tolstoy's line . . . The shining star of Soviet intelligence who eclipsed Richard Sorge and Rudolf Abel . . . A talented painter, novelist, screenwriter, and memoirist . . . A polyglot with twenty languages at his disposal, including Flemish, Turkish, Chinese, Japanese, and some African dialects . . . A victim of Stalin's purges who served sixteen years in Siberian camps and lived to take revenge on his torturers.

I would read these sensational words about my protagonist in Russian papers three decades after I met him. But on that day, September 11, 1973, on my way to his tiny Moscow apartment on Vernadsky Prospect, I knew nothing about him. Not even his name . . .

A few days before, my father-in-law, a tailor working in a shop for the Ministry of Defense, called me with some news. One of his customers, while trying on his suit and talking about this and that, had learned about me and my profession. He took an interest and asked my father-in-law to give me his phone number.

I wasn't surprised. It often happened that people hoping to win a fight with a Soviet bureaucrat would seek the help of the press. Under my pen name, Emil Abramov, I had published articles and stories in *Izvestia* (*The News*), *Literaturnaya gazeta* (*Literary Gazette*), *Komsomol'skaya Pravda* (*Komsomol Truth*), *Trud* (*Labor*), and other newspapers and journals, as well as in the satirical journal *Krokodil* (*Crocodile*), so all sorts of people contacted me from time to time.

I called. In a light baritone, my father-in-law's customer asked me to come and see him at home. He gave me no reason. This, too, was not unusual in Moscow. I went to the meeting wondering what a man who had his suits made at the Ministry of Defense tailor's shop could possibly want from me. After all, you couldn't criticize that ministry in print.

A tall, broad-shouldered man in his early seventies, a bit stooped, with blue eyes, the well-groomed gray beard of an academician, and boyish dimples, greeted me at the door. I entered, and while helping me off with my raincoat he introduced himself: "Bystrolyotov. Dmitri Aleksandrovich."

Bystrolyotov . . . What an unusual name! The son of a fast flier—that's what it meant in Russian. I looked at the old man again. Despite his age and the somewhat uncertain motion of his limbs, he was sprightly and had sparkling eyes. He might have been a fast-flying man in his younger years.

Meanwhile, trying not to offend his guest by showing mistrust, my host smiled pleasantly and asked, "I assume you have a press card on you?"

I showed him my membership card from the Union of Soviet Journalists. "Will this do?"

Still smiling, he nevertheless carefully examined it before nodding. "Good enough. Would you care for some tea?"

He sat me down at the table in his living room, which was no more than fifteen by fifteen feet. There was enough space for a cupboard of polished wood, a few bookshelves, and a table.

He resembled one of Moscow's many cultured retirees who frequent libraries and concert halls. I couldn't figure out anything more about him. Yet something about him was mysterious. Perhaps his dignified and pleasant demeanor struck me as unusual for an ordinary Soviet citizen.

We began drinking tea Moscow-style—the tea leaves brewed for a while in a small porcelain teapot and poured into glasses in tin holders, with small dishes of strawberry jam alongside. My host's hands shook slightly when he raised his glass, but there were no other signs of aging. His mind was clear and agile. He told me the reason for his invitation. He was looking for someone to assist him in writing his life story.

The rest of the evening I spent listening to him.[1]

In a slightly rasping voice he recounted that back in 1919, during the Russian civil war when he was a sailor, he had been approached and recruited by the Cheka, the first incarnation of the Soviet Secret Police and a predecessor of the current FSB. At first he was sent to Europe as a sleeper with nothing more to do than familiarize himself with the territory. Then, in the mid-1920s, he was activated to do intelligence work. Like all beginners, he made mistakes but got better with time. He operated in many European countries: England, France, Germany, Spain, Switzerland, Czechoslovakia, and others.

His specialty was the recruitment of agents who had access to diplomatic codes and ciphers, and his modus operandi involved women. "I was young, good looking, knew several European languages. And I knew how to treat a lady," he added with a smile. Once he recruited a French diplomat, once a German countess, another time a Gestapo officer—all women.

"Once I received an order that came straight from Stalin: find a short man with a red nose in Paris. A short man with a red nose . . . That's all I knew about him. Nevertheless, I found him. By sheer logic."

Later Bystrolyotov successfully carried out a similar task involving the British Foreign Office. At a time when Hitler was just beginning to build the Nazi war machine, my host stole many German military secrets for the Soviet state. In the course of his work, he crossed European borders hundreds of times. A British lord, a Hungarian count, a Greek merchant—these were a few of his many disguises. His assignments took him not only to European countries but also to Brazil and the United States.

On one of his missions, he told me, he twice crossed the "gray hell" of the Sahara and the jungles of the French and Belgian Congos. In 1935, he had been sent to Africa to see whether French Foreign Minister Louis Barthou, who sympathized with the Soviet Union, could deliver on his promise, in the event of a German invasion, to bring over several hundred thousand African mercenaries.

"It was dark in the forest," he recalled, shaking his head. "Only here and there rays of sunlight would break through. Suddenly a vine would drop on your head, and you'd think it was a snake," he laughed. "Little crocodiles the length of your arm in the grass. Leeches dropping on you from the trees and sucking into your flesh."

Then he told me how his career ended. His successes in foreign intelligence didn't save him from trouble. At the height of Stalin's purges, when he returned to Moscow, he was arrested and accused of working for the enemy. In Soviet practice, the way to prove an accusation was to extract a confession, and the way to extract a confession, especially for crimes one hadn't committed, was to apply torture. "Well, young man," Bystrolyotov said, "take it from me. They make everybody talk. Some talk early, others later. But everybody eventually talks."

He was sentenced to twenty-five years: twenty years of hard labor in Siberia and five years of exile inside Russia. Thus he entered the Gulag, the vast complex of Soviet prisons and labor camps, and he served nearly all of his term—sixteen years. His arrest and conviction ruined his family and his health.

By the time of our meeting, in the fall of 1973, I knew quite a bit about the Soviet camps. Aleksandr Solzhenitsyn's *One Day in the Life of Ivan Denisovich* had been published in Moscow, and Radio Liberty had broadcast chapters of his *Gulag Archipelago* by shortwave into the Soviet Union. A few other stories by former camp prisoners had appeared in the state press and also in private editions, called *samizdat* (self-publishing). But all that had happened back in the liberal 1960s, and now in the reactionary 1970s such literature was forbidden. All the more exciting, therefore, was the fact that for the first time in my life I was sitting across the table from someone who had lived through the horrors of the Gulag.

Meanwhile, sipping his tea, my host turned his gaze to the present. Despite the tremendous injustice done to him by the KGB, he had managed to patch up the relationship to some degree. His small apartment was arranged for him after the agency intervened with the Moscow housing authorities on his behalf, and from time to time they invited him to come to the KGB school to pass on his experience to the cadets. He pointed to an honorary plaque on the wall, given to him on the occasion of the agency's anniversary.

But there was disappointment, even resentment, in his voice when he mentioned all these ego-gratifying little things. "Why," he asked several times in the course of the evening, "why did they give Manevich the award of Hero of the Soviet Union? He didn't achieve too much. The only good thing he ever did was not give away our agents and network when they caught him in Spain and tortured him. That's all."[2]

Bystrolyotov was also upset about the way the profession of espionage was trivialized in the Soviet media. A month before our meeting, a TV miniseries titled *Semnadtsat' mgnovenii vesny* (*Seventeen Moments of Spring*) had begun running. It presented a fictional version of the Soviet intelligence effort behind the German lines during World War II. It was an instant hit, and its star, a handsome Russian actor named Vyacheslav Tikhonov, became a household name. He played the part of a Soviet spy disguised as a Wehrmacht officer.

My host had nothing but ridicule for the show. To him it was full of clichés and far-fetched assumptions about intelligence work. And it glossed over the harsh realities.

"In real life," he said, "there's no need to penetrate the upper echelons of the enemy structure to gather simple information. Butlers, secretaries, housekeepers know as much about certain things as their employers." He took Heinrich Himmler, head of the SS and the Gestapo, as an example. "To confirm a rumor that Himmler was planning to go to Zurich for some negotiations," he said, "it would be enough to get to know his driver. You treat him to a fine cigarette. Ask him how things are going. People love to complain. Most likely the driver will tell you with a sigh that in a day or two he'll have to get up early, at the crack of dawn, to take his boss somewhere. Where? To a remote Berlin airport. And we know that from that airdrome they usually fly to Switzerland."

Bystrolyotov went on disparaging the TV serial. Referring to the romance between two Soviet intelligence officers working undercover deep in German territory, he sneered: "What nonsense! The radio operator gets pregnant and delivers a healthy baby! Such things couldn't take place in real life. If an intelligence worker got pregnant, she had no option. They ordered her to get an abortion right away. End of discussion."

Then he talked about his futile attempts to publish his memoirs, which were self-censored and watered-down, as I learned years later. He began to make fun of an editor of *Oktiabr'* (*October*), a well-known literary quarterly, and I caught a glimpse of his superb acting skills and sense of humor.

"He says to me, 'Here you write: *I drew my pistol*... You can't write that. A Soviet intelligence officer acts only in a humane way ... Then you write: *I pulled out a roll of bills* . . . Our intelligence officer doesn't bribe anyone . . . *I introduced the SS officer to a girl*? How horrible! Our intelligence officer would never do that. He operates by Marxist-Leninist persuasion alone."

When our meeting ended, I assumed that we would meet again. I went home and wrote down in my notebook as much as I could of our conversation. Considering the times—the Brezhnev regime was still going strong—I didn't dare transcribe the most sensitive parts of Bystrolyotov's story. In fact, I wrote his name down in pencil, in case I'd have to erase it . . .

I never heard from Bystrolyotov again. In October of the following year, I left Russia.

Since then, at various times over the years, I have recalled that unusual meeting. Bystrolyotov became fixed in my mind as the most remarkable man I had ever met. I thought of my notes and planned to do something, but my literary interests took me elsewhere. I wrote short stories and books on Russian folklore; I taught Russian literature and prepared a textbook of modern Russian poetry. Bystrolyotov's story began to fade from my memory.

Then, in the summer of 2002, on a trip to California, I visited an old friend, Gary Kern. At the time he was finishing a book on Walter Krivitsky, another pre–World War II Soviet spy, and as he told me about it, I thought I would mention my meeting with a Russian intelligence officer. "What's his name?" Kern asked. "Bystrolyotov," I replied. "What!" He nearly jumped out of his seat. Bystrolyotov, he told me, was legendary, one of the "Great Illegals." We spent the rest of the evening talking about him.

Returning back home to New York, I went through my files and pulled out a brown tattered notebook with my account of the spy I had met at the end of my former Soviet life. After rereading the notes, I decided to track down the facts in his case. Bystrolyotov, I discovered, was long dead. He had died of a heart attack in 1975, less than two years after our meeting.

Fifteen years later, during the period of Gorbachev's *glasnost'* (openness), his name was made public in Russia. First an article in *Pravda* paid tribute to his exploits, then other periodicals told various parts of his story.[3]

In the West, some of his most successful operations were known, but the person behind them was shrouded in mystery. Thus a 1986 book by William Corson and Robert Crowley, *The New KGB: Engine of Soviet Power*, attributes one of the most spectacular achievements in Soviet espionage—handling and controlling a British Foreign Office clerk in charge of codes and ciphers—to a Soviet agent whose code name, like Bystrolyotov's, was HANS, but whose background was quite different.[4]

As in Russia, the name Bystrolyotov did not surface in Western accounts of KGB operations until the 1990s, and then only in books coauthored by ex-KGB officers who had access to his file. None of these accounts, however, whether published inside or outside Russia, tells the full story of his life. As I read them, I became increasingly intrigued. For me the man was not just a historical figure, but a real person I had met back in my Soviet days. I dug deeper, trying to find out more. I read his memoirs, *Puteshestvie na krai nochi* (*Journey to the Edge of Night*), published in Russian in 1996.

Actually, this book, devoted to his years in the Gulag, represented only a small portion of his memoirs. It bore a preface by S. S. Milashov, who informed readers that Bystrolyotov had entrusted his papers to him. Here, I thought, was a lead.[5]

But how do you go about finding a person in Moscow with only his surname and first and middle initials? Well, I still had some old friends in the city, so I placed an overseas call to one named Boris and asked him for help. He explained that there was still no residential telephone book in Moscow, just as in the old days. And, just as before, if you didn't know a person's date of birth, you couldn't find him through the city's Information Bureau. Such was the Soviet system. Boris also doubted that the publisher of Bystrolyotov's book would be willing to reveal the whereabouts of the man who wrote the preface.

Turning to the Internet, I went to the search engine Yandex, the Russian equivalent of Google, and one by one rounded up twenty-two entries for the name "Milashov." Then I eliminated them one by one until I finally came to Sergei Sergeyevich Milashov, Bystrolyotov's grandson, or rather stepgrandson. Milashov was related to Bystrolyotov's second wife, whom he met and married in the camps.

Contacting him by phone, I told him about my connection to Bystrolyotov and asked for assistance in my research. By now, I felt committed to it, without really knowing why. Milashov confirmed that he was the guardian of his stepgrandfather's literary and personal archives and offered me his full cooperation. I could come to Moscow, he said, and get acquainted with Bystrolyotov's papers firsthand. He even offered to put me up in his apartment, although I declined. What a stroke of luck! How could I refuse?

It was hot and humid in Moscow in July 2003. Still jet-lagged, I called Milashov, and he came straight over to my hotel. A tall and agile man, an engineer by training, he complimented my spoken Russian, preserved in emigration over so many years. We struck up an immediate friendship and then went to his apartment.

There he sat me down and placed in front of me a pile of Bystrolyotov's papers. The first thing I discovered was a worn-out pocket-size address book. With a thrill, I turned to the first page and saw an entry under the letter *A:* "Journalist Emil Abramov (Draitser)." My old Moscow telephone numbers, both for work and for home, followed. My past Russian life, left behind so many years ago, came back to me in a flash. My curious meeting with the address book owner arose even more vividly before me.

Thereafter, I took the train every day to Solntsevo, the Moscow suburb where Milashov lived, to work my way through the materials. As a source of information, they proved to be difficult reading. Bystrolyotov had written his memoirs in the hope of seeing them published. To make his work acceptable to the censors, he resorted to a practice common among Soviet writers: self-censorship. I knew this practice only too well.

Talking with Milashov, I learned that he knew Bystrolyotov for the last twenty years of his life, from the time of his release from the camps in 1954 to the day of his death in 1975. Milashov credited him with exerting a decisive influence on his upbringing and world outlook. He recalled many conversations with his relative and mentor over the years, and these recollections provided me with many insights into Bystrolyotov's inner life.

Milashov also introduced me to Anatoly Razumov, a library scholar who published a study of the manuscripts Bystrolyotov deposited for safekeeping in 1968 at the Saltykov-Shchedrin State Public Library (now the Russian State Library) in Leningrad. The study contains excerpts from interviews Razumov conducted with some of Bystrolyotov's former fellow prisoners, the most famous being Lev Gumilyov, son of two of Russia's great poets, Nikolai Gumilyov and Anna Akhmatova. Her long poem about her son's imprisonment, "Requiem," is considered one of the glories of twentieth-century Russian literature. Razumov directed me to the "Prague Archive," a collection of Russian émigré documents at the Moscow State Archives. As Bystrolyotov had spent several years in Prague, perhaps it would contain something related to him. Soon I was holding in my hands a violet folder from the Russian Law Faculty of Prague containing the student file of Dmitri Aleksandrovich Bystrolyotov. It took me back in time to the youth of the old man I had met. I was getting to know him pretty well.

Back in New York, I studied my booty. While it answered many questions about Bystrolyotov's life, it prompted new ones, especially about the beginning of his tumultuous career. He began as a "legal" intelligence worker—that is, as an employee of the Soviet Trade Mission in Prague bearing legitimate credentials. The work he actually did, of course, was not legal. It was there that he began his recruitment of women as Soviet agents. His turbulent married life also started there. I decided that I would have to wait for a break in my teaching schedule and then pursue my subject in Prague.

In October 2005, I flew to the city, walked the same streets that Bystrolyotov had walked some eighty years before, and sat in a reading hall of Charles University where he had read his textbooks to prepare for his law classes. On the city outskirts, I visited a dormitory where he had roomed. I stopped by a café in the fashionable Steiner Hotel (now Grand Hotel Bohemia) that had served as a meeting place for him and his spymaster. I walked the paths of Rieger Gardens, a city park where he pursued his femme fatale, Isolde Cameron. Then, at the Czech State Archives, with the help of Anastasia Koprivova, a Czech scholar working on a book about Russian immigrants in Czechoslovakia in the 1920s, I uncovered many items related to Bystrolyotov's life in Prague: college documents, police reports, and newspaper articles.[6]

I also traveled to Istanbul and Berlin, Paris and Zurich, following in my protagonist's footsteps. I looked into the French Foreign Ministry Archives in Nantes and the British archives in London.

Meanwhile, political developments in Russia have made me increasingly aware that telling Bystrolyotov's story was no longer my private and self-imposed mission but an urgent order of the day. While I was doing my research, an ex-KGB officer became the country's president, and many features of Russian life began making a comeback from the time of Bystrolyotov's spy career, the country of Stalin. Under President Vladimir Putin, state control of the economy, media, politics, and society had tightened, and Russia has begun sliding back to its Stalinist past. And, as in Stalin's era, behind a modern democratic facade, Russian nationalism and anti-Westernism have made a full comeback. The most troublesome of these developments are the revision of history and attempts to whitewash the KGB's bloody role in it.[7]

It has become clear to me that the time has come to set the record straight about the life of a man who bore witness to Soviet history and testified about it both in ink and blood.

PART I

THE MAKING OF A SPY

TO: St. Petersburg

RUSSIA
(RSFSR)

1914   1904

Odessa
Jan 1921
Yevpatoria   Feb 1921   Akchora   Anapa

TO: Czechoslovakia

Dec 1920   June 1921   Novorossiisk

Sevastopol   June 1917

June 1919

Black Sea   June 1921

Dec 1921–
Jan 1922   Nov 1920   Aug 1919   June 1921

Batumi

July 1921

Constantinople
(Istanbul)

TURKEY

Bystrolyotov's Travels (1904–1921)

ONE | Sowing the Wind

It so happened that [young] Bystrolyotov saw his parents rarely.

—BYSTROLYOTOV'S OFFICIAL BIOGRAPHY

I [was] not a pretty little boy, but a little boy down on his luck.

—BYSTROLYOTOV, RECALLING HIS CHILDHOOD

"Where would you like to work for us?" a man with a Mephistophelian beard asked.

"I don't know . . ." Dmitri began, but, seeing that this didn't make a good impression, he straightened his shoulders and added, "I want to be where it's most dangerous!"

He got what he asked for.

The conversation took place at the end of April 1925, during the time of Dmitri's visit to Moscow as the Czechoslovakian delegate at the First Congress of Proletarian Students. His address to the Congress was published in *Pravda*. His interlocutor was Artur Khristyanovich Artuzov, head of the Counterintelligence Department of the OGPU. Although Dmitri had been involved in intelligence work at the Soviet Trade Mission in Prague for more than a year, he considered this meeting the true beginning of his intelligence career.[1]

The interview had been arranged by Soviet secret service operatives at the Trade Mission in Prague, the only institution representing Soviet interests in Czechoslovakia at that time. Before coming to Moscow, Dmitri had known next to nothing about the inner workings of the

Soviet secret service or its intricate structure and organization. He knew only that its headquarters were located on Lubyanka Square in Moscow and that the second secretary of the Prague Trade Mission was an OGPU operative. Before leaving Prague for Moscow to take part in the First Congress of Proletarian Students, he had been forewarned at the Mission that some very important people would talk to him.

The meeting took place in a mansion that had been owned by Prince Dolgorukov until the Bolshevik takeover in October 1917 dispossessed him. In his memoirs, Dmitri gives a minute description of this pivotal meeting in his life:

> They took me to a small room where a middle-aged man, tired and sleepy, lay fully clothed on a sofa and next to him sat a man, a bit younger, astride a chair, dark haired, slit eyed. They would tell me later that the man on the sofa was Artuzov and the seated one was Mikhail Gorb. They offered me the only other chair. I didn't know who those men were or what they wanted from me. But I felt that they were big bosses and that my whole future life depended on this conversation . . . Comrade Gorb's face reflected ill will. He glanced at me and gloomily looked away. But Artuzov examined me and my suit with apparent interest and a benevolent smile: "Well, let's get acquainted. Tell me everything about yourself. Don't drag it out, but don't race through it either. I'd like to know about your background."[2]

Dmitri outlined that he was brought up in an aristocratic family (although he did his own mending from age thirteen), learned foreign languages (French, English, and German), later worked as a sailor on the Black Sea, and when the Russian civil war broke out, with the outflow of refugees, fled to Turkey, eventually winding up in Czechoslovakia.

This was all true. But there was so much more in his background that he didn't—and couldn't—tell, because he would only realize its full meaning many years later. Not until the end of his life did he fully comprehend the profound effect of his formative years on the makeup of his personality and the choices he had made in life. To his credit, he knew that his lifelong troubles had begun early, and he mercilessly examined all the circumstances of that period in his voluminous memoirs, sparing no one, including himself.

Bystrolyotov's most recent official biography makes light of the fact that while he was growing up he saw his parents rarely. To begin with, this statement is misleading. He "rarely" saw only one of his parents—his mother. And he never *ever* saw his father, a situation that deeply wounded him and to which he returns again and again in his memoirs.[3]

Born January 3, 1901, in the Crimean village of Akchora (now Gvardeiskoe), the young Bystrolyotov was deprived of a father not because his mother had had an illicit love affair or because she had wanted a child but decided not to marry, but rather because she wanted to make a social statement. She gave birth to an illegitimate child only to challenge conventions. "They didn't consider the baby and his future," Dmitri bitterly remarks.[4]

"They" is a reference to his mother, Klavdiya Bystrolyotova, daughter of a provincial clergyman, and her best friend, Anastasia Krandievskaya, daughter of a liberal publisher. Both young women were affected by the ideas of women's liberation then gaining ground in Russia. In 1899, under the influence of a newly organized Society for the Protection of Women's Health, they called themselves suffragettes, began dressing in men's pants and hats, and occupied themselves with Swedish gymnastics. Such ostentatious behavior, however, was insufficient for Klavdiya, who burned with the desire "to challenge respectable society in a bolder, sharper, more demonstrative way . . . to spite the whole Victorian world." The method she ultimately chose was to have an illegitimate child.

In Bystrolyotov's view, such an outlandish idea could only arise from emotional instability. He attributed his mother's disorder to two factors. The first was Pavlovian reflexes or, as he puts it, "dominance of psychomotor stimulation of the cortex over the buffering effect of inhibiting centers." The second was bad heredity, which he traced back to her grandmother Nina and which he thought had been passed on to him as well. The daughter of an Ossetian prince, Nina had married one Ivan Bystrov, a Cossack officer who later changed his name to Bystrolyotov ("fast flyer") after the nickname friends had given him for his daring horsemanship. Nina was nicknamed Osa ("wasp"), doubtless due to her erratic and irritable character. Shortly after giving birth to a son, she became violent and had to be physically restrained. She died young.

Nina's son Dmitri also grew up troubled. His early life injuries prevented him from becoming a Cossack officer like his father, so, on a whim, he chose the priesthood. But his inborn anxiety and restlessness eventually ruined his career. Made pastor of a rich parish with a new church in town, he announced one day to his superior, the archbishop of the North Caucasus, that no one could prove the existence of God. The archbishop exiled him to Solovetsky Monastery in the Far North, where he could reflect and repent.

One of Grandfather Dmitri's children, Klavdiya was like her grandmother and father. Restless, headstrong, and erratic, she gave everybody a lot of trouble. Dmitri believed that he, her only child, carried the burden of this heredity all his life.

Upon graduation from the gymnasium (high school), Klavdiya was thrown out of her parents' house for some scandalous behavior. At age nineteen, she began her study in the humanities at a private institution called the Higher Women's Courses in St. Petersburg. But soon, due to her inborn restlessness, she switched to another institution, then another. Finally she abandoned studies altogether and turned to social activism. She served as a liaison between political exiles in the North and their families back home.

As she became better known in circles of the liberal intelligentsia, Klavdiya met Anastasia Krandievskaya, her future lifelong friend. Anastasia suggested that they join a group of young men and women from all over Russia who were heading to the Crimea to do volunteer work at Akchora, the estate of a rich landowner, Sergei Skirmunt. Influenced by Tolstoyan ideas, he was building a model village for the local peasants, complete with cottages, hospital, and school. It was there, while working on the estate, that Klavdiya and Anastasia conceived the idea of challenging polite society by openly having an illegitimate child. Born in 1866, considered a spinster already, Klavdiya nonetheless volunteered to be the mother, while Anastasia took on the task of finding a like-minded male. Relying on his mother's stories, Dmitri identifies him as Count Alexander Nikolaevich Tolstoy, at the time a minor official of the Ministry of State Properties and a descendant of the ancient aristocratic family. The Tolstoy family, in addition to Russian diplomats, scholars, and artists, produced three famous writers: Leo Tolstoy, Alexei Konstantinovich Tolstoy, and Alexei Nikolaevich Tolstoy.

In his memoirs, Bystrolyotov goes to great lengths to describe all the circumstances that made him take the surname Bystrolyotov and not Tolstoy. He painstakingly recounts all the legal obstacles that had to be overcome to make his birth legitimate. First, the laws of the Russian Empire did not allow his father to adopt him at the time of his birth. Then, two years later, when a new law made it possible, other obstacles appeared. Adoption meant granting him the right not only to carry his father's name and aristocratic title but also to inherit a share of his estate. This circumstance, Bystrolyotov believed, brought about a Tolstoy family feud. Those who did not have a share in the estate approved of the boy's adoption; those who did opposed it. When this conflict was finally resolved in Dmitri's favor, a new hurdle arose. Because his father belonged to the *titled* branch of the Tolstoy clan, his adoption required a decree of the tsar himself.

Only someone in a position to advise the tsar could have resolved the matter. Whatever were the circumstances, the question of his father's identity remains uncertain—in some of his writings he calls him Alexei Alexandrovich, while in his official Soviet documents, he always put a dash where his father's name should have been entered.[5] But it is important that Dmitri himself believed that he *was* a Tolstoy. Since he was embarrassed by the circumstances of his birth, it made him feel better about himself, although he never put an official claim on it.[6]

Little Dmitri spent the first few years of his life with his mother at Akchora, the place of his birth, at Skirmunt's estate. But at the age of three, he was separated from his mother, an event that left a lifelong scar on his psyche. It's not quite clear how it happened. According to his memoirs, it was because his father's family, the Tolstoys, paid the bills and insisted on bringing up one of their own as an aristocrat. Apparently trusting his mother's story, he reconstructs a conversation between her and his putative aunt (his father's sister), Varvara Nikolaevna Kokorina, which goes as follows:

When Klavdiya Bystrolyotova got pregnant, Kokorina invited her for a talk and laid down the following conditions: If Klavdiya gave birth to a healthy baby, she would get child support and the baby would be raised in an aristocratic family that she, Kokorina, would choose. The child's continued support would depend on his merits. A mediocre youth would be returned to his mother, but an able offspring would be officially adopted and given all the privileges of a highborn aristocrat. Under these conditions, Bystrolyotov writes, when he was three, Kokorina arrived in the Crimea and took him to St. Petersburg to live with a foster family, the de Courvals.

Bystrolyotov's recollections of his aristocratic upbringing sound quite authentic. When Artuzov talked to him, he had no doubt that he had been raised according to the highest cultural standards. However, some elements of his story are dubious. Most notably, his mother's meeting with Kokorina and the latter's subsequent visit to the Crimea could not have taken place for the simple reason that Kokorina died a few years before Dmitri's birth.[7]

Although the details remain unclear, the fact remains that the baby boy Dmitri was brought to St. Petersburg and placed under the foster protection of a widow, Elizaveta Robertovna de Courval, who had two small daughters of her own. There was no man in the household. After losing his fortune in a game of cards, Elizaveta's husband, an officer of the guards, had shot himself. Thus whoever made the arrangement for little Dmitri evidently tried to do two things at once: to help the impoverished widow and to give a fatherless boy an aristocratic upbringing. (Such a practice was not unheard of in Russian high society. For example, the famous Russian poet Vasily Zhukovsky [1783–1852], born of a captive Turkish girl and given to his father as a birthday present, was raised in the family of an impoverished nobleman.)

Despite leading a materially secure life as a child, Dmitri was anything but happy. In his early teens he began receiving books from his father on high cultural subjects: ancient Greece and Rome, medieval art and the Renaissance, the history of Russian art, the history of French art. But he never received from him even a short note, much less a letter. And he never heard that his father wanted to see him. The two never met. In his memoirs, Bystrolyotov assigns no importance to this situation: "My father is nothing for me; he's a myth. I don't have any feelings for him." Yet it's hard to imagine that a sensitive and intelligent boy would not feel hurt by his father's distance and disaffection.

His mother also was lost to sight, so he was doubly abandoned. In her case he could not hide his feelings. "I lived far from her and was out of her way," he bitterly remarks in his memoirs. With her son off her hands, she threw herself back into her prime interest—fighting for social causes. No sooner was he gone than the war with Japan broke out in 1904, and she volunteered to serve as a nurse at the front in Manchuria. When World War I broke out in 1914, she volunteered again. "She couldn't miss such a rare opportunity," Bystrolyotov remarks sarcastically. Since she hadn't bothered to adopt him officially, and since his father did not adopt him, it seems he was documented as an orphan.

This life of "privilege and prison," like that of "a bird in a gilded cage," as he characterizes it, was interrupted only by rare visits from his mother, who would take him on short trips to the Caucasus. For him these occasions were as comforting as "the whistle of a whip." His radically minded mother resented her son's life of luxury and used every opportunity to give him painful (in the direct meaning of the word) lessons in social justice, lessons he would remember for the rest of his life.

One such occasion occurred when he was about five. His mother had taken him out for a picnic, and curious peasant children came up to look. Seeing the barefoot boys and girls walk awkwardly across a field of wheat stubble, he laughed unwittingly. Klavdiya exploded. "Don't you ever dare laugh at them!" she shouted. "You live on their money." And she ordered him to remove his shoes and socks, grabbed him by the hand, and forced him to walk over the prickly stubble. "Here you go, you little master. Now you know how poor people walk on earth!"

Again, when he was about twelve, he and his mother were vacationing in the Caucasus, and they saw an old Cossack woman, who was trying to cross, fall into a turbulent mountain river. Immediately Klavdiya ordered Dmitri to jump in and save the woman at the risk of his life. When he hesitated, she scolded him, threatened to slap his face, and called him a coward. "Your Cossack ancestors would be ashamed of you!"

Prodded by his mother, he jumped into the water. After much struggling, finally he managed to grab the old woman by the hand; his mother pulled them both out. When the old woman bowed to young Dmitri and thanked him for saving her life, Klavdiya told her, "Get up, little mother, don't degrade yourself. It was his duty to do it." Dmitri forever remembered the way his mother "threw these words over her shoulder" and went to change her clothes with "a very haughty look," all the while laughing at him. His heroism had been turned to humiliation.

In 1914, with Russia entering World War I, inflation made life difficult for the de Courval family in St. Petersburg. Elizaveta Robertovna moved the household to Anapa, a small resort town on the Black Sea, where life was easier and the family still owned a villa. Young Dmitri, now thirteen, was enrolled as a cadet in the Sevastopol Naval Academy. This was a prestigious institution that prepared young men of the aristocracy for careers as naval officers. In 1916, as part of the Second Fleet Crew of the Russian Black Sea Navy, he took part in landing operations at Rize, Turkey.

After the February 1917 revolution, by decree of the newly formed Council of Sailors and Soldiers Deputies, all privileged schools in the country were closed. Dmitri could continue his maritime training in a nautical school (*morekhodnoe uchilishche*), which prepared skippers and navigators for trade expeditions. Schools of this kind functioned in Odessa, Kherson, and Anapa. He chose the latter because his mother lived there and taught at the local gymnasium. In September 1917, he began attending classes at both the gymnasium and the Anapa Nautical School.[8]

In the summers, deeply involved in social causes, his mother ran a local sanatorium for wounded officers. As always, duty bound to save the sick and unfortunate, she gave her son one more lesson in egalitarianism. One day, while cooking, she saw through the kitchen window how one of her officer patients, discharged from the sanatorium, slapped around an old coachman who mishandled his suitcase. She ran to this officer and threatened him with a ladle. "Don't you dare!" she shouted. "Don't you dare! No one here gets by without common decency."

All these episodes of his mother's behavior made deep impressions on Dmitri.

During his ten years with the de Courvals, young Dmitri received an education proper to Russian aristocratic society of the time. Instructors taught him European languages (French, German, and English) and the arts (dancing, fencing, and drawing). His aptitude for the latter skill was evident quite early in life.[9] A German instructor took charge of his physical education and ensured that the boy developed and controlled every muscle of his body. A Swiss teacher specialized in strengthening his will, a skill that would prove crucial during his future life as an intelligence officer—and as a Gulag inmate. In fact, quite early, Dmitri became fascinated with the very concept of will and what could be accomplished using its power, which may explain his future interest in Nietzsche. Among the books that arrived by mail from his father was Professor Chelpanov's *Introduction to Philosophy.* In the book, Chelpanov sides with those philosophers who assert complete freedom and autonomy of the will. One day, fascinated by this concept, young Dmitri decided to test the strength of his own will. He gathered a matchbox full of all kinds of insects and, shutting his eyes, swallowed them. For about a month, he felt nauseated at the very memory of the experiment. But he was quite proud of proving his resolve to himself.[10]

As he was growing up, his theoretical fascinations with willpower grew in sophistication. While reading Dostoevsky, young Dmitri was especially drawn to conversations between Ivan Karamazov and the Devil in *The Brothers Karamazov.* In his memoirs, Dmitri does not specify what aspects of these conversations he found so captivating in his boyhood, but certain elements of them seem obvious. In the novel, Ivan Karamazov tells his brother Alyosha a story about a certain Richard. Born out of wedlock, Richard was abandoned by his parents, who got rid of him by giving him away to some Swiss shepherds, who mistreated and exploited him. When the boy grew up, he became a vagabond and a drunkard. He ended up robbing and murdering an old man and was guillotined.[11]

Dmitri could easily identify with Richard. Like him, he was born out of wedlock, abandoned by both of his parents at a young age (he was actually half Richard's age when he experienced that trauma), and given away to live in a foster family of total strangers.[12] Physically, Dmitri closely resembled Raskolnikov, the hero of another Dostoevsky novel, *Crime and Punishment;* he was also "exceptionally handsome, above the average in height, slim, well built, with beautiful . . . eyes and dark brown hair." Preoccupied with the idea of the predominant role of the will in human behavior, young Dmitri thought of Raskolnikov as a weakling destined for failure, since, as he writes, "by asking himself whether he was a Napoléon or a louse, he proved that he *was* a louse."

One summer night in 1917, to further test his willpower, Dmitri, now age sixteen, staged another "scientific experiment." This time, the test of his will took a much more dramatic form than swallowing some insects. Saying to himself, "I'll show those fools, Raskolnikov and Dostoevsky, what a true man is," he decided to repeat Raskolnikov's act—that is, to commit a robbery. It looks as if Dmitri wished even to surpass Raskolnikov, because he set out to rob not a stranger but one of his own kin. He chose none other than his own aunt, Anna Bystrolyotova, his mother's sister. Whereas Raskolnikov's target was a "worthless old woman," despised by everybody as a loan shark, Dmitri was fond of his aunt; he called her *milaia Nyusenka* (my dear little Nyusya).

Anna worked as a cashier at a local officers' club. Late in the evening, Dmitri followed her. Dressed in a sailor's striped T-shirt, he put on his face a mask cut out of the black oilcloth cover of his gymnasium notebook and slipped a Finnish knife into his pocket. As his aunt approached her home, he quickly ran up to his auntie, grabbed her from behind, and hissed, "Money or death!" To his surprise, instead of being easy prey, his aunt put up a fight, and as people approached, the young robber ran into the bushes.

Bent on proving his resolve, Dmitri made another attempt at robbery. This time, he did it pursuing social justice, which he absorbed with his mother's milk, now Bolshevist-style—by "robbing the robber." His new target was a member of the officers' club where his aunt worked, a rich merchant.

Dmitri again failed miserably: the victim managed to get away, and his companion, an army lieutenant, shot at Dmitri at close range several times. To Dmitri's luck, he missed, but the events of that night overwhelmed him. In the coming days, he felt like vomiting every time he recalled his near-death experience. He decided to cut short his budding career as a robber.

Decades later, laughing at himself when describing these episodes to his second wife, Dmitri would attribute these youthful escapades to his inherited impulsiveness and restlessness. But it is easy to see that they were much more than that. Most likely and quite unconsciously, they were expressions of his bottled-up, suppressed hostility, resulting from his parents' abandonment of him as a young child. The first time, he chose to attack his abusive and neglectful mother's mirror image—her sister. And in his second attack, any rich male stranger could serve as a stand-in for his father, whom he never saw. After all, the very fact that he indulged in robbery twice in a row reveals the lack of a sense of conscience in his mental makeup, a known result of the absence of a consistent value-conveying figure. His decision to stop making further attempts along the same line of physical attack had hardly anything to do with a guilty conscience. As an abandoned child, he developed the elements of a sociopathic personality free of guilt. In fact, in his memoirs, he reports only that his failures at robbery left him with "the mocking feeling of a bruised ego."[13]

If not for the failing Russian economy of the time, Dmitri's life might have taken a different course, and he might never have joined the Communist camp. Due to World War I inflation, the allowance sent by his father's family became worthless. His mother's salary as a teacher at the Anapa gymnasium was hardly enough to support them both. Young Dmitri was forced to fend for himself. As a result, at the age of sixteen he was forced to begin a life of hard labor for a piece of bread. This brought him close to the lives of the unfortunate and downtrodden, whom he otherwise would never have known.

In fact, he became one of them. First, he worked at the local vineyard, where he quickly discovered that his physical training at home was insufficient for real-life work. The young peasant girls turned out to be more adept at picking grapes than he was. His pride suffered, and he found a job as a sailor on a motor launch. His social adjustment did not go smoothly, however. He was often beaten up; and his ego suffered greatly. But he had to endure it all, his teeth clenched. Here, trying to keep up with other sailors of working-class backgrounds, he went through a painful overhaul in his life values. This was the time of his personality change. "A presumptuous weak little intellectual," he writes about himself with remarkable introspection, "slowly but inescapably began turning into a rough, strong, adroit, suspicious, and internally tense and aggressive working lad."

As irony has it, a week before the October 1917 Bolshevik takeover, ostensibly as a result of the decision of his father's family finally to include Dmitri in their aristocratic clan, a letter from Petrograd arrived congratulating him and confirming his right to the title of Count of the Russian Empire. He asked himself how he would find work in the nearby Novorossiisk port next summer with the "idiotic burden" of an aristocratic lineage in his identity papers. Who would take him now? How would the sailors perceive it? Even if he found a job as a loader at the local cement foundries, it would not be any better. As a result, he never showed his identity papers to anyone. But his worries turned out to be short lived. Soon after the October 1917 Bolshevik takeover of power in the country, by special decree of the Council of People's Commissars, all aristocratic titles were abolished.[14]

A year later, in the summer of 1918, he landed a job as a helmsman on the cargo ship *Fortuna*, cruising along the Caucasus shoreline. As a sailor, he became used not only to the roaring of the waves, sleepless nights, and lugging heavy sacks but, on his own admission, "to foul language, to drinking, and to prostitutes." Now he became even more aware that his upbringing and the circumstances of his new life contradicted each other.

Meanwhile, after the October 1917 Bolshevik takeover, the new regime spread from St. Petersburg and Moscow to the country's provinces and finally reached Anapa. Dmitri landed a job as a sailor on an armed patrol boat. With the ensuing civil war already under way, he was often forced to choose sides and act against his will. Two events of that period foreshadowed his future choices in life. The first was related to the experience of shooting a human being. When one day Protapov, head of the local Soviet government, was murdered, a quick revolutionary trial took place, and all five suspects, also World War I veterans still in uniform, were condemned to death by firing squad. Now a member of the town's sentry, Dmitri was ordered to take part in their execution. Since his attempt to rob a rich merchant had ended in his being shot at, he notes in his memoirs: "Right then, spotting a discolored soldier's tunic in my gun sight, I discovered that here too life was quite unlike that described in books. Aiming at others I felt more at ease and calmer than when I had seen others aiming at me."

He was also greatly impressed at the sight of people who were proud to die for their ideals. As the civil war continued, the violence claimed new victims. One day a motor launch under a black banner carrying the words "Anarchy Is the Mother of Order" broke into the

Anapa port. After pillaging the town's wine cellars and treasury, the anarchists arrested the local commissar of justice, a former Moscow lawyer, and his wife, a schoolteacher. They brought the couple aboard a cutter and tied their feet together with rope. The couple chose to commit suicide rather than be killed by their enemies. They embraced each other, kissed, and threw themselves into the water.

Then it was the White Guard army's turn to capture the town. Their first priority was to hang the local Red commissar of finance. After that, they arrested a young man who took an active part in all Bolshevik town meetings, though most of his talk had been without much point. The commander of the White Guard regiment, General Pokrovsky, offered to spare the young man if he would ask forgiveness for spreading revolutionary ideas. The young man spat at the general, and he was hanged at once.

Big crowds hungry for entertainment attended these events. They observed executions dispassionately, "crunching sunflower seeds." "This was the style of the times; it formed my psyche as well," Dmitri comments.

In the spring of 1919, Dmitri graduated from both the Anapa gymnasium and the Anapa Nautical School. He found a job as a sailor on a coast guard boat. Considering the turmoil and depravation of revolution and civil war, he was relatively well-off, earning enough to get by. But the gnawing sense of worthlessness that had pursued him for as long as he could remember did not subside fully. One day, walking along the Anapa embankment, which was crowded with refugees from the Bolshevist north of the country, he overheard whispers: "Mathilde . . . Nicholas II's son . . ." They referred to a thin, worn-out woman, who walked through the crowd accompanied by a teenager carrying a bottle of kerosene on a string. The woman was identified as Mathilde Kschessinskaya, a former prima ballerina of the St. Petersburg Imperial Theater, who had been the object of scandalous rumors concerning her sex life. Back in 1890, at age seventeen, she had been romantically involved with the future Tsar Nicholas II. The romance lasted only three years, after which, in 1894, the tsar married the love of his life, the future Empress Alexandra Fyodorovna. Although, after that, according to rumors, the ballerina had formed a ménage à trois with two other members of the tsarist family, the gossipers insisted that her son—born in 1901, the same year as Dmitri—was an illegitimate son of Nicholas, and, supposedly—like Dmitri—the boy never knew for sure who his father was.

When the crowd expressed affection and reverence toward the teenager, it only irritated Dmitri. "I looked at the out-of-wedlock emperor's son without pity or reverence," he recalls. "At the very least, I'm legitimized now . . . And, at our coast-guard motorboat, I can get kerosene without measuring it with a bottle." He tries to reassure the readers of his memoirs—and himself—that, in the long run, the unfortunate circumstances of his birth turned out to his advantage: "No, no, I'm glad that I was born the way I was born." A non sequitur that follows this statement betrays his inner struggle to dismiss his own thoughts of later days—his subsequent career as a spy had everything to do with his emotional dependency, with his strong need to belong, developed early in life, which was exploited by the KGB: "As to my thirteen years of work in [Soviet] intelligence, it only proves the strength of my soul, my openheartedness, and my trusting nature."[15]

But the period of stability in Anapa did not last very long. Dmitri lived in the territory controlled by the White Army authorities, and therefore he was eligible for draft into military service. This made it impossible for him to be hired by a merchant ship's captain. As a result, he wound up as a volunteer first-class sailor aboard the *Rion*, a big cargo ship undergoing repair in Novorossiisk port. The tsarist government had bought the *Rion* on the eve of World War I. Soon after Dmitri came on board, it went to Sevastopol, where it was docked and partially rebuilt so that it could carry out landing and cruiser operations.[16]

With the fortunes of the civil war turning in favor of the Reds, Baron Wrangel replaced the unsuccessful White Guard army commander, General Denikin. It didn't help much. The White Army continued retreating. Discontent grew increasingly pronounced, and aboard the *Rion*, Dmitri was forced to choose his political allegiance. The ship's crew was socially divided. There were sailors like him who had volunteered to work for the Whites out of their need to earn a living. But, unlike him, all of them came from the lower classes. Given the opportunity to switch sides, they cast their lot in with the Reds. All officers aboard the ship belonged to the upper classes. With tensions between the two groups growing by the hour, Dmitri was hard-pressed to decide which side he was on. Eventually, he chose to stay with his proletarian comrades.

Soon all volunteers aboard the *Rion*, including Dmitri, received a draft call from the White Guard authorities. To avoid the draft, his new coworkers decided to flee to Turkey and he agreed. They advised him that to have enough money to survive the first week in Constantinople, he should steal their ship's compass and sell it to the captain of a schooner anchored nearby. The next morning, Dmitri dismantled the compass, hid it in a basket under his dirty linens, and under a pretext of taking them ashore to his laundress, passed the sentry.

The compass sold for three Turkish lira. He sewed the money in his shirt. At night, the Bolshevik sympathizers aboard the ship attempted to destroy the *Rion* by blowing up the dock housing. The attempt failed. In the morning, all sailors subject to the draft were sent ashore with the order to report to the local military commander. Refusal to carry out the order meant being sent to the front right away. Dmitri had to act as quickly as possible. He climbed aboard the *Tsesarevitch Constantine* ship bound for Turkey. First, he hid in the ship's lavatory; then he jumped into the hold. For the first time in his life, he left his native land behind. He was full of anxiety. In August 1919, still a teenager, he was on his way to a foreign country with no idea that it was only the beginning of his long and troubled life.[17]

Unaware of it, he thus began a new cycle of separation in his life, now not only from his mother but from his Motherland as well. At this point, life pushed him away from fulfilling his strongest need—the need to belong. For him, who had been given away by his mother and totally ignored by his never-seen father, this unfulfilled need to belong would play a fateful part in his life, forcing him to make bad choices that, eventually, would result not only in the wasting of his inborn talents but also would bring him to the verge of physical destruction.

But, for now, coiling up in the hold of a Russian ship, he was leaving his native land.

TWO | A Leaf Torn from a Branch

Against his will, he was brought into the White Volunteer Army as a civilian sailor. In 1919, . . . on the ship Constantine, *he was taken to Turkey.*

—BYSTROLYOTOV'S OFFICIAL BIOGRAPHY

A leaf torn from a branch, I was carried by storm to an unknown faraway land. Twirling in the wind, I ran on because I couldn't stop.

—BYSTROLYOTOV, IN HIS MEMOIRS

Dmitri's life in Constantinople began with a stroke of luck. Soon after the ship he was traveling on dropped anchor in the port, and he had climbed out of the ship's hold covered in coal dust, he ran into his classmate from Anapa Nautical School, Evgeny (Zhenya) Kavetsky, who had fled to Turkey a few months earlier. Kavetsky was employed as a boatswain on the schooner *Eglon,* formerly *St. Sergii.* The ship was privately owned and used for commercial purposes. Its crew consisted of destitute men of many nationalities who had fled their native lands in the course of World War I and the Russian civil war. Besides a Russian boatswain, there were three Estonians, Captain Kaze, and two machinists, August and Martin, as well as Turk, Arab, and Greek sailors.[1]

Luckily for Dmitri, the position of ship's cook was vacant, and he was hired at once thanks to his friend's recommendation. The trouble was that Dmitri didn't know how to cook. Kavetsky wrote down recipes for him on a piece of paper. Because it was damp in the kitchen, the ink ran, and the recipes soon became illegible. Naturally, angered by the inept cooking, the crew members came close to throwing the new cook overboard many times. Luckily, boatswain Kavetsky intervened on Dmitri's behalf.

Little by little, Dmitri learned how to cook. His living conditions on board the schooner were harsh. As maritime tradition dictated, a cook was assigned the worst berth on the ship. Dmitri's bed near the hold was always damp. Tired from working all day, he slept, often jolted out of his dreams by cold rat tails scurrying over his body.

The ship's owners took full advantage of the lawlessness reigning in the country at the time. In 1918, following the defeat of the Ottoman Empire in World War I, British, French, and Italian troops had occupied Constantinople. Soon afterward, General Mustafa Kemal (Atatürk) waged the Turkish War of Independence against the Entente Powers (1919–23). As the war raged on, wartime profiteering flourished. The most lucrative business consisted of transporting refugees running from the advancing troops of Turkish nationalists to the Bulgarian and Greek coastlines.

The schooner's Captain Kaze worked out a modus operandi—he sailed along the shores looking for distant smoke, which usually came from Greek and Armenian settlements burned by Atatürk's troops. Once he spotted the smoke, he knew it wouldn't be too long before, in a frantic attempt to escape over the sea, scores of refugees would stream to the beaches. When the lifeboat was packed to capacity, those who couldn't squeeze in knew that they were doomed to death, and they howled like animals. As the lifeboat cast off the beach, the refugees—their faces distorted, fists raised to the sky—jumped into the water and tried to cling to the boat's sides. In frantic pleas for their lives, dangling in the water, choking on it, they offered whatever valuables they had to the sailors. Since the boat was usually already overloaded, the crew bashed the desperate swimmers over the head with the oars until, one after another, they disappeared in the water.

Dmitri witnessed a scene during one of these operations that would haunt him for years, eventually causing paroxysms of incapacitating depression.

> [At that time] only one young woman with a baby
> is left behind the boat . . . I see her face; it's an arm's

length away . . . She pushes her baby over the side into the boat toward us and looks at the baby, holding on to the rocking boat with her thin fingers. One of the sailors crushes them with his oar. The bones of her fingers crack. Smiling at her baby, the woman is slowly sinking . . . I'm rowing the boat and see her hair in the clear water. It twines about her face like snakes . . . She smiles and looks at me from under the water. Then she disappears.[2]

In the fall of 1920, to supplement their income from trafficking in refugees, the owners of the *Eglon* also speculated in goods, such as tins of tea and sacks of sugar stolen by the French quartermasters in the Greek army fighting the Turks. One day, the schooner was caught in a storm. To avoid capsizing in the heavy winds, the crew cut down the ship's masts and got rid of the sails but couldn't stop water from seeping through the cracks. For the next three days and nights, huge waves pounded the ship; it was a matter of sheer luck that it didn't sink. Finally, the storm subsided, and powerful currents pulled the schooner into the Bosporus. The exhausted crew was still recuperating from its ordeal on the open sea when the shipowners, concerned about nothing but profit, ordered the crew to repair the masts and sails without delay and return to sea. The sailors argued that the ship's condition was too poor for a new raid. In need of substantial repair, her damaged body wouldn't survive the next big storm. In response, the owners threatened to fire anyone who refused to follow their orders. With several hundred thousand refugees flooding into Constantinople, it would be impossible to find another job of any kind, so the crew grudgingly obeyed their masters. "That was my lesson in political literacy," Dmitri writes. "That [incident] drove home my first passionate political convictions."

Back out on the open sea, the ship soon encountered powerful winds. To escape a new storm, the crew hastened to pull into the nearest small port, which was already in the hands of the Turks. Captain Kaze began long negotiations with the authorities. Toward morning, the ship slipped away into the foggy sea, and the fate of everybody on board again looked quite bleak. Resenting the dirty business he was forced to be part of, Dmitri was looking for a chance to escape. He persuaded his boatswain friend Kavetsky to join him in taking over the ship's command and sailing it back to the Russian shore. One day, when bringing dinner to the captain's suite, Dmitri managed to get hold of his pistol. Handing it over to Kavetsky and arming himself with a crowbar, the two confronted the captain and demanded that he head the schooner toward the Crimea. To their surprise, Captain Kaze didn't object to the change of course, and the crew turned out to be equally indifferent to the ship's destination. Despite the ship's poor condition, after a few days of sailing, the *Eglon* made it to the Crimean port of Yevpatoria.

By that time, the defeated Baron Wrangel's White Army troops had left the Crimea and fled to Turkey. The Crimea was in the hands of the Red Army. Here, in Yevpatoria, Dmitri had his first ominous brush with the most powerful institution in Soviet history—the Cheka, a vernacular version of VChK, an abbreviation for the All-Russia's Extraordinary Commission for Combating Counterrevolution and Sabotage. Founded in December 1917, shortly after the Bolshevik takeover, it soon became the most dreaded of Soviet institutions. From the outset, it carried out both punitive and intelligence functions. The local Cheka summoned Dmitri and his fellow sailors and ordered them back to their ship to carry out an important mission: they were to take on board a group of important Red functionaries and deliver them to Odessa.

Neither shortage of fuel nor scarcity of food in Yevpatoria presented any problems for the almighty Cheka. The ship was fully resupplied and headed for Odessa. It was a risky and dangerous undertaking. In the course of the civil war, the White Guards and Entente troops had mined all water approaches to the Odessan port, and the mine chart for the area wasn't available. The crew placed their hope on the ship's shallow draft, about two feet above the usual mine submersion level, and their fingers crossed, they eventually reached Odessa unharmed.

Odessa was also hit by cold and hunger. The ship's stay was cut short: the Cheka charged the crew with a new mission, this time a secret one. They had to take on board two Red commissars and their wives and, after swinging by Sevastopol, where they had to pick up a suitcase with valuables expropriated from the Whites, take them to the Bulgarian port of Varna and, at night, on a rocket signal, land on a remote beach. The operation was part of the political agenda set by the new Soviet government—to spread the Russian Revolution across the globe. The commissars were to orchestrate a proletarian uprising in Bulgaria.

On December 31, 1920, after picking up the suitcase in Sevastopol, the schooner headed for Bulgaria. Poorly repaired after the storm lashing in Turkish waters, the ship's sides yielded to the pressure of the icy sea, and in the middle of the night, water suddenly gushed into the hold. With the ship's sinking imminent and only one four-person lifeboat available, everybody panicked. To get hold of the boat for the secret mission party, one of the commissars drew his handgun. Condemned to perish in the icy waters about to rush over the ship's sides, the sailors drew their pistols as well. The situation grew tense. Gunfire seemed inevitable. One of the commissar's wives fell on the deck crying that she couldn't move. The commissar aimed his gun at Dmitri's chest and ordered him to take her to the boat. As Dmitri carried out the orders, sheer luck again saved him and his fellow crewmen. The captain of an Odessa port tugboat passing nearby noticed the ship in trouble and rushed to its rescue.

(During my meeting with Bystrolyotov, he described his first encounter with the Cheka differently. Upon his return to Yevpatoria, the Cheka approached him and asked whether he was a patriot of his Motherland and wanted to serve her. When he enthusiastically agreed—Bystrolyotov made it clear to me that, at the time, he had a rather vague idea what the Cheka was all about and where Russia as a country was heading—they proposed that he become their sleeper abroad. To do so, he would have to go back to Turkey and wait. They would find him and let him know what to do next.)[3]

While the ship underwent repair, Dmitri fell ill with pneumonia. After a long recovery, he and Kavetsky felt they had had enough of sea adventures and asked the Cheka to relieve them of their duties. After some deliberation, they received permission provided that they surrender their Turkish documents and their sailors' clothing. These items were passed to the commissars, who planned to use them to blend in with the rest of the schooner's crew.

In February 1921, Dmitri and Kavetsky headed for Novorossiisk, where they hoped to find work. Their journey from Sevastopol to Kerch on a horse-driven cart, over the frozen and deserted steppes, turned into an ordeal. The horses tired often, and they had to brandish their pistols to get fresh horses in villages along the way. Biting cold combined with fierce winds caused Dmitri to fall ill again. Kavetsky again proved a good friend. He removed his peacoat and wrapped it around Dmitri's shoulders; to keep warm himself, he ran next to the cart.

En route to Novorossiisk, Kavetsky also fell ill with pneumonia. With much difficulty, Dmitri arranged for a horse-driven cab to take his friend to a hospital. While his friend stayed in the hospital, the local authorities appointed Dmitri to the post of chief of the Anapa Lighthouse. The lighthouse had an extensive library that had belonged to Dmitri's predecessor, before he ran away with the Whites. During the long night hours, Dmitri admired the colorful brochures featuring Switzerland. He had no inkling then that, in time, his future spy work would take him to these very places shown in the brochures, and he would wonder where he had seen them before.

After Kavetsky's recovery from pneumonia, both he and Dmitri succeeded in being relieved of military duty. They finally made it to Novorossiisk but could find no work there. In the spring, on a motor launch carrying an American trade union delegation headed by one Melnichansky, they went farther south along the coast and eventually reached the port of Batumi in the Republic of Georgia. In July 1921, hungry and lost, and along with other refugees, they boarded the Italian liner *Roma* and departed for Constantinople for the second time. Exit visas posed no problem. To get rid of the unemployed and hungry, the new administration let them go without any formalities.

In Constantinople, luck again graced Dmitri and his friend. At the Seli-Bazaar pier, Kaze, their former captain, spotted them in the midst of the crowd of jobless sailors. Remembering that Dmitri and Kavetsky had saved him from the hands of the Cheka, Kaze reprimanded them strongly for taking over the ship in the first place but took them back on board. Soon, with a load of stolen army blankets on board, their schooner was on its way to the Mediterranean seaport of Izmir.

Here Dmitri's fortunes changed for the worse. At night, an American destroyer accidentally ran into their ship and ripped it in half. Suddenly, along with the rest of the crew, Dmitri found himself in the water. He grabbed the ship's mast floating nearby, pulled himself onto it, and lost consciousness. In the morning, Dmitri and his shipmates, minus two who had drowned, were picked up by the Americans and taken to Constantinople's Navy Hospital.[4]

The situation in the city was even worse than before. With the National War for Independence raging and Atatürk's troops controlling half of the Turkish territory, Constantinople was awash in refugees, over one hundred thousand Russians among them. Without proper documents, it was almost impossible to get work of any kind. Kavetsky was only able to find employment as a deep-sea diver recovering the remnants of sunken ships. One day, because of strong currents in the Bosporus, the air-supply pipes of his diving suit became entangled. He was trapped underwater for too long and suffered extensive bleeding. With the money received as compensation for the damage to his health, he bought an American passport on the black market and left for the United States.

Seeking some help in finding employment, Dmitri visited the Russian consulate in Constantinople. The consul, one Professor Gogel, was willing to oblige his compatriot and issued him a passport in the name of "Walt Antonio Guerrero." Now, having a passport with a Spanish name, Dmitri finally landed himself a job as a stoker on the *Farnaiba*, a huge Brazilian dry-cargo ship that made regular trips to Alexandria and farther into the Red Sea to the port of Djibouti.

Work aboard that ship proved to be another trying experience for Dmitri. It was already summertime, and as the ship passed through the Red Sea, the heat became unbearable. Working near the furnaces felt like being in hell. There, on the *Farnaiba*, Dmitri discovered that he had acting ability. He would often use this talent in his future intelligence work, but here, aboard a cargo ship, it helped him to survive. Despite his having experienced many rough times, the other stokers, a bunch of hoodlums, perceived him as a cultured youth and made him a routine target of their insults. He felt like "a lamb surrounded by wolves," as he put it.

Dmitri realized he had to come up with some survival strategy, because if he allowed their insults to go unchallenged, they would eventually kill him. At a stopover in Alexandria, he bought a long, "sinister-looking" knife and hid it in his clothes. One day, at mealtime, his persecutors began throwing crusts of bread at him. Dmitri figured out a way to avert their attacks. At the dinner table, he sat opposite one of the weakest and least aggressive of the stokers. When he was hit right on the forehead with a bread crust thrown by a huge stoker sitting at the far end of the table, Dmitri shouted at the stoker sitting across from him, "Last warning! One more time, and I'll slash your guts out."

"I don't know what you're talking about," the man said. The huge stoker threw another crust at Dmitri. Making a wild face, Dmitri jumped to his feet and pulled out the gigantic knife. Shrieking, "Now you're going to die!" at the top of his lungs, he ran around the table toward the innocent man. To give the other stokers enough time to grab the hand with the knife in it before he reached his target, he purposely entangled himself in the chairs. When ten stokers caught up with him, Dmitri roared and tossed about in their strong arms as they calmed him down and reasoned with him to "forgive" the innocent.

His strategy worked. The incident earned him a reputation as a man of violent temperament, and no one bothered him after that. "I was going on twenty. I was alone abroad, without my Motherland, without help. Among the wolves, first I pretended to be a wolf, and then I became one."

After a few trips, Dmitri lost his *Farnaiba* job and joined the vast ranks of the homeless, sinking into Constantinople's lower depths. Here he witnessed and experienced the horror of destitution and its effect on human morality. In his book *Sredi emigratsii* (*In the Midst of Emigration*), a Russian refugee, A. Slobodskoi, who lived in the city about the same time as Dmitri (1920 to 1921), describes the sad state of affairs in the milieu of Russian refugees. Besides quarrels and gossip, drunkenness became rampant and widespread: "Everybody drank. Those [émigrés] who were penniless sold their belongings and their rations. They sold their military uniforms and everything else they could put their hands on. They earned money by chance through work that was unbelievably hard to come by, and they drowned it in drink as soon as they got it. Nothing could stop it. As a result, thievery flourished. An idle and animal-like way of life pushed women to shameless [behavior]. Marriage ties collapsed."[5]

Dmitri observed the humiliation to which the destitute Russian refugees were forced to subject themselves:

> For a dollar, an American sailor could smear a [White
> Guard] officer's face with black and red shoe polish.
> For two dollars, he could make him climb a tree and
> urinate on the heads of passersby. For three dollars, he
> could take part in "cockroach races" [a gambling enter-
> prise widespread in Constantinople]. For five dollars,
> customers could get into a "Turkish pasha's harem,"
> where naked wives of [defeated White Army] officers
> reclined on carpets, offering hashish and opium . . .
> On the wet, dirty steps [of the back alleys] thousands
> of refugees lay, children crawled about, old people, sick
> and wounded, died one after another.[6]

In Tartush, the seediest part of the old city, now extinct, there were gambling joints and bordellos. A Jewish woman from Odessa, Madam Rosa Leizer, who owned one of those places, let unemployed Russian sailors sleep in an empty room. Moreover, in their motherly concern for the poor Russian sailors, Dmitri among them, the ladies of the house mended the homeless men's jackets and darned their socks. To escape the drabness of their lives, his fellow unemployed sailors resorted to crude entertainment. Lodging on the second floor of the bordello, they drilled holes in the floor and watched the action below. When they saw that the lovers had reached the highest point of oblivion, they took turns urinating on the customers' heads. The enraged customers ran upstairs and engaged in fierce fistfights. At that time in his life, Dmitri experienced the first stages of his mental illness. "Everything seemed to me like a dance in a fiery fog," he recalls. "I realized that I was falling into an abyss."

However, there was no time to find out what was happening to his mind. Hunger prompted him to act. Many Russian émigrés in Constantinople made a meager living through trade of any kind. The long Pera, one of Constantinople's main streets, teemed with his equally destitute compatriots, fellow Russian émigrés. They sold any items they had brought from Russia that had some value: engagement rings, watches, gold chains, earrings, table silver, pillows, blankets, and dresses. The formerly rich sold the expensive carpets they had brought along. There were also those who tried to sell their last torn boots, military uniforms, and underwear donated by foreigners and stolen from the refugee warehouses.[7]

Because of his aversion to commerce of any kind, to survive, Dmitri had to resort to manual labor. Such work was very difficult to come by. From time to time, he would land a job for a day or two, using the same trick over and over. At the labor exchange, he pretended to be an expert in any profession for which there was an opening. By claiming that he was an ex-chef for the Russian grand duke, he cooked for a while at Doré, a posh French restaurant. As an "expert plasterer," he repaired the walls of the Black Rose, a cabaret owned by a famous Russian émigré singer, Alexander Vertinsky, who also performed there.

Once, posing as a professional auto mechanic, Dmitri got a job repairing trucks at the British military base. The employees were paid at the end of the workweek, on Saturdays, but they were fed quite well every day. He ate "for ten people" at the job and stole food. He dragged out this job for as long as he could without revealing his incompetence. He managed to disassemble some truck engines and clean the parts, but he couldn't put them together, and thus he didn't make it to payday. At other times, he was paid half a lira for a day's work removing seashells from ship hulls. The money was hardly enough to buy a shish kebab made out of dog meat.

At the lowest point of his Constantinople life, while roaming over Galata Street, near the port, Dmitri ran into an old friend, Georgy Georgiev, a St. Petersburg naval cadet. At the time of their meeting, Georgiev was studying at the Constantinople gymnasium of the All-Russia's Union of Cities (Vserossiiskii Soiuz Gorodov).[8]

The school was organized in early 1921 to serve Russian children uprooted by the calamities of civil war and emigration. Since Russian émigré organizations were short of funds, foreign philanthropists, mostly American, took part in setting up the gymnasium. On the high hill overlooking the bay, they rented a shabby thirty-two-room mansion with surrounding grounds complete with several terraces planted with fig and quince trees. Since Constantinople was teeming with homeless Russian children and raw youth who, not unlike Dmitri, were poorly dressed (in dirty soldiers' overcoats, torn underwear) and malnourished, the gymnasium was set up as a boarding school, a shelter.[9]

Georgiev brought his old friend to the gymnasium at once. At the time of this lucky encounter, Dmitri was already nineteen, but his age wasn't a problem: there were many other overage students. The school's founders understood that some young men couldn't complete their education because of the wartime. In his memoirs, Dmitri claims that Georgiev arranged for him to be accepted into the graduating class not of the Russian gymnasium, but of some "college for Christian youth" run by the American Red Cross. He also claims that he completed the college in a year, obtaining a bachelor's degree. However, his personal file at the Prague Archive of the Moscow Central Archive of the Russian Federation tells a different story. Later on, in the spring of 1922, when he applied to the Russian Law Faculty (*Russkii iuridicheskii fakul'tet*) in Prague, the only evidence of his prior education he could submit was a certificate of completion of the Constantinople Russian gymnasium. Moreover, the certificate shows that he graduated from the school after just a month of studies (from July 31 to September 2, 1921). With several of the classmates at the "American college" (Georgiev, Chavchavadze, Tolstaya, Dolgov, Avtokratov, Klodt, Yurevich) he mentions in his memoirs, Dmitri is listed among the Constantinople Russian gymnasium's graduates. Dmitri's description of his "American college's" location and school life also matches that of the Russian émigré gymnasium.[10]

It is obvious that Dmitri's duplicity toward his readers in this section of his memoirs comes from the fact that he was not eligible for admission to that gymnasium, having already completed the Anapa gymnasium two years before. But who could blame him for trying to survive by any means possible? There was another reason why, in his memoirs—to be read by Soviet censors, for he longed to publish them in his lifetime—he calls the Constantinople gymnasium an "American YMCA college." He had to avoid being accused of affiliation with the White émigrés, a political sin that was unforgivable by the Soviet regime of his time. To reassure those anticipated censors, he states, "I was starving and worked as a day-to-day laborer, but I didn't contact Baron Wrangel's people [White émigrés]."[11]

Accepted to the gymnasium, he felt he had entered a paradise. Now he slept not on the floor of a Constantinople bordello, but on a bed with a mattress. In contrast to his meager existence of the past few years, he was now clothed and fed "like a king." His breakfast consisted of American canned stew with eggs and hot rice cereal topped with condensed milk; he also had jam made of fresh figs, oranges, and lemons and drank a big cup of cocoa. The lunches and dinners were no less abundant and delicious.

However, the mental illness that he had suffered from at Madam Leizer's establishment for the first time now revisited him with renewed force. This time, he knew what had caused it. It came from the trauma he had experienced witnessing the agony of Armenian and Greek refugees running for their lives from the advancing Turkish troops. "[At the time of the Black Sea adventures] everything I had seen was etched in my memory without reaching consciousness: there was no time to think, I didn't have a breather," he recalls. "Later when I did, the impressions gushed with such might that they bowled me over, and for the first time, I [truly] lost my mind. After all, is it my fault I saw all that?"

The scenes of ruination of human lives began haunting him, producing nightmarish visions. One especially vivid scene of that past experience tormented him the most: "As I was lowering my eyes to a starched tablecloth . . . , I saw the lifeboat's side and the young mother's thin fingers, blue from cold, and the oar, crushing their bones . . . I saw her eyes full of love [for her baby] and grief [at parting with the baby]. I saw her smiling mouth through the cold blue water . . . The past kept holding me by the scruff of the neck. It refused to set me free."

To fight off the disturbing vision, he indulged in love games with young female students. But this helped only for a short while. The image of the drowning woman kept haunting him. When classes were over, the students came to the luxurious villa of the Turkish general who had run away with Atatürk's troops. "It was there," Dmitri recalls, "at the moment of full relaxation that the hidden mental illness, planted in me by my grandmother, 'the Wasp,' and my mother, overwhelmed me . . . Unbearable pain tore me inside out. I was obsessed with the vision of the young mother swimming up to our boat, overloaded with refugees, through strangers' legs, pushing her baby into the boat and then drowning in front of everyone, smiling happily and looking at me from the water with her radiant eyes."

Of course, the incident of the drowning woman would have been an extraordinarily traumatic event for any witness. But Dmitri's post-traumatic stress disorder was amplified by the episodes of his own life, not only that of his near drowning in the open sea but also—and, perhaps, even to a much greater degree—that of his mother urging him to jump into the rapids to rescue the drowning woman when he was twelve. And there, in the Black Sea water, he witnessed another mother who was the direct opposite of his own. Whereas his mother hadn't thought twice before abandoning her baby (him) for the sake of some "higher cause," in front of his eyes, the young Armenian woman sacrificed her own life for the sake of her child. No wonder that her face before she drowned, happy because she knew her child was safe, stuck in Dmitri's mind.

In fact, he couldn't shake off this vision no matter how hard he tried. Before falling ill, he had made a new friend, Konstantin (Kotya) Yurevich, a proprietor's son from Odessa, who now took care of him. He would take Dmitri to the seashore and sit him on the beach. Indifferent to everything, Dmitri sat there, his head helplessly drooping on his chest.

At the end of 1921, with the Turkish troops approaching Constantinople, the League of Nations appealed to all countries to help Russian émigrés. Among others, the newly formed republic of Czechoslovakia, a country populated with brotherly Slavs, offered to host Russian students. When he had somewhat recovered from his psychosis, Dmitri paid a visit to the newly created Soviet Mission in Turkey. There, he told one Comrade Kudish, working at the Mission, that back in 1919, "to avoid fighting against the Red Army, along with a group of revolutionary-minded sailors," he had fled to Turkey and was now headed for Czechoslovakia. He asked him to write to the Soviet Mission in Prague on his behalf.[12]

From Dmitri's writing, it is not clear what the purpose of that visit to the Soviet Mission was. Why did he want to assure the Soviet official of his loyalty to Red Russia while planning to move even farther away from her? If homesickness was his major problem, he could have tried to scrape up the money for a boat ticket and go back, as hundreds of his compatriots did a few months later in the spring of 1922. With the beginning of resettlement of the defeated White Army and numerous refugees abroad, the dream of repatriation occupied the minds of the vast majority of émigrés. If that was the case with Dmitri, then, like many other desperate Russians in his situation, Dmitri would visit the Mission to ask for permission to go back. He could have emphasized the political nature of his escape from Russia as a plea for good treatment upon his return. (According to rumors, often well founded, that circulated among Russian refugees in Constantinople, the White repatriates often faced ruthless reprisals upon reaching Soviet shores.)[13]

His behavior at Comrade Kudish's office makes sense only if you fill in what he couldn't write about in his memoirs, which he hoped to see published in his (Soviet) lifetime, and what he confided to me during our private meeting—that, trying to remain a patriot of his country while living abroad, he considered himself already recruited by the Cheka. He visited Comrade Kudish just to remind them about himself, to inform him that he was that young man whom the Cheka had sent as a sleeper with the flow of refugees. From the outset, besides their direct trade functions, Soviet trade missions abroad were involved in intelligence and agent recruitment. By paying a visit to the Mission, Dmitri prompted their recognition of him. That's why Comrade Kudish heard him out, encouraged him to proceed to Czechoslovakia, and promised to write him a letter of recommendation.[14]

On December 18, 1921, Dmitri and the rest of the gymnasium students boarded a train headed for Prague.[15]

Bystrolyotov's Travels (1922)

THREE | In the Grips of Holy Wrath

For an intelligence agent, it's best to pose as a student. It gives you freedom. You don't draw any suspicion when appearing on the streets even at nighttime.

—BYSTROLYOTOV, IN CONVERSATION
WITH THE AUTHOR

Dmitri arrived in Czechoslovakia on January 8, 1922, with other students of the Constantinople gymnasium. As part of the Czechoslovakian government's Russian Action program, the graduates received Czechoslovakian entry visas and could apply to any Czech institution of higher education. Dmitri first applied to the Komensky University in Bratislava. He studied there for only one semester. Then the Russian student program there ended, and he moved to Prague, where he applied to the newly organized Russian Law Faculty. On May 22, 1922, he was accepted there as a full-time student.[1]

The school was set up to train émigrés in Russian law. The program was based on that of prerevolutionary law departments of Russian universities, and former professors of those universities now living in Prague as émigrés constituted the school faculty. Studying Russian law in earnest at this school made sense only for those who strongly believed that the Soviet regime wouldn't last for too long. Otherwise, knowledge of the laws of an empire that no longer existed would render the school's degree worthless. For many, including Dmitri, it was a temporary refuge, a social niche that provided them with the support of the Student Welfare Committee set up by the Czechoslovakian government as part of the Russian Action program. They also received legal status in the country, being granted Czechoslovakian citizenship. At the time, no other Russian educational institution in Prague could provide these benefits to the Russian émigré students.[2]

The classes were to begin in early October. Meanwhile, Dmitri stayed in the gymnasium dormitory housed in army camp buildings, vacant since the end of World War I, near Moravská Třebová, a town 160 miles southeast of Prague. Here his depression returned with renewed force. During the first months, the "fresh impressions" of his adopted country helped him to recover from the disease that had attacked him so powerfully in the last months of his Constantinople life. But his condition weakened when the White Army veterans among the gymnasium students learned about his escape from the White Army ship and his subsequent, albeit short, service in the Red fleet. They began harassing him. At night, they would smear his clothes with dirt, spit at him, and make his life miserable in every way possible. Despite his physical strength, Dmitri had difficulty thwarting these attacks because of his emotional vulnerability. The attacks depressed him and even made him suicidal.[3]

The depression caused by the hostility of his classmates was exacerbated by the sense of disaster on a grand scale produced by the news of hunger in the USSR. Czech and Russian-émigré papers were filled with reports on the subject along with photos of emaciated Russian children and their mothers begging for bread on the streets. Ostracized by the rest of the students, frustrated, and desperate, Dmitri became obsessed with his dying compatriots. With his native land on the verge of perishing, he felt compelled to return home to die along with his countrymen. His mother's letters containing eyewitness accounts of hunger reached him in Prague and served as a trigger for action. "Psychopaths are the most energetic people," he writes in his memoirs about that moment in his life. He threw himself into action. In June 1922, he sold whatever decent clothes he had and bought an old suit, a blue cap, a pair of rough boots, and a train ticket to Berlin. There he found the Soviet naval attaché and told him about his desire to return to Russia.[4]

Wary of letting saboteurs or spies seep into the country, the naval attaché sent Dmitri first to the town of Velikie Luki, a detention center where thousands of other repatriates—former World War I prisoners of war, Ukrainian peasants from Argentina, Polish Jews, and others—were held for clearance. Once cleared, Dmitri went first to the Russian naval base at Kronshtadt on the Baltic Sea. There, on July 4, he was assigned to the Baltic Sea Transportation Department and then to Sevastopol, the Black Sea naval base. However, the civil war was over, and neither place needed sailors. Left on the streets of Sevastopol with no money, Dmitri set out on foot and reached Anapa, where his mother lived.[5]

He didn't get a warm welcome from her either. She scolded him, calling his return to Russia "foolish, senseless, and criminal." Why had he come back? He had a chance to get an education, and he'd behaved irresponsibly. Civic minded as always, she told him angrily, "Your place is in Russia, of course. But only if you become useful to your country . . . It's time to end your wanderings. Settle down and get a profession." She repeated Lenin's call to the nation's youth: "Study and study and study." With these words, she gave him her last bits of bread and salt pork and saw him off to the outskirts of town. "I went down the road but then looked back, thinking that my mother was still standing and waving good-bye. But she lay in the grass, her body shaking with sobs."[6]

On the road again, Dmitri went to the port of Novorossiisk. There was no work there either. He managed to board a little steamship and, in search of work, stepped ashore in every port on the ship's route south to Batumi. One night he overheard a conversation about the rebirth of Russia between two passengers, both Communists. That conversation helped him to clarify his world outlook, realize his place in life, and situate himself politically. He felt that now his duty was to go back to Prague and take the enemies of his country, the émigrés, by their throats. He was emotionally set up for it on a personal level: after all, they had been the people who spit in his soup and pricked him at night with safety pins.[7]

Late September 1922, the Italian liner *Roma* was anchored at one of the Batumi piers, and it gave him an opportunity for escape. Unlike before, the Soviet borders were now sealed. The entrance to the ship was heavily guarded by customs officials. How could he sneak through? A plan came to him at once. He picked up an Italian newspaper lying on the pier and put it in his pocket so that its banner would show. Then, his teeth clenched, "a tiger hitting its own sides with its tail," as he describes himself, he moved toward the customs guards. When one of them demanded his documents, hands in his pockets, he pretended he was an Italian sailor and that he didn't understand Russian. He smiled, pulled out—instead of his documents—a pack of Italian cigarettes, took out one for himself, and offered the rest to the guards, saying, "*Prego, signore, prego!*" The guards took the bait. Dmitri jumped into the rowboat.[8]

Once on board the ship, he hid in a nook on the upper deck for three long days and nights to escape the ticket collectors. He found scraps and pieces of food at the bottom of a garbage can, quickly shoved them into his pants and jacket pockets, even into his cap, and returned to his nook on the upper deck. He ate hastily and fell asleep. In the morning, he discovered that the ship's rats had eaten his cap and gnawed holes in the pockets where he had stuffed bits of food. Then the ship's stokers discovered him. They forced him to load coal into furnaces around the clock, until he was about to collapse from exhaustion. Then the stokers' boss told him, "You don't have money for a ticket, and you don't have strength to work it off." He pulled out his knife and extended it to Dmitri: "Take it, boy, and cut your throat yourself. Why go on living? Help yourself."[9]

But Dmitri's will to live won out one more time. He forced himself to get up, grabbed his shovel, and went to work. Finally, after endless hours, his shift ended, and he was allowed to take a shower. His slavery seemed to be over, but when he asked for money to buy some food, one of the stokers gave him a terrible kick in the face. He fell and lost consciousness.[10]

When he landed in Constantinople, he had no documents that would allow him to travel across Europe back to Prague: he had surrendered his Czech passport upon his visit to the Soviet naval attaché in Berlin. With premonitions of atrocities at the hands of the nationalist forces led by Atatürk, Westerners fled the city any way they could. Those who lacked proper papers took the office of the International Refugee Committee by storm. In the confusion of the time, Dmitri managed to obtain a Dutch passport in the name of "Hans Galleni" (he would make use of it in his future intelligence work).[11]

On the roofs of trains, crisscrossing European countries—Greece, Bulgaria, Serbia, and Hungary—he finally reached the Czechoslovakian border in early November 1922. There, in response to a customs officer's question about his belongings, he handed over the only item in his possession—a pencil stub. One of the female passengers saw his clothing eaten through by rats, took pity on him, and gave him her bathing suit to use for underwear. "The customs officials and the gendarmes looked with surprise at me, an emaciated boy in a woman's bathing suit, which showed through the holes of my sailor pants," he recalls.[12]

He came first to Brno. His fellow Russian émigrés who had settled there earlier, Konstantin Yurevich of the Constantinople gymnasium and others, collected some clothes for him; one gave him a shirt, another a tie, yet another a cap. On November 18, 1922, Dmitri returned to Prague and paid his first visit to a two-story building behind a stone fence on the far side of Rieger Gardens, a fashionable city park. The building, known in Prague as Villa Teresa, housed an institution that would play a sinister role in his life—the Soviet Trade Mission.[13]

This outpost of Soviet power in Czechoslovakia, as well as Soviet trade missions in other European countries at that time, served as a center of Red propaganda and a cover for the OGPU operatives. Moreover, these missions were charged with doing everything they could to undermine the political and civic stability of the host countries. Even today, secret instructions to those missions shock with their Machiavellian hypocrisy:

> In capitalist countries with a bourgeois and politically
> right-wing population, the Soviet [trade] mission
> premises and stores must be luxuriously equipped and
> all receptions must impress [their guests] with luxury
> and abundance. By all means possible, it's necessary to
> make them believe that the Soviet government is so
> close to the capitalist system that its official recognition
> would benefit capitalists, not blue-collar workers.[14]

In other words, the Soviet trade missions had to imply that the official Soviet statements of being a "country of toiling masses" were just a cover for the true (read: capitalistic) nature of the newly formed USSR. In the spirit of its political agenda at the time, bent on exporting revolution throughout the world, the Soviet government instructed its trade missions abroad to "spread rumors about the possibility of military conflict [with the Soviet Union] and agitate against [the host state's] government." The missions' most important task was to "purchase weapons and ammunition; [and] seize every opportunity to buy arms of all kinds. Ammunition had to be stored in areas where it would be easiest to recruit and arm detachments of blue-collar workers."[15]

Because of Czechoslovakia's strategically important location in the center of Europe, the Soviet Trade Mission in Prague was designated by the Soviet government as a center for espionage in neighboring European countries as well. In planning a Red Army offensive, the Mission was charged with determining measures that would assure its success in the Carpathian Mountains, the Danube Basin, and the Balkans. With Czechoslovakia as a natural source for upgrading Soviet armament during the planned Red Army attack, the secret instructions marked the Czech army, which was well organized and equipped with state-of-the-art military technology, as the prime target for intelligence work. The Soviet agents were charged with full assessment of the country's capacity to produce ammunition and artillery. The Škoda plants, the main manufacturer of military equipment and arms, were the prime targets for industrial espionage.[16]

All these tasks required a constant supply of spies recruited from every possible quarter. However, on this first visit to the Mission, Dmitri, emaciated and ragged, was met at the Villa Teresa with suspicion. The head of the Soviet Mission, Comrade Alexandrovsky, heard out his feverish story and told him, "You're either a spy or a lunatic," and threatened to call the police.[17]

Ironically, Dmitri's enemies, the anti-Bolshevik Russian Émigré Student Union, did want to listen to him. They thought he would give an eyewitness report on hunger and atrocities in Red Russia and invited him to speak at one of their meetings. Despite the danger that such a venue posed for him, Dmitri decided to use his talk as an opportunity to advance a political goal of his own. Instead of describing the horrors of Soviet life, he assured his listeners that their homeland was returning to normal and called on them to repatriate and take part in the reconstruction efforts.[18]

It seems that, speaking to the émigré students, Dmitri did not believe so much in what he was saying, but he desperately *wanted* to believe in the future of his country. Although undoubtedly the hardship and social injustice he experienced during the years of his vagabond existence played an important part in forming his political convictions, there were no less powerful emotional reasons for his attachment to Russia. The Soviet secret service as a whole, and his spymasters individually, took the place of the father he never knew. His strong craving to belong, whatever the consequences, would induce him to risk his life many times in his future intelligence work.[19]

As he could have foreseen, the effect of his speech was explosive. Deeply disappointed, the émigré students attacked him physically. Miraculously, he survived, escaping with minor cuts and bruises, but he didn't give up on his political convictions. When he began his studies at the Russian Law Faculty, he refused to accept support from the Czechoslovakian government's Russian Action program because he considered the program hypocritical—a way of keeping "Russian money" in the Czechoslovakian government's pocket. He believed the Soviet claim that, during the civil war in Siberia, fighting on the side of the White Army, the Czech Legion expropriated a considerable amount of Russian gold. And now the Czech government was giving the very same money back to émigré Russians in the form of support for students, among whom were not only White Guardsmen but also those who, in his view, had nothing to do with Russia proper—Jews and Ukrainians from Poland and Romania.[20]

He also refused to accept a free dormitory space offered by the program, instead renting a tiny, cold room in the attic of a building overlooking the Škoda plants on the outskirts of Prague. To support himself, he dug graves in the Olshan Cemetery and occasionally gave Russian lessons to members of rich Czech families. His day-to-day life consisted of attending his Russian Law Faculty classes and spending most of his time in the State Library, located in the old Jesuit monastery near the Charles Bridge. Here he not only prepared for his classes but also worked on a series of articles on Bolshevik ideology. Although they didn't promise much income, the articles helped him to develop theoretically the world outlook he had already formed emotionally.[21]

At that time, he wasn't alone in embracing the Bolshevik ideology. At the beginning of the civil war, the politics of the Russian emigration, mirroring political life before the Bolshevik takeover, represented a wide spectrum of political views. However, toward the end of 1921, with the final defeat of the White Army, increasing numbers of destitute refugees turned toward Bolshevik Russia. Homesickness engendered idealization of the changes that the country was undergoing. Deprivation, near starvation, and the separation of many refugees from their families in the homeland speeded up this process.[22]

Besides his hand-to-mouth existence during the past few years and his need to feel attached to his Motherland, young Dmitri embraced Communist ideas because, as he admits himself, by giving him hope, they made his life seem easier. In the late afternoon, he would make the rounds of the stores in the center of the city. One storeowner would give him scraps of meat; another offered a loaf of stale bread. As he would recall years later, walking amid well-dressed Czechs along Prague's main streets, he felt "not envy but great anger, a holy wrath that one day would overturn the world."[23]

Since he couldn't pay for electricity, he hurried back to his room before dark. He had dinner, spreading an old newspaper on his bed. There was no kitchen, so he ate his meat raw. Usually at that hour, the fever, which he attributed to early stages of tuberculosis, resumed. The fever made him feel exalted and enthusiastic. He read his beloved poems aloud and argued with imaginary opponents. In his head he composed apt phrases for his articles on Nietzsche and Lenin, "on good and evil, on the birth of a new man, who, renewed and restructured, will be God." In these feverish hours, he thought he could "deliver the new word to the indifferent world," which seemed to him "a bulwark to be taken by storm." He anticipated the time when the "new men" wouldn't know the horrors of poverty and loneliness. He imagined the "heroic symphonies of uprising," and the flames of the steel furnaces seemed to him "victorious banners waving."[24]

Apparently, composing those articles, especially on Nietzsche's work, had a profound effect on the half-starved, lonely, and otherwise deprived young man. It shaped his character and guided his actions, both consciously and unconsciously. It seems that now, reading Nietzsche, Dmitri had been prodded further into buying the new morality that had begun taking root on Russian soil at the end of the nineteenth century, first, in the artistic milieu, and then among radical politicians. According to that morality, pity had to be rejected as a sign of weakness, and love for "the most distant" was by far more important than love for neighbor. Sacrifice and suffering became the ideal mode of behavior. Among radical political thinkers, populist terrorism began to be seen as a heroic tradition to be emulated by the new generation of revolutionaries. (We will encounter Dmitri's fascination with the heroic images of populist terrorists in tsarist prisons at the time of his own imprisonment in Soviet ones.) Fulfilling these high ideals gave birth to a revolutionary immorality in which the end justifies the means. An ethic of everyday life was deliberately omitted. It was assumed that the ordinary, everyday aspects of life would be radically transformed.[25]

Dmitri's stoicism lasted a few months. Eventually, he was forced to join other émigrés and move to a Russian émigré students' dormitory, a five-story building, Svobodarnia, in Strašnice, a Prague working-class district. Formerly the residence of workers at a Škoda plant, the building consisted of tiny rooms with just enough space for a bed and a stool. The wooden partitions didn't reach the ceilings; privacy was impossible. Not surprisingly, Dmitri's sympathies for Red Russia proved hazardous there. Soon after moving in, he became the target of relentless, at times life-threatening, attacks. The students beat him up often. At night, they attached wires to his body and gave him electrical shocks. Once they even tried to throw him out of a fourth-floor window. He survived only thanks to his physical strength and the help of his old friend, Georgy Georgiev, who also lived in the dormitory. Georgy notified the Czech police, and the attack was stopped before it was too late.[26]

The hand-to-hand fighting between Dmitri and his fellow students came to the attention of the OGPU operatives at the Soviet Trade Mission. Instructed "by all means possible to foster quarrels in various [Russian] émigré circles and to publicize these quarrels, disagreements, and scandals," the operatives acted accordingly. They also used the opportunity noted in these instructions: that some Russian émigrés could be "bought at little expense because most of them [were] destitute."[27]

Evidently, what also helped to establish Dmitri's loyalty was the arrival of a letter from Comrade Kudish of the Constantinople Trade Mission, in which he vouched for Dmitri. The head of the Prague Mission, Comrade Alexandrovsky, had a change of heart toward the young man and took him under the Mission's wing. Since Dmitri's pro-Soviet activities twice caused public disturbances and made him a candidate for deportation, the Soviet Mission intervened on his behalf and gave him cover. In August 1923, they helped to restore his Soviet citizenship, and he became permanent secretary of the Union of Student Citizens of the USSR Living in Czechoslovakia, organized by the Mission. The union's task was to divide and demoralize the émigré students, most of whom had opposed the Bolsheviks. The Mission also charged the union with putting pressure on those students who were undecided about repatriation, which the Mission had begun promoting since June 1922. Another of the union's tasks was finding prospective intelligence agents.[28]

Dmitri led an active pro-Soviet propaganda campaign among the students. His most aggressive actions were reported in the Czechoslovakian press. For example, on January 25, 1924, a few days after Lenin's death, all the major Prague papers ran the story of the fight he picked with a monarchist student who wanted to tear down the deceased Soviet leader's portrait, displayed in a store window.[29]

Because of Dmitri's knowledge of foreign languages—Czech acquired locally, French, German, and English studied first with private teachers in his foster family and then in the Anapa gymnasium, and Turkish learned from his nanny and improved during his long stay in Constantinople—the Mission made him a freelance translator in its press department. Gradually, they involved him in intelligence work. He was asked to collect information about politics and the economy not only from a variety of open-press organs but also from his Czech acquaintances. Then they gave him a part-time job as a librarian. Soon he got a full-time position as the Mission's registering clerk. "For the first time in my life abroad," Dmitri underscores in his memoirs, "I ate my fill, moved to a decent apartment, and clothed myself well."[30]

At the end of April 1925, in Moscow as a delegate to the First Congress of Proletarian Students, in Prince Dolgorukov's former mansion, his true consecration as an intelligence operative took place. Dmitri didn't know at the time that the man who interviewed him, Artur Artuzov, wasn't so much testing him as a potential agent abroad as making sure Dmitri wasn't a Czech spy, recruited from the White émigré community in Prague.

Dmitri would learn many years later in the camps that, unbeknown to him, the Czech secret police had considered recruiting him as their agent, which very fact the OGPU might have learned through their own agents in Prague. Thus, already employed by the Mission, Dmitri was sent to Moscow to be cleared of that suspicion first of all. This also explains the rather cautious attitude toward him during the interview on the part of the other interviewer, Mikhail Gorb, at that time assistant to the head of the Foreign Intelligence Department of the OGPU. [31] He wanted to determine whether, once recruited by the OGPU, Dmitri would become a double agent.

Apparently, on hearing Dmitri's story, Artuzov trusted him and said to Gorb, "We'll use him in the upper circles [of European society]." It was then that he asked the young Dmitri what kind of intelligence work he wanted. Dmitri returned to Prague sworn in as a full-fledged operative of the OGPU Foreign Intelligence Department (INO). As his employment record shows, his cover job title was "translator."[32]

Prague wasn't only the city where his career in intelligence was launched; here he would also meet and fall in love with two young women who would play a dramatic role in his life. He would marry one and be brought to the verge of murdering the other.

FOUR

Looking for Love in All the Wrong Places

Dear God, spare me from love. And I'll take care of the rest of my troubles.

—RUSSIAN PROVERB

"Has that hobo gone yet?" These words rang in his ears long after he heard them. They belonged to a woman who would play a sinister role in his life, although at the moment he met her he never would have guessed this. Little did he suspect that in a year or so he would fall in love with her, hopelessly and fatally. He heard the scathing remark sometime in late 1922, soon after returning from his impulsive trip to Russia. It was at the time when, having refused support from the Czechoslovakian government, he was leading a dismal existence and living in a poorly heated attic on the outskirts of Prague. He read all day long, leaving his hideout only for law school classes or to search for work of any kind. One of his few sources of income was tutoring in Russian one Mr. Fischer, a wealthy Czech businessman. That was how Dmitri met a young Englishwoman, Miss Isolde Cameron, a governess in charge of Mr. Fischer's two adolescent girls, Camilla and Evelyn.[1]

It was hardly love at first sight. Moreover, his first impression of Miss Cameron was highly unfavorable. Her svelte figure, her energetic and pale face, and her shiny blue eyes notwithstanding, he found the young woman obnoxious and haughty. Although, like himself, she was a poor foreigner working for a rich Czech man, she showed nothing but contempt for the destitute young Russian. One day, as he stood on the balcony of Mr. Fischer's luxurious apartment waiting for his pupil to come for their scheduled lesson, he overheard the governess asking the housemaid, "Has that hobo gone yet?" The words made him uncomfortable. For a while, he couldn't even force himself to come in from the balcony for fear of being ridiculed on account of his patched-up pants and tattered shoes. But what happened next had ramifications that he could hardly have foreseen. He was about to leave the balcony when, through the lace curtains of the girls' bedroom lit from inside, he saw the governess undressing Mr. Fischer's young daughters. Unaware of being watched, she dropped on her knees and began passionately kissing intimate parts of the girls' bodies.

The scene was hardly a shock to Dmitri. Several months in Constantinople bordellos had exposed him to every imaginable form of human sexuality. Leaving Mr. Fischer's house, he dismissed what he saw as "sweet poison," a metaphor for homosexual sex he borrowed from Charles Baudelaire, whom, together with other decadent poets of the late nineteenth and early twentieth centuries, both French and Russian, he had eagerly read in his youth:

What a dizzying pleasure—
Through these new lips,
The most exciting and beautiful,
To infuse you with my poison, my sister![2]

Before leaving the quarters of his pupil, he called the housemaid and angrily demanded to be paid for the lesson: it wasn't his fault that Mr. Fischer hadn't shown up for it. The episode set the stage for his later fixation on Mr. Fischer, who duplicated his father in an emotional sense. His father had paid for his privileged upbringing but never took any interest in him personally, and by skipping a lesson without advance notice, Mr. Fischer also undermined Dmitri's feeling of self-worth.

Soon dramatic changes in Dmitri's life eclipsed the unpleasant episode in his memory. With the beginning of his employment at the Soviet Trade Mission in Prague, his daily struggle for survival ended and, with it, so did the ascetic phase of his life. Under the wings of the Trade Mission, he finally gained a sense of belonging. Self-disciplined and industrious, he quickly rose in rank. His full-time Mission employee salary made it possible for him to move to a decent room, where, in a matter of a few months, a shy and ragged fellow turned into a strong and self-confident man.

His participation in intelligence work at the Trade Mission was enhanced. Besides doing research work by scanning open publications behind the desk, he became personally involved in collecting industrial secrets, using his aristocratic manners and good looks. For that purpose, he began rubbing elbows with members of the Prague business community. Of course, after a decade of destitute life, he had to brush up on his manners and dress appropriately. He gave his efforts an ideological twist: he considered dressing fashionably not an exercise in vanity but part of his armor in the class struggle, which would eventually lead to the victory of those from whose ranks [he had] recently emerged:

> Previous ascetic ideals of stern self-restriction now
> seemed to me a harmful sectarianism: to eat well didn't
> mean to commit treason in relation to the hungry, and
> an elegant suit could be useful in my new work [as an
> intelligence operative] . . . For all my foreign life, I didn't
> have even a gulp of alcohol, didn't smoke a cigarette,
> and didn't visit a night joint *just for myself.* I learned to
> do it [to fight] *them* [the bourgeoisie], and I did it well
> as though these habits were second nature to me.[3]

Soon he excelled in drinking whiskey without getting drunk and learned how to behave in the chic restaurants and expensive nightclubs that abounded in Prague in those prosperous years of the First Republic. Founded after the collapse of the Austro-Hungarian Empire in the aftermath of World War I, the Republic of Czechoslovakia inherited a productive industrial and financial infrastructure. Under the leadership of its first president, Tomáš Masaryk, the country found a healthy balance in its economy and politics. Enlarging markets for its products was the only problem that the Czechoslovakian business community strove to solve. Engaged in reconstructing an economy ruined by revolution and civil war, the Soviet Union was a large potential buyer of Czech industrial products and equipment.

Pictures from his archive taken during 1924 and 1925 show how Dmitri gradually changed his appearance—from a poor law student to a well-groomed and fashionably dressed businessman with a clipped moustache. Although he calls these the "work clothes" of his newly acquired intelligence employment, his own description of himself preparing for a stroll in the city betrays his true enjoyment of his elegant looks for their own sake: "Over a gray English-made suit, I throw on an oversized spring coat and carelessly knot a multicolored scarf. I don a fashionable hat and tilt it slightly. Done? Yes, also a pair of light suede gloves. A pack of cigarettes in a pocket. Well, now I seem to be ready."[4]

He would retain this penchant for good clothing for the rest of his life. Even after serving sixteen years in the inhuman conditions of Siberian camps, already a broken man, his health permanently ruined, he was nevertheless always well-groomed and, insofar as he could afford it, made it a point to have clothes from the best Moscow tailors. (As the reader may recall, I owe my acquaintance with Dmitri to the fact that, instead of buying a ready-to-wear suit, usually poorly made, in a Soviet store, as the vast majority of Soviet citizens did, he had his new suit made in a tailor's shop of the Ministry of Defense where my father-in-law worked.)

But Dmitri's social advances turned out to be insufficient to compensate for the absence of a personal life. He had an unclear, unconscious need for something that he himself couldn't understand. To suppress this mysterious need, he engaged in sports of all kinds. But neither swimming nor tennis nor fencing nor skiing in the mountains helped much. His strange feeling of emptiness kept growing. At this point in his life, what had seemed to be a permanently discarded memory returned to him and began haunting him with an unanticipated power. The incident that triggered it and set it in motion took place in the winter of 1924 to 1925, during one of his ski trips to the Sudeten mountains, a luxury he could now afford thanks to his new line of work. Shortly before sunset, returning to his hotel, he stopped for a moment to take in the beauty of the landscape, and right there, on the top of a hill, he spotted a statue of the Madonna. Describing the moment in his memoirs, he does not register any religious feelings. For him, the statue was not that of the mother of the Christian God but that of a "svelte girl pressing a baby to her chest."

The immediate image that came to his mind was that of a woman who was nearby and whom the statue resembled—another svelte young woman whom he had met two years earlier, Miss Isolde Cameron, the governess of the children of his former Russian pupil, Mr. Fischer. (In turn, with her "high forehead, a falcon profile, and a daring and strong-willed facial expression," she strikingly resembled his own mother, Klavdia Bystrolyotova; it's easy to see the same features on Klavdia's photographs and in his drawings of her.)

On a train returning to Prague, he couldn't wait to see Isolde. He rushed to Mr. Fischer's home only to find that she had quit her employment there. Since the maid who opened the door didn't have the former governess's home address, he obtained it from the city's information bureau. In the evening, he paced the sidewalk in front of her residence thinking about how he would make her believe that he had run into her by chance. Finally, after hours of waiting, Isolde appeared on the street. His heart skipping a beat, he even forgot to bow politely, as she walked by without even glancing at him.

He could hardly wait for another day to pass, a day spent feverishly rehearsing openers with which he hoped to engage the object of his obsession in a conversation. But standing outside her home, when he tried to talk to her the next evening, she dismissed him right away, saying in a tone that left no room for hope, "I'm sorry, but I don't know you. And I don't talk to strangers on the streets."

He wasn't one to give up easily. Since Mr. Fischer's maid had mentioned that, after quitting the governess job, Isolde had taken a teaching position at the English College, he signed up for her class: with his good command of the language, he hoped to attract her attention.

He dreaded spoiling things with an overeager attempt made too early, so he waited a few months before summoning the courage to approach Isolde again. But he failed again and failed miserably. The young woman not only replied that she didn't remember him but also made it clear that she wasn't interested in seeing him outside of the classroom. Tormented by her rejection, he spent day and night with no more than glimpses of hope against a background of solid despair.

The intensity of his pursuit of Isolde speaks volumes about Dmitri's need for affection at that time in his life. Clearly, it was more than a plea for a woman's love. Isolde was the emotional surrogate for his mother, who had been distant, cold, and punishing for most of his formative years. His pursuit of the young woman became an obsession, a desperate attempt to fix the relationship with his mother after the fact.

Finally, after his futile attempts failed again and again, Isolde's coldness stopped him. However, the experience changed him in one respect: he abandoned the self-imposed sexual abstinence he had practiced during his first Prague years. His sexuality awakened, he began pursuing other women. "I was young," he recalls, "and once reminded about women, I couldn't stop. Girls were looking for me themselves, and easy victories supplanted a troubling feeling of emptiness."

His sexuality was hardly abnormal, but he would sustain his interest in women even in the horrific conditions of Siberian camps. ("He didn't pass up any opportunity to speak to a beauty," Milashov said, smiling, during our interview. He recalled how, when walking with him on Moscow streets, already a broken man, an invalid, Bystrolyotov would give his stepgrandson, then a young boy, pointers on how to attract the attention of a pretty girl who passed by.)[5]

At that time in Prague, tall, handsome, well dressed, and well groomed, emanating an air of respectability, Dmitri had no problem attracting women. In hindsight, he realized that he had hardly been an ugly duckling back in his youth. He recalled now that, at the age of eighteen, shortly after he had fled from war-torn Russia for the first time, dressed in a sailor's uniform—"a sparkling white tunic with a blue collar, a beret with pom-pom dashingly moved to the side" [his schooner *Eglon* flew a French flag]—he was irresistible to women in seaport hangouts. They all vied for his attention and offered him their embraces "for half the price, for a quarter of it, even for free." He didn't succumb to the temptations then, because, as he recalls, "amid the coarseness and filth of a sailor's life," he "still preserved a shy innocence and a naive belief in a woman's purity."[6]

But, like everything else in his life from the time of his employment at a Soviet institution, his renewed pursuit of women wasn't a matter of his personal life. No longer the "leaf torn from a branch" at the time of fleeing Russia in 1919, now he willingly subordinated the whole of his self to the higher cause. He wanted to please his kindhearted Motherland, which forgave him his trespasses—leaving her in the trying time of the civil war—and now took him back into her bosom. And he was eager to prove his loyalty to her. His willingness to serve his country with self-abandon was in line with the traditional

Russian intelligentsia's belief in the primacy of the good of the society at large in the life of an individual. After all, back in his early days, his mother gave him ample lessons on what should be of supreme importance in his life.

His allure to women came in quite handy now, when the orders of OGPU operatives at the Trade Mission heavily involved him in economic and industrial espionage. Since the main article of Czechoslovakian import to the Soviet Union at that time was heavy machinery, to facilitate doing business with the Soviets, several machine-building firms created a company called the Continental-Kern Concern. For a small fee and, in his own words, "compensation in intimate relations," the Concern's young secretaries and typists supplied him with technological blueprints, production data, and engineering calculations. He saw to it that the flow of information was never interrupted: if one of his informants married or moved to another job, she would assist him in finding a replacement.[7]

Most of his spy activities took place in Prague itself. But some of the Mission's assignments took him out of town. Thus, as the Soviet shoe industry was beginning to develop, one of his orders was to obtain the technology for the leather varnish production of the famous Batia shoe factories. To fill this order, he traveled to the Moravian town of Zlín, where these factories were located.[8]

Intelligence work made him happy. By his own admission, he "reveled in it, despite the danger; a new world opened for [him]." The apparent ease with which he operated within the Czech business community made it sensible for the OGPU operatives to invest in him. Now, as he socialized with many prominent businessmen, it was necessary to maintain his image with appropriate living arrangements. The OGPU rented a large and comfortable apartment for him with a balcony overlooking Rieger Gardens in the center of Vinograds, the city's bourgeois quarter, so he could invite his business associates to his home. To add to his respectability, a bona fide "prim" housemaid was hired.

After a while, the same apartment was used for even more daring operations: capitalizing on his fluency in English, Dmitri began posing to Czechs as a visiting American businessman. This was risky: Prague wasn't a large metropolis; there was always a danger that he could be identified as an employee of the Soviet Trade Mission. But, as he recalls, "I believed in myself, my intelligence, my cunning abilities, and my bravery." He seemed happy. At night he would sit with his books, studying as the "days passed joyfully."

One hot summer evening in 1925, after dining alone in a good restaurant, he walked into the Rieger Gardens, the city's central park. Here and there couples sat on the benches kissing. Glancing at the lovers, he recalls that "an unsettling feeling of chaos and dark desires" arose in him.

He was moving along poorly lit alleys when suddenly he spotted a lesbian couple: a young woman sitting on another woman's lap. In the semidarkness, he couldn't see their faces, but the crocodile-skin purse on the bench was familiar. His throat dried up: the purse resembled the one that belonged to Isolde. As he moved closer, he recognized the voices. One of them, girlish, belonged to Mr. Fischer's thirteen-year-old daughter Camilla and the other was . . . Isolde's. First he felt like taking revenge on her for rejecting him. But, to his own surprise, he couldn't help feeling joy at seeing her again. He felt "crazy tenderness" and something else that he couldn't identify, something "bitter and sweet."

He couldn't move as he tried in vain to decide upon some kind of action. Meanwhile the couple got up. He was about to follow them when, from the bushes in front of him, a man's figure emerged. It was Camilla's father, Mr. Fischer himself. When his daughter and Isolde left the park, he began stalking them along the streets. Dmitri tailed him all the way to the doors of Mr. Fischer's villa. There the lovers embraced and parted. Seeing Isolde threw Dmitri into emotional turmoil, which kept him awake for the rest of the night. He wandered the streets till dawn.

Now he decided to force her to see him by blackmailing her, taking advantage of her Achilles' heel: child molestation. The next day he phoned Isolde. Without identifying himself, he asked her what kind of cocktail she preferred and invited her to meet him at the bar of the Steiner Hotel, located on Vaclav Street. She would recognize him by a Paul Verlaine volume in his hands. She was ready to hang up when he offered to read her one of Verlaine's poems, "Pensionnaires," from his famous *Parallèlement* cycle. Perhaps, he said, she might reconsider her refusal to meet him:

The younger one is thirteen, the older is twice older,
And both share the room where they repose.
It happened in September, toward the evening time.
Both fresh and rosy, as a little apple, sweet-scented,
    golden,
Disposed from underwear, transparent, laced, restraining
    movement
The underwear emitting fragrant odors,
The young one twines in front of her older sister,
Who kisses her breasts, her whole youthful body.
Then she pressed herself to her partner's hip and,
Her arousal a par with her insanity,
She pressed her lips, against her will,
To the shadow under the light fleece.
Then, in the measure of waltz, giving themselves up to
    the touch of little fingers,
In a palpitating movement, they merged into one being.[9]

To make it clear why he was reading this poem, he substituted the ages of the girls in Verlaine's original text, who are fifteen and sixteen, with the ages of Camilla and Isolde. He finished reading the poem and asked politely, "What do you say to that?"

After a short pause, Isolde replied, "I see that you're an exceptional scoundrel." She called his actions by their name, blackmail, and asked him what his demands were. He replied that he had only wanted to caution her that she was in trouble: her former employer had seen her in the company of his daughter Camilla the night before. "Oh God," Isolde sighed. Now she agreed to meet Dmitri.

He arrived at the café earlier, and to calm himself, he gulped down two shots of brandy. Deeply in love with Isolde, he brushed off the fact of her sexual liaison with Mr. Fischer's daughter as a prank, a temporary indulgence in a "fashionable vice." He believed that his passion for Isolde, the passion of a true man, would eventually prevail over her lust for young girls.

Finally, she appeared in the café and joined him at his table. To cover up the awkwardness of the moment, she began smoking; she opened her cigarette case, plated with dark gold, and offered him a cigarette. As Dmitri took it, he let his eyes linger on the case. He spotted an inscription on the inside of the front cover: *Am loving you only and all my other loves are but nothing.* The inscription astounded him, and as he admits in his memoirs, it "later became the curse of [his] whole life." Isolde, whom he had idealized as a "pure and untouched flower," turned out not to be the Madonna. Was she in fact a "secondhand item"? He hoped he had just misread the inscription. To have a chance to read it again, he pretended to drop his cigarette and asked for another one.

There was no more doubt now. His heart sank, and he asked Isolde about the inscription. She said that it had been made by an extraordinary person. Having already decided that he would fight for Isolde's heart, he asked her whether that person was strong, and she replied that the opposite was true. She said that she preferred weak people. They can't control themselves well, and therefore, they live more vibrantly than the strong, who are able to stifle their desires.

"I'm weak myself," she said, "therefore, my passions are strong."

"I wish I could meet that person," he said.

She laughed. "That's quite simple. I exchanged identical cigarette cases with this person, and they both have the same inscription. If you ever come across another who owns such a cigarette case, look at that person, and you'll know that I'm in front of you, in the body of that other person. We are inseparable."

The conversation went on. He was already no longer able to separate his private life from his professional one, and he talked to her not as if she were his love interest, but as another Czech business contact whose trust and confidence he had to gain. To win her over, he had to convince her that they had something in common. Without thinking it through, he told her that on the night he had seen her with Camilla in the park he was not alone but in the company of a young male friend. And he offered his help in fighting Mr. Fischer, because people like him and Isolde, that is, homosexuals, have to stick together and form a common line of defense. "Today I help you," he explained, adding, "tomorrow you'll help me."

The tactic seemed to be working: Isolde's fingers squeezed his hands in appreciation. She reciprocated with a confession of her own: she had quit working for Mr. Fischer because he had pursued her sexually. Dmitri promised to think up a plan of action against their common enemy, and they parted.

Dmitri did resent Mr. Fischer, but of course, it had nothing to do with the reason he gave Isolde. Although in his memoirs Dmitri states that he was glad he had been "free from the prejudices, passions, and extremes peculiar to the class-bound world of Russian society," his caricatured portrayal of Mr. Fischer recalls Soviet propaganda posters directed at representatives of the bourgeois class. On that fateful day when he had met Isolde for the first time, walking away from Mr. Fischer's apartment, he thought, "Somewhere far away a luxurious car quietly rolls along the beautiful Prague prospects. Returning home, a fat Mr. Fischer calculates in his head the profits of the day. He's sure of himself. Business is good, and the firm of Fischer and Co. will stand forever like the Tower of Babel. He doesn't know that, underneath it, a mole is digging; it will undermine his power. The tower will collapse and bury Mr. Fischer in the trash heap."

Of course, here Dmitri is just paraphrasing Marx's prediction that capitalism was doomed to be buried in the dustbin of history. Thinking about what he had just witnessed through the lace curtains of Mr. Fischer's children's room, Dmitri gloated about the fact that the businessman's daughters had been molested. For him, it was but more proof of the inevitable demise of the bourgeois class: "[Mr. Fischer's] kin were already marked by doom: both his girls are poisoned with the sweetest poison; they'll perish. Yes, that's life's wise revenge."

Yet, Dmitri sought approval from the very man he despised. He felt special satisfaction when, during one of the Soviet Trade Mission receptions for the Prague business community, Mr. Fischer approached him, just recently a nobody, a destitute young man, and asked him about the prospects of getting a contract for his firm with the Mission. Later on, the two men ran into each other at the city theater, and Dmitri enjoyed the fact that, noticing his well-crafted and fashionable suit, Mr. Fischer asked "obsequiously" for the name of his private tailor.

Before getting down to the business of placing Mr. Fischer in a compromising position, Dmitri informed his spymaster (*rezident*) at the Soviet Trade Mission about his plans. He followed the ironclad rule imposed by his superiors—to report every new social contact—a rule he would always follow to the letter. The rule played a double role: it served as a means of enlarging the pool of potential recruits, and it kept Soviet intelligence operatives in check. The OGPU bosses never fully trusted their own employees. A failure to report any new contact raised the suspicion of double play.

Dmitri's spymaster at that time was "Comrade Golst," second secretary of the Trade Mission, the position traditionally occupied by Soviet foreign intelligence officers. "Golst" had the code name SEMYON, but his real name was Nikolai Grigorievich Samsonov. Before his Prague assignment, he was a seasoned spymaster who had directed Soviet intelligence operations in Estonia, Latvia, Germany, and Turkey.[10]

"Golst" gave Dmitri the go-ahead for his plans under the condition that the operation wouldn't create too much noise and break into an open public scandal, which could jeopardize his subordinate's reputation. When, as anticipated, Mr. Fischer phoned Isolde and demanded to see her on "very important business," on Dmitri's cue, she invited her former employer to her apartment.

In staging the scene, Dmitri seemed to draw his inspiration from the silent film melodramas of the time: an old rich man and a young poor man were to vie with each other for the heart of a damsel in distress. To play the part of the young lover, Dmitri solicited the help of his friend, Georgy Georgiev, whom he had already recruited as a Soviet intelligence agent. At the time, Georgiev had completed Prague's Commercial College and was working as a traveling salesman for a Czech firm.

Dmitri and Georgiev arrived at Isolde's apartment and planned their moves, step-by-step. As soon as Mr. Fischer knocked on the door, they hid in the bedroom. The first thing Mr. Fischer did as he entered the apartment was threaten to report Isolde to the police for child molestation, which he saw with his own eyes. "You're a criminal!" he shouted. "But I, a father, am ready to forgive your defiling of my underage daughter . . . in exchange for your love for me." He promised to protect Isolde from the law if she agreed to go away with him to any place of her choice—to Paris, to the Riviera, to Switzerland.

He offered her first money, then friendship, and finally, marriage. He dropped to his knees in front of the young woman and sobbed. Since Isolde remained silent, unable to restrain his desire anymore, he grabbed her, crying, "Answer me! Yes or no?" Trying to escape his embraces, Isolde retreated and fell onto the couch. Her dress tore, leaving her shoulders bare, and Mr. Fischer began kissing them passionately. At that moment, at Dmitri's prompting, Georgiev stepped out from the bedroom and exclaimed, "Well, you daughter trader, this time your tricks took you too far . . . [For] a husband you're too old and for a lover too ugly . . . Leave my girl alone. I'll be the one to kiss her. Not you!" That was too much for the businessman. He rammed Georgiev and pressed him against the wall. Then he grabbed the young man by his throat. They began to fight, overturning armchairs and smashing a porcelain vase.

Georgiev pulled out a gun. Fischer reached for it and tried to turn the barrel toward the young man's chest. A shot resounded, and Georgiev fell to the floor. The landlord, his wife, his guests, and their children ran over from an adjacent apartment to find out what was going on. Bursting in the door, they froze in horror. Dmitri's description of the scene also reads like a silent film melodrama: "Oh, what a picture it was! Isolde reclining on a sofa unconscious . . . Her dress torn, bits of the vase and pillows from the couch scattered all over the floor . . . Lying on the carpet, his face and chest covered in blood, was Grishka [Georgiev] . . . Above him, a mountain of meat, a pistol in his hand, stood Mr. Fischer. After a short pause, women and children began screaming."

At that moment, Dmitri himself stepped into the room. When the landlord asked what was going on, he dramatically pronounced, "A man was murdered while defending his girl from rape!" Mr. Fischer ran out of the apartment in dismay. Dmitri and the landlord put Georgiev on the couch. As soon as the landlord stepped out of the room to get a basin with warm water to wash off Georgiev's blood, Dmitri quickly disposed of the empty container of cherry syrup hidden in his friend's chest pocket and replaced the gun clip containing blanks with one containing bullets, one of them missing. Dmitri handed the landlord the gun, along with the empty cartridge, and advised him to keep it for police inquiry.

Then he went to Mr. Fischer's office and offered him his services as a lawyer. Dmitri misrepresented himself, of course. At the time, he was only a student of law who, too busy with his intelligence work, was falling behind in his academic studies and on the verge of being expelled from the Russian Law Faculty. Whatever knowledge he obtained in that school was useless in Fischer's case anyway: the school's program was geared toward preparing lawyers for the now-defunct Russian Empire.[11]

Evidently, Mr. Fischer was not aware of this. Believing he had committed murder, he was already dictating his last will to his secretary before planning to take his own life. Dmitri assured him he would see to it that the story was not publicized. In exchange for his assistance, Mr. Fischer wrote a letter of recommendation for Ms. Isolde Cameron, praising in particular her high moral qualities in bringing up his girls. Dmitri, Isolde, and Georgiev spent that evening in a restaurant celebrating their victory.

Apparently, when he had asked permission from "Golst" for this operation, Dmitri spared him the details. Otherwise, it is doubtful that an experienced spymaster would have approved an action potentially fraught with trouble. It looks as if Dmitri's emotional vulnerability impaired his judgment: his hatred for his father transferred onto Mr. Fischer, and his obsession with the young Englishwoman (a lesbian and a child molester to boot!) made him act irresponsibly. Indeed, this operation could easily have gone awry and done more harm than good. For one, Mr. Fischer could himself have had a gun, loaded with real, not empty, shots, which could have led to *real*, not fake, bloodletting. It is also not quite clear how Dmitri prevented an open scandal and avoided a police investigation, which could easily have established his affiliation with the Soviet Trade Mission. It already had a poor reputation with the Czech government as an outpost of Communist propaganda. Dmitri's involvement in a criminal case could have had grave political consequences. At the very least, it would have cost him his job.

But it seemed he was lucky. Everything worked out as planned, and he had something to offer to his masters in return. While the ordeal brought him closer to Isolde, it also made it easier to recruit her. After Dmitri tipped off "Golst" to that effect, the elaborate process of clearance for a prospective agent began. First, through a Soviet spymaster in London, they checked out her background. They found nothing suspicious. Then, Soviet agents like Dmitri who were part of the Prague White Guard student milieu tried to involve her in a bogus White Guard terrorist organization. When she didn't take the bait, on orders from the Soviet Trade Mission, the Czech Communists posing as agents attempted to persuade her to work for French intelligence. She also turned down this offer. A "rich man" pretended to fall in love with her and offered to take her with him to America.

When none of these traps worked, Dmitri tried to recruit her as a Soviet agent. But he also failed: Isolde wanted neither money nor adventure. When Dmitri appealed to her on idealistic grounds, she turned him down. "I don't have political convictions," she said. "I'm not quite sure of my own morality, but I want to keep my hands clean. I don't want to smear them either with somebody else's blood or with gold, and I don't want to belong to anyone." When Dmitri reported the results to "Golst," he was instructed to remain in contact with Isolde. She gave English lessons to some prominent officials of the Czech Ministry of Foreign Affairs and directors of the country's leading firms and banks, as well as their families. She might prove to be useful one day.

The order suited Dmitri's personal agenda. Although he had failed so far, he did not totally discard his hope of finding a way into the young woman's heart. Though his designs on Isolde were amorous in nature, the way he planned to proceed was not much different from the technique he learned as a recruiter—"to get to know her better, to make her open her soul to [him], so that it would be easier to control her later on." He was obsessed with uncovering his rival's identity, so as to challenge this person's power over Isolde. But weeks and months passed, and Isolde refused to reveal anything about the identity of her one and only true love. Dmitri decided to change tactics. To lower her guard, he began acting as if they were just brother and sister. He took her to dance halls, but he "danced with her as if she were a relative, that is, nicely, but without much enthusiasm." Once, when she was bathing, he carelessly walked into her bathroom and, without apologizing, took a towel and walked out with an indifferent expression on his face. A few times, under various pretexts, he slept on a couch in her apartment.

Eventually, he achieved the desired goal: Isolde became totally relaxed in his presence. He had convinced her that he had no sexual designs on her. One day she revealed to him that the reason for her homosexuality was an aversion to men that she had developed in childhood. She told him that, by accident, she had witnessed her widowed father raping one of his young female servants, and her father's animalistic behavior appalled her and made her forever avoid men. Although this seems implausible according to our current understanding of homosexuality, Dmitri seemed to believe her and didn't abandon his hope of becoming her lover.

Finally, his patience expired. One day, when they were dining in a restaurant, he tipped the waiter and told him to make Isolde's drinks stronger than usual. After she became considerably intoxicated and fell asleep, he brought her to his apartment and put her in his bed. He took a shower and lay down next to her in his pajamas, foretasting his victory: when his beloved awoke next to a true man, she would respond to him with desire. Waiting for this to happen and tipsy himself, he fell asleep. When he woke up, Isolde was sitting up in the bed, furious, full of animosity and contempt for him. She told him that, if he wished, he could proceed with his plan—but he should know that she would hate him forever for this, and now it was all over between them, once and for all. His heart sank. He had blown it. Months and months of obsession went down the drain. He admitted his defeat and left the room.

Although, on the surface of things, Dmitri's decision to pursue Isolde romantically looks sudden and rash, in psychoanalytical terms, it is a classic case of an unconscious attempt to heal childhood wounds. The chain reaction of Dmitri's emotions was triggered by seeing the sculpture of the Madonna during his ski trip, whose physical features reminded him of both Isolde and his mother.

While, as research has shown, physical resemblance to our primary caretaker in childhood plays a major role in whom we pick as objects of erotic desire, Isolde resembled Dmitri's mother not only physically but emotionally as well. She shared her negative traits as they were imprinted in Dmitri's brain from childhood: from the outset, she was equally dismissive and scornful toward him. On his own admission, his mother's rare visits to him at the foster family burned in his mind like the "whistling of a whip." Thus, the very coldness with which Isolde met all his advances made her even more desirable: the more she pushed him away, the more relentlessly he pursued her. The childhood wounds reopened and begged to be taken care of.

As psychologists of today observe, our motivation for seeking a mate is often directed by our unconscious urgent desire to heal childhood wounds, to find one who will help to undo the psychological and emotional damage of childhood, to reclaim our lost selves by proxy. This explains why, in most cases, our spouses' negative personality traits closely resemble the personality traits of our primary caretakers.

As psychologist Harville Hendrix explains it, "[one's] time-locked, myopic, old brain [is] attempting to return to the scene of [one's] original frustration so that [one] could resolve [his or her] unfinished business." [12]

It is, therefore, noteworthy that, describing the moment of his sudden decision to pursue Isolde erotically, Dmitri recalls that seeing the statue "*painfully* touched [his] heart: [he felt that] something wanted to awaken in [him] but couldn't." And the scene he had observed through the lace curtains of Mr. Fischer's apartment flashed in front of his eyes. Even in this, Isolde resembled his mother. Child abuse is an ambivalent act: the abuser loves the child but at the same time abuses him or her. That is why Dmitri's need for intimacy with the young woman became an obsession, and he decided to get her no matter what.

After finally giving up and making his decision to stop pursuing Isolde, Dmitri thought that he had seen her for the last time. But he was mistaken. A few years later, Isolde would reemerge in his life again and again until their final, deadly standoff. But then, in late November 1925, at the time of their last date, Dmitri did not have much time to lick the wounds of his male ego. Soon, he had to fulfill his spymaster's order and put his male charms to professional use again.

FIVE | Marriage and Other Calamities

When you're in love, you're at the mercy of a stranger.

—AMERICAN PROVERB

In his memoirs, Bystrolyotov calls his new target for recruitment "Countess Fiorella Imperiali, the first, and so far the only, woman diplomat of Fascist Italy." "Golst" characterized her as "pretty, educated, proud, rich, capricious," ten years older than Dmitri, and an important and difficult target. "Golst" himself and another, younger member of the Prague Mission staff had tried approaching her but failed. She was interested in neither money nor flings. "Golst" advised Dmitri not to spoil things by acting crudely or hastily. He gave him a year or two before actually attempting recruitment.[1]

"I was young and not bad looking," Bystrolyotov recalls. "The assignment seemed only a curious adventure, and the countess a fortress that I lacked both the skills and the strength to conquer. After all, I was only a youthful twenty-six, and she was a worldly woman, a Roman, one of those ladies I could see only from afar."

In real life, the woman was neither Italian, nor rich, nor a countess, nor a diplomat. And her name was not "Fiorella Imperiali." Marie-Eliane Aucouturier attracted the attention of Soviet intelligence because, as a typist at the French Embassy in Prague, she had access to confidential diplomatic material. At that time, the Soviet Union was fighting for full diplomatic recognition of the new proletarian state and was anxious to look into the files of all European power brokers. In his memoirs, Bystrolyotov substituted World War II adversary Italy for World War II ally France, still not disclosing secrets that, as he thought, could have political ramifications even decades later.[2]

In writing about her, Dmitri builds up Marie-Eliane as an insurmountable fortress, citing the gap between them in terms of age and social standing, but in reality there was not much disparity between them on either count. Born on July 10, 1900, Marie-Eliane Aucouturier was about the same age as Dmitri and of a modest petty bourgeois background.[3]

The only true thing in Bystrolyotov's description of her is that she was attractive, and unlike little secretaries and typists of the Škoda plants, the Continental-Kern Concern, and the Batia factories, who easily succumbed to his charms, she wasn't interested in sex without commitment. Her father, a blacksmith in the village of Les Frauds of Brie-Larochefoucault community, Departament Charente (evidently, LAROCHE, her future code name, connoted her birthplace), instilled in her and his three other children a strict bourgeois morality. At the outset of World War I, he moved his family to Paris, where he worked for the city, shoeing streetcar horses, and his wife owned a haberdashery store. Times were tough, and the couple managed to give their children only a high school education. Marie-Eliane followed her brother, Gustave Aucouturier, to Prague.[4]

Besides wanting to make his victory over the young woman look more impressive, Dmitri had another reason for giving her the name "Countess Imperiali," a character from Schiller's tragedy *Fiesco; or, the Genoese Conspiracy*. As with his other literary allusions, hoping to see his memoirs published in his lifetime, he followed a long Russian literary tradition that had evolved over centuries of draconian censorship—he turned to Aesopian language.

This tactic made it possible for him to talk more freely about his life than the KGB censors would allow. Indeed, the device works successfully: there are many parallels between Bystrolyotov's life and Schiller's play. The historical events on which Schiller based his play—the conspiracy against the house of Daria, the sixteenth-century Genoa imperialist dynasty—could easily be seen as a metaphor for the Soviet conspiracy against the imperialist order of the day, of which France was considered a part. Both cases, the plot of Schiller's tragedy and the real-life OGPU plot, involved feigning love to a woman related to the target of the corresponding conspiracies: Countess Imperiali to the house of Daria by blood (she was the patriarch's daughter) and Marie-Eliane Aucouturier to the French Embassy by employment.

By giving Marie-Eliane the name of "Countess Imperiali," Dmitri invited readers to infer that his own role in the events was similar to that of Schiller's protagonist Count Fiesco. The men resemble each other in more ways than one. Just as Schiller's hero comes from a long line of nobility, Bystrolyotov believed himself to be the descendant of an ancient aristocratic line, the Tolstoys. Even physically, the resemblance of the two was uncanny. Schiller's portrait of Fiesco could easily describe Dmitri as he appears in passport photos of that time: "A tall, handsome young man; his character is that of dignified pride and majestic affability, with courtly complaisance and deceitfulness." The last quality was hardly negative in Bystrolyotov's eyes: after all, dissembling feelings was one of the most important talents of a successful recruiter.[5]

Assigning him to the case, "Golst" gave Dmitri a blueprint of actions. According to preliminary observations, the target related to the Soviet people "without prejudice," so Dmitri was to make casual acquaintance with her at a social function. He was to engage her in a conversation about the new Soviet way of life, a subject that intrigued cultured Europeans at the time. As their relationship developed, he would pretend to fall in love with her and act along the lines of the scenario "Golst" had laid out for him. He would propose to her and offer to take her first to Moscow and then to Washington, claiming that he would be appointed second secretary of the Soviet Embassy for ten years. He would have to paint his bride-to-be a picture of the leisurely and beautiful life that awaited them. After she took the bait and craved physical intimacy with him, he was to tell her sadly, with tears in his eyes, that his superiors insist on some proof of her loyalty to her new country. First, he would ask her for some trifle—a couple of decoded diplomatic telegrams, then more and more of them.

"She'll give you one finger," "Golst" instructed. "Demand another one and then the whole hand, and after she is compromised, take her whole. We need [the French] Embassy's ciphers and codes, all of the diplomatic correspondence."

Dmitri immediately threw himself into action. It was easy to become casually acquainted with Marie-Eliane: her brother, Gustave, a Slavist who had come to Prague as a journalist, a correspondent of the Havas Agency, was close to the same circle of Russian émigré intellectuals as Dmitri's colleague at the Trade Mission's Press Department, Roman Jakobson, a well-known literary scholar. (With the outbreak of World War II, Jakobson later moved first to Scandinavia and then to America, where he would teach at Harvard University and the University of Massachusetts.)[6]

As instructed, Dmitri began courting Marie-Eliane at a restrained pace. He took the advice of "Golst" to heart and avoided rushing; by building up the target's trust, he slowly brought the relationship to the point where proposing marriage would come naturally. Physical intimacy was an important step in that direction. Unlike his easy victories over the young secretaries and typists at the Continental-Kern Concern and Prague's Škoda plants, it took Dmitri at least half a year to get this far. But something totally unexpected happened: in the course of two feverish days, he fell in love and married a total stranger.

On May 1, 1927, in the course of the May Day demonstration of the workers' parties in Prague, he met the woman who was soon (too soon!) to be his wife. He knew that he should follow the Soviet Trade Mission's instructions to its employees and avoid any open contacts with the Czechoslovakian Communists. It was bad enough that their leader, Clement Gottwald, had blown the cover of his direct ties with the Soviets when he declared during a speech at the National Assembly, "In reality, Moscow is our external revolutionary headquarters. We travel to Moscow to learn from the Russian Bolsheviks how to destroy you. And they are masters at that."[7]

But the sunny day called for a stroll. Elegantly dressed, full of energy, on his way to the Mission to help prepare for a large diplomatic reception on the occasion of the big Soviet holiday, he stopped for a smoke at the city center at Vaclav Square, near a group of Prague Communists preparing for a demonstration. Bystrolyotov describes what happened next: "At that moment, I noticed something that delayed me for only a half hour—but later, in a fateful manner, broke my life." He noticed a beautiful young woman standing on the back of a truck and handing out Communist propaganda leaflets. Her finely shaped hands and exquisite demeanor did not seem to belong to the crowd of blue-collar workers who surrounded the truck.

Dmitri admired the very things his newly embraced Communist ideology considered bourgeois and, therefore, contemptible: her fashionable clothes. He appreciated her elegant ensemble—her sporty suit, black suede beret, matching gloves and shoes. Already a connoisseur of fine clothing, he was prompted by the woman's attire to think of London's Bond Street or New York's Fifth Avenue boutiques. Was she a foreigner? If so, what was she doing handing out Communist leaflets here in Prague? He also noticed her fine brooch, in the shape of a heart stung by a scorpion. Bystrolyotov recalls the details of that brooch not by chance. Looking back at the circumstances of his meeting with his future wife, he sees the symbolism of the brooch's shape: in time, his own heart would be stung as treacherously as if by a scorpion. In hindsight, he recalls it as an omen of disaster coming to his personal life, which he seemed to notice right away but ignored, as many people do when they're in love. Together with the woman's high forehead and small, childlike mouth, he saw that her wide-open eyes were cold, the color of ice, and appeared empty. As she looked above the crowd, she made an impression of being "either blind or clairvoyant." He thought her head resembled that of Medusa Gorgona. He decided she was "a bit crazy . . . healthy people don't have such eyes," but he was mightily intrigued about the identity of this mysterious female.

At the moment, Georgy Georgiev, his friend and confidant, happened to pass by. He noticed Dmitri's interest in the young woman and tried to talk him out of pursuing her right then and there. An experienced "skirt chaser," as Dmitri characterizes him using the English term, Georgiev guessed that the woman was equally promiscuous. In fact, he had seen her before, in the company of his boss's wife, Mrs. Goldberg, his occasional lover. The two women had recently traveled to America and had become friends during the trip. Dmitri couldn't bear his friend's talking in the same breath about the stranger with a Medusa look and some vulgar Mrs. Goldberg. He was already smitten. He dryly asked Georgiev not to meddle in his private affairs. All he wanted him to do was to find out the young woman's name and address as soon as possible.

But he couldn't wait. He rushed along Italska Street to Villa Teresa, to the Trade Mission, where he knocked on the office door of Comrade Weisskopf, a young German Communist. The Mission's press secretary–attaché, Weisskopf knew many people in town. Dmitri described the young lady he had just met. When he mentioned her blind eyes, Weisskopf told him her name right away—Maria Milena Iolanta Shelmatova. Devoted to the Communist cause, she frequented the Mission. Later in the day, Dmitri phoned her and asked for a date. She told him that she planned to attend the All-Workers' Ball that evening.

In anticipation of their meeting, Dmitri dined at his favorite restaurant and decided that this young woman was the one he had been waiting for all his life. "All my ability to love was longing to be released," he recalls. At the ball, he took another look at Iolanta. (From the outset of their relationship, Dmitri addressed her by her third name, Iolanta—using the short forms Iola and Iolochka ["little Iola"], the Russian diminutive and endearing form of the name, perhaps because the word also means a "little spruce," that is, a thing both beautiful and prickly at the same time.) Although he had initially dismissed Georgiev's impression of her, now in this different setting, he did, indeed, see something unsettling about her. For one thing, she was dressed inappropriately for the occasion. Blue-collar workers with their families looked disapprovingly at her provocative décolleté and her bare back. And she behaved too forwardly for a lady as she talked to the group of young men swirling around her.

Only one thing remained unchanged from his first impression of her—her sad eyes. He knew that she saw him, and her sadness made him think the young woman's frivolous behavior was her way of stopping his pursuit of her. Now she reminded him of one of those "American vamps, making themselves up for a movie shot: sophisticated . . . thrilling . . . they embodied the ideal of [those] depraved times."

Much taken with Iolanta, he approached her and invited her for a stroll. They took a table in a restaurant, drank, chain-smoked, and talked all night. He dropped flower petals from a bouquet on their table into her glass. It was about three in the morning when he walked her to her place on the Mala Strana on the other side of the Vltava River. As they walked over the Charles Bridge, he told her how intoxicated he was with his life, full of adventures. Of course, he talked about them in general terms, without revealing their nature.

Sitting down at the base of one of the statues on the bridge, they continued talking. Still melancholy, Iolanta told him she did not share his enthusiasm about life. In her view, life was only a temporary stage, and a "big black hole" awaited everybody. She said that six

years before, at age nineteen, she had received a diagnosis of acute tuberculosis. The disease made her indifferent to everything in life. She
cited the engraving on King Solomon's ring—"This too shall pass."[8]

Her words relieved Dmitri. As he had hoped, it was illness, not
depravity, that made her sad and pessimistic. He would nurse her
back to health, and eventually she would cheer up. Meanwhile, Iolanta professed her love for heroic outcasts—"prophets beaten up by
stones, Prometheuses, and Quasimodos." Only selfless heroes were
high on her list. "I shy away from people with double chins, a hero's
certificate, and a check for their heroic deeds neatly folded in their
pockets," she declared.

Dmitri spoke in equally grand and abstract terms. He rhapsodized
about a life full of big ideas, about the beauty of struggle, victory or
death. He prattled on about everything that was on his mind at the
time. His own talk intoxicated him and made him oblivious to the
passing time. Writing about that episode four decades later, he finds
his own image of a man pontificating about politics on a first date
rather humorous: "I provided a firm base of scientific Socialism to
human dreams, quoted the classics of Marxism and Leninism, re-
futed bourgeois criticism and its reformist distortions, tied the general theoretical premises to the revolutionary practice of the moment,
and finally, enthusiastically concluded [my speech] with slogans developed for the May Day celebrations."

It's no wonder that Iolanta fell asleep listening to him. Carried
away with his talk, he noticed she was asleep only when she cuddled
under his arm. As he wrapped his coat around her, he thought of her
as a trusting child. But a few hours later, when the skies lightened up
and Iolanta awakened in his arms, he was disillusioned again. The
first thing she asked when she opened her eyes made his heart sink:
why hadn't he taken advantage of her when she was sleeping? She
laughed at his gentlemanly behavior. "Oh, it's all too clear to me,"
she said. "You're impotent. Yes, sir, you're impotent. You should see a
doctor right away."

Then, as if that weren't bad enough, she pulled down the top of
her dress and bared her breasts, saying in a cute voice, "And you,
poor little ones, are you alive or has this idiot frozen you to death?"
Dmitri was taken aback. "A whore," he said to himself. But then, as
he walked her home, he changed his mind. He decided that she was

too sad for a vulgar vamp. As they passed a hot dog stand, Iolanta said she was starving. She ate hot dogs and gulped milk from a bottle, like a puppy, and once again, for him she was just a child he had to protect.

They parted at the doorway of her building. At the last moment, she gave him one of her brooches, a silver one shaped like a rose. As he stepped onto the roadway, a passing truck nearly killed him. Luckily, a passerby pulled him back to safety. The brooch wound up in the mud. Four decades later, recalling that moment, he exclaims, "'What a menacing omen!' I should have shouted then. But, in his wandering, a human being is incapable of unraveling the mysterious signs of his fate. A dark shadow of my future crossed my path, but I stepped over it, not understanding anything."

The next day, he ran into Iolanta again on the steps of Villa Teresa. She asked him to take her to a theater that evening. Excited, he immediately offered to meet her an hour earlier for dinner before the show. The moment she agreed, he suggested meeting even earlier to make time to visit the Mission and register their marriage there. "Why did I say it? I don't know," he recalls. "But, in the dark depth of my ego, a clairvoyant gaze found the truth. Suddenly, I felt at ease and calm." Iolanta agreed. Later that day, the Mission's Council, Comrade Kliavin, recorded their marriage. At the moment when Dmitri excitedly signed his name, he produced a big ink blot and exclaimed, "What the hell!" In much dismay, his new bride told him she had mentally decided that the first word he uttered after signing their marriage papers would become symbolic of their future life together.

Disaster struck instantly, the moment he and Iolanta signed the marriage papers. He was still trembling with the excitement of this pivotal event in his life, when, to calm him down, Iolanta suggested that they have a smoke together. She opened her gold-plated cigarette case. It looked familiar to him. He caught a glimpse of the engraving inside the front cover—*Am loving you only and all my other loves are but nothing*—and he froze in horror. "If you ever come across another who owns such a cigarette case," Isolde's words flashed in his mind, "look at that person, and you'll know that I'm in front of you, in the body of that other person. We are inseparable."

In dismay, barely talking to his new wife, he took her home. She invited him up, but he abruptly said good-bye and left. In his memoirs, Dmitri gives two conflicting accounts of what happened next. In the first account, as soon as he reached the Charles Bridge a few blocks away, he changed his mind and returned to Iolanta. He found her crying, consoled her, and spent the rest of the night with her. But elsewhere in his memoirs, he gives a different—psychologically much more convincing—account of the events of his wedding night: while he did return to his new bride, it wasn't right away but several hours later. He spent these hours in the company of another woman, the French Embassy typist, Marie-Eliane Aucouturier.[9]

(Nine years down the road, when Dmitri revealed this fact to Iolanta, he sugarcoated his infidelity by presenting it as an example of his personal sacrifice to the higher cause. But it was true only to a point. He had pursued the French Embassy worker for nearly six months under orders, and meeting Iolanta had mixed up his plans and delayed that important step in Marie-Eliane's recruitment. Still, it's hard to believe that he had no choice but to seal his and Marie-Eliane's friendship with intimacy on his own wedding night. It is not too difficult to surmise what happened that night. Shocked and traumatized by the sudden discovery of his newlywed wife's past, he did something to assuage the blow to his male ego, to mend his broken heart. So he turned to another young woman who was ready to embrace him. A psychological nuance makes the last scenario ring true: after he disclosed his long affair with the Frenchwoman to his wife, Iolanta immediately responded that she knew when he had slept with Marie-Eliane for the first time, that it was on their wedding night. It is no wonder that she remembered her new husband's bizarre behavior.)

If the whole story in Dmitri's memoirs about the cigarette case sounds too contrived, as if taken from a B movie, the reader should bear in mind Nabokov's notion about life imitating art, even if, in this instance, it's low-grade art. At the same time, it is also possible that Dmitri invented the cigarette case connection between Isolde and Iolanta to conceal the fact that he had known (or perceived) all along that these two young women were lovers. It could have happened that at some point during his relentless pursuit of Isolde he had seen the women together (after all, Prague was not such a huge metropolitan city at that time). In that respect, his rush to marry Iolanta could easily be explained in psychoanalytical terms. After failing to erotically conquer Isolde and thus assuage the pain felt in his "old" (childhood) brain, when he met Iolanta, he unconsciously began to pursue her as a means to achieve visceral gratification: if he could not have Isolde, Iolanta would do. Moreover, he married her hastily because of his need to secure that psychologically important conquest. (As will be seen in the way their relationship developed in the coming years, the ease with which he separated from her on many occasions, at one point even nonchalantly handing her over to another man, makes this scenario of the outset of his marriage plausible.)[10]

Whatever scenario joined him with Iolanta, upon his discovery of the inscribed cigarette case, which jolted him back to the reality that Iolanta was not, after all, Isolde, it took Dmitri several days after their wedding night before he was able to compose himself enough to confront his newlywed wife. Until the last moment, he hoped he had misread the engraving, that Isolde was no more than his wife's close friend. When he finally brought himself to ask her, Iolanta responded evasively. She began talking about love in vague and general terms, claiming that this emotion defies clear-cut definitions. No two loves are alike, and her love for him was unique. As a way to calm him down, she offered to view Isolde as a test of strength of their marital love. And, in return, she promised to treat any young woman who might appear in his life in the future the same way. She insisted that true love cannot be possessive; it is a contradiction in terms. She also swore she would step aside if that theoretical other woman ever made him happier than she, Iolanta, was able to do, adding that she expected the same selflessness from him.

Elusive as her response was, after much hesitation, Dmitri accepted it. Deep down he hoped that his strong will would keep in check his physically and emotionally fragile wife, whom he saw more as a child—charming, but sick and unhappy—than a mature woman.

Describing his life in that period, Dmitri tries to project his image as a confident man in full control of his fate. In reality, nothing was further from the truth. From the moment of recruitment, a Soviet intelligence worker relinquished control of his life to his spymaster and, through him, to the Soviet state. Dmitri no longer fully belonged to himself and would not be able to regain his freedom for most of the rest of his life. As an intelligence operative, he not only had to report each and every social interaction but also had no choice of place of work or residence, not to mention having no control over such important decisions as marriage, which in some instances was even arranged as a means of a cover.

Writing in the 1960s and wary of censors, Dmitri glosses over the fact that even his marriage, the pivotal event in his life, had to meet his spymaster's approval. Intelligence operatives' marriages usually posed no problem. A family made agents even more dependent on their controller: now they had more to lose in case of defection or double-dealing. It also made them less susceptible to counterintelligence ploys involving sexual bait, which first compromised them and then coerced them into changing sides. But a potential bride's background had to be thoroughly checked to ensure that she did not present a security risk. Iolanta was cleared quickly, which is why Dmitri was able to marry her the next day. Not only did his bride work for the Mission on a voluntary basis, but her father, Josef Shelmat, was a staff member on the Central Committee of the Czechoslovakian Communist Party.[11]

In his memoirs, Dmitri passes over in silence how he managed to reconcile his marriage with his assignment to recruit the French Embassy secretary, Miss Aucouturier. After all, according to the "Golst" scenario, he had to seduce her by convincing her that he had serious intentions toward her. His marriage to Iolanta could jeopardize his assignment. To prevent derailment of the important task of obtaining French diplomatic codes and ciphers, and unable to talk the enthralled bridegroom out of marriage, "Golst" had to step in and take precautionary measures. While Dmitri's Soviet citizenship made the marriage fully legitimate, registering it at the Mission instead of the Prague City Hall made it low profile. Most likely, Comrade Kliavin, head of the Mission's chancellery, who conducted the quick ceremony, was ordered to keep it secret. After all, some Mission employees, Roman Jakobson in particular, belonged to the same social circles in which Dmitri's courtship of the Frenchwoman was undoubtedly known.

All this makes Dmitri's assertion that after their marriage he and his new wife led an intense social life—attending all sorts of parties and nightclubs—seem rather dubious. After all, appearing in public with another woman, never mind his wife, would have undermined his efforts to recruit Marie-Eliane, a woman of strict moral standards. That could explain why, in contrast to a general statement about his extensive mingling in Prague society with Iolanta, Dmitri goes into a detailed and lengthy description of what seem to be the true events: in secret from his friends and colleagues, and provided he had a cache of plausible excuses for not seeing his French "fiancée," he often escaped with Iolanta to the countryside, to secluded areas in the surrounding mountains and forests.

Tenuous as his hope of keeping Iolanta under his control was, Dmitri's gamble seemed to work during the first year of married life. Gradually, he and Iolanta grew closer. Decades later, he recalled that period of his life as truly happy.

But one day a new disaster struck. Iolanta returned to that sad state of mind he had noticed when they met. Her eyes sorrowful, her gaze empty, she withdrew from the world around her. Her condition worsened day by day. Finally, she refused not only to talk to anyone but even to eat. Alarmed, Dmitri summoned a physician. The doctor examined Iolanta, found nothing wrong with her physical health, and recommended a consultation with a psychiatrist. Writing about this many years later, Dmitri describes the psychiatrist's visit in inordinately minute detail, as if he wanted to persuade himself that the decision he had made during that visit was the right one.

Unsuccessful in his attempts to establish eye contact with the patient, the doctor asked Dmitri about his wife's family history. Dmitri told him what he knew. Iolanta came from a troubled family. Both her parents suffered from tuberculosis; in fact, her mother had died of a pulmonary hemorrhage. She also had a nervous disposition and often flared up easily. Iolanta's kindhearted and weak-willed father was prone to drinking. Her older brother was a gambler and a suicidal alcoholic. The other brother was also an alcoholic who refused to get an education. Iolanta's younger sister, Bozhena, whom Dmitri had met at the All-Workers' Ball shortly after he met Iolanta, took the radicalism of the Communist ideology, which the whole family embraced, to its extreme. Since the ideology called for contempt toward bourgeois respectability and propriety, Bozhena totally neglected her appearance; at the ball, she looked like a scarecrow indeed. As Iolanta put it, her sister combed her hair with "her fingers only" and wore "antediluvian black stockings recovered from the city dumpsters." Her breasts were "pulled tight by bandages so that, God forbid, she wouldn't appear either a bourgeois or a girl at all."

Summing up his findings, the psychiatrist explained Iolanta's withdrawal from the world as a psychotic episode characteristic of a borderline patient going through a depressive cycle. Based on what was known about borderline personality disorder at the time, he also guessed something about Iolanta that Dmitri had already known—that she was bisexual. The doctor warned Dmitri that his wife was dangerous, because there was an "eternally smoldering spark of madness" in her. "Your charming spouse is a Pandora's box," he said. "Never forget it and beware!" He recommended immediate hospitalization and told Dmitri that Iolanta's condition was a solid basis for divorce.

There are no simple answers to the question of why Dmitri reveals these highly private matters of his domestic life, sparing no clinical detail. Did he just want to get off his chest something that had troubled him for so many years? And why did he remain married to a mentally ill woman who gave him grief from day one (it could even be said, minute one!) of their marriage?

While we may never know all the answers to these questions, a close reading of his memoirs sheds some light on them. It seems that Iolanta's mental disorder served as an aphrodisiac to Dmitri. The psychiatrist read him the following passage from a textbook on patients with symptoms similar to his wife's: "The very nature of mental disturbances of these patients makes them extraordinarily sensitive and highly vulnerable. From here come their natural gifts, pure-heartedness, and charm. As they shy away from everything earthly, weak and defenseless, they are capable of evoking the most passionate love in others without much effort on their part." Dmitri commented, "Amazing! You just drew Iolanta's portrait."

Even motionless and withdrawn, Iolanta seemed to arouse him: "Deadly immobile, she looked at the sunset with her unseeing eyes," he writes. "Something horrific was in her—and seductively exciting for me, as always. Her transparent nightie bared her, taunting me. While hiding the details of her body, her heavy velvet robe revealed the perfection of her general outlines. She was a wonderful vessel from which, with my thirsty lips, I drank the sweet poison of enjoyment."[12]

Apparently, Iolanta's melancholic beauty fit Dmitri's aesthetic ideal of femininity, shaped by his early readings of fin de siècle French and Russian poetry. In fact, Dmitri precedes the account of his romance with Iolanta with the lines from Charles Baudelaire's poem "Madrigal triste" ("Sad Madrigal"): "Que m'emporte que tu sois sage? Sois belle, sois triste." (What do I care whether you're sane or not? Be beautiful, be sad.)

Dmitri's addiction to the "sweetness of danger" was a strong motivation in his daring intelligence operations, especially in the years to come, which affected his choices in his personal life as well. Perhaps in answer to himself about why he had stayed with the mentally troubled Iolanta, he quotes another decadent poet, this time a Russian, Aleksandr Blok:

> It's frightful, it's sweet, it's inevitable, it's a must
> For me—to throw myself into the mighty and foamy
> billows
> And for you—as a green-eyed naiad,
> To sing and splash near the treacherous rocks.[13]

Without much hesitation, Dmitri decided against divorcing Iolanta and took her to a hospital. However, to his chagrin, their relationship failed to improve after her discharge. Moreover, his wife mysteriously disappeared on a regular basis. Despondent, Dmitri confided his domestic troubles to his close friend (and fellow OGPU agent) Georgy Georgiev. He learned something from his friend that he wished was not true: his wife and Isolde had resumed their relationship some time ago. They were meeting at the apartment of Georgiev's employer, Mr. Goldberg, whose young wife, Lea, herself a bisexual, had turned her quarters into a meeting place for her lesbian girlfriends.

Desperate to get his wife back, one day Dmitri came up with an idea to gain control over her. He decided to involve her in his espionage business, thus leaving her neither time nor energy for extramarital affairs. He made her privy to the true nature of his job at the Mission and revealed that his job as a translator at the Trade Mission was a cover (his code name was "Zh/32" at the time). He proposed that Iolanta join the ranks—it was the best way she could serve the Communist cause that she claimed to hold so dear.[14]

Excited, Iolanta agreed immediately. The work promised danger, to which she seemed equally addicted. Dmitri set only one nonnegotiable condition: she had to end her relationship with Isolde once and for all. Iolanta swore she would. As a symbolic gesture of her resolve never to see Isolde again, he asked her to commit the damned cigarette case to the waters of the Vltava River, to throw it down from the Charles Bridge. She laughed, finding the gesture unnecessary. But since he insisted, she passed the cigarette case to him and let him do it himself. On Dmitri's recommendation, Iolanta was employed as a secret agent under the code name MILENA. His gamble seemed to work. In time, the marital bliss of their first year together returned. He felt happy again.[15]

But when he told Iolanta about his true occupation, he withheld an unpleasant detail: carrying out his assignments involved cheating on her regularly. For several months, he was sleeping in the beds of both his wife and the French Embassy secretary. He often came home late at night when Iolanta was already soundly asleep.

Something else happened along the way that surprised him a great deal and complicated his life significantly. His professional interest in Marie-Eliane did not make him immune to developing genuinely warm feelings toward her. Seeing her often, he got to know her better and grew to respect and admire her. He found himself truly attracted to her in more ways than one. The premeditated duplicity of sexual espionage turned into true love. He not only writes about that development openly in his memoirs but also finds it necessary to add an artistic touch. While for security reasons he gives Marie-Eliane the name of "Countess Imperiali," he makes it clear to the reader that in real life the woman did not resemble the vain and coldhearted Schiller character, "a mere piece of woman-flesh, wrapped up in a great-great patent of nobility," as her own brother says to her face in the play. To underscore that difference, Bystrolyotov replaces the first name of Schiller's countess (Julia) with a name that, in the context of his memoirs, sounds special and expresses his affection—*Fiorella* ("a little flower," in Italian).[16]

"Slowly, without rushing, I wove a web of the finest treachery around [her]," he writes with much anguish. The guilt of eventually breaking Marie-Eliane's heart at the demand of his job tormented him for the rest of his life. "Even now, so many years later," he recalls in his memoirs, "I'm ready to kneel before her and ask her forgiveness."

But back then, in Prague, the young Dmitri was apparently able to compartmentalize his passion for his new bride and his feelings for Marie-Eliane. Cheating on both of the women he loved, he consoled himself with the thought that, after all, he was doing it not for personal gratification but as part of his sacrifice to the higher cause he had embraced: "There's no struggle without sacrifice, and all three of us were its victims." In fact, he thought himself even more victimized than the women: he had to split his heart in two.

But there was one more woman in his life at that time whom he truly adored. Thinking back on that period, he writes, "More than anything in the world I loved that gray and untidy woman in glasses with a thick volume of *Das Kapital* under her arm—the goddess of social revolution and class struggle."

Finally, the day came when he had to begin recruiting Marie-Eliane. They were already engaged, and following the "Golst" scenario, he had told her about his Moscow and Washington assignments to a diplomatic post. Now it was time to ask her for a minor favor. Would she be so kind as to bring him something from her office desk that would prove to the Soviet authorities that she had made her choice and could be fully trusted?

Overcoming revulsion for her own actions—betrayal of her country—the next day she brought him some documents from her desk. He found them too innocent.

"That's not enough," he said. "You have to burn your bridges."

"But I'm an honest person," she said.

Marie-Eliane struggled with herself. When Dmitri insisted that she pass him the French Embassy's ciphers and codes, she cried and begged him to spare her this.

"I love my country. Do you want to make me a spy and a traitor?"

"No," he said, although she was obviously correct regarding his intentions. As if to prove his negation, he added, "I want to make you a patriot of another country."

Much torn between her love for a man and her love for her country, Marie-Eliane finally delivered what he asked for—all of the French

Embassy's cipher books. "I remember that evening," he writes. "She stood in pink rays of sun, and her distorted facial expression made me shudder."

"Please," she begged him. "You can keep it for only an hour. One hour only!" An hour was plenty of time for Dmitri to photograph the documents.

Cursing himself, he followed the OGPU scenario for a long time. What Marie-Eliane thought to be her one and only violation would be just the beginning. Dmitri kept coming up with stories of red tape that prevented them from getting married and leaving Prague. And he demanded more and more confidential material from the French diplomatic pouches, which Marie-Eliane provided him in the course of two years.

When Dmitri could seemingly have taken pride in his achievement—he had enabled the Soviet government to read the contents of French diplomatic correspondence on a daily basis—he experienced a shocking disappointment. It was the first big hole in the romantic veil in which intelligence work had wrapped him. Combined with other setbacks and failures, it made him feel at that time that his days in the intelligence service would soon be over.

But a day came when he realized that, on the contrary, his career as a spy was only beginning in earnest.

PART II
MASTER SPY AT WORK

SIX | Going Underground

All countries of the world would open before me.

—BYSTROLYOTOV, ON THE OFFER TO BECOME
AN ILLEGAL OPERATIVE

A new and sharp turn in Dmitri's life came late at night at the end of January 1930, with a knock on the door of his luxurious apartment in the upscale Prague neighborhood of Vinogrady. Dmitri and Iolanta were packing their suitcases and burning papers in the fireplace. They were about to leave Prague forever. For successful work at the Trade Mission, Dmitri was recommended for postdoctoral studies at the Academy of Foreign Trade in Moscow.[1]

But late on the eve of their departure for Moscow, "Golst" visited them and offered Dmitri a change of destination. Transferred to Berlin, "Golst" suggested that Dmitri follow him there. But in Berlin, he would have to become an "illegal" operative, that is, work underground, under an assumed name. Iolanta could join him later.

"Golst" left. Dmitri and his wife didn't sleep all night. She begged him to leave everything behind and go to Moscow. "I paced anxiously about my room from corner to corner, like a beast in a cage," he recalls. He stepped into the wintry Prague night. Once outside, as was his habit over many years of his stormy life, he took stock of the events of his past two years in the Czechoslovakian capital.

A few years earlier, at the end of 1927, things still seemed to be going well for him. He obtained a new spymaster. Instead of "Golst," the OGPU cover position as the Mission's second secretary was passed to another operative whose alias was "Dneprov" (code-named MAKAR). His real name was Pavel Matveevich Zhuravlyov. Born in 1898 to a well-to-do peasant family, he had studied at the Kazan Medical Institute, where he took part in the student radical movement. After the Bolshevik takeover in October 1917, he joined the Red Army and soon began his career in the Cheka ranks. When the civil war ended, he worked first in Kazan, then in the Crimea. He arrived in Prague after a short stint at the central apparatus of the foreign intelligence in Moscow, where he wound up after being expelled from Lithuania for espionage activities.[2]

At the time of his arrival in Prague, times were difficult for Soviet spies in Czechoslovakia. The country's highly popular president, Tomáš Masaryk, took a strong anti-Soviet stand. Since for the Soviet Trade Mission trade was secondary to spreading Communist ideology and conducting a wide range of propaganda activities, the Mission was put under tight police surveillance. To keep it under its watchful eyes at all times, the police installed a tobacco booth next to the fence of Villa Teresa occupied by the Mission. Both Soviet and Czech citizens entering the Mission were often detained for questioning. With the exception of the Czechoslovakian Communist Party paper *Rude Pravo*, the pages of the Prague press bristled with such headlines as "Soviet Diplomat Spies," "When Will Villa Teresa Be Clean?" and "Another Soviet Trade Mission Provocation."[3]

"Dneprov" suggested changing the course of Soviet intelligence work in Czechoslovakia. Because of the significant presence in the city of Russian émigrés who had fled from the Bolshevik troops at the end of the civil war, Prague was a breeding ground for various anti-Soviet groups. These émigrés from Russia still hoped to reverse the tide of historical change and bring back the old order in their homeland. Working toward that goal, these groups prepared secret agents for penetrating Soviet territory.

Mingling in Prague high society, Dmitri established contact with the son of a privy councillor of the Czechoslovakian Ministry of Foreign Affairs. This man not only provided him with the minutes of confidential sessions of the Ministry but also tipped him off about a school for spies operating in Prague. Russian émigré General Inostrantsev and his wife ran the Higher School of Russian Language as a private business and offered much more than linguistic drills. The school was a training ground for blending into Soviet society. Under the general's guidance, by closely examining Soviet newspapers and newsreels, the students learned the everyday behavior and manners of Russians of different walks of life—Party functionaries, military officers, industrial managers, members of the intelligentsia, blue-collar workers, even members of the underworld.[4]

Inostrantsev assessed his students' physical and other personal characteristics and helped to cast them in the most appropriate cover roles. He supplied them with the corresponding clothing, including such accessories as an embroidered skullcap (*tiubeteika*) for a person intended to penetrate one of the Soviet central Asian republics or a thin leather waist belt for a future man of the Caucasus. The school had operated since 1919, and its first students were officers of the defeated White Army who wanted to contribute to the struggle against the Bolsheviks by means of covert operations. But, as Dmitri learned, recently the school was attracting professional intelligence officers from England, France, Italy, and Sweden.[5]

Under an innocent pretext, Dmitri struck up a casual acquaintance with two of the school's students—a senior lieutenant in the British Navy, Edgar Young, and his wife, Geraldine. The couple planned to infiltrate the Soviet Union together. To get a helping hand in cracking the school secrets, Dmitri recruited one Joseph Leppin (codenamed PEEP), a law student from Prague University and a member of the Czechoslovakian Communist Youth League. Born in 1906 in Prague, he was fluent in English and French, tall and slender, had the demeanor of an intellectual, and was interested in art. He became Dmitri's most reliable assistant in many operations. With him and his friend Georgiev, Dmitri placed the school under around-the-clock surveillance and photographed all students entering or exiting the premises. As Dmitri discloses it in his thinly disguised account of his spy work in the form of a film script, titled "Shchedrye serdtsem" ("Generous Hearts"), eventually he broke into the Inostrantsevs' apartment and photographed the school documents, complete with addresses and fingerprints of both the current students and the school alumni.[6]

Parallel to his intelligence work, Dmitri continued to pursue his education. Back in 1925, he had been forced to stop attending the Russian Law Faculty. Working at the Soviet Trade Mission full-time and heading the Union of Student Citizens of the USSR Living in Czechoslovakia were hardly compatible with attending classes that prepared lawyers for the Russian Empire soon to be recovered from the hands of the Bolsheviks. As his student file shows, in the academic year 1924 to 1925, he took and passed only one exam. In October 1925, the school administration summoned him for questioning about the reasons for his lack of academic progress. He gave no explanation as to why he neglected his studies; he filed no petitions on his own behalf; and he was soon expelled from the school.[7]

His further education during that period is not quite clear. His memoirs briefly mention a short period of medical studies at Prague University. Then, in the summer of 1927, he entered another émigré law school, the Ukrainian Free University (Ukrainskii Vil'nii Institut), the working language of which, apparently, was Russian. In 1928, he defended his thesis, titled "The Origin and Formation of Law in the Light of the Teachings of Marx, Lenin, and Engels." As a result, Dmitri was promoted to the position of the Mission's economics adviser. He wrote and published several articles in specialized journals and edited the Mission's bulletin on economics. Knowledge of economics of Western states would benefit him greatly in his future intelligence work.[8]

All his professional success notwithstanding, at that time, Dmitri was not yet aware of the unquestionable fact, of which he would be reminded quite painfully later in his life, that no one in the Soviet secret police was trusted fully; everyone was a subject of constant suspicion. As his KGB file reveals now, on March 5, 1926, the first signal of mistrust had come from his native turf, from the North-Caucasian Authorized OGPU representative. It took the form of a letter to the Foreign Intelligence Department of the OGPU in which the local representative called to the attention of his Moscow colleagues that Dmitri Bystrolyotov's employment at a Soviet setting in Prague might be a mistake. The letter suggested a course of action to rectify it: "to allow Bystrolyotov to come to the Soviet Union, particularly to Anapa, where he will be arrested."[9]

Nevertheless, responding to this signal, the very same Artuzov who had seemingly checked Dmitri out and blessed his intelligence career, while asking that Dmitri not be arrested if he stepped on the Anapa soil, followed it up with another letter requesting that "in case of Bystrolyotov's arrival, if possible, put him under surveillance and report the results." Dmitri was also unaware that his letters to his mother were routinely opened. And on December 12, 1928, the North-Caucasian Authorized OGPU representative again reported to Moscow about Dmitri's pending vacation in June of the next year and asked for instructions concerning whether "measures have to be taken toward his secret seizure."[10]

Although he had not been arrested, toward the end of 1929, Dmitri seemed to be running out of luck professionally. He went through a number of setbacks and failures in his spy work. First, he accidentally blew the cover of one of his Czech agents, a Škoda engineer, presumably the one through whom he had obtained the secrets of gun tube hardening, which Dmitri was credited for.[11]

One day, Dmitri wrote him an innocent letter, a signal to meet at the usual place of contact, the café-bar of the Steiner Hotel. Overwhelmed with work that day, he instructed the Mission's porter to take the letter to the city and drop it in one of the street mailboxes, the usual precautionary measure he employed himself. Busy with his other duties, the man put the envelope into the Mission's outgoing mail pile. When the engineer appeared at the café-bar a few days later, Dmitri saw that something bad had happened. This usually obedient and submissive man could hardly hide his fury. Instead of saying hello and asking permission to join Dmitri at his table, he slammed the envelope down on the table and hissed, "Is this your letter, sir?"

"Mine," Dmitri replied.

"Look at it again!"

"Mine."

"Well, then what's that, may I ask you?" He flipped the envelope over. As on other pieces of Soviet Trade Mission mail, an advertising sticker with a red star read, "Drink Russian Tea!" With the Czechoslovakian government closely monitoring activities of the Soviet Mission, receiving a letter with that sticker compromised the engineer as a "source." Most likely, he had already been under police surveillance.[12]

Next came another failure, no less embarrassing. Although Soviet agents provided the Mission with a wide range of confidential information on Czechoslovakian economics and technical know-how, "Golst" directed Dmitri to enhance the quality of industrial espionage by recruiting the secretary of the influential Czech Union of Industrialists. Privy to the most sensitive information, the man (identified in Dmitri's memoirs only as "polished Pan Doctor") fit all the characteristics of a "soft" target for recruitment: he lived beyond his means and was heavily in debt. "Golst" instructed that he be cultivated immediately and, without much ado, offered him a substantial sum of money in exchange for his cooperation. Dmitri had a casual acquaintance with Pan Doctor in the course of a few years, meeting him at various Prague bars and theaters. He followed the instructions from "Golst" to the letter. He invited the man to his office, locked the door, and put a thick packet of money on the desk before Pan Doctor, who responded swiftly—and unexpectedly. He got up and spat in Dmitri's face. Already a seasoned spy, Dmitri was able to separate his personal dignity from his professional work. "Out of agitation, he missed," he remarks in his memo for the KGB nonchalantly. "But this didn't change a thing: I became a finished man in Czechoslovakia."[13]

However, the harshest and most painful of his setbacks in Prague was related to his French Embassy operation. In fact, the wound it inflicted on him never healed in full. Every time Dmitri had delivered his loot—photocopies of the most sensitive French diplomatic correspondence—"Golst" couldn't have been happier. He assured Dmitri that the Center would greatly reward his efforts.[14]

But one day "Golst" summoned Dmitri to his office and told him that the Center had instructed him to let the French "source" go. Dmitri was both flummoxed and devastated by this news. It was one of those rare instances in his career as a spy when he could not help but protest his superiors' inhumane treatment of him: "I'm a living person," he said to "Golst," "not some fish stuffing. How can I let go of the 'source' that I've been working on so hard for three years? I've defiled three human souls—my lover's, my wife's, and my own. For three years, I've been a scoundrel. And now, when I've finally procured the secrets for my Motherland, you tell me 'We don't need them?' Where were you before?"[15]

"Golst" shrugged. He speculated that the order to close the French "source" could have come from a traitor who would face exposure by those who read confidential French diplomatic mail. "That's for the better!" Dmitri exclaimed. "Then we'll catch the bastard!" "Golst" hypothesized that the traitor could have wormed his way into the higher echelons of Soviet power and, therefore, was untouchable. "I didn't understand a thing," Dmitri recalls, "because I was an idealist and a fool. The situation was revolting, but nothing could be done to change it."[16]

He came to see Marie-Eliane for the last time. He told her they had to part forever: he had suddenly been recalled to Moscow and had to leave Prague at once.

The Frenchwoman's reaction to this news tormented him for the rest of his days. Apparently she was unable to accept that the man she loved was part of a trap the Soviet intelligence had set for her from the very beginning. She fell on her knees, embraced Dmitri's legs, and cried. Through her sobs, she asked him why they hadn't let her know before that he could be recalled at any moment, before she had blotted her conscience by giving away her country's secrets. "I stood in silence," Dmitri recalls. "Then I tore her hands from my legs and left her lying on the floor."[17]

This was the last straw. Dmitri called it quits. On his request, the Prague Trade Mission gave him a letter of recommendation for post-doctoral study at the Moscow Academy of Foreign Trade. He had other plans as well. Quite early in his life, he had developed artistic ambitions. Even at the most trying moments of his life, he never missed a chance to draw a sketch or jot down some notes. It was his way of coping with the overwhelming impressions his turbulent life kept throwing at him. Now it was time to give his long-suppressed creative urges a chance to realize themselves in full. He also wanted to capitalize on his firsthand experience of life abroad and write a satirical book about Western bourgeois life. He already had some literary experience. In 1924, he had published articles about the White emigration in Prague newspapers. In 1927, as he resumed his studies at the Ukrainian Free University, he began contributing to journals specializing in economics. Bit by bit, he gathered material for his future book. Toward the beginning of 1930, the manuscript was ready. He couldn't wait to take it to Moscow and see it through publication.[18]

And now came the offer from "Golst" to put all of his plans on hold and resume his spy career in Berlin. The offer didn't come totally out of the blue, however. Back in the summer of 1925, after his trip to Moscow and interview with Artuzov and Gorb, Dmitri had been ordered to make a short trip from Prague to Helsingfors (now Helsinki). There, in a small café, he met secretly with Mikhail Trilisser, the head of the Foreign Intelligence Department at that time. Good recruiters were hard to come by. At that meeting, Trilisser tested the waters of Dmitri's feelings about their plans to move him to Germany. Dmitri may have forgotten about it, but now, several years later, when his mind was set on going back to Russia, it looked as if they had decided to act on it after all.[19]

Regardless of that meeting, the reason for the offer from "Golst" was a massive Soviet effort at the time to create a new pool of OGPU illegal operatives to be infused into Western countries. There were good reasons for it. In the spring of 1927, the global Soviet spy network experienced serious damage. In the course of a few months, Soviet spies were rounded up in eight countries: Poland, Turkey, France, Lithuania, Switzerland, Austria, Japan, and Great Britain. In the wake of these scandals, the last of them, Great Britain, which the Soviets considered their most dangerous adversary, even broke off diplomatic relations. Stalin, by that time in full control of power, was convinced of a well-developed conspiracy of Western powers to destroy the Soviet Union. And he attributed the lack of evidence of such a conspiracy to a dearth of Soviet intelligence efforts in that direction. He demanded drastic strengthening of such efforts. In accord with his wishes, in January 1930, the Politburo decided to reorganize foreign intelligence and intensify its work.[20]

Since most arrests of Soviet agents involved those who worked in the Soviet missions and resided legally in the countries of interest, to prevent a repetition of similar scandals, the emphasis was on shifting the main spy activities to illegal operatives. In the case that such a spy was arrested, any official affiliation with him could be flatly denied. Thus, a knowledge of foreign languages and an ability to blend into the upper circles of Western societies became the most desirable qualities for a prospective agent recruiter. With mass persecution of the old aristocracy during and after the civil war, individuals with such qualifications were hard to come by. Apparently, at that point, Artur Artuzov, the newly appointed deputy head of the Foreign Intelligence Department, thought of the young man of aristocratic upbringing whom he had screened back in the spring of 1925, Dmitri Bystrolyotov.

Dmitri attributes his decision to accept the offer to his romantic vision of the cloak-and-dagger profession: "All countries of the world would open before me. I'd fly around the world for about five years, and then I'd go to Moscow, to the Academy, but as a different man, more experienced and useful."[21]

There was another, even more powerful incentive. Unlike his previous position as an employee of the Soviet Trade Mission, where he enjoyed the security of his diplomatic immunity, working underground under an assumed name presented an enormous risk. He could expect no protection and would have to rely solely on his own wits. And, as Artuzov had warned him during the interview, a recruiter's job was the most dangerous of them all. He would have to tread the waters carefully and be an excellent judge of people's characters. The very nature of his task required that, at his own risk, he reveal himself to the prospective agent before the latter decided whether to change sides or not. A recruiter's mistake could turn fatal.[22]

The OGPU chiefs believed that Western counterintelligence worked the same as their own agency and also had a free hand over a foreign spy's life. They believed that, once caught, a spy would be tortured, imprisoned, and even shot without due process of law. Therefore, before sending one of their operatives abroad, the Soviet secret police made sure that he was aware of the mortal danger. If captured, they encouraged him to behave "like a man," that is, to commit suicide.[23]

The danger of his new assignment not only did not repel Dmitri, it made the job more attractive to him, even irresistible. It served as a powerful cultural incentive. Soviet spymaster Alexander Orlov attests that "the dangerous work in the underground [was] surrounded in Moscow with such an aura of heroism, that many an intelligence chief, irrespective of his previous service abroad in an official capacity, tr[ied] to get the hazardous assignment as a matter of honor and personal pride." In addition, for Dmitri, a hero's halo promised to end the gnawing sense of inferiority he had felt from the early years of his life.[24]

Although he cites the following lines from one of Pushkin's *Little Tragedies*, "A Feast Amidst Plague," much later in his memoirs than the actual time of his decision to accept the offer to go underground, he does relate it to his spy work abroad. Indeed, it was one of most powerful reasons for that fateful decision:

> There is an intoxication in battle,
> And on the edge of a dark abyss,
> And in the raging ocean,

Amidst terrifying waves and stormy darkness,
And in the Arabian Desert sandstorm,
And in the breath of Plague.
Everything, everything that threatens with ruin
Is fraught with inexplicable delight for a mortal's
    he art—
It is, perhaps, his pledge for immortality.
And lucky is the one who, amidst tribulations,
Could find and know these thrills.
Thus—glory to you, Plague![25]

First, when Iolanta expressed her unwillingness to go to Berlin and tried to talk him into going to Moscow, he agreed. But when in the morning "Golst" appeared at his door again, Dmitri (unexpectedly even to himself) answered, "Yes." At night he burnt his manuscripts and all his literary work. He left Iolanta temporarily behind in Prague, boarded a train to Moscow, and at the first station hopped on a train heading to Berlin. Comrade Dmitri Bystrolyotov disappeared. Now, he became an illegal operative under the code name ANDREI, which was later changed to HANS.[26]

The first order of business in going underground was to assume a new identity. "Golst" tipped Dmitri off about an opportunity to obtain a legitimate passport. It involved a trip to the city of Danzig (now Gdansk), which since 1919, under the Treaty of Versailles, had been considered a free city under the protection of the League of Nations. The doyen of the Diplomatic Corps in that city was in a position to issue a passport at his discretion. Diplomatic councils of various countries carried out the doyen's duties on an alternate basis. That year, the consul general of Greece, one Henry Habert, presided over the corps. "Golst" advised Dmitri not to take the man's grand appearance seriously for, as the OGPU had learned, he was a crook, a member of an international gang of drug dealers who had wormed their way into the League of Nations. Habert himself was not even Greek, but a Jew from Odessa.[27]

Dmitri already knew that he could act. To remind the reader, he had once crossed the Soviet border in Batumi by making the customs guards believe that he was not a Russian, but an Italian sailor. To escape harassment by the *Farnaiba* crew, he successfully feigned un-controllable rage. And, when Mr. Fischer was compromised, he acted as a powerful lawyer who could get him out of trouble.

"Your Excellency," Dmitri said in English as he entered the doyen's luxurious residence. He sat on the edge of a chair in front of the imposing old man, who wore a monocle in his eye, a false shirtfront, and white garters. "Please help your unlucky compatriot. My briefcase along with my passport has just been stolen."

"Where were you born?"

"In Saloniki."

"Do you have a birth certificate?"

"Alas! It was burned in the city hall fire a decade ago."

(Back in his Constantinople days, Dmitri had heard about the Saloniki fire that destroyed many birth records.)

"Which of the Greek embassies know you?"

"None, I regret."

"Can anyone in Greece vouch for you?"

"Alas, I never saw my homeland. My parents fled the country when I was a baby."

"What's your name?"

"Alexander S. Gallas."

"Do you speak Greek?"

"To my shame, no. Not a word."

"Well," Habert said, "I'm afraid I can't help you. Good-bye!"

Dmitri put two hundred dollars on the doyen's desk.

"What's that?"

"For the poor people of Danzig."

"This is not a charity. Take your money and get lost."

When he realized that he was failing his first assignment, Dmitri decided to act more aggressively. Apparently, he was inspired by American movies of the period: in 1928, *Lights of New York,* the first all-talking film, about a chorus girl involved with gangsters, had already appeared in Europe. His face assuming a vile expression, he pulled out a pack of American cigarettes, stuck one in his mouth, and struck a wooden American match over the papers in front of the doyen.

Habert looked at him in outrage. In a hoarse voice, Dmitri barked at him in American slang, "Button your lip. I need an ID. In a flash!"

Habert turned pale. "Where are you from?"

A few days before, Dmitri had read in the Berlin papers about an international scandal: In broad daylight, the chief of the British police, a colonel, was gunned down in downtown Singapore. The assassin escaped, but the police established that he was an American mobster, a drug dealer, and a spy for Japan.

"Singapore," Dmitri said.

"Do you know what happened there?"

"I do."

"And do you know who killed the colonel?"

"Yes. Me."

His fingers trembling, Habert filled out a blank passport as Dmitri dictated. "Take it. That's all."

"No, that's not all. Give me that Greek king's portrait," Dmitri pointed at the doyen's desk.

Habert was about to remove the portrait from its frame wrapped in ribbons, the colors of the Greek flag, white and blue, but Dmitri stopped him. "Don't touch it. I want it with the frame. For the idiots at customs. Got it?"

Habert saw his visitor to the door. Here Dmitri made a wrong move: he switched back to the image of the polite Greek refugee who had presented himself at the beginning of his visit. That made the doyen suspicious. He suddenly grabbed Dmitri firmly by his waist and asked in Russian, "Vy tol'ko chto iz Moskvy?" (Are you straight from Moscow?)

Taken by surprise, Dmitri was about to reply in Russian but managed to switch to English at the last moment. "I . . . don't understand Polish."

"Ah, forgive me," Habert said. "I'm tired. It was a mistake, sir."[28]

Dmitri considered his visit to the doyen the first little victory of his new underground life. Moreover, he found the character of the American gangster working for Japanese intelligence quite effective, and he used it in future operations.

Getting a legitimate passport was only the first step in creating an operative base in a foreign territory. Now Dmitri had to come up with numerous details to make his assumed personality blend with the surroundings. Here one could not be too careful. As Dmitri told this writer in the course of our interview, "If you pose as a herring salesman, you should be able to tell one herring from another—a Norwegian herring, an ocean herring, a bloater. You should learn how a herring salesman moves and talks. You should reek of herring." Because he decided to present himself as a Greek merchant, he first made the rounds of Greek shops in Berlin and made casual acquaintances with several shop owners. To justify his lack of Greek, he repeated the legend he had come up with during his meeting with Habert: his parents had fled Greece when he was a baby. But he kept telling everyone that, nevertheless, he felt himself Greek in his bones.[29]

Then he joined the parish of the local Greek Orthodox Church. He made friends with exchange students and tourists from Greece attending the services. When they returned to their homeland, they sent him letters and postcards with Greek stamps. On the walls of his apartment, he hung pictures of his "home city," Saloniki. In case of police inquiry, the very presence of all these items corroborated his Greek image.[30]

Now a legitimate business cover had to be established, one that would allow him to move around the country and abroad without raising any suspicions. The cover also had to identify his source of income. First, the OGPU made him the sales rep of a Danish businessman, one Skau-Cheldsen, who traded in top-of-the line neckties. However, after making some calculations, Dmitri found that such a cover was too thin. His commissions would hardly justify his considerable living and travel expenses. He needed to create a legitimate business, profitable enough to finance intelligence operations.[31]

Utilizing his economics knowledge, he suggested creating an import-export company trading in cloth waste. Locating it in Amsterdam would make it convenient for the Soviet intelligence network in all West European countries. To that end, the OGPU brought Dmitri into contact with one Baruch (Bernard) Dawidowicz, an uncle of the OGPU *rezident* in London. The man had some knowledge of Polish import rags and wastepaper technology. Dmitri appointed him director of the newly formed firm; its name, GADA, was composed of the first two letters of Dmitri's alias (Gallas) and the director's surname.[32]

To facilitate opening the new business, Dmitri struck up an acquaintance with an influential banker and businessman, Israel Pollack. He happened to be a patron of an underground bordello operating in the neighborhood where Dmitri rented a spacious apartment. He won the man's confidence, charmed him, and soon, on his recommendation, opened an account at an Amsterdam bank and joined the City Chamber of Commerce. For his part, Dawidowicz became a member of a local temple and, through other congregants, soon established the necessary business ties.[33]

GADA's official business was wholesale trade in wool cloth. But in reality the cloth was counterfeit. First, the firm collected high-quality wool clippings not only all over Holland but also in Belgium, England, Denmark, and other Scandinavian countries. Then, the raw materials were shipped to Lodz, where Dawidowicz arranged to mix them with a generous amount of cotton. The end result was "high-quality" wool cloth. A Belgian artist (perhaps, a member of the local Communist Party; Dmitri calls him "Comrade Gan van Looi") employed by one of the major British textile firms provided GADA with the next season's patterns. The counterfeited cloth produced in Lodz resembled the real thing. To make it look thoroughly authentic, the rolls of that cloth were transported to a shop in England where a machine stamped "Made in England" along its borders. The cloth was then sold for a solid profit in remote areas, such as the African continent and South America. Thus, as GADA representatives, Dmitri and other OGPU operatives obtained a solid base for both a verifiable occupation and the financing of their covert operations in Western Europe.[34]

With his solid cover and financial base, Dmitri joined the "flying squad," a mobile group of Soviet undercover operatives capable of crossing the borders of many European countries, without arousing any suspicion, frequently and with ease. His immediate assignments came from the OGPU illegal *rezidentura* set up in Berlin and headed by Boris Bazarov (code-named KIN). His true name was Boris Shpak. Eight years older than Dmitri, he came from a similar background. A military officer by training, during the civil war he first fought on the side of the White Army, but after the defeat of General Denikin in the south of Russia, he ran away to Turkey and later settled in Berlin. As Dmitri had done in Prague, disappointed in the "White cause," Bazarov offered his services to the OGPU *rezident* in Berlin and began his career as an intelligence officer. He knew several European and Slavic languages (German, French, English, Bulgarian, and Serbo-

Croatian). His appearance was perfect for a spy: a short, red-haired man with an agile facial expression, he was shy and unassuming, and he could easily blend with a street crowd.[35]

Although based in Berlin, Bazarov controlled illegal Soviet agents not only in Germany but also in other countries, including England. His group hunted for information on British economic development, the state of the country's relationship with Germany, and other state secrets.

Dmitri settled down as an illegal operative in Berlin and had begun working under Bazarov's supervision when disaster struck on his home front. Four months after he left for Berlin, Iolanta was called to duty as a Soviet agent and given a risky mission. She had to travel to Hungary first and then cross the Hungarian-Austrian border under a forged British passport carrying a package of secret documents. Apparently, she was under police surveillance. At a small railroad station on the Hungarian side, gendarmes tried to remove her from the train. Iolanta put up a fight and shouted in English. Observing the scene, American and British tourists on the train decided that the lady was being violated by the awful Hungarian watchdogs for no reason and interfered on her behalf. Iolanta managed to lock herself up in the compartment. Meanwhile, the train began moving. When finally the gendarmes made their way to Iolanta, the train had crossed the border. On the Austrian side, she was arrested and her luggage confiscated. Dmitri characterizes the contents of the luggage rather vaguely, as some "quite blameworthy material, from the point of view of Austrian authorities." During her trial, other "weighty pieces of evidence" appeared against her, and her fate was sealed: an Austrian military court sentenced her to five years of confinement in a military prison.[36]

Iolanta's arrest had a devastating effect on Dmitri. As his description of the first four months of that new life attests, his dream of a hero's halo notwithstanding, he hardly knew where his life was going and what was happening to him. He describes that time as "one stormy night with two people [him and his wife] running through it. And now, when one of them fell down, the other kept running alone. Stumbling and falling, and stubbornly getting up again, that person ran on and on until he disappeared in black darkness that led to . . . Where? Oh, if only he had known it then!"

Because of the security risk, Dmitri could not visit Iolanta at the time of her trial in Vienna and followed the proceedings by reading the Viennese papers. Through go-betweens, he hired a good lawyer for her. When Iolanta was sentenced, he sent her parcels with everything she needed or might need. But, as he later regretted, he failed to visit her *right away*. Again giving the higher cause priority above personal life, he was busy carrying out various pressing OGPU assignments. He traveled extensively all over Europe—to Istanbul, Oslo, Warsaw, London, and Lisbon. He calmed his conscience, talking himself into believing that he had sacrificed everything for the sake of the common cause to which he and Iolanta had both sworn allegiance when they began their life together.

One day, Bazarov commented regarding Dmitri's continuous postponement of a visit to his wife in prison: "You behave like a hero."

The remark woke Dmitri up. He put all his business aside and rushed to Vienna. When he came to the fortress where Iolanta was serving her term, he realized what a grave mistake he had made by delaying his visit. The vacuum of love he had created was already filled by his old rival for his wife's heart, Isolde Cameron. She was in the visitors' room. Her body language revealed how much she suffered at the very sight of her beloved behind the prison bars. Seeing them together deeply wounded Dmitri. For the first time a thought flashed in his mind that the only way he could get rid of his rival for Iolanta's heart once and for all was by murdering her.

But Dmitri did not have time to sort out his personal problems. Grudgingly, he had to put his private life on hold. Now, with his presence in Berlin legalized, he was called to urgent action.

SEVEN | Hunting Down a Man with a Red Nose

To locate that man was like finding a needle that has
vanished in a haystack.

—BYSTROLYOTOV, IN CONVERSATION
WITH THE AUTHOR

Indeed, this was no time for Soviet intelligence to be idle. After a relative relaxation of international relationships during the years immediately following the end of World War I, the early 1930s were marked by a considerable buildup of international tension in Europe. There were several reasons for this development. The Wall Street crash of October 1929 was followed by economic depression across Europe. Extremist political groups (Fascists and Nazis) used the crisis to promote their agendas and grew in popularity. Mussolini in Italy and Hitler in Germany promised economic growth to their peoples. These leaders pursued aggressive foreign policies, presenting them as a necessary means to assure their countries' prosperity.

In addition, there was the unresolved issue of what to do with the newly born Soviet Union. Coming to power as a result of the Bolshevik takeover in October 1917, the Soviet state proclaimed the export of revolution as its official foreign policy. This agenda made the Western powers wary of Soviet expansionist tendencies, especially when words became practice. Communist attempts to seize power in a number of European countries—Germany, Austria, Hungary, and others—only strengthened the appeal of the volatile new political movements, Fascism and Nazism, among many segments of the European populace.

In turn, the Soviet government was also at a loss as to the intentions of the major European power brokers. By the early 1930s, now already in full command of the Soviet domestic and foreign policies, Stalin was sure that a plot to attack the USSR was in the works. He was frustrated about the lack of reliable information that would confirm his expectations.

All these developments made the early 1930s a time of intense diplomatic maneuvering. It also dramatically increased the espionage activities of all parties involved. Codes and ciphers of correspondence between high-level officials of major European powers became the most coveted target of world intelligence services. Enabling Stalin to peek into the playing cards of the main adversaries of the Soviet state became the most pressing order of the day for the Foreign Intelligence Department of the OGPU.

The hunt for these secrets was spearheaded by a recruiter whose task was to make the initial approach toward a new "source" and begin cultivating him or her. The recruiter's efforts were assisted by both illegal OGPU *rezidents* (Boris Bazarov in Berlin and Theodor Mally in Paris) and legal *rezidents*, that is, the OGPU operatives with diplomatic immunity occupying official positions in the Soviet Embassy; at the time, they were first Samsonov (code name SEMYON) and then Boris Berman (code name ARTEM) in Berlin and Stanislav Glinsky (code name PETR) in Paris. The efforts of this group were supported by photographers and messengers. The group used photography and cryptography as a means of keeping the Center informed; there was no direct radio connection.[1]

In August 1929, Soviet hunters for diplomatic secrets had a lucky break. A modestly dressed short man, the cuffs of his jacket worn, paid a visit to the Soviet Embassy in Paris and asked to see the military attaché. He introduced himself as "Charlie," a typesetter in charge of printing copies of the deciphered British diplomatic dispatches from around the world for distribution among the members of the British Foreign Office. For a fee of 10,000 pounds, he offered to make an extra copy of these dispatches for the Soviets. He made it clear that, if the deal went smoothly, he would also be willing to serve as a middleman in selling copies of the British diplomatic codes and ciphers. Asked why he chose the Soviets as his potential customer, "Charlie" cited safety: in his view, unlike other embassies, the Soviet one was least likely to be infiltrated by British secret agents. The man set only one precondition: he wanted to operate incognito and threatened to end delivery at the first attempt of shadowing. He brought to the Soviet Embassy two books, one titled *Foreign Office Ciphers* and the other *Colonial and Dominions Office Ciphers*. The visitor's facial expression was one of "last and utter desperation."[2]

At first, the transactions with "Charlie" (code name ARNO) proceeded smoothly. But then, under various pretexts, the man decreased the quantity and quality of the documents. Picked randomly, the material often turned out to be of little interest to the Soviets. Also, the Brit dragged his feet on his promise to sell British diplomatic codes and ciphers. Besides, his insistence on remaining anonymous only reinforced the conviction that he was not just a typesetter. For a man with a rather humble station in life, the agent showed a quite independent spirit. The OGPU believed that the only way to assure an agent's full cooperation was to bring him under total control. But, despite many attempts, the walk-in's true identity remained a mystery.[3]

To get a firmer hold on ARNO and wrestle from his hands once and for all the initiative of choosing material of interest to the Soviets was impossible without finding out who he actually was and what his true position at the British Foreign Office was. This task was given to the illegal OGPU *rezidentura* in Berlin headed by Boris Bazarov. Dmitri's first major assignment was to give Bazarov a helping hand in bringing ARNO into line. First of all, it was important to establish the man's true identity. That could lead to his source of classified information and make it possible to eliminate him as a middleman from the costly deal.[4]

Bazarov and Dmitri developed a game plan for bringing "Charlie" under full control. They decided to use the classical "good cop–bad cop" routine. Bazarov took upon himself the part of the "bad cop." He was to act as a merciless Italian Communist (cover name "Da Vinci"), fanatically devoted to the Soviet cause and acting under direct OGPU orders. Dmitri was cast as the "good cop" whose game plan was to win "Charlie's" confidence. For that purpose, he had to become his comrade in misfortune. Moreover, he had to present himself to the Brit as a man on equal footing, which would flatter his ego. Totally in the dark about who exactly "Charlie" was, they assumed that an employee of such a prominent institution as the British Foreign Office must be an aristocrat. Bazarov and Dmitri decided to make use of Dmitri's aristocratic upbringing. The Center supplied him with a Czech passport issued in the name of a real impoverished Hungarian count, one "Lajos József Perelly."[5]

To make his new assumed personality look as authentic as possible, Dmitri had to get inside the skin of an impoverished Hungarian count. An avid reader since his early days, he perused several books on Hungarian history, culture, economy, and everyday life. To facilitate his conversion into "Count Perelly," the Center spared no means. The prospects of obtaining the innermost British diplomatic secrets were worth it. With his passport acquired in Danzig and issued to the name of Greek merchant "Alexander Gallas," Dmitri went to Budapest. There, he attended places frequented by the local landed gentry—diplomatic receptions, opening nights in the theaters, popular horse races, and important church services—making note of the local aristocracy's manners and customs. To blend with that crowd, he ordered himself several suits from the best Budapest tailors, purchased a few pairs of fashionable shoes, a dozen ties, a few rings, and some other accessories. A set of his smoking pipes carried his family's (i.e., the Perelly family's) coat of arms. As dictated by the Hungarian landlord fashion of the time, he embellished one of his hats with a characteristic little brush.[6]

Then he toured the country taking pictures of himself against the background of the best-known Hungarian sites. While on the road, he seized an opportunity to solidify his legend. He learned that the Hungarian cardinal would take part in one of the forthcoming church processions. Studying the real Count Perelly's family tree, Dmitri had established that the cardinal (although nameless in Dmitri's memoirs, this was apparently József Mindszenty, born József Pehm) was the count's uncle. Dmitri feigned a fit of religious fervor and stepped out from the crowd in front of the cardinal, who smiled and blessed him. A street photographer hired for the occasion took a snapshot of the moment. The picture proved to be invaluable. Casually stuck in Dmitri's "Perelly" passport, it never failed to impress customs officials at many European borders.[7]

Dmitri already felt well prepared to play his part in handling ARNO, but he became sidetracked by a short-term reconnaissance mission in the Norwegian fjords. One possible purpose of his trip was to assess the feasibility of using the fjords as submarine hideouts in case of a military conflict in Europe. (Apparently, it was there that Dmitri posed as a herring salesman.) He also took Norwegian language lessons from a pastor's daughter. This served to explain at the border why he was in the country.[8]

While he was there, his mission was suddenly aborted by a contact from the OGPU illegal *rezident* in Oslo, who invited him to a secret meeting at the Hotel Viking. At this meeting, Dmitri received an order from Abram Slutsky, the OGPU Deputy Chief of Foreign Intelligence, to leave for Moscow at once and, immediately upon arrival, report to him. Following the OGPU instructions for all illegal operatives, Dmitri traveled to Moscow not directly, but in a circular manner. This was necessary to avoid giving away his Soviet connection to foreign counterintelligence by having a Soviet customs stamp in his passport. He visited several European countries before contacting the illegal OGPU operative at the last stop (apparently in Geneva), where he exchanged the passport he had used to travel to Norway, made out to the name of some Austrian textile engineer, for his genuine Soviet one.[9]

Dmitri was allowed to spend only a few hours in Moscow. From the railroad station, he went straight to Lubyanka. As he walked into Slutsky's office at the OGPU headquarters, his boss opened a book lying on his desk and asked Dmitri to read a marked-up paragraph. The book, titled *Na putiakh k termidoru* (*On the Way to Thermidor*), was the memoir of an old Bolshevik, a former chargé d'affaires of the Soviet Embassy in Paris, Gregori Bessedovsky, who had defected to the West in October 1929. The paragraph in question was devoted to an episode involving a walk-in to the embassy that had taken place a year before ARNO's visit, in August 1928.[10]

A short man carrying a heavy briefcase asked to see either the Soviet military attaché or the first secretary of the embassy. Posing as one of them was the embassy's OGPU *rezident* Vladimir Voinovich (aka Yanovich and Volovich). The walk-in offered for purchase the contents of his briefcase—a set of codes and ciphers of Italian diplomatic mail. The asking price was two hundred thousand French francs. Since, for security reasons, the ciphers were subject to yearly changes, he also offered to provide a steady supply of new ones in years to come.

Voinovich took the briefcase to the embassy security room. There, using the set of codes, he read some samples of coded Italian diplomatic letters and found the goods genuine. He passed the codes to his wife, also an OGPU operative, who photographed the whole set of material. Then Voinovich took the briefcase back to its owner, threw it at him, and outraged, called the walk-in's behavior a provocation and threatened to call the police. Voinovich's superiors hailed his cleverness, which saved the country a bundle in hard currency, and awarded him a thousand-dollar bonus.[11]

Dmitri finished reading the passage and shrugged. What had he to do with it? "Do you know whose handwriting it is?" Slutsky pointed to a word—"Restore!"—penciled in the book margins. "The Master's himself. It's Stalin's order. You should act right away. Find that shorty and arrange to get his wares on a permanent basis."

Dmitri gasped in astonishment. "There are zillions of short men in the world. Where the hell would I find him?"

"That's your business," Slutsky said. "If we knew, we would manage it without you. Get as much money as you need, but time is limited. You have no more than six months to get it done. Good luck!"

First, Dmitri went to Paris and interviewed the embassy employees, asking them to recall whatever details they remembered about the man in question. All they came up with was that the man's little nose was reddish. Dmitri nicknamed him "Nosik," which means "a little nose" in Russian.

Dmitri chose Geneva as his operational base. On a bench at the bank of Lake Geneva, feeding swans, he began thinking. Where should he start looking for the man about whom he knew so little? So far, only one thing seemed certain: to have access to diplomatic codes, "Nosik" had to be attached to one of the Italian embassies.

Anxious to fish him out as soon as possible, Dmitri first cast too wide a net. On his request, the OGPU Foreign Intelligence Department supplied Dmitri with a list of employees of every Italian embassy that interested him. Their physical descriptions were also on the way from Moscow.

But Dmitri, unable to wait, rushed into action. He summoned his assistants, Dr. Joseph Leppin (PEEP), whom he had recruited back in his Prague years, and his new wife, Erica Weinstein (code-named

ERIKA), also an illegal OGPU agent. Erica was a licensed nurse, a profession she used frequently as a cover. Like Joseph, she was also Jewish. A vivacious and plumpish green-eyed brunette, she was transferred from another illegal OGPU spy group. Both she and Leppin knew five languages and were excellent photographers, radio operators, and shooters. Most likely, the marriage had been arranged as a cover-up: Leppin was often seen in the company of an Englishwoman.[12]

Dmitri ordered the couple to begin picketing Italian embassies in European capitals, one after another. Posing as street photographers, they had to take pictures of all small-built employees of these embassies. Dmitri's first impulse was to start with the larger European capitals and gradually move to smaller ones. But then he shortened the list after concluding that, considering the risk involved and the amount of money commanded, "Nosik" could hardly be attached to an embassy in a small country.[13]

Of course, it was still a long shot, and as his assistants had left, Dmitri began thinking further. It was also possible that "Nosik" was not an embassy employee at all; he might be the subject of embassy security surveillance. The man in question could just as well be a high-ranking official of the Italian Foreign Ministry Cipher Department.

The lack of progress made Dmitri restless, and he rushed to Rome himself. Once in the city, he passed by the ministry building a few times but couldn't think of a way to find the cipher man working there. Here, he realized that his assumption that the walk-in belonged to the diplomatic corps could be wrong; he could be just a middleman and not necessarily an Italian. He could be just the agent of some Italian traitor, a go-between of some other nationality.

These questions unanswered, Dmitri returned to Geneva. Leppin and Erica came back from their assignment empty-handed. But a letter from the Center arrived with some more details about the ill-fated walk-in. First, it was reported that the man wore a red carnation in the buttonhole of his jacket and behaved with undue familiarity. Second, his face had a golden suntan.

The first detail confirmed Dmitri's hunch that "Nosik" wasn't a schooled diplomat. It also dawned on him that the man's suntan resembled one that could be seen on many people's faces in Geneva, where mountain skiing was a favorite pastime. Thus, the reddishness of the Paris walk-in's nose could be explained not by an inordinate love of hard liquor, as he assumed initially, but by a sunburn. Thus, "Nosik" could either be Swiss or a foreigner living in Switzerland.

The next question to be answered was where an agent of a highly placed Italian traitor could possibly position himself in that country. By the nature of his business, he had to have contacts with intelligence agents of many countries. It was logical then to assume that the targeted man had to spend lots of time in Geneva, the home of the League of Nations, a town teeming with diplomats but also with knights of the cloak-and-dagger from all over the world.

If that were true, Dmitri asked himself further, where would all these foreigners entertain themselves in Geneva, in his assessment a "boring and prim Calvinistic town"? Sorting out Geneva bars and restaurants, he thought of two of the most popular places where people like "Nosik" spent time: an expensive "International Bar" and a cheaper "Brasserie Universal." Staking out these two places promised good results.

But how do you keep such places under surveillance without arousing any suspicion? Among many autographed pictures of celebrity patrons that covered the walls of both places, Dmitri spotted sketch artists' works. That gave him an idea. An avid artist himself, he solicited the help of his collaborator from the time of setting up the OGPU cover company in Amsterdam, a Soviet agent of Dutch origin code-named COOPER. His true name was Henri Christian ("Han") Pieck, and he was also a talented artist.[14]

As soon as Pieck arrived in Geneva, both men sat down with their pads and pencils, Dmitri at the International Bar, COOPER at the Brasserie Universal. They sketched all of the patrons who resembled the physical description of "Nosik," and rather quickly, in one day, both of them spotted him. The man was short but strongly built, handsome, and energetic.[15]

Before approaching the man, Dmitri followed his own rule of learning as much as possible about his target. Already an International Bar habitué, Dmitri knew that the barman, Emile, was in the business of selling bits of his bar patrons' background information to many foreign intelligences. According to Dmitri, the barman's true name was Emilio Spada. He had come from a Sicilian family, part of the local mafia. In Geneva, he ran a ring of waiters, maids, and shoe-shine boys who served foreigners in big hotels. Every move of the unsuspecting guest was under close surveillance. The precise coordination of these servants' actions made it possible to ransack suitcases, briefcases, pockets, and wallets without the danger of being caught.[16]

Later, when they began working together, Emile revealed to Dmitri that when he had just begun his spy business, at first he could not believe his luck: all those vaunted diplomats and professional intelligence agents were real dimwits. Here they would forget to destroy a document, there they would tear it so carelessly that the parts could easily be glued together. It would even come to sending a bellboy on a secret mission to drop a letter somewhere on the outskirts of the city. Before it reached that mailbox, the letter would manage to spend some time in Emile's hands. On top of all this, as a barman, he knew quite well that alcohol was a bad guard of secrets. As a result, a great deal of information made its way to him. Each of the bits was just a speck, but together, the specks often gave the whole picture of a foreign agent's interests and activities. (In time, while visiting Moscow, Dmitri would make the same mistake himself, apparently forgetting to be on guard even on his own soil.)[17]

Dmitri slipped a large tip to the barman and learned a few things from him about his target. "Nosik" was a habitué of the bar; everybody knew him as "Rossi." (This name became the agent's code name in OGPU files as well.) An Italian on his mother's side, he was born in Switzerland, served in the Swiss Army, and retired with an officer's rank. He had strong family connections in Rome: allegedly, his mother's uncle was one of Rome's cardinals. ROSSI claimed to be a representative of General Motors in a number of European countries—Switzerland, Italy, Bulgaria, Yugoslavia, and Romania. However, his real surname was not established precisely. It sounded like "de Rue" or "de Ry." Dmitri also learned that the man owned a house and lived in one of the southern Swiss cantons.[18]

To uncover ROSSI's true identity, Dmitri sent his assistants to search for the man's house. Judging by his Italian-sounding nickname and French-sounding surname, most likely he resided in a canton with either a predominately Italian or French population. Leppin took care of the Italian canton Ticino, and Erica headed for the French mountain cantons. They visited the landlord associations of these cantons and, under an innocent pretext, checked the list of house owners. They found no listing for "de Rue" but three for "de Ry." One of them, Jan, age sixty-seven, was listed as a merchant whose house was located in Nyon. Age-wise, he could not possibly be ROSSI. Another one, Victor, age thirty-two, was a Swiss Army captain and had a house in Sion (in the canton of Valais).[19]

First, Dmitri decided that Victor was ROSSI. He immediately dispatched Leppin and Erica to Victor's house to stake him out and take his picture. When the agents came back and developed their film, Dmitri was disappointed: the man did not resemble ROSSI in any way. The third "de Ry" turned out to be a woman named Valerie. She was married and had four children living with her in the resort town of "St. Alberto" (in his writings, to avoid disclosure of the real place of action, Bystrolyotov replaces the real name of the Swiss town with the invented one). This was the last chance. Dmitri sent Pieck to the town to find out all he could about Valerie de Ry.

To approach the target of his reconnaissance mission inconspicuously, Pieck traveled to the picturesque town, taking along his easel and brushes. He positioned himself in a corner of the town square and began painting, counting on arousing the curiosity of the locals. The plan worked. Soon, a group of the town's children surrounded him. Pieck joked and fooled around with them. Once he got the children in a playful mood, he engaged them in a game that consisted of a child telling his or her name, first and last, in exchange for a piece of candy.

The ploy paid off: soon he got who he was looking for. One of the girls was "de Ry." Expanding on the game, Pieck offered her another piece of candy in exchange for her parents' names. "Valerie and Giovanni" was the child's answer. As luck had it, the girl turned out to be talkative and told him more than Pieck expected, things she had learned around her family's dinner table. She said that their house actually belonged to her mother, not her father, and that, from time to time, they took in boarders.

After a while, the artist wandered with his easel and palette around the town and, chatting with a local fruit seller, asked him to recommend a good boarding house for a few days' stay. Among two others, the seller suggested Valerie de Ry's house. He also passed to Pieck the town gossip confirming what he already knew: that the house belonged to Valerie de Ry herself, not to her husband. The fruit seller told the artist that this was a result of scheming on the part of Valerie's husband, Giovanni. Ousted from the Swiss Army for some improprieties, to protect the house from the possibility of being confiscated in case of his trouble with the law, he had bought it in the name of his wife. That way, nobody could touch property that did not belong to him personally.

Back in Geneva, Dmitri ran the town rumors by barman Emile. The barman told him that he had also heard them and added that, as far as he knew, ROSSI managed to keep a connection with the Swiss Army Headquarters by watching over the diplomatic and intelligence crowd swarming around the League of Nations. The barman also warned Dmitri that ROSSI was a cheat and an insolent fellow and that he could be dangerous.

That did not stop Dmitri, who, by the time of this operation, had been through many life-threatening situations that made him a fearless and courageous man. Now, when he knew as much as he possibly could about his "Nosik," there was no other way but for Dmitri, at his own risk, to approach the man. One day, while posing as a sketch artist at the entrance of the bar, Dmitri saw ROSSI enter. Putting away his drawings, Dmitri followed him all the way to the counter and sat down next to him. ROSSI ordered a double whiskey. To draw the man's attention, Dmitri not only repeated his order word for word but also imitated the man's mannerisms of speech and gestures. The maneuver worked. "Nosik" turned toward Dmitri and began scrutinizing him. To impress him, Dmitri opened his solid-gold cigarette case, took out a cigarette for himself, and offered one to the man. "Nosik" took a cigarette. Dmitri clicked his lighter. "Nosik" asked the stranger, "What's next?"

"Next is a heart-to-heart conversation," Dmitri replied. "We've known each other for a long time."

"Really? I can't recall your face," "Nosik" shrugged. "Who introduced us?"

"Not who—but what!" Dmitri paused, blew several smoke rings, and then whispered into the man's ear, "Italian ciphers!"

"Nosik" winced, but he got hold of himself right away. He paid for his and Dmitri's drinks and, as soon as they walked out, grabbed his elbow in the manner of a policeman dragging a hobo to the precinct. "Well?"

Dmitri laughed. "By the way, would you mind letting go of my elbow? I'm quite good at karate. And I can get an ace from ten steps, shooting through my pocket."[20]

Dmitri was not bluffing. Although as an agent recruiter he did not have to bear arms, he saw his work as a romantic endeavor. Carrying a gun made it more exciting for him. Soon after going underground, while on business in Lichtenstein, he had bought a revolver and in his spare time taught himself to shoot in the manner of American gangsters in Hollywood movies—through his jacket pocket. He wasted lots of old jackets but finally learned to do it well.[21]

Dmitri also informed ROSSI that he knew everything about him, including his home in "St. Alberto." ROSSI let go of Dmitri's elbow.

"Let's assume," he said, "that my name's Johnny."

Dmitri replied in the same tone, "Let's assume my name's Jackie."

He knew that telling ROSSI the truth—admitting he was a Soviet intelligence officer—would be counterproductive. Most likely, it would only turn ROSSI off. It was logical to assume that, after the dirty trick played on him at the Soviet Embassy in Paris back in 1928, he would hardly be willing to have anything to do with the Soviets who had cheated and humiliated him.[22]

Therefore, Dmitri decided to work under a "false flag"—to pretend that he represented not Soviet intelligence but the intelligence of some other country. He recalled the character of an American gangster working for a Japanese spy agency he had created back in 1930 on the spur of the moment while visiting with Mr. Habert, the dean of diplomats in the free city of Danzig. The image had worked well for him then. It was worth using it again. And he told ROSSI that, since their complexion and other physical features of their race constrained them in their European operations, the Japanese hired him to procure Italian diplomatic ciphers.[23]

Dmitri rightly assumed that ROSSI would not ask how he knew that he was in the business of selling the ciphers. This information could come from many quarters other than the Soviet Embassy in Paris. A flourishing black market of international codes and ciphers in Geneva made such a question superfluous. Dmitri's brash handling of the man paid off. ROSSI offered him some fresh goods that had come into his possession for a short time: reports of Mussolini's advisers and ciphered Italian diplomatic dispatches.[24]

Soon, ROSSI began supplying the OGPU with Italian diplomatic codes on a permanent basis. He also sold contacts with informers and agents in Geneva for five hundred dollars apiece. But, as Emile the barman warned Dmitri, ROSSI turned out to be a shady character indeed, a cheat and a liar. Apparently, to cover up the fact that he was selling the same ciphers to many other foreign agents, he invented a story that Mussolini's son-in-law, Count Ciano, was the organizer of underground trading of Italian diplomatic codes. Presumably on his instructions, ROSSI made the rounds of embassies of the great powers in European capitals and sold Italian diplomatic ciphers at the highest price. After taking the cream of the profit, he turned to mid-size countries, eventually selling the ciphers to the smallest possible bidders. When all possible profits had been taken in, Count Ciano changed the ciphers, and the whole business began anew.

Moreover, ROSSI insisted that the Duce himself was aware of the scheme and profited from it. To make his story believable, ROSSI also told Dmitri that after Bessedovsky's defection and his publication of a book in which he revealed the offer of Italian ciphers, a scandal seemed imminent. To prevent it, on Ciano's cue, his agent at the Italian Embassy in Berlin hid the cipher book in the cabinet in the embassy restroom and reported its disappearance. Ciano ordered an immediate search of the premises, "found" the cipher book, arrested the poor Italian cipher clerks, and sent them to the Italian equivalent of Alcatraz, on the "Devil's Island" of Stromboli, one of the Eolie Islands (Lipari Islands), in the Tyrrhenian Sea near northeastern Sicily. They all perished there. Then, the scandal was successfully suppressed. Indoctrinated in Soviet ideological dogma, according to which the bourgeois West was thoroughly corrupt, Dmitri and the Center easily believed that tall tale.[25]

But when it came to money ROSSI had no scruples whatsoever. At their first trade interaction, he suggested that, instead of two hundred thousand genuine francs, he would accept a million counterfeit American dollars. More than once he tried to get advance payment for making contacts with information sources that were not there. He also tried to sell the same ciphers twice. If money were involved, he didn't think twice, even though he could run into serious trouble. Once, traveling with Bystrolyotov, he was almost caught by customs guards smuggling a wad of Brussels lace into Great Britain.[26]

Later on, he even turned dangerous. When the Japanese intelligence in Tokyo bought some diplomatic ciphers from him and, soon after, Bystrolyotov purchased the very same ciphers from him, ROSSI realized that he had been duped twice by the Soviets. He decided to get even with them by murdering their slick agent. After one of their meetings in Geneva, ROSSI invited Dmitri to stop by his place for a cup of coffee to see how he lived. Though he knew that ROSSI's home was in the provinces, Dmitri thought that the man might also have some city quarters and accepted the invitation. ROSSI brought Dmitri to a gated mansion in the depths of one of Geneva's parks, where a servant in livery opened the gates.[27]

As he walked through the hall, Dmitri immediately suspected that he was trapped: antique furniture, sculptures, and expensive pictures on the walls were covered with dust. Dmitri had a feeling that nobody had lived in the house for a long time. ROSSI took Dmitri to a guestroom, offered him a seat, and sat down himself on a couch a few yards away. While Dmitri was marveling over the fancy interior, a gun appeared in ROSSI's hand. The self-satisfied grin on his face made Dmitri realize that he had fallen into a trap. His first thought was that ROSSI would try to extort money from him. But things turned out to be much worse than that. "I brought you here," ROSSI hissed, "to finish you off. I've suspected all along that you're a Russian spy. And I hate Russians. Now, I'll turn you into ground meat right this minute."[28]

First Dmitri tried to reason with him. But when this didn't work, trying not to lose self-control, he looked at his watch and said as calmly as possible, making sure that ROSSI heard him clearly, "My people are in cars all around this park. If I don't leave this house in fifteen minutes, a dozen brutes will break in here. They'll turn you and your pictures into such ground beef that all the butchers in Geneva will applaud in delight."

This worked. ROSSI stopped grinning. "What cars? What?"

"Only thirteen minutes left before you'll see for yourself," Dmitri said, looking again at his watch. "Take away your stupid cannon and let's talk business."

"It was a joke," ROSSI said, hiding his gun. "Can't you take a joke? Sorry, old man."

"I don't like jokes of that kind," Dmitri said firmly. "Try to refrain from them in the future."[29]

Despite the danger that ROSSI could come up with some other threat, Dmitri did not break with him. Of course, he duly informed the Center about the incident. But he accepted the danger in dealing with his agents as an occupational hazard, as part and parcel of his intelligence work.

And the risk Dmitri took in his dealings with ROSSI paid off handsomely. The agent possessed a wealth of knowledge about the inner workings of the international black market in codes and ciphers. In the future, he gave Dmitri numerous leads to other sources of important information and recruitment opportunities. This made the ROSSI line the most productive in Dmitri's spy career.[30]

One of the first people ROSSI introduced Dmitri to was a French foreign intelligence agent and recruiter, Rodolphe Lemoine. Born Rudolf Stallman, he had come from a wealthy family of Berlin jewelers but, after travelling around the world, had become addicted to the thrill of espionage. In 1918, he became a French citizen and was recruited by the Deuxieme Bureau, French military intelligence, where his code name was REX. Lemoine's looks and personality made Dmitri cringe. Although, at the time of their meeting, the man was just in his late fifties, according to Bystrolyotov, Lemoine looked old, ominous, and repulsive. In "Generous Hearts," he describes his profile as "strange-looking, as if cut out of cardboard and daubed with yellow and brown paint." His full face also resembled that of a "villain and scoundrel in theater makeup. Dead eyes set deeply under gray brows streaked with red."[31]

But the connection turned out to be very important. Lemoine's method was not selling diplomatic ciphers of various countries but exchanging them for similar material of countries he did not have. That way, later on, the Soviets obtained ciphers of diplomatic mail from Austria, Belgium, Hungary, and Czechoslovakia. Through him, the Soviets could also identify the sources of confidential information leaks from the USSR.[32]

Pressed by the necessity to return to his prime responsibility—handling "Charlie" and keeping the OGPU out of the equation when dealing with foreign agents—Dmitri made another "false flag" move. He introduced Lemoine (code-named JOSEPH) to one "Walter Scott," an agent of "American military intelligence."[33]

His true name was Ignatii Stanislavovich Poretsky (1899–1937). Born to a middle-class family in Austria-Hungary, he took part in the revolutionary movement in Europe. After the end of the Russian civil war, he worked as an illegal operative in central and eastern Europe and was awarded a Military Red Banner order. At the time he and Dmitri met, Poretsky (legal cover name "Ignace Reiss," code-named RAYMOND) began his West European assignment for the Soviet Foreign Intelligence. Judging from the fact that Poretsky was one of three intelligence officers who would write a letter of recommendation for Dmitri to join the Party and the high responsibility it carried, they were in close collaboration. (Moreover, the time would come when the recommendation would become Dmitri's liability after Poretsky's defection to the West in 1937.)[34]

Meanwhile, ROSSI and Dmitri agreed to see each other in Berlin in a few months' time to discuss the terms of selling Italian ciphers. Now Dmitri could go back to what he had already been prepared to do: to close in on ARNO.

EIGHT | Handling "Charlie"

It's easier to deal with a fool than with a drunkard.

If, in finding and handling ROSSI, Dmitri showed his ingenuity, ability to take risks, and perseverance, all of these qualities were even more pronounced in his most celebrated case: controlling "Charlie" (code-named ARNO), the British agent with access to diplomatic material.

Having passed the Lemoine contact to "Ignace Reiss," Dmitri went to Paris, where Bazarov and "Charlie" had already been meeting regularly. Dmitri showed up at a restaurant where Bazarov and ARNO were together and pretended that he had mixed up the time of his own appointment with "Da Vinci" (Bazarov). Later, when Hungarian "Count Perelly" (Dmitri) approached "Charlie" on his own, he could speak with him not as a stranger but as a colleague working for the same boss. The Hungarian count confided his life story to "Charlie." Ruined by "that awful war" and down on his luck, the count had first found a temporary haven in Bolshevist ideology. To maintain the same lifestyle he had before the war, he took money from the OGPU, thus winding up in its claws, from which it was difficult to extricate himself.[1]

Handling "Charlie" was a delicate job. The trick was to ensure his cooperation. Scaring him off could cause him to sever the connection or, even worse, to leave the Foreign Office, escaping the pressure altogether. Therefore, Dmitri's story was intended to make the Brit believe that he and the count were in the same boat: two mixed-up decent people of the same social standing, comrades in misfortune, who had to stick together while working for the same master. Dmitri explained that having been assigned to work with "Charlie," he was following the orders of "that cruel and angry Bolshevik, 'Da Vinci,'" only out of necessity. "Count Perelly's" only hope of ever getting out of this mess was to rely on his new British friend's cooperation. If "Charlie" wouldn't give "Da Vinci" whatever he wanted, the proud Hungarian count would pay the price. The Soviets threatened to move him away from his beloved Europe to work in some uncivilized place, in some godforsaken part of the world. He dreaded even thinking about such an unfortunate turn of events.

Though sympathetic to the count's predicament, ARNO continued to guard his true identity zealously, and Dmitri decided on active pursuit. After one of their meetings, he shadowed "Charlie," again bringing in his assistant couple, PEEP and ERIKA. Joined by Bazarov himself, all four tried many times to track down where ARNO was staying in Paris by stalking him, but they failed miserably time and again. The Brit seemed to know the Paris streets thoroughly and foiled all attempts to pursue him. This fact alone convinced Dmitri that "Charlie" was misrepresenting himself: such a skill hardly fit the image of a modest typesetter.

During one of their next meetings in a restaurant, Dmitri tried to slow "Charlie" down by getting him drunk. It was easy: the man seemed to like alcohol a great deal. But all attempts at surveillance failed again. Though considerably intoxicated, the man spotted his pursuer in the crowd, approached him, and laughingly told him to "stop playing the street spy." Instead, he suggested a new place for their next meeting—his Paris relatives' apartment—and he gave him their address. The next day, Dmitri rushed to find the place but, much to his dismay, realized that ARNO had played a practical joke on him. The address turned out to be a vacant plot of land on the site of a demolished building.[2]

This only fueled Dmitri's desire to track the man down no matter what. Finally, the group's persistence paid off. One day, ERIKA spotted ARNO running into the entrance of the Hotel Napoleon near the Arc de Triomphe. First she thought he was just trying to lose his tail. But then, through the glass door, she saw him take a key from the front desk and enter an elevator. She went into the hotel hall and asked the concierge whether a man in a light suit had just walked in.

When the concierge answered affirmatively, she asked where she could find him. "Room 86, third floor," he answered. ERIKA pretended to be going there but, in fact, stayed in a corridor for a half hour and then inconspicuously slipped out of the hotel. The news reconfirmed Dmitri's hunch that ARNO had lied both to him and to Bazarov: a typesetter could hardly afford to stay in such an expensive place.[3]

Dmitri rushed into action. He checked into the hotel himself and soon learned that "Charlie" was registered there under the name of "Ernest H. Oldwell." Full of hope, Dmitri went to London. Through the city address bureau, he found several men of this name, but none of them fitted ARNO's profile. Obviously, "Oldwell" was the man's alias.

Searching for clues to the Brit's identity, Dmitri hypothesized that the initials of ARNO's real name were the same as those of his alias. Recalling his own experience, he observed that people tend to cling to the familiar. To check out his hunch, one day, shortly before "Charlie" had to leave his hotel room for their meeting, Dmitri ran up to the room and burst in. The move was risky but calculated. It violated the condition ARNO set for meetings with any OGPU agents—his right to privacy had to be honored. But Dmitri decided that since "Charlie" hadn't been paid yet for his recent delivery of the British diplomatic dispatches, he would hardly make good on his threat to break with the Soviets. He asked "Charlie" to excuse him for intruding, citing "an emergency," which was to notify him about a sudden change of the place and time of their meeting. He, "Count Perelly," had just received orders to go to Turkey on an OGPU emergency assignment. At first "Charlie" became angry, but the count's explanation seemed plausible to him, and he softened up. They set another date for their next meeting and Dmitri left, politely bowing and asking again to be excused for his intrusion. Before leaving the room, Dmitri spotted what he was looking for. It was ARNO's travel bag lying in the corner of the room. On it he clearly made out its owner's embossed initials—"E.H.O." Bingo!

The rest of the task to find out ARNO's real name was a matter of logic. Since he had most likely traveled to Europe on business related to his place of work, the British Foreign Service, it was natural to assume that he was a member of the large British delegation, which, a few days after the postponed appointment, was to take part in the next session of the League of Nations. The OGPU already knew that British diplomats usually stayed at the Hotel Beau Rivage in Geneva. Dmitri went there and, scanning the list of delegation members posted near the counter in the hotel lobby, found one that fit the initials "E.H.O." It was Ernest Holloway Oldham.

Such a close match of the first name with the alias and the exact initials "Charlie" had used in his Paris hotel ("Ernest H. Oldwell") left Dmitri with little doubt about "Charlie's" identity. Waiting patiently for ARNO's appearance in the hotel lobby, he finally spotted him taking a seat at the hotel bar. As in his recent handling of ROSSI, Dmitri again made his appearance before his target as dramatic as possible. Without saying hello, he took a seat on the stool next to ARNO. Oldham paled in horror. Now he realized that his cover was blown, and he was no longer in control of his relationship with the OGPU.

In early September 1931, Dmitri and Bazarov went to London to find everything they could on Oldham. It was an important step toward carrying out Stalin's order to open British diplomatic pouches. Consulting Britain's *Who's Who*, they found out what they had suspected all along: their "Charlie" was not a typesetter but a staff member of the British Foreign Service, a decorated officer, a retired army captain. The book also revealed that the man owned a sizable mansion in the upscale area of Pembroke Gardens in Kensington. A visit to his home would send the message that his days of independence were over. His cover blown, now he had no choice but to submit to all OGPU demands.

Once they settled in London, in preparation for the visit, Dmitri dressed in the style of a regular London official—a bowler hat, a dark gray jacket, and striped pants. Looking him over before he stepped out to the street, a nervous Bazarov blessed Dmitri, "May God be with you!" When Dmitri arrived at Oldham's estate, a pretty maid answered the door. Dmitri gave her his business card, that of a Dresden bank representative, embossed with his Hungarian count insignia, and slipped her a pound bill as a tip.

But the effect of his appearance was diminished by the absence of the master of the house. His wife, Lucy, met the stranger rather coldly. In Dmitri's account, she was a "beautiful woman around fifty years old who tried to look younger than her age." (In fact, Lucy was almost twelve years older than Oldham, whom she married after her first husband had died, leaving her with their two boys. To hide this discrepancy in their ages, both Lucy and Ernest lied on their marriage certificate, stating that she was four years younger and he was five years older.) She also gave the impression of being haughty and not too bright. Dmitri respectfully introduced himself and explained that, due to a volatile stock market, her husband's valuables were at risk. In the interest of its clients, the bank had sent him for an urgent meeting to discuss the situation privately. Softening at the mention of money matters, Lucy explained that her husband was out of town.[4]

Dmitri made his next move. As he often did during his intelligence career, he played his "innocent abroad" card. "I'm sorry," he said to Oldham's wife, "I'm not very familiar with British etiquette, but I hope it's not out of line to invite you to lunch with me at the Ritz Hotel." It was the most expensive place to eat in London, and the lady was duly impressed.

Toward the end of their lunch, during the course of which he ordered a bottle of high-priced Burgundy and coffee with cognac, Lucy became totally disposed toward the elegant and attractive visitor. She even felt comfortable confiding to him that the reason for her husband's current absence was his inordinate love of alcohol. On doctor's orders, he was undergoing treatment at the Rendlesham Hall near Woodbridge in Suffolk. She felt hopeless about her husband's addiction to drink and asked the count to try to convince him, for his own good, to take the treatment seriously.

The next day, she sent the family's luxurious car, complete with a uniformed chauffeur, to pick up the count. As the car reached the private sanatorium, which looked like a medieval castle, Dmitri found drunken Oldham in the hall sleeping in one of the ancient armchairs. A servant wanted to wake him up, but Dmitri stopped him. Making himself comfortable in another chair, he calmly waited until "the typesetter" woke up. When Oldham finally opened his eyes and saw the Hungarian OGPU agent near him, he was crushed. Now, he had nowhere to run. "God damn you!" was his only reaction. According to Dmitri, he stayed in the sanatorium for about a month until Oldham completed the treatment. Little by little, Dmitri learned what he had suspected all along: that ARNO wasn't some modest typesetter, but a Foreign Office specialist in developing cipher codes and deciphering them. They returned to London together. From that time on, ARNO didn't budge, and although from time to time he cursed "that awful Bolshevik Da Vinci" behind his back, he carried out his orders to the letter. Dmitri stayed close to him and watched his every step. He even accompanied him on recreational excursions. On one of their visits to a cinema theater, afraid of being exposed as a Soviet agent, Oldham had a nervous fit when Dmitri hesitated for a moment before jumping to his feet the way everybody else did as the first chords of "God Save the King" played before the screening started.[5]

As anticipated from the start of Dmitri's involvement in the case, ARNO's wife (code-named MADAM) took a liking to the young and handsome Hungarian count. She insisted that he stay at their home and convinced her husband to extend his invitation as well. Moreover, she promised to introduce the count to Oldham's colleagues among the Foreign Office officials. This opportunity for the Center was hard to pass up. Although it was established now that ARNO wasn't a "mere typesetter" but a Foreign Office functionary himself, he was still believed to be a go-between for "the source," that is, someone in charge of the entire flow of British diplomatic correspondence. Establishing the identity of that man would make it possible to eliminate ARNO from the loop. That way, the OGPU could achieve two objectives at once: to speed up the delivery of information and save on commission paid to ARNO.

But it was not expected that Oldham's wife wouldn't wait for the Hungarian count to make a pass at her. Apparently, long neglected sexually by her alcoholic husband, MADAM took the initiative and approached Dmitri. On the eve of ARNO's return from the clinic, she offered herself to Dmitri, as KIN's report to the Center expresses it, quite straightforwardly: with the "spirited gesture of a seaport hooker, rolling up the hem of her dress, spreading her legs, and begging him not to waste any time." Dmitri told his stepgrandson three decades later that he'd been caught by surprise and simply succumbed to the temptation. The moment it was over, he locked himself in the bathroom, overwhelmed with shame. "I looked in the mirror. I'm sweaty; my tie shifted to one side. My God, what do I tell my superiors?" As KIN's report to the Center shows, Dmitri gave a plausible excuse for his unauthorized action. He informed Bazarov that he had to make a split-second decision: since MADAM was needed as a source of information for future dealings with ARNO, if he had rejected her, she might have become hostile toward him. His refusal to oblige her could make access to ARNO difficult, if not impossible.[6]

Meanwhile, for his own protection, ARNO tried to make Dmitri's presence in his family as inconspicuous as possible. Since Oldham had to take packages of confidential materials across the British border himself and deliver them to Bazarov in Berlin, he entrusted the Hungarian count with the care of his younger stepson, Raymond. Dmitri took the boy to Germany and placed him with a family living in a villa near Bonn overlooking the Rhine River. This gave ARNO a legitimate pretext for his periodic trips abroad—visits to his son. Gradually, Dmitri's relationship with Oldham's family grew to the extent that he was entrusted with the most intimate of family affairs. When ARNO's daughter-in-law, the wife of his older stepson, Tommy, exceeded the time limit for obtaining an abortion in England, Dmitri took her across the channel to Berlin, where he arranged for the unlawful operation.

Wary of the possibility that British counterintelligence was watching Oldham, the meeting places and intervals between them were changed often. Madrid, Paris, a beach near Ostend (Belgium), and a Swiss resort area (near Brienz, in the canton of Bern) were some of the locations to which ARNO traveled with his packages of diplomatic dispatches for the OGPU.

Overall, things were going smoothly, but from time to time mishaps occurred. Once when ARNO brought the next book of diplomatic ciphers and codes to Paris, tired after an all-night photography session in his hotel room, Dmitri cut his finger while pressing the pages with a piece of glass. A large bloodstain appeared on one of the pages. No matter how hard he tried to lick it off the surface or wash it off with a wad of cotton, the blot refused to disappear. By luck, when Oldham returned the books to his office, nobody noticed anything suspicious. In his KGB memo, Dmitri explained this oversight, saying that British Foreign Office functionaries—mostly aristocrats— knew each other from their Ivy League school years and trusted each other too much.

It is apparent that, while being able to penetrate so deep into enemy territory, Dmitri didn't know much about Oldham's background. From the outset of the operation, both Bazarov and Dmitri were wrong in assuming the agent's aristocratic standing. In truth, Oldham was of humble origin: his parents were schoolteachers, he didn't go to university, and he entered the civil service at the age of nineteen. What seemed to make an impression of Oldham's high station in life was the spacious house in Kensington, complete with a maid and a uniformed chauffeur driving a luxurious car, and Oldham's penchant for dressing in expensive suits, with matching shirts adorned with monograms. All these signs of belonging to high society were of his wife's, Lucy's, making. The daughter of a wealthy man herself, before marrying Oldham, she inherited considerable funds after the death of her first husband, Thomas William Wellsted, a rich gold-mining engineer. It was her money with which the house was purchased and domestic help hired. Apparently, something happened to her inheritance (risky investments?); she lost her fortune—but not the taste for high life. It looks like she was the one who prompted Oldham to do whatever he could to support the level of life she was used to, which brought him to the doors of the Soviet Embassy in Paris to begin with.[7]

Meanwhile, it became clear that sooner or later, ARNO would be trouble. Squeezed by the OGPU, worn out from the fear of being caught, and tormented with pangs of conscience, ARNO again took to drink, this time very heavily. Yet, it was at that time when he managed to do a great turn for Dmitri. In the summer of 1932, Dmitri learned that Oldham was personally acquainted with the British Foreign Secretary, Sir John Simon, and decided to use this connection. Perusing the Canadian press, he established that the second son of Lord Grenville, Robert, was born at his father's estate in Canada, Points North, and decided to obtain a British passport issued in Robert's name. Preparing himself for a possible British counterintelligence inquiry, and as was his method when assuming a new identity, he immersed himself in books on Canada's geography, history, economy, and everyday life. Once he felt sufficiently prepared, he signaled ARNO to proceed in getting the passport. On its delivery, ARNO boasted that as an exception and a sign of special attention, Sir John signed the passport himself, allegedly saying, "Hm, I didn't know that Lord Robert was here in Britain again."[8]

It was truly a stroke of luck. At the time, customs officials across Europe considered British passports most reliable. Traveling abroad, the Russian poet Vladimir Mayakovsky observed that British passports were treated with great reverence. It is known that Kim Philby took advantage of this circumstance in smuggling radical Marxist literature across West European borders. Dmitri resorted to this passport generally when he was carrying the most dangerous materials. He made a point, however, not to stay in any country for long because that would require a visit to the local British consulate, where his thick accent would give him away.[9]

During that period of summer 1932, the bulk of material collected by ARNO and passed on to the Soviets was related to the Lausanne Conference, which took place between June 16 and July 9 and concerned a whirlwind of diplomatic and behind-closed-door activities of many European countries. It was an important conference aimed at relief of international tensions caused by Germany's burden of paying World War I reparations, especially in view of the worldwide depression triggered by the Wall Street crash of 1929.

Even before the crash, it had become increasingly clear that the defeated nation, Germany, would have a hard time meeting the obligations stipulated by the Treaty of Versailles. In fact, back in 1923, with its economy unable to sustain war reparation payments, Germany defaulted on them. As a punishment, French and Belgian troops occupied the Ruhr River valley. This occupation of the center of the German coal and steel industries struck at the heart of the German economy and contributed to the country's hyperinflation.

After the failure of several additional attempts to solve the problem of war reparation payments, in a final effort to find an orderly solution to the issue that had caused so much political tension, representatives of Germany, Great Britain, France, and Japan convened the Lausanne Conference.

What was the nature of the information received from ARNO? On this point, there are discrepancies between Tsarev and West's book, *Crown Jewels,* and its Russian version, *KGB v Anglii.* According to *Crown Jewels,* in a Foreign Office cable of June 28, 1932, the British ambassador in Berlin, Sir Horace Rumbold, reported that he "had held confidential discussions" with the chancellor of Germany, Franz von Papen, about the "imminent" Lausanne Conference and the "approach to be taken with the French." The reader is thus led to believe that British and German officials on opposite sides of the conference negotiations conducted secret talks about how to deal with the French.[10]

However, the text of the same cable in the Russian version of the book quoted from the Bystrolyotov file does not report any "confidential talks" between Rumbold and von Papen. It merely states that Rumbold used a "secret informer" to learn about Chancellor von Papen's intention "to reach a compromise with France at all costs about all points of contention even at the price of sacrifice on the side of Germany." It states that Rumbold also learned through the same secret informer that the German "cabinet insists that a firmer tone be taken in Lausanne." It adds that "on the day of von Papen's return from Lausanne, during the cabinet meeting before signing the treaty, a secret session took place during which General Schleicher insisted on the necessity to come to an agreement with France on the question of armament, stating firmly that Germany cannot exist any longer with an army of one hundred thousand serving a twelve-year stint."[11]

Another document procured through Dmitri's efforts was a copy of a telegram from the Foreign Office about information collected by the Belgian military attaché and passed on to the British attaché concerning Germany's diplomatic maneuvers to offer a compromise that would persuade France to lift limitations in armament.

The Russian version of Tsarev and West's *Crown Jewels* also extensively quotes Bystrolyotov's handwritten memorandum of that time. Without citing any sources, he describes the behind-the-scenes political maneuvering of British Prime Minister and Leader of the House of Commons Ramsay MacDonald, French President of the Council and Minister of Foreign Affairs Édouard Herriot, and von Papen. This memorandum makes it clear that von Papen used the threat of Hitler's possible rise to power as leverage in persuading the French to make political concessions to Germany during the Lausanne negotiations.

Knowing the minute details of these and other diplomatic maneuvers was of great importance to the Soviets. The diplomatic activities between Germany and the Western Allies aimed to establish guarantees for stability of the borders west of Germany, leaving the country's eastern borders to possible revisions in the future. Although bound by the 1922 Treaty of Rapallo on cooperation and territorial integrity, the Soviet Union and Germany did not fully trust each other. Each party feared that the other would find a way to create a strong alliance with the French Third Republic, at the time considered the greatest military power in Europe.

The importance of these documents for the Soviets explains the OGPU gesture of gratitude toward Dmitri for his work at that time. By order no. 1042/s of November 17, 1932, "for successfully carrying out several assignments of major operative value and exceptional persistence in doing so," he was awarded a personal gun bearing the inscription: "For a merciless fight with the counterrevolution from the OGPU Collegium. OGPU Deputy Chairman Balitsky."[12]

The Russian modifier *besposhchadnyi* (merciless) is rendered as "relentless" in Tsarev and West's *Crown Jewels* (69) and "unstinting" in Andrew and Mitrokhin's *The Sword and the Shield* (48). But "merciless" is truly the only way to describe the treatment of the OGPU British "source," Ernest Oldham, especially in the course of actions that followed after the end of the Lausanne Conference when it became clear that ARNO was falling behind in his ability to be useful to the OGPU.

Dmitri, for whom attachment to his Motherland was a psychological imperative, was truly merciless in his attitude toward anyone who betrayed their own country, as his "sources" did. They interested him only while they worked, that is, while they were "selling out their country."[13]

Meanwhile, on July 27, 1932, ARNO delivered a British passport to Dmitri, but not only was he ten days late for their meeting, he brought nothing else of value. He assured Dmitri that his "source" was busy with the Lausanne Conference papers and, therefore, hadn't the time to get his hands on anything of interest to the Soviets.

The relationship with ARNO continued deteriorating rapidly. He missed appointments, and when he did come what he delivered was often worthless. To make things worse, he began failing physically. When he came to Berlin to see Dmitri in the last week of October 1932, he was in exceptionally poor shape. Although he swore he would continue to bring British diplomatic mail in the future, in Dmitri's judgment, he couldn't last more than a few months before becoming fully incapacitated. During their meeting, ARNO was totally apathetic, vomited, and often couldn't even move. Dmitri decided on having a decisive talk with him during their next meeting, also set in Germany, but a week later, when he hoped the Brit would be in better shape.

But the meeting never took place. On November 11, 1932, instead of ARNO, his wife, Lucy, came to Berlin. It is doubtful that Soviet intelligence would ever have found out much about ARNO if Dmitri had not won Lucy's full confidence by becoming her lover. At that meeting, she delivered bad news: her husband had failed to inform the count that he was no longer employed by the Foreign Office. Moreover, he hadn't left on his own volition—he was fired. According to Lucy, the reasons given to Oldham for his dismissal were his heavy drinking and careless work for the past two years. Over the past six months, he had also taken confidential papers home and lost them. For months, he had failed to respond to the inquiries of other officials of the Foreign Office.[14]

As Dmitri would learn a year later, Oldham's former assistant and friend Mr. Kemp had told Lucy that until mid-1932 her husband was not suspected of any wrongdoing. Considered a capable official, albeit lacking in discipline, he was tolerated at work although everyone was aware of his alcoholism. He was even given a leave of absence to get treatment. But one day, they found some code books missing from the safe in the basement of the Foreign Office. It was established that Oldham had visited the Cipher Room for no apparent reason. It was also established that he had used the side entrance to the building—the "ambassadors' entrance." Though no formal charges were filed against Oldham, they fired him "just in case."[15]

As if that weren't bad enough, the very way he was let go was highly alarming. Lucy was outraged that her husband, a distinguished official of the Foreign Office and a war veteran, after twenty years of service, was thrown into the street without even a partial pension. This would not usually happen to a Foreign Office employee even if he were fired for carelessness. Dmitri recalled ARNO's having told him about two other cases of employees fired by the Foreign Office without a pension (one took place in Beijing and the other in Oslo). In both cases, the fired workers were suspected of espionage. There was a good chance this was the case with ARNO as well.[16]

Lucy also told Dmitri that their family finances were in a terrible state. Since ARNO had very little money to his name in the bank, she planned to leave him after selling their house, the luxurious car, and whatever else she could get some money for. She thought of settling at some French resort area where many Brits resided and finding employment as a home companion. Moreover, she told Dmitri she was so desperate that she would also consider becoming a prostitute, not an easy task considering her age (at the time, fifty-two). She begged Dmitri to help her in one way or another.

Reporting this meeting to the Center, Dmitri suggested the following plan of action. Considering that ARNO had been fired from his job and that he was sick and incapable of working for the Soviets in any capacity, he should be offered a lifetime pension in exchange for making a direct contact with "the source." One can only marvel at how, even on the brink of total collapse, Oldham was capable of continuing his game of deception with the OGPU by holding on to his original plan—presenting himself as only a go-between for another Foreign Office employee, some "retired captain" whose name he couldn't reveal to anyone as a matter of honor.

When Dmitri checked with Lucy, she told him that her husband's story was total hogwash. She knew of no such man in the Foreign Office. Moreover, she told him that he lied about almost everything and that there was no reason to believe any of his stories. Clearly, ARNO could become a liability for the entire operation to penetrate the British Foreign Office. Intoxicated, ARNO might start talking. Now, when he was apparently suspected of treason, he could do considerable damage, the least of which was to alert the Foreign Office regarding OGPU activities.

Of course, the most reasonable way of handling the situation would have been to sever all ties with ARNO. But then, the most important task of establishing direct contact with "the source," whose existence the OGPU still believed in, would be hard to achieve. Andrew and Mitrokhin rightly point out that the OGPU's blindness regarding Oldham's true place in the Foreign Office was due to the Russians' ignorance concerning the overall structure and functioning of the Foreign Office and other branches of British government.[17]

To find a replacement for ARNO, Dmitri decided to return to England to extract enough information from him about his colleagues, even though it meant putting himself in harm's way. Shortly before Christmas 1932, he went to London. There he found ARNO on a nonstop binge. In an alcoholic stupor, he paid no attention to Dmitri's pleading that he get hold of himself. The pressure only irritated him intensely. Dmitri told Lucy to give her husband no more alcohol under any circumstances. When he visited the Oldhams on Christmas Day, ARNO was in terrible shape: unwashed, hair uncombed, eyes sunken and pinched looking. He looked like an alcoholic who had totally let himself go. Dmitri had to shake him considerably to wake him up. Without opening his eyes, ARNO groped around, found a bottle of cognac, took a gulp from it, and, apparently taking Dmitri for his wife, said, "Get lost, you old bitch!" Then he fell asleep again.

Dmitri told Lucy not to give him any more cognac and that when her husband woke up she should call a doctor. At night, Oldham came back to life and demanded another drink. When Lucy refused him, he grabbed for her throat and began strangling her. By luck, a doctor, for whom she had called sometime earlier, arrived. He gave ARNO a strong dose of morphine. With Dmitri's help, the man was transported to a sanatorium in the countryside. After his departure, Lucy had a nervous fit and wanted to end her life. During the next three days, Dmitri succeeded in talking her out of doing away with herself. With bruises from ARNO's fingers on her throat, she finally took to bed, and the doctor injected sedatives to soothe her.

After treatment in a sanatorium, ARNO felt better, but after a while, he resumed drinking and beating his wife.[18]

Toward the end of 1932, before going to London, Dmitri took a short break from his spy work. He was informed that since her tuberculosis had reactivated, Iolanta's sentence had been commuted, and she was about to be released from jail. Crisscrossing the European continent on OGPU business (Berlin, Amsterdam, Paris, London, Geneva), Dmitri had been feeling uneasy about being so seldom able to visit his wife, who was serving her term in an Austrian military prison. Overwhelmed with assignments, barely once every couple of months did he manage to swing by Vienna to see her. Of course, he was always attentive about providing her with whatever she needed in captivity. But, busy as he was, to be efficient, he had to rely on a trustworthy assistant. And there was only one person who could fill that role—Isolde Cameron. As soon as she had learned from the papers about Iolanta's arrest, she threw herself at her love's disposal. To be closer to Iolanta and visit her frequently, she immediately cut loose all her business and social ties in Prague and moved to Vienna.[19]

Grudgingly, Dmitri had to accept the reality of the situation. With him being away for long stretches of time, it was only right to put Iolanta's interests before his own feelings. And Isolde's help, the help of a loving woman, was indispensable. He made an effort to suppress his animosity toward her and to find a way to deal with her for their common good. They agreed to cooperate: he financed everything that Isolde undertook to mitigate Iolanta's conditions in prison.

As time went by, doing good things for the sake of the same person improved their relationship. First openly hostile and cold, they gradually became more tolerant and respectful of each other. Both knew that Iolanta's health was fragile, and they avoided doing anything to worry her. To coordinate their efforts for Iolanta's benefit, Dmitri phoned Isolde when he was coming to Vienna. They would meet in some café or restaurant to discuss what they could do next for Iolanta. After a while, they met out of habit without having any chore at hand related to her. Their mutual hostility began subsiding; at times they would even joke and laugh in each other's company. Once, they went to see a play together. Seemingly, whatever had divided them several years ago had faded from memory.

In the fall of 1932, when Iolanta's lawyer filed a petition to grant Iolanta amnesty on the grounds of poor health, the upsurge of hope to see their beloved free again created a truly warm relationship between Dmitri and Isolde. They seemed to feel close to each other as never before. When the day of Iolanta's release was announced, in an expression of shared joy, they hugged each other. Enthralled, they began making plans about how to take care of Iolanta once she was out of jail. During these meetings, they came up with the idea of settling Iolanta in the Swiss mountains, where her weak lungs could recuperate faster. Dmitri gave money to Isolde, who ordered train tickets and made all of the other arrangements.

Excited and jubilant, Isolde suggested that now they could sigh in relief that Iolanta would soon be free and out of danger—it was time to celebrate the occasion. What followed was a replay of their last meeting back in 1925. But, this time, the roles were reversed. Isolde took the initiative, taking Dmitri on a spree of dance clubs and restaurants; they danced and drank all night long.

What happened next can perhaps be explained by Dmitri's peculiar state of mind in that period of his life, the first years of his underground existence as an OGPU spy. On one hand, he was excited by the romantic new life that was full of danger. He was a doer, a man of action who welcomed challenge and rushed to tackle the most difficult problems demanded by his job as an illegal operative. On the other hand, judging by his own perception of his life at that time—"a lonely run in the darkness of a stormy night"—he hardly knew where life was taking him. And this was far from an exaggeration. The tension of his new life began taking a toll on him. Unlike the relative security of walking the city streets as an employee of the Soviet Trade Mission, as he had done back in Prague, his life was totally different—now in Berlin, now in London, now in Geneva or Paris, with a passport in his pocket issued in a name not his own. Following OGPU instructions to the letter, he always had to be on his toes. Any unexpected encounter with a familiar face was a source of around-the-clock worry. Once in any public place, be it an open-air market or a hotel lobby, a concert hall or a nightclub, he had to routinely scan the crowd. There was always a chance that someone might take an unusual interest in him.[20]

His life became lonelier than ever. Like other illegals, he not only couldn't visit any Soviet embassy but also had to avoid associating himself in any way, whether formally or informally, with anyone on its staff. He couldn't get together for a chat over a cup of coffee with a fellow underground operative who happened to be nearby. Even meetings with his controller Bazarov or his assistants Leppin and Erica had to be prearranged, with every measure of precaution in place. All such meetings had to be brief and to the point, dealing with an intelligence task at hand. His mother's letters (she still lived in Anapa), sent to a safe address in Prague, reached him months later and, as a precaution, had to be destroyed immediately upon reading. He couldn't keep them to read again later. If he were arrested, the letters could blow his cover.[21]

Homesick, longing to find relief from the tense and lonely life and the grim atmosphere of the underground, he asked for a short leave to visit his mother. But his request was denied, based on the urgency of the situation. A man of action, he continued carrying out his orders with persistence and resolve. His country needed him. He turned the danger of his new life into a drug of sorts, which made him forget about how lost and lonely he was again after his wife's imprisonment.

And now in Vienna with Isolde, he got the news that his beloved wife was about to join him. Happy and exhilarated as he hadn't been for a long time, he allowed himself to lose his self-control and to in-dulge in celebrating the end of his loneliness. Without noticing, he found himself so intoxicated with hard liquor that he didn't see at what point the nightclub walls had become the walls of Isolde's apart-ment. Moreover, he found himself in pajamas and lying in bed next to the naked Isolde.

When he opened his eyes, she told him that she had taken every precaution for privacy so that he could finally get what he had wanted since long ago. She was ready to give herself to him, but only under one condition: for her sake, he would give up Iolanta once and for all. As he records it in his memoirs, at that moment, his decision to do away with Isolde wasn't just wishful thinking. He clearly realized that no other course of action would ensure Isolde's disappearance from his life forever.

Upon her release from prison, Iolanta was very ill. Her tuberculosis was active, and she was slowly dying. Dmitri took the incapacitated Iolanta to Berlin and placed her in a local hospital. Her tuberculosis in the acute stage, she was barely alive as he took her for consultations with the best doctors he could find. On their advice, she underwent two unsuccessful operations that were supposed to help her—abla-tion of the lung nerves. She barely survived the surgeries.

As he learned about Iolanta's condition, Boris Berman, the legal OGPU *rezident* stationed in Berlin, exclaimed, "Very well!" And he suggested moving Iolanta to a resort area in the Swiss Alps to cure her tuberculosis. But it wasn't a mere act of compassion. Iolanta's gen-uine illness made her presence in the heart of Europe look natural, and she was entrusted with a keepsake cache of forged passports used by members of the "flying squad."

Dmitri was appalled by Berman's remark. He never forgave Boris those words, but he followed through with the plan. First, he brought Iolanta to the small town of Arosa and then moved her to Davos to a sanatorium for tuberculosis patients. There, behind a cabinet in her ward, she hid money and false passports for the OGPU European spies.

Now Davos became Dmitri's semblance of home. During his many shuttle missions across European borders, he stopped there to see his wife. This didn't happen too often, though. His selfless dedication to work often kept him away for months on end. In time, he would pay a stiff price for it. But for now, he had what he wanted in his life.

When things settled down, he responded to Isolde's plea with as much cool as he could muster. He sent her that fateful cigarette case, with its "damned" inscription, that Iolanta had given him back in Prague to dispose of as he wished. He attached the following note: "I'm returning this trifle for it no longer has any use. In my eyes, it had always been a symbol of a certain phase of Iolanta's past. But that phase is over, and there's no reason to think it will come back. Therefore, I hasten to return your gift as a symbolic gesture on my part . . . If at any time in the future you'd like to visit my spouse and me, you will undoubtedly rejoice to see our cloudless happiness."

NINE | The End of "Charlie" and Other British Agents

Only in English novels everything that [British]
intelligence service does goes charmingly smoothly, all ends
meet, and the Tower of London mercilessly swallows those
who have touched upon the secrets of the British Empire.

—BYSTROLYOTOV, IN HIS MEMOIRS

In the unsettled atmosphere in Europe, already volatile due to the effects of the Great Depression, the beginning of the new year of 1933 did not bring much relief. On the contrary, an ominous development put all parties involved on guard. On January 30, Adolf Hitler was appointed chancellor of Germany. His foreign policy, outlined earlier in his book, *Mein Kampf,* kept British diplomatic maneuvering high on the list of OGPU spies' targets. In the book, he proclaimed an alliance with England (and Italy) as Germany's security for future protection against both France, which he considered his country's "unrelenting mortal enemy," and the Soviet Union, at whose expense, in particular, he wished to enlarge Germany's "living space." Therefore, a possible rapprochement between Germany and England threatened to leave the USSR, excluded from the League of Nations, in total isolation. To make things worse, on March 19, 1933, Benito Mussolini called for the creation of the Four-Power Pact, which included Britain, France, Germany, and Italy. Although the German–Soviet 1922 Treaty of Rapallo, an agreement of cooperation and mutual security, was still in force, the USSR was justifiably worried that these countries could come up with an invincible anti-Soviet coalition.

Luckily, ARNO, the Soviet agent in the midst of the British Foreign Office, recuperated from alcoholism enough to continue selling British diplomatic secrets. In May 1933, he came to Paris and brought with him the next pack of documents. Dmitri again asked him to make a direct connection to his "source" in exchange for ARNO's retirement on an OGPU pension. ARNO replied that he had been preparing the "source" for such a transfer, but the man was still not ready.[1]

He came to Paris again on June 20, accompanied by Lucy but without any new diplomatic dispatches. He claimed that he did not have money to pay the "source." Lucy told Dmitri that ARNO did not want to come, but she had forced him to because "Count Perelly" demanded that appointments be kept at all costs. She also confided in Dmitri that ARNO had failed to kick his alcohol addiction completely. He still drank from early morning on and was heavily intoxicated all the time. He could collapse at any moment. The doctor diagnosed the early stages of delirium tremens. Moreover, Oldham had been having frequent episodes of severe heart pains, which, in the doctor's opinion, could lead to his sudden death.[2]

Facing the prospects of ARNO's physical demise, which, seemingly, nothing could prevent, Dmitri again showed exceptional doggedness in pursuing the interests of his country. In the hope of obtaining some more Foreign Office confidential documents, he decided to accompany ARNO back to London. Despite many previous failures to achieve the same goal, he did not give up the hope of restoring him as his agent by rescuing him from his self-destructive behavior. He thought of placing him immediately in a sanatorium and sending Lucy someplace else for recuperation. Then Dmitri could continue working with them, while trying eventually to get to the "source," which Oldham still guarded zealously. Forwarding his plan to the Center, Bazarov added that the plan was quite dangerous, because, to realize even a small part of it, all other means of getting the British documents exhausted, Dmitri had to stay in ARNO's home.

Dmitri arrived in London on June 23. Immediately upon his appearance in the country, bad news greeted him: Lucy told him in horror that, for some reason, Sir Robert Vansittart himself had taken an interest in her husband. "Who is he?" Dmitri asked her. "Chief of our intelligence and counterintelligence," Lucy replied.[3]

Dmitri duly informed the Center about it; it is incredible that, when trying to penetrate the Foreign Office, the OGPU did not know either the name of its head, Sir Robert Vansittart, or that there was not one combined British office of intelligence and counterintelligence. The same goes for another episode, which had taken place during Dmitri's first meeting with Lucy. She told him that her husband was in poor standing with "Monty, head of the Intelligence Service at the Foreign Office and brother of Field Marshal Montgomery." As Andrew and Mitrokhin point out, the OGPU was not aware that she had misinformed Bystrolyotov on that account as well. Combined with Tsarev and West's statement that the Center learned about ARNO's true place in the Foreign Office only after his death, it appears as if the whole ARNO operation was conducted hastily, in a thick "information fog."[4]

According to Bystrolyotov, on hearing the news of Vansittart's inquest (nonexistent at that point), the Center ordered all its illegal operatives to leave the country at once. Witnessing ARNO's decline into uncontrolled drinking, Dmitri called for medical help, which did not come quickly. ARNO would fall asleep and wake up only to begin brawling again. Once, when he was making attempts to leave the house, shouting and picking fights with his wife and even with Dmitri, to quiet ARNO down, Dmitri made him gulp down two glasses of gin. It was already after midnight when Dmitri and ARNO's wife tried to bring the troubled man upstairs, and one of the doctors finally arrived. He drugged ARNO and called an ambulance. Dmitri accompanied the patient to the hospital and then reported to Bazarov: "The worst is over. In a few days, ARNO will come to his senses and be able to walk. No. No retreat, until I carry out the assignment, I won't retreat."[5]

During his hospital stay ARNO seemed to begin recovering and expressed his willingness to continue cooperating with the OGPU, especially to make good on his promise to procure cipher books for the next year, a promise long overdue. But suddenly some new trouble emerged. Lucy's patience expired, and she made her final decision to file for divorce. She removed all the valuables from their home and hired a lawyer to get her half of the money that ARNO received from his business transactions.[6]

When Lucy's lawyer met Dmitri, who had come to visit, the man began interrogating him as the representative of a firm through which

ARNO had reportedly made two thousand pounds in commissions. The lawyer demanded the name and address of the firm as well as Dmitri's address and other relevant information. It was not simple to extricate himself from the situation. Since the lawyer could quickly and easily verify Dmitri's words, Bazarov reported to the Center his concern that Dmitri could be "liquidated" by the "enemy." As Andrew and Mitrokhin rightly point out, the OGPU bosses truly believed in the existence of Western counterintelligence execution squads that shot down foreign spies on the spot, without due process of the law. (The Center's own squads of that kind did operate in the West; one example of their activities was the murder of defecting Soviet spy "Ignace Reiss" a few years later, in the summer of 1937.)

It was at this point, according to Tsarev and West, that the Center issued the order to all illegal operatives to leave the island immediately. Whichever of the two episodes triggered the recall, both sources cite Dmitri's report to Bazarov, expressing his willingness to stay behind and complete his mission. Both the archival account and that of Tsarev agree, however, that when an order came to stop working with ARNO and leave for the continent, Dmitri asked to remain in London alone for the last push. He wanted to obtain British diplomatic ciphers for the next year.[7]

Bazarov did not press Dmitri to leave right away. In his letter to the Center, he explains, "To leave now means to lose a significant 'source,' which would be equivalent to softening our defense and reinforcing the adversary. Possible losses—today HANS, tomorrow other comrades—are inevitable considering the character of our tasks."[8]

Dmitri received permission. All other members of the group—Bazarov, Mally, Leppin, and Weinstein—left the country. Now was the time for decisive action. Dmitri took ARNO to Hyde Park and, sitting next to him on a bench, made him practice making key imprints in the paste dentists use for taking impressions of teeth. Finally, Oldham learned to produce imprints of good quality, and Dmitri "blessed him for his last battle."[9]

Oldham's declassified file at the National Archives of Britain reveals details of ARNO's actions at the Foreign Office on the fateful day of July 13, 1933. In the course of the investigation by the Defense Security Service (DSS), as MI5 was called at the time, which the Foreign Office contacted the next day, four of Oldham's former colleagues were questioned. At about 5:50 P.M., Oldham entered the Foreign Office main entrance and, spotting one of his former colleagues, Mr. B., weighing diplomatic mailbags at the scales, went over to him and chatted with him for a while. Oldham's visit by itself was not considered out of the ordinary. It was usual to let old members of the staff come in.[10]

Then, saying that he wanted to leave a note for his ex-colleague and friend, Mr. Kemp, who had just left for the day (in hindsight, it became clear that Oldham had watched him leave the building), he sat down in a room still occupied by another clerk, Mr. H. As he began writing his note, Oldham asked the clerk to open one of the cabinets where some of his personal papers still remained.

This also was not unusual. After Oldham had left the service, on two or three occasions, he was given access to his valuable papers that, for some reason, were still locked in a cabinet in one of the Foreign Office rooms. These visits usually took place at late hours when only a handful of Oldham's ex-colleagues remained at work. He stayed in the rooms long enough to have a reason for asking those who were about to leave for the day to give him the keys to other rooms, which he promised to return to the clerk on duty. During the subsequent investigation, the night staff also reported that they had seen Oldham on other occasions in various rooms, including the Cipher Room, as late as 11:00 P.M. Once, he was even found asleep in one of the rooms. On another occasion, one of the clerks found him, the keys in his hands, in a corridor leading to the exit. Apparently no one was alarmed about this episode, because it was known that Oldham suffered from alcoholism—on some occasions he even came in tipsy. They decided that he had merely forgotten to return the keys before leaving the premises. On yet another occasion, using the same pretext—that he needed more time to finish the business at hand, since it was after hours and the keys were locked up—he asked for the combination to the lock of a safe where the keys were held. Taking into consideration that Oldham had been fired from the Foreign Office for almost a year and yet had full access to the quarters, the carelessness of the staff is astonishing. (Andrew and Mitrokhin call the Foreign Office security of that time "primitive;" Richard Thurlow also notes that the office security precautions were "almost nonexistent.")[11]

On the day in question, July 13, 1933, when Oldham again asked to look over his papers, Mr. H. went back to the scale room and asked the permission of his superior, Mr. B., to indulge Oldham's request. The key to that cabinet was placed on a ring with other keys, including that of the Cipher Room. After a moment of hesitation, Mr. B. gave Mr. H. permission to take the key ring and do what Oldham asked under one condition—that the set of keys never be handed over to Oldham.

Mr. H. left. After about five minutes, he dashed back in and reported that Oldham had gotten hold of the whole set of keys and taken them into the restroom. He explained how it had happened. When he opened the safe for Oldham, he did not take the key from the ring, assuming that he would lock the cabinet in a moment. The next thing he saw was Oldham rushing out of the room saying that he had to use the restroom. As Mr. H. tried to lock the cabinet, he found that the whole set of keys was gone. Oldham had managed to remove the keys from the cabinet door quickly, without any rattling.

Caught by surprise, the only thing Mr. B. could think of was to immediately instruct the guard at the main entrance of the Foreign Office building to stop Oldham from exiting. Then both clerks rushed to the back door, the so-called ambassador's entrance, to ensure that Oldham would not escape that way.

Oldham reappeared about eight minutes later. His face sweaty and his hands shaking, he returned the key ring. As soon as he left, the clerks examined the keys one by one and, on one of them, the key to the Cipher Room, found crumbs of some substance, which looked like either wax or soap. They immediately suspected that Oldham had taken impressions of the key.[12]

Only after that were the superiors informed and the DSS called in for investigation. Oldham's home phone was wiretapped, and arrangements were made to check his mail and place him under personal surveillance around the clock. A sample of the substance found on the key was sent to the Chemical Section of the DSS for analysis.

As Bystrolyotov recalls in his "Memo," the next day Oldham visited him, his face "sallow gray." He informed Dmitri that it seemed he was under suspicion and that he was not allowed to get close to the safes anymore. But neither the bad news nor Oldham's poor health—he was bloated, and his heart barely worked—stopped Dmitri. He immediately placed the man in a private clinic again. As Dmitri explains his actions in the "Memo," he wanted to "purify Oldham's brain from alcohol and spur his heart on so that he could extract [from the Foreign Office vaults] the ciphers [for the next year] at all costs."[13]

Meanwhile, the soap from the Foreign Office lavatory was compared with the substance found on the key. But the microscopic analysis of the soap showed no traces of a red pigment found on the key. It became clear that Oldham had brought the substance with him in his pocket. (The lab never identified the substance—the dental paste that Dmitri had trained Oldham to use, as they sat together on a Hyde Park bench).[14]

On July 19, at 11:00 A.M., a phone call originating from Oldham's house was intercepted. It was Lucy calling the Foreign Office and inviting Mr. Kemp to come for lunch—"Joe Perelly" wanted to talk to him. Oldham's ex-colleague and friend, Mr. Kemp was initially on Dmitri's list of possible replacements for ARNO (in the OGPU correspondence he was code-named ROLAND). There was also a chance that he might be the primary "source" the OGPU had been trying to get to for a long time. Dmitri decided to check him out and prompted Lucy to invite him to her house for lunch.[15]

Because it was clear that Oldham's last visit alarmed the Foreign Office managers, meeting ROLAND face-to-face was a risky step. In both his memoirs and the 1968 KGB "Memo," Dmitri describes the episode as the most dramatic in his spy career. In his account, the day before, as he sat on his "usual bench near the lake" and contemplated how he should behave during the fateful meeting with ROLAND, his wife Iolanta suddenly appeared before him. She had found him there to hand over his passport in the name of Alexander Gallas. Bazarov had sent her, knowing that he might need the reliable Greek passport to quickly exfiltrate himself from Great Britain. Iolanta also gave Dmitri his pistol, so that in case of his arrest he could shoot himself. "We said farewell to each other as if before a battle," Dmitri recalls in his "Memo."

When he arrived at Oldham's house, he found Mr. Kemp already there, talking about his friend Ernest's recent strange behavior. Dmitri was nervous. Suddenly, Lucy also began talking about how upset she had been for a long time about her husband's odd actions. She told Kemp that her husband traveled in such a regular pattern that it created the impression he was going to see the same person regarding the same business. As if that were not enough reason to suspect

Oldham of shady dealings, she added that on one of his visits to the Foreign Office, he had stolen a briefcase with the designation "His Majesty's Courier." Moreover, she continued, he had managed to procure a passport for some "scoundrel," as she put it. (Apparently, she was referring to a passport issued in the name of Robert Grenville. Recalling this scene in his "Memo," Dmitri couldn't help but comment that she was "remarkably stupid.")

Naturally, highly alarmed, ROLAND began grilling Lucy about the name of the person to whom the passport was issued and his physical features. In his "Memo," Dmitri admits that at that moment, he got cold feet. But, to his relief, Lucy said that she did not remember either his name or his appearance. "That's him!" Kemp roared and banged the table. "God damn it, it's him!"

And he explained to the count that the Foreign Office investigative team had concluded that a "foreign spy was somewhere near Ernest."

"The man has to be arrested," Kemp said. "I'm entrusted to find him."

Writing about this episode three and a half decades later, Dmitri acknowledges that, at this moment, he was scared silly. He reveals his longtime observation about himself: in the first phase of fright, he suddenly gets a great upsurge of energy, his mind clears up, and he fills with resolve. In the second phase of fright, his reaction is complete paralysis, which usually comes later, after he is out of danger.

"I'll help you find him," he said to Kemp. "I know the family business situation and have some ideas about what's going on. The tracks lead to Germany, where the family owns significant property. I'll risk disclosing some family secrets, although, as the trustee of a solid bank, I'm forbidden to do so. Let's not tire our lady with boring details. May I invite you to the Ritz for lunch tomorrow, at one o'clock?"

Knowing how poorly the Foreign Office employees were paid, Dmitri used the same bait that had proved successful during his first meeting with Lucy. He assumed that it might well be the first time Kemp would have a meal at such an expensive place. The gamble worked. Kemp thought for a while and agreed. Dmitri picked up the phone and ordered a table for two. Kemp shook Dmitri's hand "especially meaningfully" and thanked him profusely for his invitation and his willingness to help. According to Bystrolyotov's own account and the KGB files, he left Great Britain early the next morning on the first flight to the continent, using his Greek passport issued to the name of Alexander Gallas.[16]

The declassified Oldham file shows that the events following the meeting of Kemp, Lucy, and Bystrolyotov were both more complex and less dramatic. After the lunch was over, later in the day, Dmitri went to see Oldham at a nursing home where he was recuperating from alcoholism and informed him about Kemp's visit. At 5:50 P.M., when Dmitri was still at the nursing home, a telephone call from Oldham to Lucy was intercepted. Oldham asked Lucy whether she had told Kemp "everything." Lucy replied, "No, I didn't, but it's about time I did." What followed was a typical quibble between spouses on the verge of divorce. She told Oldham she was about to move out of the house for he "had done nothing" for her. He denied it and offered to put "Joe" on the phone to confirm it.

In the meantime, on the very same fateful day of July 19, Kemp returned from the lunch at the Oldhams' house and duly reported what he had heard from Lucy about Ernest's behavior. A meeting was called at the Foreign Office, where the question of what to do next with Oldham was discussed at length. Two options were on the table: to arrest and charge him under the Official Secrets Act or just to interrogate him, bearing in mind that, according to the law, "any disclosures he might make could not be used against him in any future prosecutions." A representative of the office of Director of Public Prosecutions (DPP) unofficially expressed the opinion that, under the circumstances of the case, he would "deprecate a prosecution, mainly in view of the disclosures that would be made about the Foreign Office."

Sir Robert Vansittart, head of the Foreign Office, also felt that before any rush actions were taken against Oldham it would be good to discreetly search Oldham's room at the nursing home to find out what secret documents were in his possession at the time. Judging by the minutes of the meeting, in addition to what Bystrolyotov described in his 1968 "Memo," during the lunch, Lucy had told Kemp that her husband also illegally possessed a "red passport," a document given to any messenger of the Foreign Office carrying dispatches. Since it was unclear how Oldham had obtained the "red passport," even if they found him with it, he could be prosecuted for larceny only if it was proven that he had stolen it after his dismissal. But if he just retained the "red passport" given to him while he was still employed by the Office, now after his layoff, this would constitute a non-prosecutable offense, a departmental misdemeanor at best.[17]

In view of this situation, the DSS representative offered to continue observing Oldham's activities for a few more days. If anything suspicious was seen, for example, if he met someone outside his nursing home or received any suspicious correspondence, he had to be interviewed. The DSS representative also suggested that the interview be conducted along "quiet and friendly lines." Oldham should be asked whether he was in possession of a "red passport" and, if so, asked to hand it over. He should also be asked to explain the circumstances of his visit to the Foreign Office on July 13. If he would not cooperate and refused to reply, they could officially serve him with a notice of obstruction of justice.[18]

Two days later, on Friday, July 21, the officials were still at a loss about what action to take against Oldham. It turned out that, acting along the lines suggested by the DSS, if Oldham refused, then by law he could not be searched unless a search warrant was obtained. In this case, the trouble inside the Foreign Office could no longer be kept from public disclosure. It was also not clear whether Oldham could be arrested if compromising material were found at his place. And, if he were arrested, should other governmental bodies, such as the attorney general's office and the Home Office, be notified and involved? Therefore, the action was postponed again until early the following week.[19]

Meanwhile, according to the current KGB account, with the money received from the Soviets, Oldham checked into a hospital and later, in the first ten days of August 1933, left for Switzerland.[20]

Oldham's declassified file tells a different story of what truly happened. Indeed, considering that his visit of July 13 had alarmed the Foreign Office a great deal, such a tranquil denouement of Oldham's adventures was hardly possible. In reality, as the surveillance minutes show, Bystrolyotov's visit to ARNO naturally alerted him that he was in trouble. His following actions may well have been thought out together with his friend "Joe Perelly." First, he made sure to lull the vigilance of the external, around-the-clock surveillance, of which he was, apparently, quite aware. As the Oldham file shows, during the whole period from July 19, when the observation started, to July 25, no suspicious behavior on the part of Oldham was registered. Besides occasional visits from Lucy and "Joe Perelly," he made daily trips to local pubs, where he drank lots of beer and spent some afternoons on a bench in Kensington Gardens, reading and sleeping.[21]

Yet, he had a trick up his sleeve. On Monday, July 24, at 6:15 P.M., he placed another telephone call to his wife and informed her that the next day he was leaving for Vienna with "Joe." The call was duly intercepted, and an order to shadow Oldham was issued. The next day he indeed took a taxi and asked to be driven to the Victoria Station. But, at that point, the surveillance team lost him. They immediately informed the Foreign Office about Oldham's departure. The arrangements were made to inform all border controls and order them to search him if he produced a diplomatic passport or "red passport." But it was too late. At 2:00 P.M., Oldham left the country on a flight to Paris, where he was to change planes and fly to Geneva.[22]

From the documents, it is not clear whether Dmitri left in his company. But, after July 25, "Joe Perelly" was no longer observed by the Oldham surveillance team. Reporting to the Center, Bazarov informed them of Dmitri's "exceptional selfless work," that he had not left "even an hour earlier" despite the "real danger of failure with all its consequences." The Center responded in kind, acknowledging Dmitri's "selflessness, discipline, and bravery" under the "exceptionally complex and dangerous" conditions of his work over the last days with ARNO.[23]

Traveling from Geneva to Interlaken, Oldham showed up for a meeting with Dmitri and Bazarov, where he seemed surprisingly cool about what was happening back home and held his own. He continued to resist OGPU operatives' demands to name his "source."[24]

Although Bystrolyotov assumed that the Foreign Office did not know that Oldham was in Switzerland at the time, he was mistaken—they knew. His presence in Switzerland was spotted by British intelligence. The Foreign Office was informed that he had left for Paris by train and that, so far, he had not shown his diplomatic passport at the borders. After Paris, Oldham went back to Switzerland and, on August 4, flew back home from the Basel airport. His arrival in the capital was immediately reported to the authorities. On August 9, another conference at the Foreign Office was held to decide on a further course of action. Sir Robert Vansittart suggested beginning an inquest into Oldham's background, past service, and financial transactions, at least for the previous few years, and other related matters. He also instructed Mr. Kemp to get in touch with Mrs. Oldham and find out "anything he [could] regarding Oldham's whereabouts, where he bank[ed], and his present business activities."[25]

Inspection of Oldham's bank accounts didn't produce much. The only thing achieved was that, through checks paid for air travel, it was possible to establish when and where he had gone for the past two years. While, as of August 16, the Foreign Office was still unable to locate Oldham's residence in London, the KGB files show that, already on August 9, Oldham informed Bazarov that he was "safely" staying in a London hotel. It was assumed by the Soviets that he was working on his next assignment—to collect the names of British Secret Intelligence Service agents posted in other countries. In the middle of September he was supposed to return to the continent for another meeting with his handlers.

At the Foreign Office meeting, Kemp reported that, as instructed, he had seen Mrs. Oldham, who, in his view, "had definitely broken off with her husband." Therefore, it was decided to approach her to ask for Oldham's pouch and, since it was suspected that he might have photographed the diplomatic dispatches in his possession, also his camera and any films found.[26]

But nothing came of this attempt. The pouch turned out to be empty, and no camera or film was located at Oldham's house.[27]

Only on August 23, during another Foreign Office conference, a whole month from the day Dmitri had left the country, came a decision to make inquiries about "Joe Perelly." They checked the Traffic Index, but no man with a passport issued in that name had recently crossed the British borders. Then they decided to ask Mr. Kemp whether he knew anything about the man. This contradicts the KGB files, according to which, after the lunch with Lucy and "Perelly," Kemp had immediately reported the content of the conversations around the table to his superiors, who had "instructed him to establish contact with 'Joe Perelly,' secretly from Oldham, to collect everything he knew about the case and thus create a sufficient basis for arresting Oldham."[28]

Other details in the KGB files regarding the case seem plausible. They reveal that when "Count Perelly" was a no-show for lunch at the Ritz, Kemp was, understandably, alarmed. He checked the front desk of the hotel where the lunch should have taken place and found no guest registered there under this name. He began making the rounds of other hotels in the vicinity, but to no avail. It may well be that he did not report the incident because he was ashamed of being duped. Moreover, the contents of the British records suggest that, embarrassed by his own gullibility, Kemp not only failed to duly inform his superiors about what had happened between him and "Joe Perelly" but also attempted to distance himself from the count by stating that, in his view, "Perelly" was a "Jew [residing] in Vienna."[29]

In the meantime, Oldham was spotted at the Unicorn Pub on Jermyn Street, and an order was issued to "house him" if he turned up there again. Finally, on August 25, Oldham was confirmed as staying at the Jules Hotel on Jermyn Street, and all previous surveillance measures, suspended at the time of his travel to the continent, were immediately transferred to his new place of residence.[30]

On August 28, a surveillance team descended on the Jules Hotel. To avoid attracting the attention of the hotel servants to their special mission, first, one of the plainclothesmen pretended to be a "country cousin" from out of town, coming for a weekend visit to the capital. After checking into a room on the fourth floor, he came down to the lobby, where he sat in a position that allowed him to spot Oldham leaving or entering the hotel. After sitting there for quite a while, at about 5:00 P.M., realizing that his overlong presence in the lobby might look suspicious, the plainclothesman decided to call for help.

He pretended to go out for a walk in the fresh air and from a phone booth around the corner called his superior, one Captain B., suggesting that the captain join him in the surveillance to make it less conspicuous. Captain B. arrived about two hours later, and the two men pretended to be old friends who had accidentally run into each other in the hotel lobby. They sat in the lounge and "discussed their affairs over a whiskey and soda in loud tones."

Then, acting as if he were a Londoner who wanted to show his "country cousin" around, Captain B. took his partner to the local Chequers Pub. There they instantly spotted Oldham sitting in the corner alone, impeccably dressed: he wore a brown mixture suit and a brown striped shirt, with a collar and tie to match. To avoid arousing suspicion, the plainclothesmen decided not to talk to him or to the pub's owner, who was there at the time. After an hour or so, when Oldham left the bar, they also decided not to follow him back to the hotel but to leave him alone for a while.

At 9:30 P.M., the two men returned to the bar, pretending to have a good time and enjoying themselves. They found Oldham back at the bar, too, sitting in the same corner as earlier, now in the company of the landlord and some Scottish woman. Unobtrusively, as they drank and talked, they involved Oldham in the conversation as well. Oldham joined the two plainclothesmen in heavy drinking and switched from beer to straight gin. As they drank, Captain B. was able to slip into the conversation that his "cousin" was staying at the Jules Hotel, thus making his appearance there later unsuspicious to Oldham. Then, the plainclothesmen announced their intention to continue drinking after hours at the hotel, ordering drinks by room service. When they returned to the Jules Hotel, Oldham joined them. By a stroke of luck, he suggested having drinks in his room. For show, the operatives quibbled about it for a while before finally agreeing to accept his invitation.

Soon Oldham collapsed from heavy drinking. He became totally incapacitated, and one of the operatives undressed him and put him to bed.

As Oldham slept soundly, the operatives thoroughly searched his clothes and the room and made a list of what they found. Upon examination, Oldham's belongings revealed nothing noteworthy, except a dozen addresses in his papers, one of which was for a "J.P."—which could possibly stand for "Joe Perelly." The address, however, was just a post office in Trouville-sur-Mer, commonly referred to as Trouville, a commune in the Calvados département in the Basse-Normandie region of France.

The next morning, Oldham, who had a terrible hangover, accepted a lunch invitation from one of the plainclothesmen. Later, the operative visited him again and engaged in light conversation, during which Oldham said that he was staying at the hotel while his house was being redecorated and his wife was out of the country, visiting their son in Germany. The operative offered a good excuse for leaving, and he and Oldham parted as buddies.

For the next three weeks, the observation team reported having spotted Oldham receiving envelopes, one every seven days, each containing ten-pound notes. (Today the sum would amount to around four hundred and forty pounds, that is, in 1933, the notes had substantial buying power.) The security services tried to trace the sender of these banknotes, but they were unsuccessful. Oldham remained at the Jules Hotel, spending every evening in the Chequers Pub, where he drank mostly hard liquor and lots of expensive beers. He seemed to associate only with the pub habitués, among whom were female servants from adjoining rooms of the hotel, a permanently intoxicated artist, and various antique dealers from neighboring shops.

It was also observed that he usually didn't appear in public before 5:00 P.M., explaining to everyone that he had to stay in his room to receive telephone calls from the continent relating to "international currency" about which he had to make "quick decisions." When drunk, he was usually talkative; he boasted of acquaintance with some prominent people. He kept giving everyone around him the same reason for staying in the hotel, sometimes adding a few details, such as that his son had just graduated from Bonn University in Germany. In the opinion of the observers, Oldham was going down the drain.

For another week, nothing unusual was spotted about Oldham, except for a few telephone calls to and from the Jules Hotel, but the interceptors were unable to identify any of the callers on either end.

According to the British files, Oldham disappeared from surveillance on September 27, on which date he was found neither at the Chequers Pub nor in any surrounding restaurants. But the KGB files fill in the picture. In a letter that arrived on September 20, Lucy informed Dmitri that her husband had checked out of his hotel and left no forwarding address. From Kemp, who remained in touch with her as a family friend and tried to find employment for her and one of her sons, she found out that in mid-September, Oldham had sent a porter from the Jules Hotel to the Foreign Office with his passport and a note asking Kemp to indulge him as a friend and mark up his passport, raising it to the status of a diplomatic courier passport; the holder of such a passport was not subject to border-crossing disclosures.

As is known now, this request took place around the time that Oldham was supposed to return to Europe to see his friend "Joe Perelly" and deliver a list of British secret service operatives posted abroad. Whether he collected the information or not is unclear today. But he seemingly intended to take some sensitive information across the

British border. According to Lucy, when Kemp put a hold on the passport and asked the messenger to tell Oldham to come pick it up from the Foreign Office himself, Oldham became scared and disappeared.[31]

The surveillance officer reported to his superiors that the last time Oldham was seen in the pub he usually frequented was Wednesday, September 27. On Friday, September 29, an item titled "A Kensington Mystery: Unknown Man in Gas-Filled Empty Kitchen" appeared in one of the London dailies:

> The Kensington police are trying to discover the identity of a man, aged about 35, who was found dead in a gas-filled kitchen at a house in Pembroke Gardens, Kensington. Except for a table, there was no furniture in the house, but in a cupboard were a number of suits of clothes, including evening dress. The man was five feet six inches in height, well built, clean shaven, and had dark brown hair and eyes. He was wearing a brown mixture suit, and a brown striped shirt, with a collar and tie to match. The shirt bore the initials "E.H.O." It is believed that the man formerly lived at the address.[32]

Thus, according to this report, Oldham was found dead the day before, September 28. The cause of death was assumed to be suicide due to the man's financial difficulties. Indeed, as the records show, Oldham owed money to the pub owner, the hotel he was staying in, the Savoy Turkish baths, and various restaurants. Alcoholism and drug addiction were also cited as contributing factors. It was further observed that, during his stay at the Jules Hotel, before he would return to the hotel, he usually stopped at a local chemist shop and bought large doses of paraldehyde. At the time, this drug was widely used in hospitals to treat delirium tremens associated with alcohol withdrawal, and many patients became addicted to the drug. It was also used as a sedative to calm or relax nervous or tense patients and as an insomnia remedy.[33]

There was, however, something else that might have speeded up Oldham's demise. As reported by the surveillance officer, on Monday of the week that he disappeared from the hotel and the pubs, it became known that he had received a "letter from Geneva, the contents of which appeared to upset him."[34]

The letter was never found, but knowing that Oldham's OGPU controllers often chose Switzerland as their place to meet him, the letter that upset him could well have come from them. If this is true, what could possibly have been in the letter that would have made Oldham feel that resorting to suicide was the only way out? According to the published KGB sources, in the course of the past year, while playing the "good cop–bad cop" routine, as a harsh measure, Bazarov and Dmitri had threatened Oldham, saying they would "cut him off completely," the last time, during their early August meeting.

While in *Crown Jewels*, Tsarev and West do not mention the threatening of Oldham during his last meeting with Bazarov and Dmitri, in their Russian version, *KGB v Anglii*, they quote the document from the KGB files to that effect. Reporting to the Center, Bazarov wrote that he and Bystrolyotov "conducted [their talk with Oldham] in such a way that ARNO has formed the impression that we're on the verge of breaking off with him."[35]

However, Tsarev and West do not mention another, much more powerful, pressure applied to Oldham—blackmail—that is, the threat to inform the British authorities about his espionage activities. Although in his *Handbook of Intelligence and Guerrilla Warfare*, a high-ranking Soviet spy, Alexander Orlov, who defected to the West in 1938, states that, unlike Western intelligence services, Soviet intelligence treated its informants with "genuine solicitude," it was certainly not the case with Oldham. In the course of his debriefing about the OGPU spy network in the West, another Soviet defector, Walter Krivitsky, revealed that Oldham was threatened with exposure.[36]

Apparently, combined with his other troubles, already mentioned, the admixture of adverse circumstances was too much for Oldham to handle. It looks as if he chose to end his life by going back to his house, getting drunk, and after sealing off the kitchen door and window, opening the gas jets. In *KGB v Anglii*, Tsarev and West also characterize Oldham's death as suicide caused by alcoholism and depression. However, in his memoirs, Bystrolyotov writes that Oldham, "our wonderful 'source,' failed and was killed by us" (that is, the OGPU). Although there is no archival evidence to corroborate this statement, as Gary Kern rightly points out, "there was sufficient cause for foul play: Oldham was unstable and knowledgeable about current OGPU operations." If that is true, then the suicide version, recorded as the official cause of death, was highly convenient for the OGPU. Tsarev and West underscore the "naturalness" of the way Oldham's days ended: "ARNO's tragic death was not surprising to anyone who knew him. A voluntary hostage of greed and drunkenness, vices that mutually nourish each other, he was doomed to end badly."[37]

For over two months after the death of Oldham, the OGPU was in the dark about what was going on in the Foreign Office. Most important, they did not know whether his ties with the Soviets had been revealed. Though Dmitri arranged secret (indirect) correspondence with Lucy, she could not possibly write about all that was going on around her husband's death. She only wanted to be sure that her dear "Count Perelly" would not reappear in Great Britain, for they were still trying to trace where Oldham's money had come from. Dmitri invited her to the continent for a discreet meeting, and during the last ten days of December, Lucy told her acquaintances she was going to the provinces to visit her friends and flew to Vienna. As a matter of precaution, before seeing her, Dmitri made sure that she was not being shadowed.[38]

When they met, Lucy reported what their family lawyer had disclosed to her: at the beginning of October, a few days after her husband's death, the Foreign Office had asked him to collect the most complete information on Oldham's financial transactions for the past two years. Apparently, trying to conceal the fact that sensitive state secrets had long been leaked from the Office, they instigated an inquest by citing a police report about some of their employees being involved in drug smuggling. They were especially interested in establishing Oldham's ties with Germany.[39]

The German connection may have been construed from Kemp's report on his conversation with "Joe Perelly" back in July, when "Joe" had mentioned some fictitious German real estate ownership he had allegedly been arranging for Oldham. Lucy told the lawyer that she knew nothing about Germans other than the name of the main buyer of her husband's papers, "Da Vinci" (one of Bazarov's aliases). As did her deceased husband, Lucy also believed that her dear "Hungarian count" was in the hands of that "evil man." Apparently, Dmitri was able to convince her that "Da Vinci" was a German agent: working "under a false flag" was one objective of Soviet illegal operatives. Citing the need to find the count as a link to the "Germans [who had] pulled Oldham into some dirty business," the lawyer and the family guardian repeatedly pressed Lucy to reveal Dmitri's address. They explained to her that it was the only way to get money from the Germans. But Lucy denied knowing anything about "Count Perelly's" whereabouts. Besides, she insisted, he was above suspicion—he was only a go-between and knew nothing.[40]

Soon Kemp picked up where the lawyer and the guardian had failed. First, he used a soft approach. He resumed his interest in Lucy's life by visiting her and asking her sympathetically how she was managing since her husband's death. While engaged in conversation, he tried unobtrusively to change the subject to "Count Perelly" and his possible whereabouts. When this failed, he threatened Lucy with arrest as an accomplice of her husband, a spy and a smuggler. It scared Lucy. She became hysterical and told him everything she knew about Oldham's shady business except "Perelly's" address, stating that she had lost all contact with him.[41]

Dmitri informed the Center about these events, noted that Lucy hadn't given any leads concerning the investigation, and added that, in his opinion, "the time and effort of dealing with her were justified." To keep her as a connection that might be useful for any renewed attempts to penetrate the Foreign Office, Dmitri offered her an unspecified amount of OGPU money as a means of financial assistance. He told her that he was doing it "in order to save her and her children." Indeed, at the time of their meeting, Lucy was on the brink of total financial disaster. In Dmitri's words, the desperate "aging lady was about to become a prostitute," and she accepted the offer "with tears of ecstatic gratitude." Taking care of their former agents was not a philanthropic gesture on the part of the OGPU. As Alexander Orlov explains, "This solicitude toward the informant [was] based more on consideration of self-interest than on moral or humanitarian grounds." In his opinion, the Soviet intelligence "simply came to the conclusion that such a policy toward the informants benefited its cause and contributed to its success."[42]

Meanwhile, in London, everything calmed down. The Foreign Office decided to put a lid on the scandal. As Lucy told Dmitri, Kemp assumed that Sir Robert Vansittart did not want it made public that such a disaster—which in Kemp's account was extremely rare in Foreign Office history—had struck on his watch. Dmitri rightly concluded that ARNO and the whole Soviet spy ring would have been caught red-handed long ago if the inquest were conducted not by homegrown sleuths like Kemp but by "professional detectives from the Admiralty or Scotland Yard."[43]

Lax security in the Foreign Office at that time continued to contribute to the leaking of state secrets after Oldham's death. Although no longer able to appear in England without endangering the OGPU's renewed efforts to penetrate the stronghold of British diplomacy, Dmitri remained at the forefront of the OGPU offensive. Despite the considerable experience he acquired while dealing with ARNO, he was forced to pull back from the front line. He became the main controller of another front man chosen to replace him. He knew the man very well, for he had worked with him side by side while setting up the GADA company and during his search for "Nosik," the Italian adventurist and seller of black-market codes ROSSI. It was the Soviet operative of Dutch origin, Henri Pieck, code-named COOPER.

Personality-wise Pieck closely resembled Bystrolyotov—he was a painter and a bohemian, knew several European languages, was handsome, and knew how to attract women. He even had an advantage over Dmitri: he possessed genuine British citizenship and carried a legal passport. But some of his character traits were not useful for spy work. Dmitri found the man "disorderly, sloppy, and undisciplined," and also "kind, softhearted, and sentimental." That was not sufficient for the task, for he could not "put pressure on a man, grip him in a vise, break him down, blackmail him, and threaten to kill." (More evidence of the qualities that the OGPU expected in an ideal recruiter.) Taking this into consideration, it was clear that Pieck had to be guided on a daily basis in how to handle his target depending on the circumstances at hand. Dmitri took upon himself the responsibility for this part of the operation.[44]

Now the right employee had to be found among the Foreign Office staff who could successfully replace ARNO. Actually, the process had been started back in 1932: while Dmitri was still struggling with gaining full control over Oldham, the OGPU was already actively searching for the man's replacement. Some leads had already been developed. Between his travels to London, Dmitri steered COOPER's actions every step of the way. He led him first to another Foreign Office employee code-named BOY, whom ARNO mentioned as a prospect for recruitment. BOY was working in the British delegation to the League of Nations in Geneva. When his Geneva residence was discovered, Dmitri instructed Pieck to rent an apartment in the same building (in fact, it was just one floor up from the Brit). Of course, the first contact with BOY had to take place elsewhere. On Dmitri's instruction, COOPER began visiting the Brasserie Universal, which was frequented by Englishmen living in Geneva.

In a few months, thanks to his social skills and his ability to attract attention to himself as an artist, COOPER made friends with many Brasserie Universal habitués, BOY included. However, he turned out to be a tough target, requiring much cultivation before an attempt could be made to recruit him. Overly prim, he treated every person who approached him during social interactions with icy cold politeness.

Soon a prospect appeared on the horizon who looked much more promising than BOY. The new target, code-named SHELLEY, seemed to be an easy target for recruitment because of his permanent debts and inability to keep money in his pocket. Although in ARNO's opinion he was known among his colleagues for his stupidity, he was a good specialist and was often sent abroad on business trips. There was a natural way for Pieck to get acquainted with him: the man's fiancée was the daughter of the local British vice-consul, Captain John Harvey—code-named CHIEF in the OGPU correspondence. Pieck was able not only to strike up a friendship with CHIEF but also to earn his confidence. Once, CHIEF even introduced COOPER to a diplomatic courier as "our own man" who could be fully trusted.

Lacking the finances to pursue his marriage plans, SHELLEY quickly agreed to provide COOPER with some confidential material that he was made to believe would be used by a big Dutch bank for stock market speculation. In the long run, the man turned out to be too timid and was soon replaced by a perfect agent, a cipher clerk, Captain John Herbert King. He was given the code name MAG, a Russian word meaning "magician," because one of his hobbies was magic and magician's acts. At the beginning of 1935, when SHELLEY refused to continue working for COOPER, Pieck turned to MAG.

(Several sources identify another Soviet operative who had tried to recruit King before Pieck but had failed because he lacked finesse in the skills required for such a delicate operation. Andrew and Gordievsky, as well as Gary Kern, identify the OGPU illegal operative as Sergei Basov, or Basoff. His background as a sailor in the Black Sea and his proximity to Dmitri in the operation may well point to his identity as Dmitri's old friend Evgeny Kavetsky. Bystrolyotov mentions bringing him into some of his intelligence operations in Europe.)[45]

Using the situation of Captain King's dire need for money that he hoped would help to advance his son's career in high society, Pieck made his move. As someone who had already earned a reputation as a solid businessman with connections in society, he suggested to MAG an easy way to earn the money. As bait, COOPER used the same financial angle that had been used with SHELLEY. Having a solid foundation in economics (with his educational background in that area, back in his Prague days, he had served as economics adviser at the Soviet Trade Mission in Czechoslovakia), Dmitri helped Pieck to prepare the pitch in meticulous detail. COOPER told MAG that a big Dutch bank to which he had close ties needed certain political information in order to make money on the international stock exchange. With that information, financial investments could pay off handsomely. For example, if it could be confirmed that a war between Italy and Abyssinia, which was rumored at the time, was indeed going to break out, buying stock in Italian plants working for the war machine would promise the bank big returns on its investments. Information confirming that Germany's air force buildup was soon to be legalized would have the same effect. The bank's profits on investments in the German airplane industry would skyrocket. Coaching Pieck, Dmitri also supplied him with a few truly successful cases of such financial operations. He went over the numbers with Pieck several times, until he was sure the man was thoroughly prepared.[46]

To make it look natural, Pieck revealed to MAG his own ulterior motive to make a connection with the bank: of the one hundred British pounds a month the bank was ready to pay for the confidential diplomatic information, he would take forty pounds in commission. With Dmitri behind COOPER's back at every step, MAG took the bait and began working successfully. Among many exceptionally valuable confidential materials, including ciphered telegrams, Dmitri and Pieck received from MAG a copy of a report about a meeting between the minister of foreign affairs of Great Britain, John Simon, and Adolf Hitler, which took place at the Chancellor's Palace in Berlin on March 25 and 26, 1935.[47]

The last mention in the KGB files of Bystrolyotov's involvement in decision making regarding MAG is dated September 1935. At that time, COOPER was occupied on the continent and could not come to England to accept MAG's deliveries. With no one else in London to replace him, Dmitri again volunteered to step in despite the obvious risk: someone who had seen him with ARNO, for example, Kemp, still employed by the Foreign Office, might recognize him.[48]

MAG remained undetected by the British authorities for the duration of his work with the OGPU, which lasted until the summer of 1937, when his controller at the time, Theodor Mally, was recalled to the USSR. In 1940, three years after a high-ranking Soviet spy, Walter Krivitsky, defected to the West, he gave away the OGPU agent at the Foreign Office, Captain John Herbert King. Subsequently, during his interrogation, King confessed to his crimes and was given a ten-year jail term. After the end of World War II, his sentence was commuted, and he was released early.[49]

Krivitsky also provided many details about the handling of another British cipher specialist, Ernest Oldham, whose case the authorities had already forgotten. Among the Foreign Office employees, Oldham remained part of a typical "urban legend." Apparently, based on the fact that in his last days ARNO had received phone calls and envelopes with money from France, legend had it that he had been working for the French and that the British intelligence service had finished him off, camouflaging his demise as a suicide.[50]

Krivitsky also revealed Bystrolyotov's other alias, "Hans Galleni," under which he operated at that time in Britain, and that he was traveling on a Greek passport. From the debriefing, it was clear that Lucy was somehow involved in the affair and that, if still alive, she would "know a great deal about the Greek."[51]

The Oldham file does not indicate whether Krivitsky's disclosures prompted any actions on the part of the British authorities. According to it, it was fully ten years later, on May 26, 1950, when British counterintelligence made another attempt to get to the bottom of

Oldham's case. They asked Mr. Kemp, who was still employed by the Foreign Office, to recall whatever he knew about it. He remembered Oldham and his wife quite well, but he stated that he did not recall anything about "Joe Perelly." He also did not recognize him from a drawing of Bystrolyotov, at that time obtained by the MI5. Kemp said that, in his opinion, Mrs. Oldham "would certainly remember 'Perelly,'" and he suggested finding her through her son from her first marriage, Raymond, who was in the army, stationed in Belfast, and whom she had gone to join at the beginning of the war.[52]

Slightly more than a month after that conversation took place, London's *Daily Express* informed the public about a seventy-year-old woman who had drowned herself in the Thames. At the same time, a man of thirty-five, believed to be her son, was missing. There was evidence that both were in financial difficulties. The son was writing bad checks. He was soon found and arrested. There was some evidence that he had also tried to drown himself. He formerly had a distinguished army career and was put on probation for two years. The woman and her son were none other than Lucy Oldham and her son from her first marriage, Raymond Wellsted.[53]

Clearly, whatever financial assistance the OGPU had given Lucy back in 1933 after ARNO's death did not last for too long.

It is remarkable—and speaks volumes of Bystrolyotov's tradecraft—that the British security service had an active file for him as "Joe Pirelli" until 1950 and was still trying to identify him as late as 1974 (they contacted one of Oldham's stepsons for information on him).[54]

Parallel to his involvement in recruiting and handling British agents, Dmitri took part in several other covert operations on behalf of Soviet foreign intelligence, this time on the European continent.

Dmitri Bystrolyotov, circa 1915

Courtesy of Sergei Milashov

Dmitri's mother, Klavdiya Bystrolyotova, circa 1900

Courtesy of Sergei Milashov

Bystrolyotov as a sailor, circa spring 1921
Courtesy of Sergei Milashov

. . . as a helmsman, fall 1921
Courtesy of Sergei Milashov

Constantinople, ink drawing by Dmitri Bystrolyotov, 1921

Courtesy of Sergei Milashov

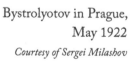

Bystrolyotov in Prague,
May 1922

Courtesy of Sergei Milashov

Bystrolyotov, 1925

Courtesy of Sergei Milashov

"Countess Fiorella Imperiali"
(code name LAROCHE)

*Reproduced by permission of Archives du
ministère des Affaires étrangères, Nantes
(document ID: CADN, Prague, consulat, 17*)*

Maria Milena Iolanta Shelmatova (code name MILENA)

Courtesy of Sergei Milashov

Bystrolyotov, 1926
Courtesy of Sergei Milashov

Bystrolyotov as "Greek merchant
Alexander S. Gallas"

Courtesy of Sergei Milashov

... as "Hungarian Count Lajos József Perelly de Kiralyhaza"

Courtesy of Sergei Milashov

. . . as "Dutch artist Hans Galleni"

Courtesy of Sergei Milashov

. . . as "Sir Robert Grenville"

Courtesy of Sergei Milashov

"Charlie" (code name ARNO)

"Greta" (code name ORLENOK)

Bystrolyotov on a reconnaissance mission in
Bellinzona, Switzerland, circa 1934

Courtesy of Sergei Milashov

Bystrolyotov's portrait of his mother (gouache, 1937)

Courtesy of Sergei Milashov

Photos from Bystrolyotov's arrest file, September 18, 1938

Courtesy of Sergei Milashov

Nikolai Yezhov, People's Commissar
of Internal Affairs (NKVD)

Bystrolyotov's self-portrait
(gouache, 1947)
Courtesy of Sergei Milashov

Bystrolyotov, before release from the Gulag, 1954

Courtesy of Sergei Milashov

Bystrolyotov in freedom, 1956

Courtesy of Sergei Milashov

Bystrolyotov with his second wife, Anna Ivanova, 1966

Courtesy of Sergei Milashov

Bystrolyotov and the author
around the time of their meeting
on September 11, 1973

Courtesy of Sergei Milashov and the author

TEN | In the Arms of the Fiercest Enemy

*It's best to appear not bright, and stay that way all
the time. One smart look, and they would suspect that
something isn't right about you.*

—BYSTROLYOTOV, IN CONVERSATION
WITH THE AUTHOR

The year 1935 began with further ominous developments in Germany. After the death of President Paul von Hindenburg on August 2, 1934, Adolf Hitler had assumed the office of *Reichspräsident* and thus became commander in chief. All officers and soldiers of the German armed forces had to swear a personal oath of loyalty to the Führer, as Hitler was now called. The Third Reich was born.

This worrisome chain of events wasn't totally unexpected. Anticipating this development, Soviet foreign intelligence had refocused its main efforts from England to Germany. In June 1933, legal *rezident* Boris Berman was recalled to Moscow, and the new *rezident*, Boris Gordon, took over his position at the end of the year. At the beginning of 1934, Soviet foreign intelligence designated the various apparatuses of Nazi Germany as targets for penetration, including the army, the police, and the Nazi Party, as well as the entourages of Adolf Hitler, Hermann Goering, and later, in 1935, War Minister Werner von Blomberg.[1]

Brought back to the continent after the end of the ARNO affair, while still supplying input on the handling of British agents who were to be recruited to replace Oldham, Bystrolyotov took part in an operation concerned with behind-the-scenes maneuvering between Nazi Germany and Fascist Italy. In both his unpublished screenplay "Generous Hearts" and his novel *Para Bellum,* describing the operation as a scheme to intercept and copy special delivery correspondence between Hitler and Mussolini, Bystrolyotov adapted the complicated real-life political situation in Europe to Soviet sensibilities at the time he was writing his work (the mid-1960s). For propaganda reasons, for decades on end, the Soviet people had been kept in the dark about the complexity of the relationship between the Führer and the Duce, which the Soviet mass media invariably portrayed as harmonious and mutually supportive from the outset of their political careers.[2]

As is known now, nothing was further from the truth. Initially, Mussolini was strongly opposed to Hitler's expansionist intentions and for some period sought Soviet help in this regard. The Soviet people had equally been kept in the dark about ideological, economic, and political rapprochement between Stalin and Mussolini in the early 1930s, as well as about the Italo-Soviet Pact of Friendship, Neutrality, and Nonaggression signed in September 1933.

Therefore, at the time of the operation in question (summer 1934), a secret correspondence between the Führer and the Duce could hardly take place. Tensions between the two dictators ran high. They had met for the first time in June 1934 and disliked each other. After the meeting, Mussolini characterized Hitler as an unimaginative little fellow whose speech reminded him of a gramophone record stuck on the same quotes from *Mein Kampf* and playing them over and over again. Also, Mussolini disapproved of Hitler's intention to annex Austria. In fact, to show that he meant business, when there was danger that Germany might invade Austria, Mussolini moved a considerable number of his troops to the Italian-Austrian border and warned Hitler that he would retaliate. Only later, with Hitler's support of Mussolini's 1935 Ethiopian campaign, relations improved, eventually leading to the formation of the Rome-Berlin Axis in late October 1936.

As Bystrolyotov mentioned briefly during our private meeting, the operation in question was concerned with intercepting secret correspondence not between Hitler and Mussolini, but between the Führer and Costanzo Ciano, the father of Galeazzo Ciano, Mussolini's son-in-law and future foreign minister. And there was good reason for Hitler to keep in touch with the man. Costanzo Ciano was one of a handful of Italian Fascist leaders who never wavered in his support of close ties with Germany. In fact, he was one of the most influential Italian Nazi admirers, and he carried considerable political clout. A decorated World War I hero, he was not only president of the chamber of deputies of the Italian parliament at that time, but most important, he was also secretly appointed to replace the Duce in case of his sudden demise. It was only natural that the Soviet authorities wanted to know what these men were up to.[3]

At their meeting in Berlin, Bazarov informed Dmitri that Soviet agents in Italy had established the identity of the courier of this secret correspondence. His name was "Gaetano Monaldi," and he was colonel of the First Legion of Fascist secret police. It was also reported that, while traveling from Rome to Berlin, "Monaldi" stopped to rest in Basel, Switzerland, where he owned a villa. A decision was made to strike at him there.

Dmitri sent his assistants, Leppin and Erica, to Basel. They had to do some groundwork: find the villa and study its guard system and the household rituals, including the names of people who made regular deliveries of food and other supplies to the villa. They also had to familiarize themselves with the city and the incoming roads. He gave them three weeks to complete the reconnaissance work.

Since it was also known that "Monaldi" was a middle-aged man and a widower, Dmitri brought into the operation an agent he had recruited earlier, soon after he moved to Berlin—a young and beautiful German lady called "Greta."

Although he describes in minute detail the circumstances of her recruitment, and in his confidential cover letter to the KGB censors accompanying the submission of his screenplay manuscript, he discloses her true name—Countess Magritte Brockdorff-Rantzau—there are unresolved problems concerning her identity. My check of her background yielded no results. According to Sergei Milashov, Bystrolyotov assured him that "Greta" was the daughter of the famous German diplomat and first foreign minister of the Weimar Republic, Ulrich Graf von Brockdorff-Rantzau. He played a significant role in Russian political history. He was instrumental in the notorious subversive operation of early 1917: securing the safe passage across Germany back to Russia of a group of Russian émigré revolutionaries headed by Vladimir Lenin. The aim of this operation was to cause political destabilization in the Russian rears, Germany's World War I adversary, thus weakening its military effort. It's no wonder that later on, after the Bolsheviks came to power in the country, they welcomed the man who had served as German ambassador to Soviet Russia for most of the 1920s; he died in 1928.

The problem with the claim that "Greta" was this man's daughter is that he was a lifelong bachelor, and furthermore, although theoretically speaking he could have fathered an illegitimate child, it was impossible for such a child to inherit his aristocratic title without being officially adopted by him. Thus, it is highly questionable that she belonged to the nobility, and her nobility was the main reason she was chosen for recruitment in the first place. Together with her youth and beauty, the title of countess was an important element of using her as sex bait in entrapment of prospective agents. Was she the daughter of Ulrich Brockdorff-Rantzau's twin brother, Count Ernst Ludwig Emil Schlesswig? The authoritative reference book on European nobility, *Almanach de Gotha,* does not list her as his daughter either. It records that he divorced his wife, Kamelita Osin von Roer, in February 1916, at approximately the time when, according to Bystrolyotov's account, "Greta" was born. Could that account for her claim that she didn't remember her father and that her mother had died giving birth to her? Or had the lady fooled Bystrolyotov himself by claiming the surname and title as her own? Though Dmitri identifies a young lady in a set of three photos (marked 1930) in his personal archive as his beloved German agent "Greta" (the photos miraculously survived the search during his 1938 arrest by the NKVD), the mystery remains.[4]

Regardless of who exactly "Greta" (code-named ORLENOK, "a little eagle" in Russian) was, her participation in the operation was essential. According to Bystrolyotov, this is how he was able to pull it off. A month before the next expected visit of "Monaldi" to Basel, "Greta" arrived there and checked into one of the most fashionable hotels in the city, Kaiserhof, equipped with several fashionable dresses, hats, shoes, and the other accessories of a stylish young lady. Her beauty, aristocratic manners, and good disposition charmed the hotel owner, who befriended her and showed all signs of respect and admiration. She told him that she planned to stay in the hotel until the end of summer for she had to recover from a long illness. Since it was known that "Monaldi" was an old friend of the hotel owner, it would only be a matter of time before he introduced him to the charming hotel guest.[5]

The plan worked. "Monaldi" couldn't resist the allure of the young German aristocrat and immediately began courting her. Under Dmitri's guidance, "Greta" played her cards carefully. Since his messenger duties prevented "Monaldi" from staying in Basel for long stretches, "Greta" had the opportunity to learn more about the man during the intervals between his visits. Among other things, the hotel owner told her she should be aware that her suitor was in dire need of money. In fact, he not only owed a lot to the hotel owner, but no local bank was willing to give him the substantial loan he needed to repair his villa. Once Dmitri received that bit of information, he knew what to do.

First, he had to find a means to penetrate the villa himself in some inconspicuous way. For that purpose, the former delivery man from the local meat shop that usually supplied the colonel's kitchen at the villa was offered a position as a waiter at one of the Basel restaurants, and Dmitri took over his place. Always wary of revealing an accent or a lack of knowledge about the details of local customs, he usually posed as a foreigner—this time, a Yugoslav man from Fiume, a Croatian town (now Rijeka) at that time occupied by Italy. Since the operation was expected to take some time, and Dmitri was simultaneously working on other assignments undercover as a Hungarian count, he had to find a place where, without raising any suspicions, he could safely transform himself from a meat delivery man into a count and vice versa. He couldn't possibly do it in a room rented on the outskirts of the city, entering as a Yugoslav meat man and exiting as a dressed-to-kill Hungarian count. A solution to the problem was found: Leppin and Erica opened a therapeutic massage parlor in a quiet area near the center of the city. (Erica's training as a nurse gave her the requisite skills to run such a business.) Because customers from all walks of life visited the office, Dmitri could safely use it to transform himself from one cover personality to another.

Meanwhile, since Dmitri had charged her with finding the location of the safe guarding the papers carried by "Monaldi," during the man's next short stay in Basel, "Greta" graciously accepted his invitation to visit his villa and dine there with him. This gave her an opportunity to look for a place where "Monaldi" might safeguard his papers. After dinner, trying to impress the young lady, among other fancy things, the Italian showed her an antique desk in his bedroom. When she expressed admiration for his exquisite taste in furniture, enamored and tipsy, with the gesture of a magician, "Monaldi" slid open the desktop, under which a small safe was concealed. "Greta" applauded in delight.

Before leaving, "Greta" expressed her deep appreciation for her reception at the villa. She found it absolutely charming. Moreover, she asked whether, the next time Signor "Monaldi" was in town, it would be possible to repeat it, only with one thing extra: instead of having dinner catered by the hotel restaurant, she asked that a genuine homemade Italian meal be prepared. And, if her gracious host didn't mind, she wanted to be present to see for herself how these magical meals were created. "Monaldi" was delighted. He immediately agreed, called in his cook, and ordered him to indulge any of the young lady's wishes.

When the Yugoslav man delivered the meat, "Greta" helped to distract the cook, and Dmitri slipped into the inner rooms of the villa.

"Greta" guarded the door to the bedroom while Dmitri worked on opening the safe and taking pictures not only of the coded letters in a small briefcase but also of the passport and travel documents belonging to "Monaldi." Though some risk was involved, the rest of the operation went smoothly.

Several weeks passed before his financial problems made "Monaldi" desperate. Already owing substantial sums of money to the local bank and to the Kaiserhof owner—both refused to give more until the existing debts were paid off—one day, deeply depressed, he opened up to the young lady. "Greta" expressed sympathy for his situation. She told him that she knew some man, her boarding school classmate's brother, a businessman who seemed to be awash in money. Perhaps "Monaldi" might try talking to this man.

"Monaldi" perked up and eagerly asked her to make the connection. Dmitri's straightforward manner in conducting the meeting with "Monaldi" is reminiscent of his last attempts at recruitment involving a Czech businessman in Prague. Though the Prague endeavor ended in fiasco, this time Dmitri was successful. When "Monaldi" came to see "Greta's classmate's brother," without saying a word, Dmitri placed a stack of money before him. The colonel was astonished, for he was prepared to give his prospective creditor a list of whatever collateral he could think of to secure his loan. Dmitri explained that this would be unnecessary, for the man had already earned the money. With that, Dmitri produced a bunch of snapshots of the documents from the colonel's safe, including his passport and travel documents.

With "Monaldi" now in the throes of despair, Dmitri offered him the chance to cooperate further—he would receive the same amount of money for copies of all new letters that came into his possession. He added that the man hardly had a choice: he was already compromised.

At first distressed and unable to move, "Monaldi" finally agreed, reluctantly. Dmitri gave him a pen and dictated the text of a binding note: "I, Colonel of the Fascist Militia, Gaetano Monaldi, confirm herewith my promise to deliver copies of documents that I bring from Rome."

Before they parted, Dmitri told him that their deal should be a gentlemen's agreement, that the young lady who had arranged their meeting had no inkling about the kind of business Dmitri was conducting, and Signor "Monaldi" should keep it that way.[6]

Soon Dmitri embarked on one of his most daring operations that brought him into the arms of the fiercest enemy possible. Into the arms—literally. On March 16, 1935, Hitler grossly violated strict limitations imposed on German armed forces by the Treaty of Versailles. The treaty called for a ceiling of a hundred thousand men under arms and the abolishment of conscription. It also called for German naval forces to be limited in manpower and naval vessels. The manufacture of weapons of all sorts, such as tanks, submarines, military aircraft, and artillery, was prohibited. Now Hitler reintroduced conscription, under which each year one hundred thousand new conscripts would receive military training. This new German army, called the Wehrmacht, swore the same personal oath of loyalty to Hitler. Although the existence of this army was officially announced on October 15, 1935, it had begun rapidly rearming months before that. Plans for not only a new army but also a new navy, full armored divisions, and an air force began being drawn up in secret.

Through a newly developed network of agents, the Berlin *rezidentura* learned that Wehrmacht Headquarters had hurriedly organized a number of safe places where they began to accumulate sensitive military information about their future adversaries. One such intelligence center was camouflaged as the documentation department of the I. G. Farbenindustrie chemical concern, which was situated at one of the concern's branch offices, Zweighalle-5. This is where all reports came in from secret German agents dealing with military industries of foreign countries, including the USSR.

The department also contained exhaustive data on the placement of new Wehrmacht orders for military equipment and weaponry at various German industrial concerns: Krupp, Junkers, Siemens, and others.[7]

The guarding of this information was entrusted to one Dorothea Müller, a woman about forty years old, who had the rank of SS-Hauptscharführer (equivalent to the U.S. rank of master sergeant). She was the clerk in charge; in the morning, she had to check out the files to the officers, whose job was to develop the information contents of the files, on the condition that they sign for them and later collect and lock up the files in a safe at the end of the day.[8]

Soviet secret agents learned that the woman preferred to be called "Doris," which, in her view, gave her name a more dignified coloring. But among themselves the Soviet intelligence group assigned the task of finding a way to the super-secret safe she guarded called her "Cerberus"—in Greek mythology, a monstrous three-headed dog, with a snake for a tail and snake heads down his back, who guarded the gate to the underworld and ensured that no living person was to enter.

The nickname was deliberate, for the woman was not only a reliable guard but also exceptionally unattractive. This is how Bystrolyotov describes her face, which had been disfigured by fire during a car accident in her childhood: "It was astonishing in its ugliness. On the right side of her face, her forehead, cheek, and chin were disfigured by huge burn scars. The skin of her face was stretched from her eye upward and downward and from the corner of her mouth to her ear." In addition, her right hand was blackened and gnarled.[9]

In fact, her repulsive appearance was one of the reasons why she was chosen for the job: her ugliness left her no hope for marriage or even an affair, and it served as the best deterrence from being recruited by foreign intelligence. Deprived of fulfilling normal sexual needs, she was embittered and unpleasant to deal with. She was also a devoted member of the Nazi Party, a fierce and fanatical believer in Nazi causes and the "idea of Great Germany." In Bystrolyotov's words, she was a "chained guard dog, a mad dog, growling at anyone who approached the secrets behind the door she guarded." And he was entrusted to tame this "dangerous beast," to find a way to transform this "Cerberus" into a "domesticated and tender puppy."[10]

Dmitri learned about Müller from ROSSI. Considering that the man traded not only in diplomatic ciphers but in contacts and leads, Soviet intelligence most likely paid him for the lead. First, Dmitri had to reestablish himself in the cover role he had decided to adopt for this operation. He put into play the legend that had worked well with ARNO and which he had enough time to get the feel of—his Hungarian count alias. First, he rented an apartment in one of the newly built areas of Berlin. As a count, he had to have an apartment spacious enough to match his title—at least three rooms. The landlord supplied him with furniture and recommended servants. His assistants, Joseph Leppin and Erica Weinstein, also arrived in Berlin. Leppin renewed his cover occupation—studying old German grammar at the university—and Weinstein found a job as a nurse in a private clinic.[11]

Of course, Dmitri realized that even the slightest commotion around the SS woman would attract the Gestapo's attention. Therefore, he had to be extremely careful. But how exactly should he approach her? To feign amorous feelings toward a disfigured and unpleasant woman wouldn't work: she would hardly believe such a crude lie. The gap between a physically unattractive, aging woman and a young, handsome aristocrat was much too wide. Moreover, any romantic overtures toward her would only raise suspicions and alarm her; she might even find them insulting and mocking.[12]

Dmitri decided to use his target's fanatical devotion to Hitler and the Nazis as her weak spot. But, as usual, before making any moves, he devoted enough time—around two weeks—to preparatory work. He needed as much information on Doris as possible. Leppin and Erica's surveillance of Müller's everyday habits did not reveal much. She lived alone in a small room near Alexanderplatz. Her workday began at 9:00 A.M. and ended at 6:00 P.M. Sometimes, she stayed in her office until ten in the evening. After work, she stopped at an inexpensive café. It was also registered that she usually occupied the same table, third from the entrance, near a window. During these two weeks she twice visited a movie theater (not surprisingly, considering her Nazi outlook, both times she chose German films). Once she visited the Berlin circus. She went everywhere alone. And she never smiled.[13]

Again, as in the first meeting with Oldham, Bystrolyotov first thought of a way just to show himself to Doris without approaching her directly. For that purpose, he involved "Greta" in the operation. On the target day, when Leppin and Erica reported that Doris was at her usual place in the café, "Greta" also went there. She knew where Fräulein Müller was sitting. After walking around the other tables, all occupied by couples, "Greta" stopped at the table where Doris was sitting and asked whether she could join her. Doris nodded. It was raining outside. "Greta" looked out the window as if expecting to see someone outside. She ordered a black coffee with liquor, looked at her watch, and said nervously to Müller with the smile of a proud, yet vulnerable, young lady, "Perhaps it's a bad sign when it rains cats and dogs on your first date."

The considerable age difference between them (Müller was almost twice as old as "Greta") made her words seem an unconscious call for a maternal cheer up.[14]

"I don't know." Müller cut her off but softened up a bit toward the naive girl, who was apparently expecting her Prince Charming.

On the other side of the window, a chocolate-colored Horch pulled up. With a foppish expression on his face, a handsome, well-dressed man scanned the café windows. Müller grinned: "It looks like it's for you."

"Look at that, he came on time," "Greta" said cheerfully. She left money on the table, nodded, and headed for the exit.

A week later, she and her man had a date at the same place again. This time, the man came early to pick up "Greta." She sent a triumphant look to Doris, who observed the scene, inviting her to share the excitement of having such a handsome and impeccably dressed suitor. One day, she introduced him to Fräulein Müller. A few times, he came to the café before "Greta" and nodded politely, acknowledging the presence of the German lady, his girl's acquaintance.

During the first encounter, Dmitri adopted the same role he had developed for ARNO, adjusting it only slightly to fit the new target. He played the part of Hungarian "Count Perelly de Kiralyhaza." Dispossessed of his considerable estates by World War I, he lived on money sent by his aunt from the United States. In fact, he had lived there for the past several years but had decided to travel and see the world. He projected the image of a man who led a dissipated life, a cosmopolite who wandered around the world to escape boredom. With a vacant look in his eyes, he politely asked Fräulein Müller to excuse his ignorance and enlighten him. As a foreigner, who would usually not be interested in politics, he could not help but become curious about what was going on in Germany. Why so much fuss about a few people in the country? Herr Hitler . . . Herr Goebbels . . . Herr Goering . . . Were they really so important? Who were they? Admirals? Professors? All these gentlemen had such sound-alike names. In America, nobody would be able to tell them apart.[15]

Fräulein Müller was horrified. She could not believe her ears! Where had this "monstrously blasphemous and ignorant" man grown up? The count blabbered his excuses, from which emerged the portrait of a rich gentleman who led a dissipated way of life and was spoiled by his easy victories over women. Müller decided that it would only benefit Germany if she made a true man out of this lightweight blockhead. She wanted to make him, if not a German patriot, at least a man who knew and respected the country in which he was spending his time so pleasantly.[16]

She began to see him carrying piles of books and articles on the nature and program of National Socialism. He looked genuinely interested. Every time they met, she patiently explained to him what Nazism was all about, what a great doctrine it was, and what a genius Germany's Führer was. She eagerly engaged in talks with the count, who, by that time, neglected seeing his young date, who could match neither Fräulein Müller's knowledge of current politics nor her passion in passing it to him. First, educating the foreigner became a habit; gradually it became an attachment. And finally, almost without noticing, she fell for him, head over heels.

Her feelings for the Hungarian count were nothing short of the true passion of a sexually awakened woman who had already given up on personal happiness. All of her unrequited need for love was now concentrated on this silly Hungarian man. It seems that Dmitri himself had not expected to evoke such strong emotions in her. "What a love it was!" With some note of awe, he registers it in his memoirs. "[It turned out that even] bloodthirsty dogs are capable of love."[17]

For several months, Dmitri and Doris saw each other on a regular basis. Throughout his writing, he generally avoids sexual innuendoes in descriptions of his dealings with women. About Doris, he writes only that when he had to kiss her for the first time he shuddered. But then he got hold of himself.[18]

After a long preparatory stage, when at last she was completely under his power as a lover, one day he became gloomy and began acting like a man in despair. Spending time in her apartment, he suggested she get drunk with him. When she asked him what was troubling him, he replied that his income, the stream of money his American aunt was sending him, had begun dwindling. "Bad times are ahead of me," he uttered. "My cash flow is going down the drain."[19]

As a nobleman, a person of a certain level of respectability, he told her he could not continue an illicit affair and that he wanted to marry her. The only obstacle was money. As a man of pride, he believed marriage had to be built on solid ground, and he needed to improve his finances. His American aunt was not sending enough.

Then one evening when he was visiting with Doris, he answered a phone call that upset him. When she asked him who it was and why the call had upset him, he answered that it was his friend and faithful assistant, one "Lajos Batory," also a Hungarian nobleman, a close friend of his deceased father. The man had literally raised him since infancy, and after his father's death, "Count Perelly" had entrusted the man with managing his estate back in Hungary. Now the man offered to help him with his financial troubles, but "Count Perelly" did not even know where to start. The man told him that good money could be made playing the stock market, if only "Count Perelly" could find a way to supply him with some "insider information." The German proclamation of universal military service had a positive effect on the securities market in Berlin. With the prospects of the country's rearmament, the dormant stock market had come back to life. "Lajos" explained to him that, knowing the plans of military industry, he would be able to make money by buying stocks of companies low, before the government orders were received, and selling high, after the orders were placed.[20]

"How the hell should I know all these things?" "Count Perelly" added in despair.

When Doris asked him to make himself clearer, he made an effort to get hold of himself and said, "You see, dear . . . I don't understand myself how it works exactly. But my friend told me that if he knew what kind of orders your government plans to place in the military branches of industry, he would be able to buy the stocks of those concerns, the value of which would jump in the near future. He would buy them now for peanuts and sell them soon at a much higher price. He told her that such an operation was fully legitimate; it's called "going long," that is, "playing on increase."[21]

Doris gave it some thought and said that it was not hard to find out these things but that she would want to meet the man and see what he was all about. Staying in character as the naive count, Dmitri suggested meeting the man in a popular Berlin café, Am Zoo. Doris rejected this idea: the café was too busy a place for a confidential meeting. She proposed bringing the man to her place.

The meeting was arranged. The illegal operative Theodor Mally was cast in the role of "Lajos Batory." Doris liked the man. He was tall, well dressed, polite, respectful, and considerate. Perhaps just a bit too dry and reserved for a stock dealer. (This could be explained by Mally's background. In his youth, Theodor had studied theology in a Catholic monastic order, was ordained as deacon, but then chose a career in the military. He finished a military academy, served in an officer's rank in the Austro-Hungarian Army during World War I, and was taken prisoner. He switched sides, joining the Red Army during the Russian civil war. Later, he joined the Soviet foreign intelligence.) "Herr Batory" told Doris he was thinking about getting into the promising area of possible stock movement—the aircraft industry. If he knew the government's short- and long-term plans for the Junkers and Messerschmitt plants, quick money could be made.[22]

Doris asked him how full secrecy of the data would be guaranteed. He replied that the whole idea of the deal was that nobody else was to know these numbers; otherwise, too many traders would jump on the bandwagon, and the profit of the "buy low and sell high" scheme would amount to next to nothing.

The next day, Doris took a few files from the safe to her office, studied them, and in the evening, made an oral report to her beloved, who passed it to "Herr Batory." After a few days, she found the procedure cumbersome and tiresome, and she brought home a piece of paper with nothing but two columns of numbers. These were the ciphered results of her study of the files in her care. She explained the simple principle of ciphering she used.

When the first round of trading brought a considerable sum, Doris asked "Herr Batory" to tell her which stocks he had bought, when, and how he had sold them. She wanted to learn the technique of the stock market game. The stock trader replied that, although the technique was not complicated, she had to be able to instantaneously gauge the mood at the stock exchange and decide what to do on the spot. It was impossible to demonstrate without stepping on the stock exchange floor. So, if she wished to, she could join him there right at the opening. Doris said that this was, of course, impossible, not only because she had to be at work at all times, but also because she could not even be seen in such a place. After all, didn't the Führer teach the German people that National Socialism and materialism were incompatible? She had no interest in the money for her own sake but for the sake of her fiancé; after all, their marriage depended on it.

"Herr Batory" stepped up the pressure and told her that if she wanted to get married sooner he would borrow more money from the banks to play the stock exchange. But it would be impossible to obtain a substantial loan based on oral assurances alone; they would want to see some supporting documents, and she would have to take them out for an hour or two.[23]

After some hesitation, Doris brought the material home. When she left, Mally quickly photographed the files, page by page. Of course, Doris knew she had bent the iron rules of guarding the material. But the files she looked in carried the "confidential" security classification; they were not marked "top secret." And, as Bystrolyotov keenly observes, "a person who is accustomed to smoking while sitting on a gunpowder barrel doesn't consider it especially dangerous to do it in a lumber warehouse."[24]

Certain measures were taken to cover the possibility that German counterintelligence might notice the frequent visits of "Herr Batory" to Doris's apartment. To justify these visits, a pack of documents was prepared and brought in from Holland. According to them, "Lajos Batory" had been commissioned by his employer, "Count Perelly," to talk to German banks and construction and repair firms regarding renovation of his family estate in Hungary. Dmitri left a few of copies of the papers, as if absentmindedly, on a shelf of Doris's bookcase. If the Gestapo happened to search the place, finding these papers would help to calm them down.[25]

While dealing with Doris, Dmitri managed to recruit another Zweighalle-5 employee. He obtained the lead by picking up just a few bits of information Doris had unwittingly shared with him. One day, during some pillow talk, Dmitri teased Doris for carrying around a pistol, part of her SS-Hauptscharführer uniform. But could she really shoot well? She flared up indignantly, stating with pride that it would be unthinkable for a true German woman not to know how to use a weapon. She even bragged about being the best markswoman in her Zweigstelle. And she would even be the best of the men, if not for that František Foster. "Who is he?" Dmitri asked out of curiosity. She replied that the man was an engineer in her department and the best marksman in the Berlin Marksmen's Union. In fact, that year, he had won first prize in the city championship, although in her judgment, in all other aspects he was a fool and nincompoop.[26]

That was more than enough information as a start for finding the man and beginning to cultivate him as a prospective agent. Dmitri charged his assistants, Leppin and Erica, with finding out as much as they could about the man. Knowing his name and place of employment, it was not difficult to obtain his address through the Berlin address bureau, where they also found the location of the Berlin Marksmen's Union. Leppin paid a visit to the union office and inquired about when and where the union members practiced their beloved sport. Charged with finding any personal data on Foster, he chatted with the union's secretary about their celebrity and picked up a bit of office gossip. A quiet and polite man, Herr Foster was still single and lived with his sick, elderly mother, who could no longer even walk by herself. Besides shooting, he had another, much quieter hobby—stamp collecting.

With Mally's blessing, Dmitri embarked on developing a new line of recruitment, and Foster was code-named ECONOMIST.[27] Dressed as a sport shooter, in a light-colored shooter's suit complete with checkered jacket, knee-length pants, thick socks, brown shoes, and a cap,[28] he went to the shooting gallery. He did not know what

Foster looked like, but that was hardly a problem: all members of the Berlin Marksmen's Union knew their champion by sight.

He waited in the foyer until Foster finished practicing and approached him respectfully. He opened with a compliment: "I was admiring your technique, Herr Foster. Did I pronounce your name right?"

The question was intended to ensure that he had the right man.

"Yes, I'm František Foster," the man replied. "I'm satisfied with my results."

"You're the pride not only of your union but of the whole Berlin population," Dmitri said and introduced himself as "Count Perelly de Kiralyhaza." And he asked whether Herr Foster would mind giving him ten shooting lessons.

"I'm flattered," Foster said but explained that he was not a professional trainer. Of course, if the count wished, he would indulge him, but he would not feel comfortable taking money for such a small favor.

"Ah," Dmitri said, "if only you collected stamps, as I do. Then . . ."

"Why!" Foster said, "I'm a passionate stamp collector!"

They shook hands in joy at having found a kindred soul.

"What kind of stamps do you collect, Herr Foster?"

"Only German ones. I'm a German patriot."

"I may be of use to you." Dmitri decided to plant a name that could evoke associations in Foster's mind. "I have a friend in London," he continued. "Alexis von Putiloff—he's also an avid philatelist. I'll bet I could get some German stamps of the past century for you."[29]

It took Foster a minute to take the bait.

"I'm very, very grateful," he said. "I have all of the German stamps of the twentieth century. But the old stamps are a big problem. They're hard to find and quite expensive."

"Well, a good turn for a good turn."

They shook hands again.

"Excuse me, Count," Foster said. "You mentioned the name of your friend. Does Herr Putiloff come from the family that formerly owned the metallurgical plant in St. Petersburg?"

Dmitri described Alexis as the son of the plant's lawful owner, who was disowned and emigrated. "Where did you hear this name?" Dmitri said, just to make the point that he knew nothing of Foster's professional life.

"I do research in the field of international economy," Foster replied.

"Ah, is that so?" The count smiled and added absentmindedly, "Well, let us return to more interesting things to talk about—marksmanship and philately."

It was the end of round one.

Dmitri immediately dispatched Leppin to Hamburg to buy about a dozen German stamps of the nineteenth century, the rarest and most expensive.

When, sometime later, he met Foster in a café, he presented him with a small album of stamps. Overwhelmed by the generosity of the present, Foster offered the count another forty lessons in sharpshooting. Understanding that Herr Foster wanted to reciprocate, the count graciously accepted the offer.

Their acquaintance soon grew into friendship: after all, they shared the same passions.

Later, "Count Perelly" accepted Herr Foster's invitation to visit him and his sick mother at their home. The guest charmed the old lady with his manners and warmth. The count saw for himself that his friend truly needed extra income to take better care of his mother. One day, traveling to the shooting range in his luxurious limousine, complete with uniformed chauffeur, the count offered Herr Foster a way to obtain funds that could pay for his mother's rehabilitation at some resort.[30]

He explained that the father of his friend, "Alexis von Putiloff," the same man who had graciously shared a few stamps from his vast collection, was eager to learn from whatever sources it would take about the current state of his plants in St. Petersburg. Herr Putiloff Sr. was ready to pay good money to know what modifications had been made to the plants to estimate their approximate market value. As an economist who followed economic development in various countries, including the USSR, could Herr Foster prepare a substantial report covering these points? Since it was quite clear that the war with the Bolsheviks was just a matter of time, their power overthrown, Herr Putiloff's ownership of the plants would be restored; naturally, he would want to know the worth of his property.

When Foster expressed his opinion that the collapse of Soviet power seemed quite far-fetched at this point, the count informed him that the Russian émigré Trade and Capital Union in Paris was taking these prospects seriously and had made a point that now was the time to set the records straight. Once the takeover had already taken place, it would be too late. It was important to have documents in hand at the moment of repossessing his stolen property.[31]

Foster contemplated the offer and replied that such a report would require quite a bit of time and effort on his part. And the count told him that he should rest assured that his work would be adequately compensated.[32]

After Foster delivered his report, the count found another client for him—one Ukrainian landlord, Alexander Ivanovich Bobrinsky. (Of course, Dmitri made up the name; it may well be that the name of Count A. A. Bobrinsky, a well-known Russian historian, ethnographer, archaeologist, and art critic, came to mind because of one of his art books Dmitri may have read back in St. Petersburg in his youth.) According to the count, Herr Bobrinsky owned lots of land on both sides of the Dniepr River, by sheer accident, in the place where the Bolsheviks had recently built a dam and hydroelectric station. When Soviet power collapsed, Herr Bobrinsky intended to claim that the dam and the station the robbers had built on his land also belonged to him.

Foster enjoyed his extra income. Soon he offered Finnish and Romanian sources, which he thought of obtaining from his friends who worked in those departments. But Mally suggested that Dmitri slow down, warning him not to accept the offer because too wide a net could run the risk that, sooner or later, Foster would suspect him of spying. He also advised against showing up with the man in public too often. All Zweighalle employees could well be under surveillance, if not constant, then at least random. Dmitri's acquaintance with another employee in the same setting could be deemed suspicious.[33]

Gradually, Foster developed a taste for extra income. He provided reports about the state of industrial production in the USSR, about the capacity of Soviet railroads, the mood of the population, and other information available to German intelligence. Studying these reports allowed Soviet counterintelligence not only to learn about the degree of transparency of Soviet defense capabilities but also to unearth German agents and their means of leaking information abroad.

No matter how successfully the operation moved along, it was clear that the game could not go on forever without risking failure. Doris had been waiting long enough for her beloved count to deliver on his promise of marriage. Besides, other Center assignments to the illegal *rezidentura* in Berlin needed Dmitri's participation.

But he could not just one day disappear into thin air from Doris without raising the suspicion of foul play. Alarmed, Doris would most likely call the police to investigate her fiancé's disappearance, thus attracting the attention of German counterintelligence as well. They would gradually get to the bottom of what had happened and what information had been leaked from the secret safe.

To avoid this highly undesirable course of events, Bazarov came up with a "newspaper variant," as he called it. One day, Dmitri told Doris that now, after some money had been made, there was no longer any reason to delay their marriage. But, as a responsible man, he needed to put things in order and place their future life together on a solid base. He would have to leave her for a couple of weeks in Berlin and go back to Hungary, where he had to settle up with his numerous creditors and put his estate in order. Then he would return to make all of the appropriate arrangements for their wedding.[34]

He left. A week later, "Herr Batory" paid an emergency visit to Doris. He was pale and could barely move his lips. He gave her the copy of a newspaper with a highlighted news item: As the result of a tragic accident during a hunting outing in the Hungarian provinces, "Count Perelly" was shot dead. His body was sent in a sealed coffin to his relatives in New York.[35]

Doris howled in despair. The deeply shaken and grief-stricken woman was saved from suicide with great effort. She went into mourning for her beloved and wore black not only as part of her SS uniform but with other attire.

But Dmitri was destined to see his SS bride one more time. After he had disappeared from her sight, a few months later, he had to pay another visit to Berlin. As he recalled many years later, he was there to meet another Soviet intelligence operative. He was about to enter a café on Leipziger Strasse, where the meeting was arranged, when, right in front of him, on the other side of the glass door, he saw his "widowed bride" staring at him in total disbelief. It happened so suddenly that they both froze, unable to tear their eyes from each other. At that very moment, a patrol of SS officers approached Dmitri, who was blocking the entrance to the café, and respectfully moved him to the side. Doris suddenly produced a wild shriek, fell to the floor, and writhed in hysterical sobbing. The officers rushed to her and bent toward the poor woman lying on the floor. A crowd of curious onlookers began gathering around the glass door. Dmitri won a few minutes, which saved his life. "One word from her," he recalls, "one slight cry or involuntary abrupt gesture [in my direction], and I would have perished." Luckily, he came to his senses first, turned around, and at the nearest street corner, hailed a taxi, which whisked him away from trouble.[36]

Meanwhile, with Germany and Italy speeding up development of their war machines, the Berlin *rezidentura* received an assignment from the Center to smuggle from Italy a sample of a brand-new model of Italian machine gun for aircraft (apparently, the newly developed model of the Breda-SAFAT series) and a sample of army gas-protection gear, complete with rubberized suit and mask. Since Italy had used mustard gas and phosgene in the course of the war with Abyssinia (now Ethiopia), which started in October 1935 and ended in May 1936, it was important for the Soviets to evaluate the effectiveness of this new means of troop protection.[37]

The items to be taken across the borders were procured by a group of Soviet agents in Italy and brought by truck to a park near Villa Borghese in Rome. Although it was known that SS guards on the German border behaved like mad dogs, there was no other way but to bring the picked-up items to Berlin's illegal *rezidentura*, which had undercover weapon experts who could thoroughly examine the samples.

A seemingly much less troublesome way was to take the items to the nearest Italian seaport and smuggle them aboard a Soviet cargo ship. But, by that time, the Germans had pressured the Italians to curtail trade with the Soviet Union. Soviet ships were under heavy surveillance around the clock; onboard searches were both frequent and thorough.

Another logical way was to take the load across the French border and then bring it to one of the French ports for subsequent delivery to the USSR. Paradoxically, the chances that the items would be discovered were much greater at the French border than at the German one. According to Bystrolyotov, in making this assignment, his superiors explained that the operation had a chance of succeeding thanks to the German servility when it comes to those higher in rank: "When a German sees a general, he tiptoes around him, full of veneration. And a French border guard doesn't give a damn about rank. On the contrary, he might intentionally turn a general's belongings upside down, just to make a point—as if he were saying, 'Watch and take it in, Monsieur General! In the barracks, you're the boss, but here at the border, I am. And I'm going to prove it to you right now.'"

All in all, it was a formidable task and a dangerous operation. On their way to Berlin, first the group had to clear Italian customs; then Swiss customs twice, upon entering and exiting the country; and finally, German customs. They chose the following route: board a passenger train in Rome to go north and cross the Italian border at Domodossola and the Swiss border at Brig. Then, passing through Switzerland, they had to reach the German border at Basel. The next stop was Berlin.

Carrying out this assignment was entrusted to Theodor Mally as the operation head, with Boris Bazarov as his assistant. Dmitri was called in to play the central part in the operation. By that time, he had already established his reputation as an expert in crossing European borders without raising suspicion. He had done it many times, carrying ciphers, codes, and copies of secret cipher-telegrams, as well as copies of secret reports and instructions. He brought into the act his reliable assistants, Leppin and Erica.[38]

From the outset, it was decided that the group could be successful only if they bluffed their way through in the most insolent way; the more bluffing the better.

To play his part, Dmitri had to summon all his acting abilities. Using watercolor paints, they gave his face a yellowish hue, with a few purple spots here and there. To prevent the paint from occasional smearing, they sprayed his face with lacquer. They wrapped him in two lap robes, in which he learned to walk in a shaking manner. In turn, he gave acting directions to Erica, who was dressed as a nun. He instructed her to keep her head high but her eyes downcast.

The group boarded the deluxe Rome–Berlin express. The nun and a uniformed aide from an American hospital in Rome (Leppin) led, supporting him under his arms on either side, a doubled-up patient, wrapped in lap robes, only his shaking yellow nose sticking out. Behind them, a tall porter (Mally) carelessly carried an elegant duffle bag, half-empty, and a suitcase. On his shoulder, he also transported a golf bag, packed with clubs. The porter, tall and athletic, put the suitcase and the duffle bag under the lower berth of the railroad car and the golf bag in a corner, accepted his tip, and left. The seeming ease with which he handled the luggage was a necessary ploy. He had to pretend that it was not much to carry, though the bag with the golf clubs, among which the machine gun barrel was hidden, and the suitcase with the gas-proof suit and the rest of the machine gun parts were too heavy for an ordinary porter, who might become curious as to the contents of the luggage.

Upon boarding the train, the nun slipped the conductor a wad of liras and, speaking in German with a heavy American accent, explained that the patient was a British lord, who, while traveling in Italy, was bitten by a rabid dog. As a result, he had become dangerously ill and, from time to time, prone to violent outbursts, which could be provoked by sharp knocking and rattling.

The conductor grabbed a bunch of towels and began to hastily tie down all objects that might make noise as the train moved: the water bottle, glasses, even the night pot. They turned the compartment into a makeshift isolation ward. They covered the walls with linens, lowered the window shades, and turned on the shaded night lamp. The hospital servant and the nun sat next to the patient, the servant watching over his every move. The nun sat next to the lamp and read the Gospel, her fingers running over her rosary beads.

The whole ploy was based on a psychological calculation. The unusual sight of the compartment and the exotic passenger were designed to distract customs attention from the patient's belongings.

When the train stopped at Domodossola on the Italian side of the Swiss border, as soon as the Black Shirt Militia stepped into the railroad car, the conductor rushed to them with the passengers' passports and begged them not to make much noise because of the unpredictable mental patient. Out of curiosity, the guards opened the door slightly, peeked inside, but did not dare to step in out of fear. When the train departed, everybody inside the railroad car sighed in relief.

The scene repeated itself with the Swiss gendarmes in Brig. During a stop in Zurich, a short and nimble doctor in a white robe with a young nurse on hand (Bazarov and "Greta") appeared in the compartment. The doctor listened to the nun's report about the condition of her patient, administered a shot to him, and left.

Then came the German border crossing at Basel. The SS border guards reacted the same as their Italian and Swiss counterparts. Nobody wanted to contend with a violent mental patient. "Death twice passed by me," Dmitri wrote many years later, recalling this operation. "One attentive look, one touch of [the luggage] with a boot tip—and everything would have been discovered."[39]

During the weapon-smuggling operation, while Dmitri was fully aware that he was in immediate danger, he didn't have even an inkling that soon he would find himself on the brink of peril again. Now, mortal danger was to come to him from the hands of an enemy he had forgotten about.

ELEVEN | The "Vivaldi" Affair

Take my wife . . . please!

—HENNY YOUNGMAN, AMERICAN COMEDIAN

With many interwar KGB files destroyed, only skimpy information about Dmitri's last operations could be culled from his writings, both published and (mostly) unpublished. All of them, in one way or another, had to do with prolonged secret negotiations between the Soviets and the French in the early 1930s.

Due to Hitler's open defiance of the Versailles Treaty limitations on the German military, international tensions in all of Europe grew rapidly, and the long-standing animosity between Germany and France became especially palpable. The war of nerves in view of Hitler's determination to rearm Germany caused France to frantically seek alliances with other countries. In the face of ominous developments in Germany, although the French governments were unstable and changed in rapid succession, all of them felt it necessary to make forays in the direction of Soviet Russia.

It was not easy to decide on rapprochement between France and the Soviet Union. Alternate French governments moved toward Russia with much reluctance and apprehension. On one hand, Russia had been an important French ally before World War I, and the Soviet Union represented a plausible Eastern counterweight against a resurgent Germany. On the other hand, after the 1917 Bolshevik takeover and its proclamation to export revolution to other countries, French right-wing politicians grew to hate the Soviet Union because of the danger it posed to social stability.

The German menace, however, was much more real and closer, just across the Rhine River. And so France gradually began to improve its relations with the despised Bolshevik Russia. In late 1932, the radical premier and foreign minister Édouard Herriot signed a non-aggression pact with the Soviet Union. In early 1934, his successor, the Socialist Joseph Paul-Boncour, concluded a trade agreement with Moscow. Conservative Louis Barthou continued the Herriot–Paul-Boncour line when he became foreign minister in February 1934. Barthou began discussing a Franco-Soviet defense pact with People's Commissar of Foreign Affairs Maxim Litvinov. Whether France liked the Bolsheviks or not, she needed the Russian counterbalance.

Although the final text of the Franco-Soviet pact did not include a supporting military cooperation agreement, apparently, during the initial stages of rapprochement between France and the Soviet Union in contemplating a defense pact, there was some discussion of military provisions in case of a German attack. Such provisions remained behind-the-scenes activities on both sides. Back in September 1933, after French air minister Pierre Cot made a short visit to the USSR, he was convinced of the great opportunities an alliance with the Soviet Union could bring to French security. He reasoned that since the USSR had the largest army and air force in the world, it could present a sufficient deterrent to German expansionist ambitions. Soviet military intelligence used Cot's pro-Soviet stand to its advantage: its agents penetrated the French Air Ministry.[1]

At some later date, Soviet foreign intelligence found an opportunity to obtain a list of Nazi sympathizers in France. Such information may have served as an enticing bargaining chip in its negotiations with France.

Since the operation required a thorough knowledge of Western banking and other financial activities, the Center called on Bystrolyotov's expertise in economics and his experience in running Western agents to carry out the operation, directed by Theodor Mally, who met with Dmitri and explained the gist of the objective. Through its agents in Germany, Soviet foreign intelligence learned that French Nazi sympathizers were serving as informers of the German intelligence, the Abwehr. So far, doing it on a voluntary basis, they were not as reliable as those on the Abwehr payroll. To tie them down and increase their productivity and cooperation, they had to be bound by money received from Germany.[2]

According to Bystrolyotov, the rationale for the Abwehr actions was the following: because bringing a large sum of money directly into France and dispensing it there would be troublesome—French counterintelligence would easily get on the informers' trail—the German plan was to find a way to send the money without leaving any traces of the transactions. What they came up with was quite similar to what, in today's terms, is called a money-laundering operation. To hide the German origin of the money, they decided to work through an intermediary firm in neighboring Holland. To avoid any suspicion of a German connection, the intermediary firm should have an anti-Nazi reputation. By the time of the operation in summer 1935, the Nazis' rampant anti-Semitic propaganda, boycott of Jewish stores, doctors, and lawyers, and banning of Jews from government service were public knowledge. It would thus be best to involve an unsuspecting Jewish financial firm in the transaction. A lump sum had to be delivered anonymously to this firm that would be entrusted with depositing the money in a Dutch Commercial Bank, which, acting in its own name, would transfer the money to France and dispense it according to the list of addresses supplied. The final goal of the Soviet operation was to obtain the list of the Nazi "fifth column" in France.

The operation was successfully carried out with the help of Baruch (Bernard) Dawidowicz, a Polish Jew who had assisted Dmitri in setting up the cover firm GADA in Holland. Because Bystrolyotov's description of the operation appeared in the open Soviet press, his manuscript undoubtedly underwent scrutiny by the KGB censors. Although the final text preserved some aspects of the operation, these details were hardly sufficient to fully access the mechanics used in tricking the Germans to give away their secret list.[3]

It is also unclear whether the Soviet government ever used this list of the Nazi "fifth column" in France in diplomatic negotiations with the French. But Bystrolyotov took part in other France-related operations and left firsthand accounts of them. One of these operations aimed at stealing secrets from the French that they, in turn, had stolen from the Germans. Due to the complex Soviet–French relationship at the time—neither party fully trusted the other—it was no wonder that both French and Soviet foreign intelligence were averse to sharing their booty about the German war efforts. Who knew on which side each might wind up in a future conflict?

Dmitri designed and executed an operation that may well be considered one with no analogues in the history of world intelligence. He describes it with such frankness that one can only guess his motive (or motives) for making it public, despite having at its heart a highly private matter. It is possible that one impetus for his writing was a desire to sort out all the motives of his past actions.

It all started one day when, chatting with him during one of their occasional meetings in Geneva, ROSSI tipped him off that a French intelligence officer was living at his luxurious villa in Locarno, Switzerland. (As he does elsewhere in his memoirs, Dmitri avoids revealing details of unacknowledged Soviet intelligence operations and nicknames the man in question "Vivaldi," whom he presents as a retired colonel from Italian Army Headquarters.)[4]

At the time of this episode, the late fall of 1935, Germany was the chief threat to French security, so it was natural to expect a heavy concentration of French intelligence activity on that country.[5] After Hitler's accession to power, intelligence gathering revolved around obtaining information on the intentions and capabilities of the growing Nazi menace on the other side of the Rhine River. The reports of secret service attachés posted to Berlin were the most prolific source of sensitive information. A subsection responsible for French foreign intelligence, the Service de renseignements (SR), operated a growing agent network in Germany. The French intelligence aimed to assess Germany's economic and political situation, an important element in the overall perception of a German threat. But efforts were no less intense in other countries through which German intelligence information traveled, and neighboring Switzerland was one of them. It was reasonable to assume that rich data about the German rearmament efforts passed through the hands of Colonel "Vivaldi." Realizing that obtaining access to this information would give a significant advantage to Soviet intelligence, Dmitri came up with a plan to get hold of the cache of reports delivered to "Vivaldi" by his agents.

Learning that "Vivaldi" was an aging, "bored widower," Dmitri calculated that the colonel would be susceptible to the charms of a young and attractive woman, a trap he had already successfully implemented in the operation to intercept the Hitler–Ciano Sr. correspondence.

But a fleeting love affair would not be enough to provide more or less permanent access to French intelligence secrets. It could only work if the woman belonged to the aristocracy, making marriage the only way for the Frenchman to have her.

It is unclear whether Dmitri struggled with himself for long before deciding to cast his own wife, Iolanta, as bait for the Frenchman. The illegal Soviet foreign intelligence *rezident* in Paris, Theodor Mally, and Boris Bazarov (who was already running the OGPU illegal *rezidentura* in America) approved the plan. The first deputy of the Foreign Intelligence Department (since May 5, 1935), Boris Berman, authorized the operation.[6]

Apparently, Dmitri's plan didn't raise his bosses' eyebrows. Although extraordinary, his readiness to place his own wife on the altar of revolution had roots in Russian cultural zeitgeist. In the famous nineteenth-century novel *What Is to Be Done?* by Nikolai Chernyshevsky, its hero, Rakhmetov, wholly dedicated to the revolution, sets an example of self-denial and ruthless self-discipline, to the point of sleeping on a bed of nails. According to him, jealousy was an unnatural feeling that should be suppressed. The novel served as an inspiration to many Russian revolutionaries who sought to emulate its hero.

In more recent times, in the 1920s, after the Bolsheviks came to power, Rakhmetov's views were echoed in public debates held in Soviet Russia about the need to do away with the old, bourgeois morality in which a woman in marriage was seen as property. Sexual freedom was part of the Soviet experiment at large. In public statements, Alexandra Kollontai, a Russian Communist revolutionary and Soviet diplomat, expressed her belief that true Socialism could not be achieved without a radical change in attitudes toward sexuality. They had to be freed from the oppressive norms that she saw as a continuation of bourgeois acquisitiveness. In her "Theses on Communist Morality in the Sphere of Marital Relations," echoing Chernyshevsky's hero, she stated that sexuality is a human instinct as natural as hunger or thirst. Like the state, when communism becomes a reality, the family unit will wither away. Kollontai admonished men and women against their nostalgia for traditional family life. (Living abroad, Dmitri fell behind the times. In the early 1930s, with Stalin's full accession to power, a period of sexual freedom deemed as the main cause of disintegration of the family had been winding down. Stalin saw to it that the institution of marriage and family was fully restored and strengthened.)[7]

Writing thirty years after that episode in his life, Dmitri does not recall hesitating for a minute before approaching his wife with this extraordinary proposition. A man of action, once he came up with a plan to subvert "Vivaldi," he didn't think twice about sacrificing his mate. He prefaces the chapter devoted to that operation with an epigraph, a line from John 15:13: "Greater love hath no man than this, that a man lay down his life for his friends." But he titles the chapter "According to St. John? . . . Hmm . . . I don't know." Often ambivalent in his feelings at crucial moments in his life, with the passage of time, he was not sure that his decision to marry off Iolanta to a stranger for the sake of the greater cause was the right one. "Was marrying Iolanta off a mistake?" he asks himself. "Was it a crime or an act of heroism?" Pondering it, he finally decides that it was a sacrifice on his part, the "biggest sacrifice [he] had ever made, much bigger than if [he] were to sacrifice [his] own life." At the time of the operation, he felt he had "given away the best of what he had, and nothing else was left." He recalls no feeling of jealousy or other bad sentiments toward Colonel "Vivaldi." In fact, he even liked this respectable and honest man and was consoled that his beloved wife was in the hands of a decent man.

Naturally, he knew it would be difficult to talk Iolanta into going along with his plan. "I had no experience in how one should marry off one's beloved wife in order to reach socially useful goals," he admits. To persuade her, he decided he would have to appeal to her Communist beliefs, as he puts it, "to raise the delicate subject at hand from the level of everyday humdrum existence, to elevate it to the height of a sacrificial and heroic deed."

They sat on a park bench in Davos, now their place of permanent residence. To be exact, she lived there all the time, and he visited her as frequently as he could, whenever his job allowed. Sometimes months on end would pass before he saw her again, as had happened during his handling of Oldham in London. Talking to her now, first he pointed out that the enormous salary they received for their work demanded that they give more of themselves, that is, not just "playing around the fire but jumping into it." Indeed, their monthly income was extraordinarily high. Dmitri received the highest Soviet monthly

salary (*sovmaksimum*) of five hundred gold rubles, and Iolanta another three hundred. Combined with their travel and hotel expenses,
Soviet Foreign Intelligence was paying them a salary more than a
dozen times that of a Soviet blue-collar worker.

So, he argued, they were morally obliged to do much more than
they had in the past so as to justify their high pay and to live up to
the expectations of their time, a time of great moral enthusiasm. He
reminded her of the time they had first met back in Prague and how
they'd sworn allegiance to the high ideals they shared. Hadn't they
promised each other they would never become "heroes with a check-
book in their pockets"? That they would be totally devoted to the cause
and fight unsparingly for the triumph of the most advanced ideas
known to humanity? If so, didn't such devotion justify "estrangement
from all things personal and worldly"? With the war coming, now was
no time for hesitation. They must act decisively and make the ultimate
sacrifices they had sworn to make.

After saying all that, he explained her part of the important operation: after she married the Frenchman and things had settled down a
bit, she would make impressions of the keys to his safe. Then Dmitri
would be able to sneak into the man's office and photograph the contents of the safe.

First, Iolanta thought Dmitri was acting under duress and his superior, Boris Berman, the very same man who had rejoiced when her
tuberculosis provided a convenient cover for the Soviet spy network
in Europe, was behind Dmitri's calling on her to "jump into the fire."
But he assured her that the idea was his alone. He expressed surprise
at her reluctance to do what was expected of her, reminding her that,
after all, they had an open marriage. Back in the Prague days, they
had foreseen that, while they would remain soul mates forever, the
nature of their work with its frequent and prolonged absences would,
realistically speaking, make it impossible for them to be physically
faithful to each other. They tacitly agreed to this, living and acting
accordingly. As an example of her de facto acceptance of these arrangements, he reminded her of an episode that had taken place back
in Berlin in the early 1930s. Visiting her in the hospital after she had
barely survived the dangerous operation of nerve ablation, seeing her
helpless and unable even to lift her head from the pillow, he felt like
crying. When he took a handkerchief from his pocket, she looked at

him and, for the first time in many months, smiled "playfully, even joyfully." Instead of his handkerchief, he had inadvertently pulled from his pocket . . . a pair of panties he had "removed from a pretty girl the night before."

And hadn't he returned the favor many times? Before visiting her in Davos, he always called from the road along the way to let her know he was coming, thus giving her time to remove all traces of her infidelities: another man's ties, socks, or whatever.

"You haven't been praying before my picture during all the years of intelligence work," he summed it up. "What's the difference, then?"

Iolanta froze for a long while, finally uttering, "Tell me, would Berman and your other bosses send their wives into somebody else's bed?"

Dmitri dismissed her point right away. It didn't matter: "Everyone's responsible for his or her own soul."

It was nighttime, and they went to bed without resolving the issue. But, in the middle of the night, Iolanta suddenly woke him up. Sobbing and getting dressed in a hurry, she swallowed her tears and said, "You want to make a whore out of me! How dare you! What did your phone calls from the road have to do with it? Those infidelities were out of necessity, out of loneliness. But what you're talking about here is sheer prostitution!"

His first thought was that, out of agitation, she might do something stupid and impulsive, which could become fatal to their undercover work. At the time she was safeguarding five passports for members of their spy network—who knew what she would do with them now?

He tried to calm her down with whatever rationale came to his mind at the moment, such as "prostitution is also a social necessity."

"You're sending me to [fuck] with some colonel!" Iolanta screeched. She threw her clothes from the wardrobe into a suitcase and before leaving said to him, this time, apparently for stronger effect, switching from Czech to English: "You're a bastard, a lousy son of a bitch!"

Realizing that the situation was going out of control, he briefly recounted the story of his affair with Marie-Eliane Aucouturier, the French Embassy typist in Prague. When he seduced her in order to recruit her as a Soviet agent, he pointed out, it was in service to the revolutionary cause, which he had placed above his personal wishes. It was a sacrifice to the revolution, being forced to cheat on his young wife. (In his memoirs, however, he admits that he hadn't told Iolanta the whole truth. He omitted the end of that affair: the French spy line was closed on orders from the Center, that is, his sacrifice had borne zero results. He hadn't told her that because "the end of that lousy story spoke against the despicable [spy] work, and it would be an argument that worked in Iolanta's favor.")

Iolanta heard him out and quieted down. But her face made him freeze. It assumed the same empty expression, resembling a blind or clairvoyant woman, he had seen for the first time many years before when they first met: "Her eyes were again the color of ice and looked at the world without seeing anything, as if looking into another world."

Iolanta became very calm and now spoke only in English. She put all her clothes back into the wardrobe and, without looking at him, asked whether his making love to the Frenchwoman had happened for the first time on their wedding night and continued during their honeymoon.

He confirmed it.

She undressed, lay down in the bed, and said into the darkness, "You're a hero. But I hope you understand that everything's over between us. You got what you wanted. I'll marry your Colonel 'Vivaldi,' but at the same time, I'm no longer your wife. You're a horrible man. Don't touch me. You're a murderer."

"Whom have I killed, Iola?" he asked.

She replied, "Me."

After that night, events ran their course without a hitch, according to Dmitri's plan. The daughter of a blue-collar worker, Iolanta could become an aristocrat only if she was married to one. Dmitri contacted his friend (and Soviet foreign intelligence agent) Georgy Georgiev, who was acquainted with a genuine Hungarian count, whom he calls "Cesar Adolph August Esterhazy." An aging homosexual, he had squandered his whole fortune and lived in Prague with his young lackey in a small house belonging to his former gardener: this was all that remained of his past luxurious way of life. For a substantial sum of money, he agreed to cooperate. They brought him to Nice, where Iolanta was already waiting for him. She was provided with a passport bought on the Prague black market in the name of "Rona Dubska." According to it, she was the twenty-five-year-old daughter of a Czech official and divorced.

Although the passport flattered Iolanta, making her nearly ten years younger, there was a snag. When they doctored the passport at the OGPU headquarters on Lubyanka, replacing the original picture with one of Iolanta, they overlooked an entry on the special features page that said the passport holder's "left leg [was] absent."

There was no time to replace the passport, and Dmitri took the risk. Since the passport entries were written in Czech, there was a good chance that a French Catholic priest wouldn't know the language.

Dmitri spared no money in subsidizing the next important step: to make Iolanta look and act like an aristocrat. He sent her to Paris, where she bought a bundle of elegant clothes and learned her new biography by heart. Then, "Countess Rona Esterhazy" traveled to Locarno. It seems that Dmitri drew his inspiration for setting up the entrapment of "Vivaldi" from a literary source, the famous Chekhov short story "Lady with a Lapdog." He planted "Rona" in a hotel in the resort town of Lugano and chose autumn as the time when the countess would appear on the embankment of the lake: the period between the summer and winter tourist seasons made the appearance of a smashingly beautiful and expensively dressed single woman (her divorce from "Count Esterhazy" had already been registered by then) more noticeable. As did the characters in Chekhov's story, "Vivaldi" and "Rona" got acquainted thanks to a little white poodle that Dmitri had given his wife.

The plan worked. "Vivaldi" couldn't resist the charms of the young Hungarian aristocrat. He immediately began courting her. It turned out that the countess didn't know Italian, which was used in this part of Switzerland, and "Vivaldi" was only too eager to help. They became friends first, and soon he proposed.

Now it was only a matter of time before "Rona" would settle down in "Vivaldi's" house and be ready to carry out her part of the operation. However, Dmitri was in for a big—and unpleasant—surprise. He had no inkling that in parting from his wife (in his mind, temporarily) he had brought back into his life a person with whom he would soon find himself in the grip of a mortal struggle—literally. Shortly after Dmitri stepped aside to let her marry "Vivaldi," Iolanta renewed her liaison with Isolde. On Dmitri's own admission, Isolde's new invasion into his private life, this time so "impudent and triumphant," inflicted tremendous pain on his ego.

It all started when Isolde sent Iolanta a ring as a wedding present. Enraged by this gesture, Dmitri now realized that what he considered a heroic deed of self-denial for the sake of a higher cause, Isolde saw as his admission of failure due to Iolanta's unwavering allegiance to her, her lesbian lover. He felt both defeated and fooled. The accompanying letter humiliated him. He read it over once, and quickly, but its words "burned him later like a slap in the face":

> I'm glad that your former spouse made such a sensible decision: your divorce from him only externally legalized his inner insolvency. He was forced to admit defeat and pass you back to me. This is how I understand his act, in that sense, not devoid of certain nobility. As I'm returning to you my previous gifts, I assume, dear Signora, that we're returning to the happy state of affairs that existed [between us] in the past.[8]

And Isolde acted accordingly. Taking advantage of the ignorance of Iolanta's new husband about the nature of his new wife's relationship with her, Isolde moved into their house as her girlfriend and permanent companion.

First, Dmitri tried to act from afar. Through some intermediaries, he attempted to remove Isolde from the "Vivaldi" residence but failed. He experienced a horrific and bitter sense of his impotence to change things. He couldn't help but spy on the couple from behind the bushes of the Frenchman's villa. One day, he saw his wife and Isolde making love. The scene had a devastating effect on him. "Simply and clearly, with my whole body and soul, I understood that this was the breaking point: from now on, I would live for one purpose only—to murder Isolde. Only her death could make my further existence possible."

In his mind, there was no longer a choice—only one of them, either he or she, would go on living. All his usual precautions in observing his stern superiors' rules of conduct for illegal operatives—he still had to report his every move to them—left him. Writing about that moment in his life, he admits, "I lost my head, and I became more dangerous than any wild animal."

Though he knew that "to murder a human being in a civilized country isn't easy," he also knew that he could do it. After all, he was a man who had gone through tough times in his life, a pistol always weighing down his back pocket, and most important, he was an intelligence operative; at his disposal was a "group of desperate people."

What followed next is not quite clear. Dmitri calls his actions regarding Isolde a misdemeanor (*prostupok*). But, in his own judgment, it feels much more serious than that: "In Switzerland I was a nobody, a man with a false passport in his pocket, and my misdeed passed unnoticed and did no harm to [my Motherland]. Nothing of what I had done harmed the Soviet Foreign Intelligence either. But there's no justification [for my deed] before my own conscience—at whose court, I admit 'I'm guilty!'"[9]

Once he decided to do away with Isolde, he spent a week devising a plan, thinking it through, and preparing its execution. Finally he felt ready to make the first move. First he thought of sending her a note with an invitation to see him. But he discarded the idea right away: a note would leave some trace of his actions. Instead, he followed Isolde to downtown Locarno, pretended to run into her by chance, and feigned surprise, even joy, at seeing her. He explained that he was in town finishing up some business before leaving Europe for good. To be more specific, he said he had decided to settle in Rio de Janeiro (indeed, one of his several passports was Brazilian). He also wanted to caution his former wife that she was in danger: Hitler's spies in Switzerland were hunting for her. Some precautionary measures had to be taken at once to assure her future safety.

To Isolde's question about the essence of the threat, Dmitri replied that he didn't know specifics and was just acting as a go-between for a former colleague of Iolanta from her Prague days. The details of what exactly had to be done to keep Iolanta out of trouble were in the hands of that man. Dmitri had arranged a meeting with him in a small restaurant in the mountains near Grindelwald.

No matter how thin his story looked, Dmitri achieved his intention: he scared Isolde. He knew well by now that she wouldn't hesitate to risk her own life to protect her beloved. His calculations proved right. Highly alarmed, without questioning Dmitri's far-fetched story, Isolde immediately agreed to do whatever it took to keep Iolanta safe. His plan was to lure Isolde into the mountains and push her off a cliff.

They agreed to meet later in the day, at 5:00 P.M., near a small bridge in the valley near Grindelwald. The previous day he had traveled to Interlaken to check out the terrain of the planned action beforehand. First, he took care of an alibi for himself. One of his Swiss contacts, a man called "Olaf," lived in the nearby town of Murren. After "doing it," Dmitri planned to go there by way of mountain trails.

From Interlaken, he went to Grindelwald on foot. Once in the mountains, he came up with a detailed plan of how he would get rid of Isolde from his life forever. To keep himself out of prison, he had to stage her death as the accident of an inexperienced hiker. He would lead her into the mountains, to a place convenient for his task. Near Upper Glacier, between Grindelwald and Scheidegg, he would stop at a tall rock as if to light a strike-anywhere match for his pipe. He marked the rock with a piece of chalk, which he had had the good sense to take along.

As soon as Isolde wound up next to the precipice, he would distract her by pointing to the top of the glacier and saying something like, "Look! There are people over there." Once he had diverted her attention, he would push her down. Her body would fall about forty yards before hitting the rocks. It would be impossible to survive such a fall, and her body would hardly show any signs of foul play.

After this was done, he would hit the trail leading to Kleine Scheidegg, a high mountain pass, and be on his way to Murren. To avoid leaving his own tracks, he thought of a creek he knew. He would take off his shoes, step into the creek, and wade downstream until he reached a larger trail to Murren. There he would step out of the creek, put his shoes back on, and rub the soles with a piece of camphor he had put in his pocket beforehand. After a while, he would stop and change his shoes for another pair that didn't smell of camphor, which he had already planted in the hollow of a marked tree.

It seemed he had thought of everything. Though he had chosen a trail that was hardly ever used, he had two provisional plans in case someone did show up and saw him. One plan involved luring Isolde with the help of "Olaf" to Holland, to a tiny desolate island in the northern part of the country, near Ijmuiden, a place he had visited when setting up the import-export company, GADA. The other plan was to trick Isolde into going with him to Venice, take her out to the open sea in a gondola, and drown her. Both ideas look more like wishful thinking than workable plans. Clearly, he was unable to think straight at the time. As he recalls, one thing was crystal clear for him at that moment: "It was I or she. Whether it took a day or a year didn't matter. I was sure she would perish by my hands."

First, everything seemed to be going according to his initial plan. Once Isolde had agreed to come to Grindelwald, he arrived there earlier and, to avoid being seen by anyone, bypassed the town and positioned himself in the bushes near the small bridge in the valley where they were to meet.

With Isolde to appear any minute, he thought about gulping a shot of cognac from the bottle he had brought along but decided against it. Now, as in his youth, when, experimenting with his will power, he had attempted a robbery, he asked himself the same rhetorical question: "Am I a louse or Napoléon?" (It looks like, twenty years down the road, no longer a raw youth but a mature man, he still had profoundly ambivalent feelings about himself.) And carefully, so he wouldn't be heard, he broke the bottle, knocking it against a rock.

Isolde arrived on time. Dmitri's attire made her wary: he had told her the walk would be short, but he was dressed in full hiking gear, as if prepared for a long haul in the mountains (as she put it, "as if about to scale Mt. Everest"). He anticipated the question and told her that, after their business was done, he was heading to visit his friend who lived on the other side of the mountain. As they walked in the gathering darkness, still wary of Dmitri's behavior, Isolde asked him why such secrecy was needed. Did he have to keep playing a scene out of a trashy adventure novel? Wouldn't it be better to invite the man they were going to see in Grindelwald to some hotel room and talk to him there? They had almost reached the marked place on the trail, when Isolde began to suspect Dmitri of foul play. She asked him where exactly he was taking her.

He made an effort to answer her calmly, without insisting on anything. An experienced operative, he knew that if the other party has any doubts, pressure is counterproductive. Isolde hesitated for a moment; her fingers trembling, she lit a cigarette, and they moved on in silence.

But soon she stopped, stating that she would go no farther. "You tricked me," she said. "Well, go back down then," Dmitri said in contempt, "and pass Iolanta into more reliable hands. March!" They stood facing each other for a long while, piercing each other with their gazes. Her face grew chalk pale. His legs trembling, Dmitri reached for his pocket and released the safety catch on his handgun.

Isolde grabbed the edge of his jacket and tried to say something but she couldn't, only managing to twist her brightly painted lips.

Suddenly, she changed her mind and continued ascending the trail.

Soon they reached the rock he had marked as the place for his deadly maneuver, and he asked her to stop for a smoke.

While Dmitri's account of the events that brought him and Isolde into the mountains is more or less plausible up to this point, his description of the following chain of events is less trustworthy and, at times, resembles the action in an adventure comic, full of cliffhanging and last-moment survival tricks. As he narrates it in his memoir, as soon as he turned away from Isolde to light a match, some huge bird took wing nearby and rushed close to him. He turned toward it for a moment, and Isolde made a quick step behind him and pushed him down. He "widely waved [his] hands and flew down the abyss, [his] face forward." He tumbled over and smashed his face against a boulder. For a moment, his hands and legs spread, he found himself glued to the rock. Then he began "sliding down, first slowly, then faster and faster." His leather jacket and his shirt slipped up and blocked his vision. He shouted as if it were his last breath of air and closed his eyes.

But he didn't plummet down the precipice. His leather jacket and his clothes hooked onto a little pine trunk sticking out from a crack in the rock. When he managed to free his face from his clothes, he saw that he was clutching the cliff. He managed to free his clothes from the trunk, examined the cracks above him, contemplating his way up, and then slowly began climbing.

It took him a long while to climb about fifteen feet before reaching the rim. Stopping, catching his breath, wiping the sweat from his eyes, he finally pulled his body back onto the trail from which he had been pushed. As soon as he felt the ground under his legs, he collapsed, losing consciousness.

When he regained it, he jumped to his feet and ran down the trail nonstop until he reached the forest. There he fell onto the grass and, reliving the moment of mortal danger he had just survived, vomited.

After this he felt better. He removed his shirt and freshened up his body in the creek water. But the thought of Isolde made his fatigue disappear without a trace.

He thought that by now Isolde must have left the town by train or some other means. He wanted to grab a taxi and get to Interlaken. Once there, he would contact "Olaf," and they would work out a plan of action. They would pin her down in Locarno. She would have to go there because of Iolanta. And there, in Locarno, she would breathe her last.

He reached Grindelwald, and as he was passing through an alley behind one of the local boardinghouses, he spotted Isolde in the first-floor window. This changed things for the better! He hid in the bushes and calculated that from where he sat he could finish her off with one gunshot. His pistol had a silencer, the alley was deserted, and it had grown quite dark, so he would be able to escape before the police arrived. But now he felt that merely killing her wouldn't satisfy him. Before, he had just wanted to get rid of her once and for all, but now, before she dies, she must see her killer. He craved vengeance.

A knife was his weapon of choice. That was the only way he could express all the feelings boiling inside him at the moment. He decided exactly how he would finish Isolde off: it was important to him that she see his face before she died. With his left hand, he would grab her hair, lift her head, and before she was able to scream, stab her, keeping the blade horizontal, making it easier to drive between her ribs. He would keep her face in front of his until she took her last breath. The last thing she must see in her life was his triumphant face. Then he would make a swift escape to Murren.

He waited in the bushes for a long time to be sure that Isolde was sound asleep. Before climbing through the window, he removed his shoes and rubbed his hands and the soles of his socks with camphor. Once in her room, he rushed to the bed and grabbed Isolde by the hair. But at the last moment before stabbing her, he realized she was dead!

Three letters were on the nightstand. Besides one with money for the boardinghouse owner and another one addressed to some attorney in Edinburgh, Scotland, one was addressed to "Countess Rona Vivaldi" at the Villa Bella Vista in Locarno. Also on the nightstand was a cigarette case, the same one that had played such a sinister part in his life, the one inscribed *Am loving you only and all my other loves are but nothing.* He took the cigarette case and the letter and left, feeling that with Isolde gone, "she needed neither [his] belated admiration nor [his] earthly love."

He spent the rest of the night walking to Interlaken. On the way, he stopped at a mountain creek, kissed the cigarette case, and dropped it into the water. He opened Isolde's farewell letter to Iolanta, which read:

> I'm leaving you forever: you're too weak for the burden
> of my love, and I'm too strong to love contemplatively
> and incorporeally. I always wanted my love to be a
> daring challenge, a delight of movement and struggle,
> intoxication with the upsurge to the Unreachable, a
> victorious jump into an Abyss. But movement of the
> storm is impossible without broken tree branches
> and trampled down flowers, and if I can topple over
> a strong one, I shouldn't harm a weak one. You need
> tranquility, and I extend it to you as my last gift. I'm
> proudly throwing poison into my wine, and raise this
> chalice high as a torch: for the last time, let it light up,
> explain, and extol my love to you and me.[10]

Reading the letter made him feel as if Isolde was "whipping him with a lash." He felt that the letter was her "triumphant cry of victory, the last thunder of the hymn of selfless love and human freedom, which are stronger than death." He closed his eyes and clearly saw death "as one that flouted the bounds of narrow earthly existence and raised up the deceased to the expanse of immortality."

And he dropped the letter into the water as well. When he reached Interlaken, it was already early morning. He wanted to go straight to the railroad station but felt exhausted. He came to a big hotel and took a room there. He went up to his corridor, but to avoid a janitor on that floor who could see his face, he stepped into a restroom. There, he fell to his knees and cried; "first soundless," his cry turned into "dull sobbing that resembled the howling of a dog."

Leaving aside the question of a slightly built young woman's easily tumbling down a six-feet tall muscular man, a former sailor (when we met, already an old man in his early seventies and a Gulag survivor, Bystrolyotov still had a formidable physical presence), other actions that took place after that moment also lack verisimilitude. Thus, since he was in full mountaineer gear (let us recall Isolde's comment that he was dressed as if he was "about to scale Mt. Everest"), he should have had on him, if not a sleeping bag, at least a backpack. That would make him finding himself "stuck" with his back to the surface of the cliff next to impossible. His numbers don't add up either: falling face forward, then tumbling over his head, he already covered at least double his height. Thus, him climbing back some sixteen feet total makes his statement of "sliding down, first slowly, then faster and faster" hard to accept at face value.

What follows after he survived his fall also raises questions. Why would Isolde stay in town after pushing a man to his death? Wouldn't she want to clear the vicinity as soon as possible? Not only the timing of her suicide but its very motive does not sound convincing. In the note, she says that she has to "go away" because she cannot accept loving Iolanta only "contemplatively and incorporeally." But Iolanta had arranged to stay with her under the same roof, and, apparently, her new husband had no inkling about the sexual nature of their relationship. From Dmitri's own account, we also know that Isolde was sure Iolanta's new marriage was the end of Dmitri in her life. It begs the question then: since Isolde had just gotten rid of the only challenger for Iolanta's heart, why would she commit suicide now, when Iolanta had again become hers alone? Did she realize that in a world that considered homosexual relationships illegitimate and scornful, her beloved would never be exclusively hers? She would have to steal moments of happiness and share her with men.

A stylistic analysis of Dmitri's writing leads us to believe that the suicide note was written by no one but Dmitri himself. As elsewhere, in telling the story of Isolde's death, his writing style betrays his method. When he describes something he has experienced firsthand, his style is realistic and precise. When, for whatever reason, he wants to avoid telling the truth and substitutes it with fantasy, his writing is at its worst. The wording of Isolde's suicide note is not only overly melodramatic—unbearably stilted, at times even saccharine—but also devoid of psychological truth. In fact, if we pick up Dmitri's story after his disposal of the suicide note, his writing again regains stylistic simplicity and psychological verisimilitude. There is no doubt that his grief was genuine. Although he sought Isolde's death for, as he admits, being the woman who "broke" him, it is also true that she was the only woman he truly loved.

It looks as though, in reality, Isolde died not by her own hand and that Dmitri is responsible. Otherwise, why would he say that he feels guilty "before my own conscience"? He also hints at his wrongful actions when he reassures the reader that whatever he did to Isolde had not negatively affected the safety of the Soviet intelligence network in Switzerland. (Citing Bystrolyotov's statement in his memoirs that his hands are in blood, Dmitri's stepgrandson, who has nothing but admiration for him, also believes that Isolde's suicide is invented, that he killed her.) Did he push her down the cliff, as he had planned to begin with, or did he dispose of her by other means, including the help of his cohorts? He acknowledges being dangerous in having at his disposal a group of "desperate men." So, was someone like "Olaf" involved in Isolde's death? In the absence of any tangible evidence, Isolde Cameron's death will remain another unsolved mystery of Dmitri's life. [11]

The only part of his story that rings true regardless of the scenario that played out in real life are his feelings toward Isolde at the time of her death. As she came into his emotional life evoking the image of Madonna, the perfect mother, so she remained at the time of her demise. Looking at her dead face, still "dear and beloved," in his description, it resembles that of his mother—"audacious, proud, and willful." Even the handwriting, "confident and bold," on Isolde's farewell letter, which he most likely invented, gives the impression of having belonged to his mother.

There was one more reason, besides the personal one, why Dmitri felt compelled to remove Isolde from the premises of Colonel "Vivaldi": her presence there jeopardized the spy operation, for which the whole bogus marriage had been undertaken in the first place. And now it was time for direct action.

TWELVE | The Last Operations: Africa and Other Gray Areas

Little children! For not a thing in the world,
Do you ever go to Africa, to Africa for a stroll.

—KORNEY CHUKOVSKY, RUSSIAN POET

When "Colonel Vivaldi" was away on business, "Rona" always knew where he was going and how long he would be absent. She managed to make impressions of the keys to his safe successfully and learned how to open it. Most secret intelligence gathering was done by the big Service de renseignements (SR) posts in Lille, Metz, Marseilles, and Belfort. Each of these posts was responsible for operations within a given geographical area. Since the Belfort post was responsible for Rhineland and Switzerland, Dmitri assumed that "Vivaldi" frequently traveled there to deposit his next batch of information as he collected it through his network of agents. After picking up the documents and reports from them, before delivering it to the SR Belfort post, he would bring it all home and take a few days' breather. This short sojourn at his villa was the time when Dmitri acted. At night before going to bed, "Rona" left one of the windows open facing the garden, and Dmitri pulled himself into the room next to the study, opened the safe, and photographed the new material.[1]

To minimize his presence in Locarno, Dmitri avoided staying in local hotels. At nightfall, he came by car from Zurich, a three-hour drive. From time to time, he could rely on his former wife as a lookout while he photographed in the study. Understandably, she was often unavailable, and Dmitri would lock himself inside the room, leaving the window open in case he had to escape. He examined the area around the house to see whether he could shoot back if the colonel pursued him through the porch (Dmitri carried a pistol with a silencer for that eventuality).

Once in the study, to avoid leaving fingerprints, he put on thin surgeon's gloves, opened the safe, and spread the material of interest on the colonel's desk to photograph it. To shut out the flash of light from his camera and muffle the sound of the shutter clicking, which, in the silence of the night, could be heard in the bedroom (Iolanta had once checked it out and concurred), Dmitri placed a thick piece of cloth over the camera with a cutout through which to focus the lens.

Although he ran the risk of being detected every time, after a considerable stretch of successful sessions, he felt that the operation of penetrating French intelligence data could go on for a long time.

But soon things changed. There was an ever-increasing threat of an outbreak of war in Europe. The rearmament of the Wehrmacht and German intelligence activity abroad rose dramatically. This impelled French intelligence headquarters to pressure "Vivaldi" to speed up delivery of the sensitive data he collected from his agents. Now he had to skip Locarno and bring his take directly to the SR Belfort post.

That meant the end of Soviet intelligence efforts to intercept the French data. After just two of these direct deposits, the Center pressured Dmitri to do something about it. They told both their operatives, Dmitri and Iolanta, that they were "eating their bread free of charge," as the Russian proverb goes, and even accused them of "extreme absentmindedness and negligence." The Center demanded that they get the data at any cost. Dmitri was ordered to go to any risk to copy the contents of the safe in the "Vivaldi" study.

On Dmitri's cue, "Rona" made a fuss in front of her husband: after all, she had the right to have her husband home for at least one night. Yielding to her pressure, the colonel altered his route reports to cover up a lull along the way to the post so he could spend a night at home.

In the middle of one of these stolen nights, when Dmitri had already made his way into the study, on some pretext, Iolanta got out of bed and joined him to stand guard until he had finished photographing.

They heard quick steps beyond the door, but it was too late to escape. The door flung open. Seeing his wife and a man with a pistol aimed at him, a camera on his desk, and the vault of his safe opened, the colonel's first thought was that his wife was being held hostage.

But "Rona" asked Dmitri to let "Vivaldi" go. She didn't want him to be hurt. Since "Vivaldi" also drew his pistol, Dmitri told him it would be useless to shoot, for he was already compromised. Dmitri spoke French trying to imitate a British accent. (Even under such dire circumstances, he attempted to mislead the man by throwing out a "false flag," pretending that he was working not for Soviet, but for British, intelligence.)

He offered "Vivaldi" a calm finish to the game—to step forward and lie face down on the carpet.

There are at least two versions of what happened next. In his memoirs, Dmitri writes that "Vivaldi" admitted defeat. He couldn't shoot both his wife and the intruder; that would make it clear that he had been duped by foreign intelligence. He told "Rona" that he would stage a car accident in the mountains and asked her to keep her mouth shut about what had happened that night. And the next day he did exactly that—he drove off a cliff, getting intoxicated beforehand and placing an open bottle of cognac next to him.

However, Bystrolyotov's stepgrandson, Sergei Milashov, who had served as his sounding board over several years of Dmitri's writing of his memoirs, recalls that a different ending was conveyed to him. Bystrolyotov expressed his respect for the way the Frenchman had acted after his discovery that he had been fooled. His reputation irrevocably ruined, the proud officer dealt with his dishonor as a soldier—decisively. He stepped into the adjacent room and shot himself. When Dmitri and Iolanta rushed to him, they found him dead.[2]

(Since Bystrolyotov usually chooses an alias for real people in his memoir based not on a whim but with some hidden meaning, it may be suggested that one reason for him to nickname the French intelligence officer "Vivaldi," besides his stated reason of avoiding the disclosure of real names and moving the action from the allied country of France to the World War II enemy Italy, was a biographical reference. At the time when Bystrolyotov wrote his memoirs, in the early 1960s, back in the Soviet Union, he drew on his early knowledge of the life of composer Antonio Vivaldi, which for a long time had not been explored historically. In his 1949 review of Marc Pincherle's book, *Antonio Vivaldi et la musique instrumentale*, music critic Paul

Henry Lang wrote, "This curious artist arrived and departed wrapped in mystery; we do not know the exact dates of his birth and death and during his life he had no chroniclers.")[3]

After the death of "Vivaldi," "Rona" made no attempts to escape: it would be dangerous for her to leave the town without alerting the Locarno police. The ensuing investigation found no evidence of foul play on her part. She attended the funeral wearing a widow's black voile.

Soon, Iolanta received permission from the NKVD bosses to take a vacation. She decided to go to the south of France. Before leaving Switzerland, she and Dmitri met in a café near the Zurich station. Waiting for their trains to arrive, his to Paris and hers to Nice, they talked. He told her that he felt badly about the part she had to play in the plot against the Frenchman. He justified it with the indisputable fact that, after all, spy work consists of "lousy episodes like that."

She told him that she was totally disgusted with such work and that she was leaving him. After her vacation, she planned to go to Moscow to live and to do some "little accountant's job." She added that she was tired of living altogether.

In her view, the times they lived in were not for her but for people like him, adding, "I repeat what I told you some time ago. You're a murderer."

After a long silence, he asked her whose life he had taken. "You killed me, 'Vivaldi,' and Isolde," she replied. "You pushed us against the wall. Isolde didn't have a choice. You killed her, you . . ." (here, again, it seems that Dmitri is alluding to Isolde's suicide).

"I hate you," Iolanta added. "For Isolde. For everyone. I'm going to Russia to die. I want to die, do you understand? To die!"

They parted badly. He realized it was his fault that he had lost Iolanta. He had no one to blame for that: he himself had pushed her away and tore apart all the ties that bound them together, seemingly forever, just because he needed to please "his own evil god." The context makes it unequivocally clear that he meant the evil god he served, the evil god of Soviet foreign intelligence.

But Dmitri was destined to remain firmly in the hands of his "evil god" for a long time still. And that god pushed him in a totally new direction. In their book, *Mitrokhin Archive II: The KGB and the World*, except for the Comintern's unsuccessful attempts to turn the South African Communist Party into an instrument for stirring revolution in the country, Andrew and Mitrokhin do not mention any Soviet foreign intelligence activities on the African continent in the 1930s. However, at least one Soviet operative, Dmitri Bystrolyotov, went to Africa on a spy mission at that time.[4]

This omission in *Mitrokhin Archive II* is understandable. When Vasili Mitrokhin looked into Bystrolyotov's file, documents related to his African trip, together with many others, had been destroyed following his arrest in 1938. That is why, in 1990, when Bystrolyotov's name as an outstanding Soviet spy was made public in a three-part *Pravda* article, its author, V. Snegirev, who had been given access to the Lubyanka files, dismissed his African adventures as too exotic to believe.[5] However, after Sergei Milashov, Bystrolyotov's stepgrandson, contacted the journalist with overwhelming evidence from his private archive—manuscripts of Bystrolyotov's memoirs, a series of African notes published in 1963 in the journal *Azia i Afrika segodnia* (*Asia and Africa Today*), as well as his numerous Africa-related photographs and ink sketches—when preparing his newspaper publication for inclusion in a book, Snegirev removed the dismissive passage. Since then, all official (and unofficial) accounts of Bystrolyotov's life include his African experience. Moreover, they commonly acknowledge that he made not one but two trips to the continent, a fact he himself had underscored when we met.[6]

According to both Milashov and Dmitri's former Gulag inmates, he made his first trip to Africa to escape from the imminent danger of arrest in Germany after his agent "Greta" was captured by the Gestapo. No details of that mishap are to be found anywhere either in Bystrolyotov's writings or the KGB files. However, when Soviet intelligence selected an operative to carry out the physically challenging African assignment, besides his stamina and strength as a seasoned sailor in the past, and his ability to take on the unforgiving impact of the continent's harsh climatic and terrain conditions, Dmitri was chosen because he was already familiar with the territory, a fact disclosed in his "Generous Hearts." During that first trip, fleeing imminent arrest by the Gestapo, he had been able to penetrate the milieu of the Tuaregs, the seminomadic inhabitants of the Sahara region. He earned their trust and befriended the chief of one of the tribes, with whom he

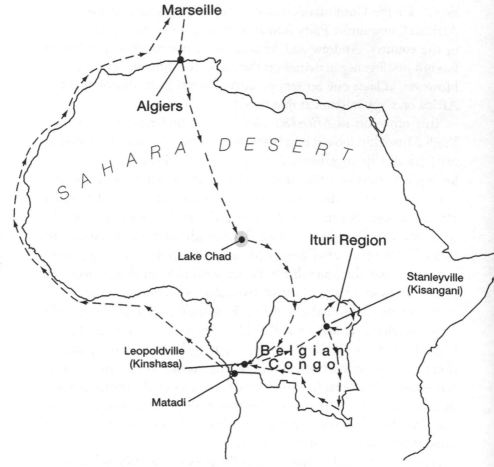

Marseille

Algiers

S A H A R A   D E S E R T

Lake Chad

Ituri Region

Stanleyville
(Kisangani)

Belgian
Congo

Leopoldville
(Kinshasa)

Matadi

Bystrolyotov's African Trip (1935–1936)

lived for a few months. His minute descriptions of the everyday life and customs of these indigenous people, whom he admired for their dignity and wholesomeness, together with several surviving gouache sketches of them, leave no doubt about the veracity of his adventure.

Of course, in his published work, duly censored by the KGB, there is no direct indication of the purpose of his second African trip. Moreover, to avoid disclosure of that clandestine intelligence operation and Bystrolyotov's part in it, the journal editors resorted to a rather clumsy cover-up. They prefaced the publication of his notes with the statement that, although the author made the trip himself and the material is nonfictional (aimed, in the spirit of the time, to "expose the imperialist exploitation of the indigenous African people"), the story is written from the point of view of a fictional Dutch artist, "van Egmont," who came to Africa in search of exotic subjects for his drawings (on the reasons for Dmitri's choice of the name later).

In time, the journal notes and the drawings became part of Dmitri's novel, *V staroi Afrike* (*In Old Africa*). In it, the author gives his fictional protagonist a more compelling reason to travel to the most remote and unexplored regions of Africa. He makes him a reporter for the European department of the International News and Photo Information Agency, "exploited by the bourgeois press thirsty for vulgar sensations." (In his unpublished work, Bystrolyotov reveals that this was his true cover during the African mission.)[7]

There are numerous other indications in both the journal notes and the novel that the traveler is, in fact, Dmitri himself. In both texts, he gives his protagonist traits of his own personality and emotional makeup, as well as his most important biographical highlights: the "always absent" father, the demanding mother obsessed with social justice, a youth full of hardships and perilous experiences, including a near drowning in the sea. In addition, sloppy editorial work sporadically reveals glimpses of the writer's personality, not his protagonist's. For example, in one place the narration suddenly shifts from third person singular to first person plural. In another, the Dutch protagonist suggests calling a dog Polkan or Zhuchka, actually Russian names for a dog. In yet another, forgetting that he is a photo correspondent with no military background, the man warns one of his fellow travelers who behaves aggressively toward him: "I shoot without missing while standing, lying down, or hanging upside down. I never go anywhere without my weapon and open fire without aiming."[8]

Thanks to all these and other editorial oversights, along with many keenly observed and minutely described scenes of overcoming the hardships of crossing the difficult African terrain, both the travel notes and the novel read like Bystrolyotov's African travelogue.

Of course, neither Soviet publication mentions the true reason for Bystrolyotov's travel to the continent. But his unpublished work does. In both manuscripts, part of his memoirs titled "Tsepi i niti" ("Chains and Threads") and his rejected screenplay "Generous Hearts," he does spell out the purpose of his African trip (which may well be one of the reasons his screenplay was turned down).

Thus, from bits and pieces of information scattered throughout the pages of his published and unpublished work, the following picture emerges.

Some time toward the end of 1935 (at least this is the year marked on the back of the photographs and sketches taken during his trip), Dmitri left Europe for an extended trip to Africa. This time, unlike his previous involvements as a recruiter and handler of foreign agents, his mission was strictly one of reconnaissance and information gathering. He was charged with his first and most urgent task: to establish the credibility of the French promise, in the event hostilities broke out in Europe, to mobilize and transport to the continent a half million black mercenaries from the French and Belgian colonies in Africa, one hundred thousand in the first echelon and the rest in four others that followed. In one part of his writing, Bystrolyotov identifies the source of this promise in general terms as the "French military"; in another, it is more concrete—French Foreign Minister Louis Barthou. It appears that Barthou had made such a promise in the course of preliminary negotiations of what later became the Franco-Soviet Treaty of Mutual Assistance, signed later, after his death in October 1934.

Since Soviet military specialists had their doubts about the feasibility of drafting and arming such a huge number of troops in Africa, Dmitri had to check on the ground the validity of the promise. In conjunction with this part of his assignment, he had to inspect the mountains in the center of the Sahara and gauge the moods of the local population, mostly Tuaregs, determining whether there was any danger that with the outbreak of war the locals could rise up against the French and thus impede troop mobilization. Since the sea paths were expected to be cut off by the German fleet, it was assumed that transportation of the projected African troops to Europe would be done overland.[9]

The other part of Dmitri's assignment was to visit the industrial region of Katanga in the Belgian Congo. His task in the area, characterized as one that "supplied the capitalist world with copper," was to gauge the political situation in the area in terms of stability of the Belgian administration. Although the initial Comintern hope for the African revolution was placed on South Africa as the most developed and industrialized country on the continent, there are indications that later the Comintern's attention turned toward possibilities of appealing to the most oppressed people in other areas south of the Sahara and encouraging them toward revolution. However, Dmitri's orders stipulated that his mission was strictly exploratory. He was specifically cautioned that he was going to Katanga not for "propaganda but for observation." Therefore, he should be careful not to "spill the beans [and to] abstain from any sharp words of criticism, and even more so, from any action, always keeping himself in the shadow, on the second plane."[10]

The third component of his assignment was more obscure: he was to "inspect the so-called white spots on the map of the Belgian Congo and determine what was hidden behind this colonialist term."[11]

And thus he set out on his six-month-long African journey. Riding in a jeep with a trailer, which, besides supplies of fuel and water, carried luggage and mail, and in the company of a driver, a guard, and three other passengers, he traveled along a north–south caravan route from French Algiers across the Sahara Desert, through the Ahaggar Mountains, a highland region in the central Sahara near the Tropic of Cancer, which was largely a rocky desert.[12]

He moved farther south, through Tanezrouft, the hottest and most arid and desolate part of the Sahara, in his description, "a desert within a desert, that is, an absolute desert within a relative desert, a dead zone five hundred kilometers long, where during fifteen days on a caravan, you not only won't come upon a well or a puddle but not even any grass. Life in Tanezrouft is totally impossible for a human or for a camel; to lose your direction and prolong your travel for even a few hours spells inevitable death. It's a dead tsardom of merciless heat and fruitless stone."

Naturally, when, in the vicinity of Lake Chad, he came out of Tanezrouft, he felt ecstatic. He then crossed the Sahel Belt, a semi-arid tropical savanna region, and eventually, moving southward, he arrived at the banks of the Ubangi River, one of the major tributaries of the Congo River. There, he and his travel companions boarded a small and dilapidated steamboat, which took them downstream to Leopoldville (now Kinshasa), the capital of the Belgian Congo (now Democratic Republic of the Congo).

After resting in Leopoldville, he traveled in a small truck across the country to Stanleyville (now Kisangani). There, he spent some time preparing himself for a long journey through the Ituri region of Congo. He studied geographical and aerographic maps of the region, bought supplies, and hired a team of twenty-three porters and guards. Along with them, he received training in rifle shooting at the local shooting gallery. He also prepared for health-threatening eventualities. At the local hospital, he procured sufficient antidotes for sleeping sickness, a disease endemic to the region and transmitted by the tsetse fly. Finally, when he felt ready, Dmitri and his party traveled through the northeastern part of the country, the Ituri Province. They followed in the steps of Henry Morton Stanley, a Anglo-American journalist and adventurer, who, hired by Belgian king Leopold II, had explored the Congo basin and, at the end of the nineteenth century, had searched for David Livingstone, the British explorer of central Africa. First, they traveled in pirogues along the Ituri River. Then, they went on foot, walking through both the fabled Ituri tropical rain forest and the savanna. It was a hard undertaking. Often, they walked in a cloud of mosquitoes and butterflies; it was hard to breathe, with the humidity at times reaching 98 percent. In this fashion, making stops in the forest and protecting themselves during the night by keeping bonfires ablaze, they crossed more than three hundred miles of the Ituri region.

While it is hard to imagine that the Soviet foreign intelligence bosses would have given him such considerable means and time (nearly six months) for a personal adventure in the jungle, Dmitri hints at a possible reason for Soviet interest in the region: after World War I, oil was found in the swamps of the Ituri rain forest. In his unpublished writings, he discloses that he had to walk through the Ituri forest, west to east on a certain route, and collect information on conditions on the ground regarding what to expect and how to prepare once the area was opened for industrial oil extraction. Two foreign companies, one Belgian and one American, had expressed interest in stepping into the area shortly. Belgians had the advantage of already having a line of trading posts in the forest. An area close to Belgian trading post 201, where samples of oil had been found, was occupied by the Mbuti (then known as the Pygmies). Dmitri visited them and became acquainted with their king, Bubu.

The Ituri expedition ended back in Stanleyville. Shortly afterward, Dmitri moved on. His next destination was the southern Congolese province of Katanga, the eastern part of which was a mining region, rich in precious metals and minerals, such as copper, cobalt, tin, radium, uranium, and diamonds. Although there is no direct disclosure of it in his writings, judging by his Katanga itinerary, Dmitri's assignment was to collect as much data as possible on the industrial capabilities of this important source of strategic materials in this part of the world. Among other places, he visited copper ore mines and ore-dressing plants in the towns of Kolwesi and Jadotville (now Likasi), sulfur mines and a sulfur-purifying plant in Elisabethville (now Lubumbashi), coal mines along the Lukuga River and in Luena, a magnetic ore-developing factory in Kasenga, uranium ore mines in Shinkolobwe, tin ore in Lubudi, and cobalt in Ruash. He noted the number of trains per day loaded with purified zinc, cadmium, wolfram, and tantalum being exported from the region.[13]

To avoid attracting attention to himself by photographing the plants, which at the time was difficult to do inconspicuously, Dmitri resorted to the sketch-artist cover he had used back in his Geneva days when hunting for ROSSI. He also made notes about the factories. After hours of observation, calculating how many railroad cars of raw material came out of the factories during three shifts around the clock, he penciled his estimates of yearly production numbers in the margins of his sketches.[14]

On the question of the Belgian administration's stability in Congo, along the way, Dmitri collected information on labor strikes and unrest at the mines and plants run by the Belgian mining company Union Minière du Haut Katanga. According to his account, such disturbances had taken place sporadically in 1921, 1926, 1927, 1931, and 1932. In his published work, he also gives an eyewitness report about a clash between workers and the police at a railroad repair plant in Upper Katanga at the time of his visit in 1935. At the same time, he also registers the relative prosperity of former tribesmen once they found employment in the Belgian-run industries.[15]

He reached a negative conclusion about the ability of French and Belgian African colonies to supply the European theater with a half-million-strong army in the event of war with Germany. Observing the indigenous way of life firsthand and making indirect inquiries along the way, he became totally convinced that Africa did not have such resources. He also consulted some published sources, which confirmed the decline of the local population at a staggering pace. Thus, he cites a series of articles by Marcel Sauvage titled "The Secrets of French Equatorial Africa" in the Paris newspaper *L'Intransigeant*. According to the French journalist, in 1911, the population of Congo was twelve million; ten years later, it went down to seven and a half million; and in another ten years, to only about two and a half million. That is, over twenty years, 80 percent of the population had disappeared. This depopulation had taken place due to indiscriminate violence against indigenous people, starvation, birthrate decline, and rampant disease, especially tuberculosis and sleeping sickness.[16]

While chatting with European officials based in Congo, Dmitri learned about the mechanics of a mobilization campaign in Africa. It was accomplished primarily by use of force. After nightfall, a village was surrounded by troops. After recruits were selected, during the day they were driven under convoy to an induction center. Sometimes, they had to be bound by rope and dragged there. At that point, the conscripts, Congolese tribesmen, considered themselves as good as dead. Their relatives even held funeral services for them, and for good reason: traumatized by fear, the drastic change of circumstances in their lives, and poor treatment, the recruits died in scores. One third of them had to be written off because of mass tuberculosis. Eventually, out of twenty recruits, only one would become a full-fledged soldier. Only a few made it to the end of their service stint. So, there was no way that the administration could possibly recruit a half million African troops. Dmitri concluded that the human resources for such an endeavor were lacking in all of Africa.[17]

Boarding a ship in the port of Matadi, Dmitri returned to Europe. He was glad to leave the continent, not so much because physical exhaustion resulting from the trying conditions of his African trip had taken a toll on him, but because, all too often, he also suffered psychologically. What tortured him most was having to contain his moral indignation when he witnessed inhuman treatment of the native population at the hands of the colonizers. Once, a group of white men aboard the boat moving along the Congo River had entertained themselves by tricking an unarmed black tribesman into jumping into the muddy water of the river to wrestle a giant crocodile. In the Ituri rain forest, a team of Africans rolled huge tree trunks as a foreman prodded them by inflicting pain on their bodies with sticks. On yet another occasion, an indigenous pregnant woman was beaten for working too slowly in the fields.

On several occasions, Dmitri was unable to control himself when he witnessed such scenes. Although he had clearly been instructed by his superiors to keep a low profile and not to interfere with any actions around him, so as to avoid blowing his cover as an impartial reporter on the African continent, he could not help protesting cruelty and correcting injustices. The urge to correct social injustice instilled by his mother in his early years became an uncontrollable reflex. At one point, he even wondered about his inability to restrain himself: "Why am I suffering?" he asked himself. "I'm not a colonizer." Once, he found himself shouting at an abuser, "Don't you dare! Don't you dare!"—the very same words his mother had shouted to an officer who was mistreating his coachman back in the summer of 1915.

The African trip produced many other indelible impressions on Dmitri that would later find their way into his book about Africa. In it, his descriptions of the inhuman treatment of indigenous people rival those of Joseph Conrad in *Heart of Darkness,* the action of which takes place in Congo as well. Dmitri's book also records the author's admiration and reverence for the culture of indigenous Africans—the Tuaregs and the Pygmies.

Apparently, shortly after his African trip, Dmitri made another trip, about which his KGB file is equally silent. His Berlin spymaster, Boris Bazarov, called on him to come to the United States, where he had been appointed head of the illegal *rezidentura.* The move was unexpected because, under unclear circumstances, the body of Bazarov's predecessor, Valentin Markin, had been found on a New York street. It was assumed at the Center that he had fallen victim to some gangster infighting. Bazarov's group had been successful in recruiting agents who had immediate access to State Department employees as well as a "source" with ties to those surrounding President Roosevelt who obtained "unique information about the American ruling circles in the period of ripening military conflict in Europe."[18]

Judging by brief references in his memoirs, Dmitri spent some time in New York. According to Milashov, Dmitri's task was mostly technological intelligence and American know-how. He also gave a helping hand to Bazarov in weaving a new spy network in the United

States. According to Hede Massing's memoirs, about that time, Dmitri's frequent assistant, Joseph Leppin, was in New York. However, there is no mention of Bystrolyotov (or anyone who resembled him) in her memoirs.[19]

His last operation that has archival support is one he took part in sometime in midsummer 1936, after his travels outside the European continent. For this operation, he again had to brush up on his sex appeal. Now he had to put his male charms to use not for cultivation and eventual recruitment of a new agent but as bait for someone who was interested not so much in money as in love and thrills.

The agent in question was Florica Titulescu, a Romanian high society lady. According to ROSSI, with whom Dmitri kept in touch from time to time and who sold him the contact with the lady, she had excellent connections. She was related to Nicolae Titulescu, the Romanian minister of foreign affairs, and she was a lover of the Romanian chief of staff (apparently, General Nicolae Samsonovici, who held the position from December 1934 to February 1937). Thus, she had access to highly valuable Romanian political and military information. As ROSSI also informed Dmitri, she worked for French intelligence, to which, via its agents in Switzerland, she passed Romanian diplomatic and military secrets. The most valuable of these were documents reflecting the political intentions of Romania toward the Soviet Union.[20]

ROSSI also cautioned Dmitri that, though wary of Germans, Florica played footsie with German agents in an attempt to secure a cushy place for herself in case Germany prevailed in winning Romania over to its side in the event of a military confrontation in Europe.[21]

Dmitri initially approached Florica at the bar of a Zurich hotel. He describes her as a "shapely, somewhat plump, brunette of dark complexion with a beautiful, albeit slightly coarse, face." As he had with ROSSI and other foreign agents, he used the same "false flag," introducing himself as "Joe Perelly," an intelligence agent working for Japan.[22]

Soon they arranged to meet over dinner, and sitting at the table, they began making the initial arrangements. With a smile on her face, Florica cautioned Dmitri that if he was going to cheat on her in some way, her powerful friends in politics and intelligence in adjacent countries would make sure that, after the very first trick on his part, "the day [he] tried to leave this country [would] be [his] last one." And he replied in the same tone that the same fate would await her if she played any tricks on him. Moreover, she wouldn't even make it to the border; she would be shot on the spot.[23]

It didn't resemble a business meeting between two counterparts as much as it did verbal foreplay between prospective lovers. At the end of their dinner, quite taken with Dmitri, Florica promised full cooperation in exchange for implied physical intimacy between them.

As he began working with her, Florica's demands for sex as a prerequisite for her full cooperation became tiresome to Dmitri. Although her lover, General Samsonovici, was not in truth a "decrepit old man," as Dmitri refers to him, nevertheless, born in 1877, he was twenty-four years older than Dmitri. Florica's amorousness wore Dmitri down; he tried to avoid intimacy with her as much as he could.[24]

Finally, he did something that his superiors characterized as carelessness and disregard for the cause. To avoid Florica's sexual demands (and without informing his spymaster, Theodor Mally), on their next date, he replaced himself with another Soviet spy, his old collaborator, Henri Pieck.

Florica threw a fit. She thought of Dmitri's actions as a trick, perhaps because she found the substitute inadequate. Although Pieck was also a ladies' man, he was not as attractive as Dmitri, because, for one thing, he was middle-aged. When Mally heard about it, he disciplined Dmitri for his prank on Florica. Although he agreed with Dmitri's assessment of her, he found his actions irresponsible and unacceptable.

For the first time in Dmitri's spy career, his job took such a toll on him that he talked back to his superiors, whose orders he had always carried out unquestioningly. He rebelled against their having used him as a sex trap, merely a tool in the callous hands of his bosses. It did not help in the least that, as Soviet high-ranking defector Alexander Orlov reveals in his book, Soviet intelligence operatives had contempt for their comrades-in-arms who were used as sex bait, nicknaming such spies "matchmakers."

When Mally reprimanded him for his poor handling of Florica, Dmitri replied angrily and gloomily, "But I'm a human being, Theodor, and I'm a decent man. Tell me, does an intelligence operative have the right to be decent and preserve his self-respect? I'll never become a gigolo."[25]

But Mally wouldn't take no for an answer. He agreed that Florica was a difficult "source" to handle. Granted, she involved herself in spying out of love for strong emotions and often acted before thinking. True, she was capricious and, at times, unbalanced. Yet, she was a very important "source" who had access to top classified material that was urgently needed.

Indeed, at the time of the action, midsummer 1936, with international tensions in Europe remaining high, the question of whose side Romania, an immediate neighboring country, would take in a potential military conflict with Germany was strategically important to the Soviet Union. The documents of the Romanian General Staff and Foreign Ministry procured through Florica could help to shed light on both the military potential of Romania and the country's diplomatic positioning among the major European power brokers.[26]

Understandably, writing his screenplay in the mid-1960s, Dmitri characterizes Romanian intentions as invariably hostile toward the USSR. The Soviet audience knew nothing about Romanian peace efforts of the early 1930s. The Soviet media always portrayed pre–World War II Romania as anti-Bolshevik, beginning with its severing of relations with Soviet Russia in 1918.

However, in truth, for a long time before eventually siding with Germany in 1940, Romania had remained on the tipping point in its orientation between Germany and the USSR. King Carol II tried to keep the country sovereign and intact territorially, which was not easy. The Soviet Union never agreed to the annexation of Bessarabia and Northern Bukovina in the wake of World War I. Hungary wanted Transylvania back, and Bulgaria claimed Southern Dobrudja. Romania hoped for French support, although it also tried to maintain good relations with Great Britain and Germany.[27]

This balancing act was complicated by infighting among Romania's own internal political forces, which tried to influence the country's foreign policy in favor of different European power brokers. But at the time of the Soviet foreign intelligence actions in which Dmitri took part, ostensibly summer 1936, Romania was closer than ever to cooperation with the Soviet Union. After informal diplomatic contacts between Commissar for Foreign Affairs Litvinov and Romanian Foreign Minister Nicolae Titulescu at the League of Nations in June 1934, Romania formally recognized the USSR. But, as was the case with France, fear of Bolshevism was an obstacle to further Romanian rapprochement with the Soviets. Furthermore, Moscow still refused to accept the annexation of Bessarabia.[28]

But the Franco-Soviet pact and the Soviet-Czechoslovak pact of May 1935 greatly affected Romanian–Soviet relations. Signing the pact with Czechoslovakia, the Soviets committed, in case of a German attack on that country, to send Red Army troops to the rescue. To do this, they had to cross Romania, with or without its permission. This development forced Romania to turn toward the idea of collective security proposed by the Soviets and to come up with some military arrangements with them. Titulescu was afraid that lack of cooperation from Romania would provoke the Soviets to invade the country and take back Bessarabia. (He also predicted that, if collective security efforts failed, the Germans would make a pact with the Soviets against Poland. As history revealed, both predictions proved true, the first in 1940, and the second a year earlier.)[29]

The Romanian Army supported Titulescu. Members of the Romanian General Staff became pro-Soviet not because of their political views but because the only strong ally, France, was too far from Romanian borders, and the USSR was their country's neighbor. The younger army officers even studied Russian to better communicate with the prospective ally.[30]

Beginning in summer 1935, the General Staff documents reveal a dramatic change in strategy with the redirection of all Romanian efforts toward securing its western borders and leaving very little protection with the borders of the Soviet Union. Moreover, in June 1936, Romania informed Czechoslovakia and Yugoslavia that Soviet troops were allowed to cross its territory. Both countries were Romania's allies in the Little Entente, an alliance formed in the early 1920s to prevent Hungary from attempting to reclaim parts of these countries' territories that had become theirs as a result of the collapse of the Austro-Hungarian Empire after its defeat in the course of World War I. France supported the alliance by signing treaties with each member country. The Romanian General Staff even worked out a provisional itinerary for Soviet troops crossing Romanian territory in the event they moved to assist Czechoslovakia.[31]

The situation became even more complicated due to political pressure at home and from abroad. Although at the time he sought an alliance with Nazi Germany, Romanian General Ion Victor Antonescu, chief of the Romanian General Staff in 1933 and 1934, was a regular army general, he exerted considerable political influence and claimed the position of defense minister (which King Carol's government granted him the next year). And it was clear what he had on his mind: among various documents procured through Florica was a photocopy of a private report from Antonescu to Ribbentrop, Hitler's Reich Minister Ambassador-Plenipotentiary at Large (1935–36).

Eventually, the German and Italian governments, naturally unhappy with Titulescu's foreign policies, forced the king not only to dismiss the foreign minister from his position but to exile him from the country. (Titulescu left the country first for Switzerland then for France, where he died a few years later.) As the Spanish civil war broke out in the middle of summer 1936, Hitler and Mussolini sided with General Franco, creating the balance of power in Europe and making Romania's immediate future even more uncertain.[32]

Thus, while Mally agreed that Dmitri had the right to some line of decency that he did not have to cross, he asked Dmitri to be patient for the sake of the cause that the whole Soviet spy group in Switzerland was fighting for at the time. He suggested that a better way to handle Florica for now would be to calm her down by promising her things.

Finally, he vowed to find and prepare a substitute for Dmitri, not only because Pieck was not a good one on account of his age, but his manners were too mild for Florica, whose imagination required someone more edgy and flamboyant.

Taking Mally's advice, Dmitri began cultivating Florica with talk of some future together, depending on his prosperity. He made some vague promises to her and told her that he wanted to create a truly worry-free life with her, for which he needed to make some money. He asked her to put him in touch with her agents, so he could buy some political information for Japanese intelligence.

And Florica took the bait. She introduced him to another agent, who called himself "Don Luis de Bourbon." According to her, the impeccably dressed man, complete with tuxedo, a monocle, and a set of diamond rings on his fingers, was the illegitimate son of King Alfonso XIII of Spain. (Most likely, the man had invented it. It is known that, in addition to seven children recognized as his own, the king had three illegitimate children, but none of them fit the profile of "Don Louis." The man called himself "Prince of Navarre." Dmitri describes him as bearing a physical resemblance to the famous French comic actor Fernandel. This suggests that "Don Louis" based his claim of relation to the king on their mutual close physical resemblance to the movie star.)[33]

Florica informed Dmitri that "Don Louis" traded in Spanish diplomatic ciphers. He could also provide Italian and, perhaps, German ones. She claimed he had many contacts with shady personalities everywhere, including Nazi Germany. He had even tried to become a go-between for Franco's Spanish government and the Nazis.[34]

Toward the end of 1936, further political developments in Europe became even more worrisome: In October, Franco became dictator of Spain and was declared the head of state. Then the Rome–Berlin Axis alliance was formed, followed in November by Germany's signing of the Anti-Comintern Pact with Japan to fight international Communism. Mally felt that if Dmitri's group operated in Switzerland for too long a time, it would inevitably appear on the radar of counterintelligence. It was time to move the group to another operational front.[35]

But, by that point in his life, Dmitri had become fed up with spying. He wanted to quit as soon as possible and go home. And he asked for permission to return.

THIRTEEN | The Return

Even the smoke of our fatherland is sweet and pleasant to us.

—ALEXANDER GRIBOEDOV, *WOE FROM WIT*

All spies are expendable.

—SUN TZU, *THE ART OF WAR*

Dear Comrade ARTEM:

I'm tired, sick, and I can't go on working without a serious rest. From day to day, I feel a growing depletion of my strength, which, naturally, lowers the quality of my work, causing sloppiness in technique. Besides, because of overwork, symptoms of the illness I suffered in 1922–1923, my depression, have reappeared. Resting on my shoulders are business of great importance and the fates of several people. And meanwhile . . . fatigue and fits of depression overwhelm me. I work only by nerves and exerting my will power. [I work] without the slightest joy of success or love of the activity, with a constant thought: "It would be good to lie down in the evening and not get up in the morning." I have been abroad seventeen years, of them eleven years on our work, of which six years in the underground. <u>Is this not enough to warrant my replacement?</u> [emphasis added]

With comradely greetings, Hans[1]

The full text of Dmitri's petition addressed to the legal NKVD *rezident* in Berlin, Boris Berman (code name ARTEM), appeared for the first time in *Pravda* at the height of Gorbachev's campaign for openness. None of the subsequent FSB publications tell the full truth about the reason(s) for Dmitri's return to Russia. One of them states that he returned to Russia after completing his assignments. Another implies that he was recalled and given a desk job for a serious mistake—the loss of one of his passports. Yet another states that he came home to rest. In the last official SVR posting, his letter pleading that he be allowed to leave is sanitized: it conveniently omits the last phrase. Since the new KGB's current policy of cleaning up its public image includes airbrushing the historical records to omit prior rough treatment of even its own heroes, the pleading and desperate tone of the concluding sentence makes it clear that this letter was not his first attempt to leave the service.[2]

In the summer of 1936, a half year after Iolanta had left for Moscow, Dmitri began feeling restless. He wanted to return to Moscow, now for good. In his memoirs, he recalls his yearning for it as strongly as the three sisters of Chekhov's play do. He re-creates his mood at the time in his unpublished screenplay, "Generous Hearts." His alter ego, the Soviet spy Sergei, says to his colleagues, "I'm dreaming of the moment before I leave for Moscow, when I can sneak onto the bank of some lake and hurl my pistol into the water."[3]

Many factors led to Dmitri's decision to quit spying and return to Russia. First, he had grown bored with the job. The lure of adventure, so strong when he had accepted the offer to go underground, had subsided significantly. By temperament, he needed tangible results and craved instant gratification for his efforts. But spy work was quiet and tedious, often demanding patience and endurance, qualities that he lacked. As seasoned Soviet spy Samsonov, his first spymaster, expressed it: "Intelligence is risk and work without firm assurance of success . . . There's no such thing as victory in intelligence work. Everything is fluid, everything changes, and at no stage of the game can you say calmly: it's a victory."[4]

Now, from the vantage point of his law and medical studies, his spy work felt primitive. Spying employed only a fraction of his abilities and talents. Back in 1930, when he had accepted the OGPU offer to go underground, he considered the move a temporary departure from the path he had envisioned for his life when he was young—to be a painter and a writer. Sporadically, between carrying out his assignments, he managed to take classes here and there: now at the Academy of the Arts in Berlin and then at the same in Paris. He also collected material for his writing. But, as any true artist does sooner or later, he eventually realized that the artist's calling requires giving oneself fully to one's talent. He cites the strong pull of his artistic calling as the main reason he was reluctant to join the Party and "even more so," he emphasizes, "to go through the formalities of becoming part of the OGPU cadres." (In time, he would pay dearly for his reluctance: the absence of proper records documenting his service to his country as a spy would—not once, but many times—bring him to the verge of peril, quite in accordance with a Russian proverb, "Without a piece of paper, you're just a tiny insect" [*Bez bumazhki—ty bukashka*]).[5]

The ethical side of his work was the most unpleasant. Eventually, he became totally disgusted with the trade's sordid practices. Decades later, he would conclude that "like imprisonment, working in intelligence disfigures your soul and life not only directly but also indirectly; it similarly affects the souls and lives of strangers who are forced to become involved in it." An idealist at heart, it seems that he had initially bought into Cheka founder and head Felix Dzerzhinsky's definition of an ideal Chekist as a man with a "cold head, a passionate heart, and clean hands." For the most part living abroad, Dmitri may have talked himself into believing that the Cheka lived up to Dzerzhinsky's expectations. Of course, Cheka practices have hardly ever been either lawful or bloodless: the Red Terror unleashed by the organization soon after the Bolshevik takeover of power claimed many innocent victims.[6]

Even Dmitri's counterpart ROSSI, an international black market code dealer, sensed that Dmitri had been holding on to some moral principles that were incompatible with spying. He told him frankly, "I don't consider you a novice, but I always feel that among us, true spies, you're an odd man. To you, this is not ethical, or that is not nice. You're stuffed with principles like a sack with potatoes. What kind of principles can you have when working with people without principles?"[7]

Although there is no evidence that Dmitri ever hesitated to handle his "source" in whatever fashion was required for the success of the operation at hand, he often acted against his own moral code and felt uneasy about it. Though the personal gun he had been awarded after handling British agent Oldham extols his lack of empathy toward the man, "For merciless battle against the counterrevolution," he was quite aware of the inhumanity and baseness of his occupation, often referring to it as "despicable work." Talking to Iolanta before her departure for Moscow, he admitted that he had often acted cruelly toward his agents, but he had done it because he believed that the high ideals of happiness for all humanity for which he was fighting justified his trespasses.[8]

But, when he told her how he had made a clean break with his German agent, Dorothea Müller, by staging his own death and how Doris had nearly died of grief, Iolanta reacted with sympathy for the deceived woman. Writing about that episode, Dmitri admits that Iolanta's reaction made him blush in shame. She told him that although his revolutionary zeal allegedly justified cruelty, he would pay a dear price for his actions in the long run. She even went so far as to foretell his future: a time would come when he would discover that the "wonderful garden" he had been heading for by "swimming across a stormy river, risking his own life, and drowning those who happen to be in his way" had existed only in his imagination.[9]

When Dmitri tried to defend himself, citing Don Quixote as an example of a hero, perhaps a comic hero, but still a hero, she replied that, unlike Don Quixote, he didn't deserve sympathy. "You're baser than him," she said. "He attacked only windmills. And you are more contemptible, for he was Sancho Panza's master, and you are his obedient servant." Describing this scene, Dmitri admits that although his inner voice told him she was right, he replied, "You are wrong, and my future will show you."[10]

In addition to "sources" he had to keep in check, sometimes by threat of blackmail, on at least two occasions he found himself in unpredictable moral entanglements involving ordinary human nature that refused to conform to the highly controlled conditions of spy work. After his successful completion of the "Monaldi" entrapment, in which "Greta" was not revealed as complicit, when she asked Dmitri what she should do next, he suggested that she stay with the man who genuinely loved her. "Greta" burst into tears: "You've used me, and now you're dumping me like a piece of rag. Shame! Not on me, on you!"[11]

It was only natural for a young and gentle woman to fall for her handsome recruiter and want to be with him. After all, although he had no intimate designs on her for himself, when he recruited her, he could hardly be totally unaware that the young lady was greatly taken with his male charms.

Another uninvited romantic entanglement involved his assistant Erica Weinstein, whose marriage to Leppin, as was indicated earlier, was most likely just a cover. Dmitri writes about an episode concerning Mally (his immediate supervisor in a number of operations), in whom, quite clearly, he saw a father figure. Mally admonished him for allowing personal feelings to develop between him and a member of his operative group.

"There must be no amorous feelings of any kind in an intelligence group," Mally said. "Think this way: if two female operatives fall in love with their male comrade-in-arms, right away a rivalry starts, then jealousy and discord. There will no longer be unity in the group! A crack forms, and sooner or later, we will all be exposed and perish. Or two men fall in love with the same woman. That's even worse. Exposure follows even faster."[12]

(As is now known, Mally spoke from experience. He had himself fallen in love with one of the young female agents recruited by Soviet foreign intelligence. His feelings weren't reciprocated, which drove him to excessive drinking. In order to keep him in check, the Center forced him to marry a woman he couldn't stand but who kept him under control.)[13]

Quite in the spirit of the revolutionary zeal of the 1920s in the Soviet Union, Mally warned Dmitri: "Chase away philistine love from your group! We're not men and women, we're fighters . . . You have no right to fall in love with one of your subordinates . . . Personal feelings . . . invite harm."[14]

Besides unwittingly hurting bystanders, Dmitri's spy work often inflicted pain on his ego as well. Though the Communist ideology he had embraced in his youth called for subjugation of the individual for the sake of the higher cause, he resented the disregard of his personal feelings when it came to carrying out a spy operation. He was treated as a puppet in the hands of his superiors. When his affair with Marie-Eliane came to an end on his bosses' orders, he was devastated. He had to suppress genuine feelings he developed for her and felt deep remorse for breaking the young woman's heart. But a few years later, when he was in Berlin, he received an order to resume the relationship. Though he felt terrible about showing his face to her again after what had happened, he blindly followed the orders and approached her. To his relief, she didn't believe a word of his pleadings. (Several years later, Marie-Eliane married, had children, and died at the ripe age of 103. Her misdeed was never discovered.)[15]

What Frederick Hitz says about Marine Corps Sergeant Clayton J. Lonetree, an American who was sexually exploited for espionage purposes during the Cold War, could equally be applied to Bystrolyotov's sexual exploitation: "He followed orders with tenacity and complete obedience . . . The loneliness and emptiness of his upbringing had left him with a low sense of self-worth and a profound feeling of insecurity. Despite his harsh life experiences he appears to have been quite naive and gullible."[16]

Then, there was also the problem of sheer fatigue, both mental and physical. Pretending to be someone else on a daily basis began taking its toll on Dmitri. With so many personalities to juggle, often in the course of a single day, he became downright tired. He often lost his sense of self:

> A Soviet intelligence operative has to change every-
> thing in himself, to root out everything: his habits, his
> tastes, his way of thinking, all but one thing—devotion
> and love for the Motherland. Psychologically, it's hard
> to take. It is not the usual actor's split personality, . . .
> You can master complex intelligence technique, you
> can get used to constant danger, but it's impossible to
> get used to your own violence toward yourself.[17]

For months he had to force himself to think in a foreign language, an exhausting task. Once when he was operating in England, one of the young ladies with whom he had spent a night mentioned casually that she had heard him murmuring something in his sleep. Naturally, this caused him great alarm. He made his comrades-in-arms listen to him after he inhaled anesthetic ether. He was relieved to learn that he did his muttering in English. (Of course, he was relieved only partially: there was no guarantee that he would mutter in the same language in regular, not drug-induced, sleep.)

Another episode shows the mental stress and the strain on him of constantly having to be on guard. In the summer of 1934, after four years of intensive underground work in the West, he was given a short vacation to visit his mother in Anapa. At that time, for one of his operations, he was undercover as a prominent Brazilian merchant. When his mother complained about the hot weather in Crimea that summer, he suddenly cried out, "That's what you call hot? Ah, Mama! If you were to live in my homeland of Brazil, you would know what truly hot weather is all about!" Only when he saw how perplexed and frightened his mother became on hearing this remark did he come to his senses and apologize for his "bad joke."[18]

"A soldier can retreat to the rear, but an intelligence officer doesn't have this opportunity," he observes in "Generous Hearts." Having been a victim of his own delusion about the romantic nature of the spy profession, he warns readers of his memoirs not to fall into that trap themselves. As he wrote about his life, he was fully aware of the deceptive image of life as a spy created by popular culture—the image of a man of leisure and material abundance who carries out his assignments as if they were a game. Irked by the stark contrast between this idealistic image and the reality he knew too well, he directly addresses his readers: "Awareness of eternal danger poisons all of the quietest, most pleasant moments of an intelligence operative's life. Dear readers! Don't ever envy an intelligence officer when, in the morning, he puts on a silk robe, at noon sits down to a well-served table, and at night heads for an expensive restaurant with a beautiful woman on his arm. Remember: in the back pocket of his trousers he keeps his Browning, so that he can shoot himself in time."[19]

Once he was close to doing just that. Staying in a small hotel in Paris, where he arrived after his trip to the Balkans, he felt especially tense: there were some indications that French counterintelligence may have picked up his trail. He carried an important document, which he protected day and night. High-strung and alert to any change in the surroundings, he kept the door of his hotel room locked at all times. And he watched the street very closely through his window. Suddenly, a police car packed with policemen came tearing along right in front of the hotel. A police officer jumped out of the car and rushed to the hotel entrance. Dmitri panicked as he heard the hurried tramping of the officer's feet up the stairs. What should he do with the document? Throwing it into the toilet bowl wouldn't do. If counterintelligence suspected that evidence was disposed of in this way, they would immediately block the building's sewage system. There seemed only one way to get rid of the document—tear it up and swallow the pieces. But he ran out of time. The police officer was already knocking on his door. Dmitri froze. A key jangled in the lock, and the officer walked in carrying a bundle under his arm. He asked to be excused for the intrusion and introduced himself as the hotel owner's son. His mother had asked him to change the linens in this guestroom, but he hadn't managed to do it the night before. Relating this episode to a fellow Gulag prisoner years later, Dmitri laughed at himself, but at the time, it was hardly amusing.[20]

During our meeting, Bystrolyotov told me about another incident when, out of the blue, he found himself on the brink of disaster:

"I was posing as a Hungarian count and standing at the Aachen railroad station next to a German I had befriended. He happened to be the SS chief of the Ruhr region, and we were at the station to meet his wife arriving from Berlin. Everything's going fine. It's a sunny day. I'm in excellent mood, sure of myself. One after the other, the trains come in and stop for border control. The SS guards go in and out of the coaches checking the passengers' documents. And then, five minutes before the express train from Berlin is due, a train marked "Paris–Negoreloe" comes in. Back then, Negoreloe was a Russian border town; all trains coming from the west stopped there, and passengers going farther east switched into trains fit for Russian tracks. I feel uneasy. I distract the SS man with small talk. But out of the corner of my eye, I see a window on the train open and a man's face, unmistakably Russian and crude, pop out and look around.

"'Hey, Mitka!' the man shouts. He's calling me, Dmitri!

"I don't turn my head. Not a muscle moves on my face.

"'Mitka, damn it!' The man persists in Russian. 'Come on over! The train's leaving in a few minutes!'

"The SS chief says to me: 'Count, I think that man is calling you.'

"Without turning my head, I reply:

"'Herr Oberst, judge for yourself. Could an acquaintance of mine possibly have such a face?'

"Although the train took off in five minutes, it felt like ages," my host laughed. "But I got through it. Of course, I recognized the man on the train. He was a Soviet diplomatic courier I had known back in my Moscow days. He didn't know about my secret work."

The constant stress of his lifestyle revealed the draining nature of spying: he compares the exhaustion of an intelligence operative with that of a long-distance truck driver. In time, a wrong move was inevitable. He may well have had in mind his own mistake, which he calls "sloppiness in his work" in the letter asking permission to return to Russia: around that time, he lost one of his numerous passports. Oleg Tsarev gives the following account of the circumstances surrounding the loss: Aboard a train heading for Paris, Dmitri gave his passport to the train conductor so that he could affix an entry stamp. The passport was presumably a false Austrian passport Series 500 issued to "Joseph Schwerma," one of Dmitri's frequently used aliases. As was customary at the time, Bystrolyotov asked the conductor to send his passport to the Paris hotel he would be staying in. For reasons that are not quite clear, the conductor sent it not to the hotel but to the Austrian Consulate in Paris. Since Bystrolyotov did not go to claim it from the consulate, the consulate authorities became suspicious and forwarded the passport to Vienna for inspection. When the Center learned about this, it immediately issued an order warning its network to stop using all Austrian passports Series 500. This act significantly impaired the illegal crossings of the European borders by several Soviet operatives.[21]

(During my interview with him in July 2003, Sergei Milashov dismissed Tsarev's scenario for the simple reason that the passport in the name of "Joseph Schwerma" wasn't produced in Lubyanka; it was a genuine one, bought for Bystrolyotov on the black market at the beginning of his underground work. Moreover, none of Bystrolyotov's passports abroad were false; all were either purchased on the black market or obtained legally, as in the case of his passport in the name of Lord Grenville. Milashov admitted that Bystrolyotov did lose one of his passports; it just slipped out of his pocket during a visit to Vienna. Whatever the circumstances of the passport loss, they were highly uncharacteristic of the master intelligence operative known for taking extra care with every move.)[22]

Dmitri's stress increased after Iolanta left him. A new onslaught of loneliness descended on him. He felt even more isolated than before. The rules of the spy game forbade socializing with members of the spy community. Their meetings had to be brief and related only to the business at hand. To protect the whole network, all other contacts were reduced to a strict minimum. Besides the normal human need for companionship, this lifestyle left Dmitri in the dark about current political developments in his homeland. An illegal operative received his orders specifying his target and his task, but he was never informed about the big picture; he was unable to feel the daily pulse of his home country. While other "illegals" received letters from their friends in Russia through official channels, at least until 1936, when this window of information was slammed shut, Dmitri did not have this luxury.[23]

Since the summer of 1922, when he had returned to Russia for a few months in a fit of psychotic effort to save his Motherland from hunger epidemics, he had only fleeting impressions of the country's affairs during brief visits when he was summoned to Lubyanka. Only once, back in 1929, when he was given permission for a short visit to his mother in Anapa, did he have some glimpses into Soviet reality at the time. On his way from the railroad station, passing through the large Cossack village of Nikolaevskaya, he found the whole settlement deserted, with only two watchmen on either side of the road running through it. With the collectivization campaign under way, most Cossacks had been deported to Siberia, and their houses stood there empty and boarded up. While staying with his mother, every morning Dmitri witnessed one and the same scene: the hungry—children, old people, and women—lined up on their knees at the window, waiting as his mother gave them each a slice of bread. She was not in need herself, because Dmitri regularly sent parcels and hard currency from abroad.[24]

Since he had lived abroad his whole adult life, other than his mother, who sent occasional postcards, Dmitri had no one to keep him abreast of developments in Russia. He had to rely on information obtained in the Soviet press or the Western media, neither of which he fully trusted. This did not make his decision to return any easier.[25]

But from what he did know he had more than enough cause for alarm. In the summer of 1936, the first tide of the new waves of repressions that later became known as the Great Terror hit the country. From August 19 to 24, 1936, the first of Stalin's show trials of sixteen members of the so-called Trotskyite-Zinovievite Terrorist Center took place in Moscow. The chief defendants, Grigory Zinoviev and Lev Kamenev, two of the most prominent former Party leaders, along with the rest of the group, were sentenced to death and executed on fabricated charges of having acted on Trotsky's orders. The defendants were also accused of participating in a plot to murder the head of the Leningrad party organization, Sergei Kirov. Along with the other defendants, they were also implicated in a conspiracy to kill Stalin, Voroshilov, Zhdanov, Kaganovich, and other top Soviet leaders. In his closing arguments, the public procurator of the USSR, Andrei Vyshinsky, indicated that during interrogations of the accused, they had revealed the complicity of several other prominent Soviet leaders such as Bukharin, Rykov, Radek, and others, making it clear that more such trials would be initiated. Soon after, in late September 1936, Stalin replaced Genrikh Yagoda, whom he had proudly called "the sword of the Revolution," with Nikolai Yezhov as People's Commissar of Internal Affairs (NKVD). That could mean only one thing: a new approach to running the repressive mechanism of Soviet power.[26]

Dmitri was not the only Soviet intelligence operative abroad who was at a loss about what to do with his life at this point. As Elsa Poretsky, the wife of another of the "Great Illegals," Ignatii Poretsky (also known as "Ignace Reiss"), recalls in her memoirs, many of her and her husband's friends and comrades-in-arms agonized over what to do next. They all suffered from the fear of emptiness, and they wavered at the tough choices they had to make. Quitting their spy work abroad also meant quitting their Party—the high cause to which they had pledged their allegiance and dedicated their lives.[27]

In his memoirs, British spy Kim Philby also discusses the hard choices he had to make. He cites Graham Greene's novel *The Confidential Agent*, in which the heroine asks the hero whether his leaders are any better than others. "No, of course, not," he replies. "But I still prefer the people they lead—even if they lead them all wrong . . . You choose your side once and for all—of course, it may be the wrong side. Only history can tell that."[28]

The same way of thinking characterized Bystrolyotov. Early in life, he had also embraced the idea of fighting for the victory of world Communism. Although, as he came to realize later, he had chosen the wrong side, he stuck to it anyway. Once and for all he attached himself to the cause he believed in. Although he knew that his return could be his undoing, the Nietzschean Übermensch who sacrifices himself for the sake of the future served as his inspiration.

For Soviet spies abroad who agonized over the decision to return or not, the fear of hurting their loved ones back home was legitimate. If they defected, they would have to relinquish their families. (Some spies, like Poretsky and Krivitsky, had their families with them in the West, which made a great difference. In fact, it was the crucial factor in their decision to defect, which took place a year later, in the summer of 1937.) Back in 1929, on November 21, the Soviet government had passed the law on defectors. It characterized flight from the Soviet Union or any of its agencies abroad as high treason. Later, on June 8, 1934, a decree was passed specifying the responsibility of all relatives of the defector. If they had facilitated the defection in any way or had even just known about the intention to defect and did not report it to the authorities, they were to be punished by confiscation of all of their property and five to ten years of confinement. Other relatives were to be exiled to the remote regions of Siberia for five years.[29]

Before his return to Russia, Dmitri was aware of this danger, as he confided to his fellow camp prisoner, Konstantin Ivanov. However, defecting would not have guaranteed his personal safety either. In his *Gulag Archipelago*, Aleksandr Solzhenitsyn cites the case of a Soviet man kidnapped abroad, in Brussels, Belgium. He also recalls the notorious kidnapping of Russian émigré General Kutepov in 1930; the general was snapped up in broad daylight from the streets of Paris by OGPU operatives. (Perhaps Theodor Mally had that event in mind a year later, in the summer of 1937, when he decided to go back to Russia. One of Mally's reasons was that the NKVD would murder him anyway, whether he returned or not.)[30]

Besides, at the time of his trip back home, the end of December 1936, Dmitri could not possibly have known yet about the special mobile groups of assassins created to take care of Soviet spies who, once recalled, refused to follow orders and were hunted down and eliminated on foreign soil, as would happen to Ignace Reiss in the summer of the following year. There were many others among intelligence officers in this situation who couldn't fully grasp what a devoted Soviet man, who had selflessly subjugated himself to his country's interests, often risking his life, could possibly be incriminated for.[31]

Perhaps the most compelling reason of all for Dmitri's decision to return was that he was unable to disassociate himself from the Motherland, which would have permanently violated his sense of belonging. This was the sense that, after his years of abandonment as a child, he had obtained for the first time when he rang at the doors of the Soviet Trade Mission in Prague back in 1922, a homeless young man, a prodigal son of his native land. The only undisputable and sacred concept for him was the Motherland. "Motherland remains Motherland," he repeats many times in his memoirs. (Even after he had not only witnessed but experienced firsthand—"on his own skin," as the Russian expression goes; and in his case, in the direct meaning of the phrase!—what was in store for those Soviet diplomats and intelligence officers who didn't defect but, following orders, returned to the Soviet Union, he remained adamant in his outrage at those who betrayed the Motherland by refusing to return.

For example, such was the case of Fyodor Raskolnikov, a Soviet diplomat who, in 1938, refused to return to the USSR for fear of being arrested. Dmitri wasn't able to accept as a mitigating circumstance that the man was betraying not their Motherland but its usurper, Stalin; Raskolnikov wrote an open letter to the dictator, accusing him of betraying the revolution. By the same token, he praised another diplomat, the Soviet ambassador to Romania, Mikhail Ostrovsky, who could easily have fled for freedom but, as Dmitri would soon do himself, returned to Russia to his own doom. What Dmitri didn't know was that Ostrovsky hesitated before making this fateful decision and opted to return only after Kliment Voroshilov himself, Marshal of the Soviet Union, personally guaranteed his security. Ostrovsky was seized the moment he crossed the Soviet border and later died in the camps.)[32]

Now Dmitri had finally made his fateful decision to return, but he discovered he was not at liberty to do so. To quit the Soviet foreign intelligence was not a simple matter. Now he realized that back in 1930, when they had offered him the opportunity to stay in Europe and work underground, the OGPU had entrapped him (as it had its other émigré recruits) with false promises that they would let him go at a later time. (Years later, serving his term in the Gulag, he would come to the sobering conclusion that the "OGPU has an entrance door but does not have one for exit.") Now, in the summer of 1936, tired and sick, he found that he had to fight for permission to leave his job, which was slowly killing him. He had to fight the authorities and fight hard. Sticking to the current policy of ennobling the KGB post factum, in the last version of Dmitri's biography, the FSB (the KGB's successor) makes it seem that his wishes were readily accommodated. To that end, they airbrushed from the record the fact that the response to his plea for replacement due to exhaustion and illness was a harsh reprimand. The suppressed document that refutes this picture-perfect treatment of their hero was made public under Gorbachev:

> Dear Comrade Hans:
> I ask you to gather patience and hold on to your job
> for a month and a half or two . . . More than anything
> else I'm surprised at your being unnerved . . . Though
> I understand that I might cause you a few unpleas-
> ant moments, I must state that these thoughts of total
> despondency are completely unworthy of our [NKVD]
> worker, no matter how hard his circumstances are and
> how badly distraught he is in performing his work . . .
> Cast off your dejection and in the two remaining
> months do not smear all of your many years of work
> in the past. Artem[33]

The harsh reprimand of a valuable worker for reporting that he was tired was nothing unusual; in fact, it was characteristic of the prevailing Soviet moral standards. The attitude toward human limitations as a sign of ideological weakness was indicative of the high ideological spirit of the time in which the revolutionary, self-denying spirit prevailed. In fact, Felix Dzerzhinsky was nicknamed "Iron Felix" for his self-sacrificing ways of serving the revolution: reportedly, he had died of a heart attack, widely assumed to have occurred because, in his fierce fight with the enemies of the revolution, the man refused to rest for even a moment.

They made Dmitri wait several months before he finally received permission to return. In his words, he "succeeded in breaking away from work" and arrived in Moscow on the eve of the new year 1937. He met the new year at one of the secret dachas belonging to the top NKVD brass. In his memoirs, he does not relate how he and Iolanta got back together. There is no question that she loved him, and perhaps this was enough for her to forgive him all his transgressions. He could hardly wait to start the life he had always longed for, the life of an artist and writer. When he returned home he brought along two book-length manuscripts—one journalistic in nature and the other related to the medical field. He even brought with him a set of lithographic plates for the latter, which he had prepared in Paris. He also brought fifty paintings, mostly done during his African trip. He applied for membership in the Union of Soviet Artists and was accepted unanimously. His personal exhibition was scheduled for the coming fall season. He submitted his manuscripts to publishers and was ready to devote himself fully to artistic life.[34]

However, "circumstances of a higher order," as he characterizes them, forestalled his plans. He was promised that, to compensate him for several years of work with no break, upon his return he would receive a year of paid vacation and then be allowed to leave his job. But, citing the urgent need for his language skills, they did not allow him to quit the NKVD. They assigned him a desk job in the twentieth sector at NKVD headquarters, headed by Colonel Karl Gursky (code-named MONGOL). Dmitri worked there as a translator. As always, trying to do more than was required of him, he made use of his expertise to write two chapters for the first textbook to be used in the Soviet school for intelligence officers. He chose the subjects on which he was considered a supreme master: the best ways to legalize a spy's presence in a foreign country and devices to avoid blowing one's cover. He received an in-house official commendation for this contribution, and instead of the permanent relief from duty he had been promised, they began processing his official attestation for the NKVD cadres. He was to be awarded the rank of senior lieutenant of the NKVD (which was equivalent to the rank of an army major), and he had to join the Party. Three of his comrades-in-arms submitted their recommendations—Ignatii Poretsky, Theodor Mally, and Boris Bazarov.[35]

Then they made him take another trip abroad. Dmitri does not disclose the nature of this assignment, only mentioning that he "made a round through Estonia, Latvia, Lithuania, Germany, Denmark, Norway, Sweden, and Finland, and safely returned home." Next came another, even more important assignment from INO head Abram Slutsky. This time, his orders were to go via Japan to Canada, and from there to England, the country he knew well from the years he had handled Oldham, the Foreign Office functionary. Now, under the assumed identity of a forest industrialist, Dmitri was assigned to work with another British agent, John Herbert King, a British official connected to the Cambridge and Oxford groups of Soviet agents. After all, not only had Dmitri known him for a long time, but the NKVD had recruited King on his recommendation.[36]

It took four months to fully prepare for the trip. With Iolanta, still an NKVD operative, he traveled to the White Sea region, to the Karelian Autonomous Republic of the Soviet Union, and photographed himself next to a local log warehouse and sawmill. Since there was a chance that their luggage could be searched as they went through customs or during a hotel stay, they made sure that every item of clothing was of Canadian make. Since Dmitri and his wife had no children, to make them look like a solid family, Iolanta carried a staged photograph of her with a well-groomed young boy provided by the Foreign Intelligence office staff; they nicknamed him Encio.[37]

When he was ready for the mission, on March 27, 1937, Abram Slutsky, chief of Foreign Intelligence, reported the details of Dmitri's assignment to People's Commissar Nikolai Yezhov, head of the NKVD. Yezhov listened carefully, approved the assignment, and said to Dmitri: "We're giving you our best 'source.' You should appreciate it. You've been given the rank of senior lieutenant of state security. Apply for Party membership. We'll accept you. And don't worry about your mother: we'll help her with whatever she needs. You may go abroad in peace. Remember: Stalin and the Motherland won't forget you. Good luck to you." He hugged Dmitri and kissed him three times in the Russian style: on either cheek and on his lips. Dmitri left Lubyanka excited and inspired.[38]

He returns to this episode several times in his memoirs and takes understandable pride in the honor bestowed on him by Slutsky and Yezhov in entrusting him with another highly important assignment. But it may well be that Yezhov's kisses were those of Judas. As Dmitri could not have known in his time, but as we know now, soon after the scene he describes took place, a secret operation directed at destroying Soviet foreign intelligence officers of his generation began. To avoid alarming their comrades-in-arms who were still abroad, the recalled operatives were summoned to headquarters and given new assignments, usually to a faraway country. Soon after they began traveling, during a stop, they were removed from the train, arrested, and hidden in one of the secret NKVD prisons. For months, nobody knew what had truly happened to them.[39]

Apparently, at the time Dmitri was called in, this operational procedure, not yet fully developed, was still on the drawing board, and his trip was postponed. But the atmosphere in the country was growing increasingly ominous. Between January 23 and 30, 1937, soon after Dmitri's arrival in the country, the anticipated second show trial, now known as Trial of Radek and Piatakov (Trial of the Seventeen) took place in Moscow. Top Soviet leaders Yuri Piatakov, Karl Radek, Grigori Sokolnikov, and fourteen other distinguished party members were accused of organizing acts of sabotage and murder in furtherance of a plot between Trotsky, Germany, and Japan to overthrow the Soviet government and restore capitalism. All but four defendants were shot, and the others given long prison terms. Elsa Poretsky, who visited Moscow about the time of Dmitri's return, describes the atmosphere of total suspicion by everybody of everybody, the devastating impact of mass arrests, and the paranoia of those who expected to be arrested at any time, who froze even at the sound of a telephone ring. Surveillance and denunciation to the police became everyday occurrences.[40]

People around Dmitri began to disappear almost daily. First, some clerks from his Foreign Intelligence Department were arrested. Then, officers of the NKVD central apparatus began to be eliminated one by one. One of the first victims was the outstanding operative Felix Gursky. Even though quite recently, on January 2, 1937, after being recalled from abroad, Gursky was awarded the Order of the Red Banner, they came to arrest him. Knowing well what awaited him in Yezhov's chambers of torture, he ended his own life by jumping from his office window on the ninth floor of the Lubyanka building.[41]

Then the two prominent NKVD officers who had blessed Dmitri in his intelligence work back in 1925, Mikhail Gorb and Artur Artuzov, were arrested (Gorb on April 29 and Artuzov on May 13, 1937). Accused of taking part in some anti-Soviet plot, they were sentenced to death and shot on the same day, August 21, 1937. (As was widely practiced at the time, Artuzov's wife would later be informed that he had died on July 12, 1943, while serving his term.) In August 1937, Dmitri's first OGPU controller in Prague, Nikolai Samsonov, was also arrested, accused of espionage, and shot. The fact that he knew the arrestees firsthand was a great surprise to Dmitri, and he was overwhelmed by the sheer magnitude of mass imprisonment, which seemed to be seizing the whole country. Coming home, he discussed what was going on with his wife, wondering how his country had come to be infested with so many traitors and spies.[42]

By the end of summer 1937, as Stalin's cult of personality reached its apogee—the entire Soviet media spared no efforts in praising him as "our father, our Sun, our Soviet leader"—his campaign of witch hunt and terror was also in full swing. About forty officers were recalled from abroad and dealt with in short order. Those who refused to follow orders were hunted down by mobile NKVD groups organized back in December 1936 when the whole operation to eliminate the old guard of spies devoted to the ideas of world revolution was still on the drawing board. One such dissenter, "Ignace Reiss," was murdered in Switzerland and his body thrown out of a car going at full speed.[43]

After the whole contingent of foreign spies had been taken care of, it was the turn of the INO head, Abram Slutsky. On February 17, 1938, Slutsky ("Comrade Abram," as Dmitri warmly referred to him) died suddenly under suspicious circumstances. The official version was that the man had suffered a fatal heart attack while visiting the office of Mikhail Frinovsky, the first deputy of the NKVD head, but rumor had it that Slutsky was suffocated with a pillow as he sat in his own office. (It has since been established that Slutsky was murdered in Frinovsky's office but in a slightly more sophisticated way. First, he was subdued with a chloroform-soaked patch pressed against his nose, and then he was injected with poison.)[44]

On February 25, 1938, Dmitri was suddenly laid off by the Foreign Intelligence Department and transferred to the State Chamber of Commerce. There, thanks to his working knowledge of nearly twenty languages, he was made head of the Translation Bureau. In March 1938, the third show trial, "The Trial of the Twenty-one" (also known as the Rykov-Bukharin trial), took place in Moscow. As expected, Bukharin, Rykov, Yagoda, Krestinsky, and seventeen other prominent party cadres were accused of cooperating, under Trotsky's direction, with German, Polish, and Japanese intelligence to commit acts of sabotage and diversion in industry, transport, and agriculture and to commit murder and terrorism, with the goal of overthrowing the government, dismembering the USSR, and restoring capitalism.[45]

As the trial proceeded, on March 7, 1938, Dmitri learned about the fate of another spymaster, one of the country's most distinguished, who had directed several of his operations abroad: Theodor Mally had been imprisoned. (As Dmitri would learn decades later, two days after his own arrest, Mally was sentenced to death and shot immediately.) In June 1938, Boris Bazarov, who had directed many of Bystrolyotov's operations in the West, was recalled to the USSR and, on July 3, arrested and accused of espionage. One after another, the most talented and courageous operatives working undercover abroad were brought back to the country and thrown into jail.[46]

The waves of arrests of good and solid workers from all walks of life continued nonstop. Clearly, it was only a matter of time before they would come after Dmitri, too. Now he couldn't help but recall some ominous signs that he too was targeted for persecution. He recalled an incident that happened during a short vacation to see his mother in Anapa. Carrying a passport issued in the name of a foreign engineer, he stopped in Moscow on the way and checked into the luxurious Hotel Metropol, where foreigners usually stayed. Every evening his supervisor, Colonel Karl Gursky, and other NKVD bosses visited and used Dmitri's hard currency, which they lacked living in Moscow, to carouse in the hotel restaurant. The INO department secretary used the occasion of his appearance in Moscow to cleanse his file of unneeded documents and pictures. She gave him the packet of documents with instructions to tear up the obsolete papers into small pieces and furtively dispose of them in one of the street garbage cans. He chose to dispose of his old service card from a short stint in the Red Fleet during a hasty trip to Russia back in 1922 and a few photos he had bought to use in an article for the Soviet press. He didn't heed the secretary's warning—he tore everything up but threw it into the wastebasket in his hotel room.

Of course, he also remembered Geneva barman Emile, who had taught him that the scraps of paper could be retrieved and glued back together, but this precaution, which he would undoubtedly have taken if he were working abroad, seemed silly at home, on the soil of his Motherland. Nontheless, he noticed some rather crude attempts at trapping him into doing something illegal. Thus, a pretty hotel cleaning lady turned to him and, cursing the Soviet authorities in French, asked him to take some papers out of the country, a major offense in Soviet times. He cut her short and left for Anapa. On his way back when he called the INO department, Gursky roared with laughter: "Are you still alive? Haven't they shot you yet?"

At first, Dmitri laughed, too. But then his feet went cold. In the evening, when Gursky came over with his lover and they went as usual to dine at the Metropol restaurant, Dmitri learned what had happened. The cleaning lady glued together the pieces of documents he had discarded and passed them to the NKVD Operative Department. The head of the department quickly cooked up the case that a foreign spy with forged documents was heading for Crimea, Sevastopol, the location of the major Soviet Navy base on the Black Sea. He asked for permission to liquidate the spy. Luckily for Dmitri, Abram Slutsky, still in power at the time, checked things out and saved Dmitri from the meat grinder into which Slutsky himself would fall a few years later.[47]

Now, Dmitri found that anticipating arrest was torture in itself. He lived with his wife and his mother in the settlement of Sokol, on the Moscow outskirts, in a building occupied by NKVD employees. Every night, black Marias (the nickname for the cars that took arrestees to their prison cells) rolled up to the building. It was impossible to fall asleep. Their apartment was on the first floor. The beams of headlights and the grinding of motors kept them awake all night long. Through the drapes, they watched their recent comrades-in-arms being taken away into the darkness of the night.[48]

At the break of day, numb and exhausted, they would fall back into their beds and sleep for maybe a couple of hours before going to work, dreading the next nightfall. Every morning, the caretaker of the building had the sad duty of blacking out the names of those who had been arrested from the tenant register board in the entrance halls. As was the custom in all households at the time, in preparation for her husband's possible arrest, Iolanta put together a bundle of warm clothes, a bowl and a spoon, and a food package containing some sugar and butter. No matter how much they discussed it, they couldn't find a reason for the nightmare they were going through.

During this highly volatile and suspenseful time, with the question of life and death hanging by a thread, it looks as though his nerves finally snapped. He picked up the phone and called his former employer, the Foreign Department of the NKVD. Since Dmitri had been dismissed before his full attestation took place, he worried about not having documents that proved his service to the country as an intelligence operative (in fact, his work record book shows only that back in 1930 when he began his undercover work, he was hired simply as a senior translator), and he asked the person who took his call how those documents could be obtained. That turned out to be a truly life-altering move, the grave consequences of which he could possibly have avoided if he had continued to keep a low profile, as he had since leaving the agency for the Chamber of Commerce: acting on instinct, he had not contacted his former comrade-in-arms. That proved to be the right tactic. As a precautionary measure, foreign intelligence officers knew only the code names of their colleagues. Therefore, when Bystrolyotov was dismissed from the Foreign Intelligence Department, nobody in the office knew exactly where he went. In the leapfrog of the agency's bosses that followed the murder of Abram Slutsky, Dmitri disappeared from their radar, at least temporarily.

Recently published archival materials from Russia's State Archive of Social and Political History (RGASPI) disclose with clarity the chain of events triggered by Bystrolyotov's fateful phone call. Renowned Soviet spymaster Pavel Sudoplatov, at that time an operative executive (*operupolnomochennyi*) of the department, picked up the phone and was taken by surprise when he heard Dmitri's voice. A few days before Dmitri's call, Sudoplatov had asked the new acting head of the department, Zelman Passov, who replaced his predecessor, Sergei Shpigelglas, under whom Dmitri worked for over a month, about the whereabouts of HANS. Passov replied that he had been arrested, which was a quite realistic assumption on his part. After all, at that time, the meat grinder of terror aimed at the first generation of Soviet foreign intelligence operatives of various ranks was in full swing, with many operatives at Dmitri's level being thrown in jail on an almost daily basis. (Passov's own turn would come a few weeks after Bystrolyotov's; he was arrested on October 23, 1938.)

The rest followed in quick succession. Sudoplatov told Dmitri that he would make inquiries about the documents and invited him to call back in a few days. The moment Dmitri hang up the phone, Sudoplatov duly reported the incident and Dmitri's arrest became imminent. (In fairness it has to be stated that, in the paranoid atmosphere of the time, Sudoplatov hardly had a choice: if he chose not to report Bystrolyotov's phone call and it were discovered later on, he would inevitably be arrested for attempting to harbor an "enemy of the people." In fact, at the end of the year, Sudoplatov himself would barely escape the purges.)[49]

It may well be that Dmitri, a man of high intelligence, knew perfectly well what he was doing when he picked up the phone. In his memoirs, he recalls tremendous relief that the torment of dreadful anticipation was finally over. He was even elated, and a paradoxical thought registered in his mind: "What a joy! I've been arrested!"[50]

PART III
AFTERLIFE

FOURTEEN | In Ink and Blood

If the facts aren't confirmed, too bad for the facts.

—JOSEPH STALIN (APOCRYPHAL)

"Do you want to write your testimony in ink," the NKVD officer asked him, "or in your own blood?"

Dmitri knew he was innocent; he found himself incapable of self-incrimination. He refused to write in either.

At midnight, two hefty prison guards walked into his cell, twisted his arms behind his back, and dragged him, his head lowered, through the prison corridors to the interrogation room. There, investigator A. P. Solovyov and his young assistant, Fyodor Shukshin, were waiting.[1]

After a short talk, during which Solovyov stated that NKVD officers like himself were the strongholds of Comrade Stalin, the beatings began. The two wardens again twisted the prisoner's hands, and with two precise jabs, Solovyov knocked out the teeth on both sides of Dmitri's mouth. Then he began kicking the prisoner in the shins with his boots. Meanwhile, the assistant removed Dmitri's shoes, and Solovyov began stomping on his toes.

After that, they handed the prisoner over to the security guards, who hammered him from the left and right. Dmitri's face swelled up, and all he could discern were his torturers' fists, smeared with his blood, as they came in for the next blow. (As Dmitri sarcastically remarks in his memoirs, at that moment the only other things he was able to see clearly were the Komsomol pins on the guards' uniforms.) Next, they threw him down on the floor and began kicking his abdomen with their boots.

Finally, they grew tired. Their hands and faces covered with Dmitri's blood, they washed themselves at the sink and asked again, "Now, will you write it?" Dmitri tried to say no but his lips were so swollen that he couldn't speak. Solovyov decided this was enough for the first time, and Dmitri was dragged back to his cell.[2]

As Dmitri would realize decades later, September 18, 1938, the day of his arrest, cut his life in half. That was the day he crossed the line separating his life from the "afterlife." He even titled the opening chapter of "Zalog bessmertiia" ("The Key to Immortality")—his memoir covering his first period of imprisonment—"How I Died." There was good reason to call his postarrest existence the "afterlife," for life as he knew it, the life that made sense to him, would be over, once and for all. He would gradually turn into a shadow of himself, a ghost descending into an underworld filled with millions of ghosts like him: the netherworld of the Gulag.

On the night of his arrest, when the door of his cell in the Butyrka prison slammed shut behind him, Dmitri's first thought was that he had been imprisoned by mistake, and he was agitated, so for starters, they put him in a solitary cell. There he tried to calm himself and figure out what possible reason there could be for his arrest. The NKVD men who brought him in hadn't given any clues.

First they had taken him to Lubyanka, the NKVD headquarters in the center of Moscow, and locked him up in an "envelope," a tiny room the size of a phone booth.

Then they led him through several narrow corridors and threw him into a cell containing four beds. However, only one prisoner was there, a middle-aged man. He introduced himself as chief of the construction sites in Norilsk, a town in the Far North, beyond the polar circle. "After the trial," he said to Dmitri, "if you aren't shot, they'll send you there. You'll wear a padded jacket, and with a crowbar in your hands, you'll be crushing permafrost." This pronouncement irritated Dmitri. No way it would happen to him. He'd been arrested by sheer misunderstanding. "I bet you're here for some serious offense," he said to the man, "and you should anticipate a harsh sentence. As for me, I'm not guilty of anything. And, in the Soviet Union, they don't convict an innocent man. Unlike in the capitalist countries."

The man, enraged, jumped to his feet, ready to fight, but instead the two men got hold of themselves and decided to talk. From first-hand experience, the man told Dmitri to prepare himself for things to come. If he were lucky enough to escape a death sentence, like thousands of others, he would likely be sent to Norilsk as a prisoner.

Talking at length, the man gave Dmitri as much useful information as he could. But afterward, busy with thoughts of his wife and mother and going through the rituals designed for the newly arrested—a thorough body search, filling out numerous documents, being photographed and fingerprinted, having all his hair cut off, and undergoing a medical examination—Dmitri didn't pay much attention to what the man had said. (A year later, when he actually did arrive at Norilsk as a prisoner, he came to deeply regret his disregard of the man's advice—essentially spurning that "extraordinary gift" fate had sent him soon after his arrest.)

The next night, Dmitri and a group of other prisoners were driven through the Moscow streets to the infamous Butyrka Prison, legendary for its brutal treatment of inmates. Butyrka had a long and sad history, stretching as far back as the seventeenth century, when, during the reign of Peter the Great, its quarters were used to imprison rebellious troops (the Streltsy). In the nineteenth century, hundreds of participants in the Polish uprising of 1863 were incarcerated there, as were members of the radical group "The People's Will" in 1883. Before the October 1917 Bolshevik takeover, among Butyrka's famous inmates were the revolutionary poet Vladimir Mayakovsky and Felix Dzerzhinsky, future head of the first Soviet secret police (the Cheka)—one of the few who managed to escape from the prison. At the time when Dmitri was brought there, Butyrka functioned as a place of internment for political prisoners as well as a transfer station for those sentenced to the Gulag.[3]

To his total disbelief, shortly after being thrown into a cell big enough to accommodate seventy-six prisoners, Dmitri recognized Konstantin Yurevich, his former classmate at the Constantinople gymnasium. To Dmitri's surprise, the first thing his old and trusted friend did was to ask his forgiveness for testifying against him. He had told his investigator that both he and Dmitri were involved in terrorist activities against the Soviet Union back in their Czechoslovak years.

Moreover, Yurevich insisted that Dmitri follow suit and repeat the same lie when facing his own investigator. Still unable to comprehend why he should invite trouble and act against his own best interests, Dmitri studied his decrepit old friend and decided that he must have gone mad.

Meanwhile, Yurevich did whatever he could to set Dmitri up as comfortably as possible in the cell. He arranged for him to get a wooden bed next to a prominent prisoner, the pioneering Soviet aircraft designer Andrei Nikolaevich Tupolev, who had been arrested in 1937 and was accused of being a member of the Russian Fascist Party. (He would only be fully rehabilitated two decades later, in 1955, two years after Stalin's death.)[4]

Yurevich urged Dmitri, for his own good, to accept once and for all, no matter how preposterous the charges against him turned out to be and no matter what he did to try to deflect them, that the authorities had arrested him for good, and his fate had been sealed behind locked doors. And if this advice wasn't outrageous enough, Yurevich then told him to get ready to follow the practice of the day—cooperate with the investigator in drumming up charges against himself. When Dmitri responded that he would rather die than dishonor himself, his old friend reasoned with him, making an even more foolish statement: Dmitri's refusal to confess would only serve as proof to his investigator of his malicious anti-Sovietism. In the twisted jailers' logic, if the arrested man was a true loyal Soviet citizen, it was his duty to help his investigators, thus showing his loyalty to the Soviet authorities.[5]

Dmitri had a hard time believing his old friend; it was just too outrageous. Yurevich must be crazy, or a coward, or a slanderer. *No torture could possibly take place in our country.* Time and again, he sifted through the multitude of his actions as a foreign intelligence operative. His past was impeccable. There was nothing in his work—nothing!—that could possibly incriminate him.

Finally, he calmed himself down with the thought that his arrest was just a precautionary measure. They would go through his file, page by page, and release him. The procedure would take no more than two months, and the current nightmare would be over. In fact, his life would be even better than ever before—free of any anxiety, the life that he, a devoted Soviet citizen, was entitled to. Despite the arrests of many people he knew, he still believed that in his country they didn't arrest people without a reason. He reassured himself again and again: "I'm innocent, it's crystal clear."

Meanwhile, along with the rest of the inmates, he was brought to a bathhouse. Here something strange took place. Before they left the bathhouse, their clothes disinfected with hot steam, they were informed that the whole group had been stripped of yard privileges, because one of the prisoners had written the word "Lenin" on the wall. He realized that he had entered a topsy-turvy world in which fresh air was a luxury and merely inscribing the pen name of the leader of the revolution on the wall was considered a misdemeanor.

This convinced him that the hell he'd descended into was a real one. He decided that Yurevich had been placed in this cell for one purpose only—to undermine his determination to fight off the charges against him. He began distancing himself from his old friend. He wouldn't be caught by their bait.

On his third day in Butyrka, Dmitri discovered that besides admitting their guilt in general terms, those who "cracked" were expected to cooperate by providing the investigators with detailed accounts of their "crimes." Some veteran prisoners had even established a wild racket: for a fee, ranging from one to three bread portions, they would coach novices in writing self-incriminating testimonies.

Dmitri decided that he wouldn't require these bizarre services. His case was different, and he would find his own ways to defend himself. To his relief, he noticed that the investigators didn't treat all prisoners in the same way. While one man brought back to their cell after interrogation had deep wounds on his back, his broken ribs sticking out from under his flesh, Tupolev returned from one session smiling and carrying a few apples. This gave Dmitri some hope.

But other observations were less encouraging. He searched for a common denominator among the reasons for his cell mates' arrests—but he found none. The cell was crowded with people from all walks of life and backgrounds: Spanish Communists who had fought Franco, Chinese Communists brought to Moscow for military training, heroes of the civil war of all ranks, not to mention illiterate peasants and blue-collar workers oblivious to any kind of politics. No matter how hard he tried, he couldn't comprehend why all of these people had been arrested. Who could possibly have benefited from their imprisonment? As the days passed, he gradually came to his senses and accepted the fact that Yurevich was, as always, his true friend and not some investigator's stooge. Now, totally confused, Dmitri began to suffer from headaches and insomnia.

At last, the day arrived when it was Dmitri's turn to face his investigator, who turned out to be not some monster but a young, innocent-looking man in an NKVD uniform with no insignia—apparently an intern waiting to be accredited and given his first rank. He showed Dmitri excerpts of testimony from eleven people, all members of the Union of Student Citizens of the USSR Living in Czechoslovakia. They all testified that Dmitri Bystrolyotov, the Union's secretary from its very beginning, had recruited them for anti-Soviet work, giving them various spy or terrorist assignments. No specifics were given, however; all charges were stated in the most general terms.[6]

When Dmitri pointed out that some of the dates in these testimonies couldn't possibly be accurate, because at the time of his alleged actions he wasn't living in Czechoslovakia, the intern calmly rewrote the date. Astonished, Dmitri asked him how he could change somebody else's testimony, to which the young man replied with a straight face, "I can do anything." Then, to Dmitri's bewilderment, he calmly picked up a novel lying on the desk and began reading it.

Similar interrogation sessions repeated over several weeks. Dmitri would be brought in, the intern would sit there reading his book, and most of the time, not much else happened. Yurevich explained that this wasn't unusual: to look solid, an investigation should take a certain amount of time. The intern just accrued hours, which were recorded in Dmitri's file and counted toward the length of service the intern needed for accreditation.

After three months, during one of these silent sessions, a middle-aged NKVD captain walked into the room. Dmitri didn't like the very look of him and mentally nicknamed him "Toad." The officer, A. P. Solovyov, asked the intern what the prisoner was accused of and how the case had been progressing. The intern reported that Dmitri was charged with espionage, and Solovyov left.

The next night, when they came for Dmitri, the guards ordered him to put on his coat and hat and drove him to Lubyanka. They brought him into the interrogation room where another NKVD officer sitting at his desk remarked that three months had been wasted, and it was time to get down to business. The officer stated as an irrefutable fact that, in a matter of a few days, Dmitri would confess to all of his crimes. The only question remaining for the prisoner to clarify was the method of his confession. This was the moment when the officer asked Dmitri which he would prefer: to write his testimony in ink or in his own blood. He gave Dmitri twenty-four hours to consider his options.

Back in Butyrka, Dmitri began discussing the situation with his cell mates. They split into two groups. One group advised him to co-operate with the investigator, and thus save his life, in the hope that an opportunity to prove his innocence would come up in the future. The other group felt that the threat of torture was just that, a threat, and by standing tall, he had a chance of proving his innocence.

Agonizing over this fateful decision, Dmitri made the rounds of the cell. In the end, he came upon a homely and quiet Jew, a Party member, formerly an engineer in a state forest export firm. The conversation he had with this man made a deep and lasting impression on Dmitri, reshaping his world outlook and serving as a guide through many future perturbations in his life. When the prisoner asked him how he would characterize his work as an intelligence operative abroad, Dmitri answered with three adjectives: "filthy," "bloody," and "heroic." He explained, "We did base and cruel things for the sake of the future . . . I fought for my Motherland, and that says it all. We did evil things for the sake of the good."

The Jewish prisoner mulled over Dmitri's words and replied, "If you understand that you did evil things, then I'll tell you the following: evil deeds must be atoned for." Besides doing evil things abroad, wasn't he guilty of evildoing in their homeland? Hadn't he, with many others, raised his hand when voting to condemn the "enemies of the people"? After all, the two of them had built their Soviet home, "both its beautiful rooms and its stinking toilet," where they had now ended up. In his view, millions of other honest Soviet people imprisoned now should feel responsible for their own misfortune.

The engineer reasoned that there were only two options: either to "spit at [themselves] and become Fascists [read: anti-Soviet] or to keep going forward along the honest Soviet road to the end and see what else was there, even if that turned out to be something still more horrible." He found that to denounce oneself right away, without fighting, was despicable. "Let's get to Lefortovo prison [where torture awaited them—E.D.] and see what they're doing there," the prisoner said. "Together we built Lefortovo, too; it's part of our Soviet home, and we are responsible for it. If they let us live, let's go to the camps to work, atone before our people, and gain a new understanding of how to live and what to do in the future. We'll keep on building our Soviet home as if we are free. In the name of the evil you did abroad, don't make it easy for yourself."

He went on encouraging Dmitri to believe that the Party itself, not necessarily its Central Committee members, would finally find the right course of action. Sticking to the Communist ideals would mean remaining at his post, thus making himself immortal. Dmitri's encounter with the Jewish engineer had a lasting and profound effect on him. As do many men who grow up with absent (or weak) fathers, Dmitri often sought advice from strangers he subconsciously substituted as father figures. Although he doesn't acknowledge it openly in any of his memoirs, his readers will find endless retellings of the ideas expressed by the Communist Jewish prisoner during their conversations. Those ideas, an odd mixture of Communists' belief in the eventual triumph of their just cause and Judeo-Christian notions of atonement for sins committed while fighting for that cause, helped Dmitri to resolve his inner conflict caused by the clash of the proclaimed ideals of Marxist-Leninist teaching and the realities of the mass terror that enveloped the whole country.

Finally, after much emotional turmoil, torn between one inner voice telling him it was "better to be a living dog than a dead lion" and another demanding that he prove his innocence, he made his decision. He let the twenty-four-hour deadline lapse, tacitly choosing the torture alternative. As promised, the guards came and took him to Lefortovo prison. Built in 1881, it was used mainly to conduct investigations. Named after the Lefortovo District of Moscow, where it was located, the prison was well known for its harsh treatment of political inmates. Over the decades of Soviet rule, among many prominent political prisoners incarcerated in Lefortovo were Raoul Wallenberg, Yevgenia Ginzburg, Alexander Dolgun, Vladimir Bukovsky, Natan Sharansky, Andrei Sinyavsky, and Aleksandr Solzhenitsyn.[7]

To begin with, Dmitri was placed in a dark squalid cell containing two beds with no mattresses. A middle-aged man was lying on one of them. After a while, feeling the need to exchange at least a few words with another human being, Dmitri turned to the man, only to discover that he was talking to a corpse. He realized that this was his captors' attempt to break him down psychologically. After a prolonged struggle with himself, he gathered all his will to show that the proximity of a dead body had no effect on him. He even forced himself to hum a song under his breath. A few more days passed until, finally, what he had been dreading the most began in earnest. One midnight, his captors took him to another cell, and the beatings started. They sat him on a high chair and shone a huge lamp in his face. They repeatedly threw him against the wall. Once they made him stand on his feet during the whole seventy-hour-long interrogation session while shouting furiously into both of his ears simultaneously. He was physically fit, and because of years of underground work abroad, he'd grown used to the thought that, sooner or later, he would wind up in enemy hands and die a painful death.[8]

During that first beating they broke his breastbone and his stomach muscles had begun to give way. They brought him back to his cell. After a few days, he gradually came to his senses and found that, if he lay still, there was no pain; if he dared to move, the pain resumed. He became preoccupied with deciding how much damage to his health he could endure before he would be forced to surrender. "In our villages, in old times during Shrovetide," he writes, recalling his thinking after that first round of beatings, "[during ritual fist fights] our young Russians inflicted such pain on each other just for fun. Will my suffering now justify my surrender later on?" He decided to endure the pain for as long as he could. Otherwise, he would feel ashamed for giving in too soon.

Several more days passed, and the beatings resumed on a regular basis. Each time he would assess the damage and again tell himself that it hadn't been enough to justify his surrender. One day, during renewed beatings, People's Commissar Yezhov, the head of the NKVD, suddenly entered the interrogation chamber. Solovyov jumped to his feet to salute him. Yezhov didn't (or pretended not to) recognize Dmitri as the man whom, just a few months ago, he had blessed before sending on his next intelligence mission abroad. Now he just asked the investigator, "How many foreign intelligence services has he admitted to spying for?" Solovyov lied, "Four." "Not enough," Yezhov said and left the room.[9]

After every new thrashing, Dmitri ransacked his memory, recalling other beatings he had endured in his life. One that came to mind had taken place in his youth. At one time, during the civil war, having wound up in Turkey, he worked as a cook on a boat. In an act of mischief along with other sailors, he stole the geese that the Turks had brought for the market in Constantinople. One day the Turks caught the sailors in the act and began beating them over their heads with boards. A nail in one of the boards punctured Dmitri's skull just above the bridge of his nose. He screamed, which frightened the Turk who had hit him and made him run off. Dmitri's friends led him away with the board still stuck in his forehead, but he suffered no lasting injury. These were just regular sailors' pastimes, he thought at the time, and recalling that episode, he told himself again, "No, I haven't had enough! Not yet!"

The beatings continued. He was reaching the point where he felt he could stand it no longer. His racing heartbeat indicated that his heart, not too healthy to begin with, had started to give way.

One night, Solovyov said he was running out of time and his bosses had given him permission to finish Dmitri off if he kept refusing to sign the papers. To prove that he meant business, Solovyov raised the level of violence, now using an "instrumental approach" (Dmitri's euphemism). He took a hammer out of his briefcase, wrapped the head of it with cotton, and secured it with a bandage.

"That's for your stubborn noggin," he said. "I'll knock all the foolishness out of it once and for all." He also took out a three-foot length of steel rope with a ball bearing attached to its end with wire. "This is for your back," he said. "I'll whip you to death with it." The security guards stripped Dmitri to the waist. Hammer in hand, Solovyov came around the desk and hit him on top of the head. Dmitri collapsed onto his face. The young intern Shukshin sat on his neck, the guards sat at the other end on his legs, and Solovyov began flogging Dmitri's back with the steel rope. From time to time, he turned the prisoner over on his back to kick him in the stomach with the heels of his boots.[10]

The bearing eventually broke during the beating, and the two balls lodged inside his rib cage (he would never be able to remove them). They also broke two of his ribs and destroyed several nerves. This caused paralysis of his limbs, and for a while he couldn't urinate. (During our meeting, when Bystrolyotov related that episode of his life to me, he pointed to the short black felt boots on his feet, the kind of boots that, in my Soviet life, old Russians wore in the streets when it was wet and cold outside: "As a result of that beating, my circulation's still poor. I have to wear these things even at home. My feet freeze.")[11]

At this point, for the first time Dmitri felt that he might die soon, and death would make it impossible for him to prove his innocence. He began thinking that resistance could also be flexible: not only "do or die" but also "he who laughs last laughs best." He decided not to let them murder him. At the break of dawn, he gathered what remained of his strength and whispered to Solovyov's assistant, Shukshin, that he was ready to give his testimony.[12]

After that, he was taken to the hospital. He spent a few days there and, when he had somewhat recuperated, was returned to his cell, where he was given a week's rest before he was to begin working on his file with the investigator.

The day came for this meeting with Solovyov, whom Dmitri found in good spirits, ready to write down whatever Dmitri cared to tell him. Solovyov even offered him sweetened tea with sandwiches. Since Dmitri had decided to survive, at least for the time being, it made sense to take every possible opportunity to restore his strength. He ate the sandwiches and drank the tea, while telling Solovyov whatever he thought was expected of him. Prompted by Solovyov, he soon admitted that, during his Prague years back in the 1920s, he had belonged to the Union of Student Citizens of the USSR Living in Czechoslovakia. This was easy to admit, because it was true. What wasn't true was that, as Solovyov claimed, this student group had served as a cover for a counterrevolutionary organization set up by the Czech police; in fact, the union was the brainchild of Soviet intelligence.

But this wasn't going to be good enough. Solovyov searched for other, more damning, accusations. Looking through Dmitri's papers, he found a photo of Dmitri's mother in the company of her old friend, General Baratov, a commander of the Cossack "Wild Division." The investigator suggested that Dmitri admit to being the general's son, and since it was known that Baratov had hanged Bolsheviks during the civil war, he, Dmitri, had to confess to taking part in those executions.

Eventually, when all other possibilities were exhausted, Dmitri was formally accused of belonging to the Socialist-Revolutionary (SR) party and recruiting other Soviet students living in Czechoslovakia to join it. Organized in 1901, the SR party had gained much support among Russian peasants, playing an active role in both the 1905 and 1917 Russian revolutions. One party member, Alexander Kerensky, eventually became head of the Russian Provisional Government, which was abolished by the Bolshevik takeover in October 1917. In 1918, the SR party tried to revolt. Its defeat led to the arrests and mass persecution of its leaders and regular members. In response, some of them again resorted to violence: on August 30, 1918, a former SR member, Fanya Kaplan, made an attempt on Lenin's life. Many SR party members fought for the Whites and Greens in the Russian civil war. When it ended, some SR party members joined the Communist Party. Others left the country and created several opposition centers abroad. Dmitri Bystrolyotov was accused of spying for one of these organizations in Czechoslovakia.

Now, nothing remained to be done but to await sentencing. Long days stretched out, one after another. From time to time, Solovyov called for him. To make the case look solid, he tried to beef it up by adding some new details.

An episode that took place during one of these meetings stuck in Dmitri's memory. He would go back to it time and again for the rest of his life. In his memoirs, the echo of that episode is heard every time he asks himself the key question about his life: Had he done the right thing in coming back to Russia at the end of his spy work in the West? One day, fearing that his captors might change their minds and charge him with espionage that would call for capital punishment, Dmitri decided to slip the investigator another, more benign, self-incrimination. He began saying he had been a regular embezzler of state funds, of moneys sent to him for their underground spy-ring operations in the West. He claimed that he had stolen three million French francs from the funds given him by his former boss, Theodor Mally.

At first, Solovyov brushed off this testimony as total nonsense. He didn't believe Dmitri's words, for he knew damn well that Dmitri was an honest man and a good intelligence officer. The higher-ups' decision to persecute him had nothing to do with embezzlement. Then, as he listened to Dmitri repeating his made-up story again and again, Solovyov finally asked whether he'd heard right: "You had a foreign passport and enough money to slip away to some distant corner of the world and live there as you please for the rest of your life? And still you came back here?"

"Yes, I did. I came back even though I could surely have expected what has happened to me. The foreign press reported the mass arrests taking place in the USSR, and we, all of us operatives working abroad, were well informed."

"Why did you return then?"

"Because Russia is my Motherland."

"Moron!" the investigator cried out. "What a fool you are! To exchange hard currency for a Soviet bullet! You had everything—money and a passport—and yet you dragged yourself here? What a reptile! You have neither a soul nor a brain. 'Motherland!' Oh, what a jackass! What a fool! Well, stay in prison then, you insensible animal!"

This exchange with his investigator would haunt and torment Dmitri for a long time. Indeed, what had caused him to make that fateful decision? Why had he come back, facing almost certain ruin? What had led him to choose his earlier life as a spy in the first place? The answer would gradually come to him after years of going over the events of his dramatic life and writing his memoirs.

When our country orders us to be a hero,
Any one of us becomes a hero.

—FROM A POPULAR SOVIET SONG OF THE 1930S

Happy that he had finally broken the stubborn prisoner's resistance, the investigator Solovyov gave Dmitri his file to examine and sign. Besides his own testimony, the file contained two others, both incriminating him as a double agent serving the OGPU as well as the Social-Revolutionary (SR) Center in Prague. One of these was the testimony of Igor Kedrov, who had worked at the INO department of the OGPU since 1931, someone Dmitri had never met. Kedrov's testimony is absent in Bystrolyotov's current court case, indicating that it was most likely fabricated to intimidate him and discarded later, after serving its purpose. In February 1939, Kedrov himself (along with another OGPU official) wrote to the Central Committee of the Communist Party regarding the NKVD's "violations of Socialist law and unacceptable methods" of investigation. Characteristically for that time, he was arrested, accused of espionage, and shot.[1]

The other testimony was that of the former acting head of the INO, Sergei Shpigelglas. A seasoned Soviet spy in his own right, he had acted as an illegal operative around the globe—in China, Germany, and Spain. His most daring operation took place in 1930s France. Running a fish shop near Montmartre in Paris as his cover, he directed the kidnapping of Russian émigré general E. K. Miller from the streets of Paris and delivered him to Moscow. Later, Shpigelglas coordinated the exfiltration from France to Spain of another émigré general, N. B. Skoblin, who had served as the OGPU agent in the Russian émigré community in Paris. Under the code name DOUGLAS, Shpigelglas personally directed the smuggling of top secret military documents, including those from German General Headquarters that revealed the German military doctrine regarding the USSR. Shpigelglas's testimony against Dmitri was likely written under pressure: he was arrested six weeks after Bystrolyotov and also accused of high treason, conspiracy, and espionage. He was shot on January 29, 1940.[2]

Since Dmitri hadn't yet regained full command of his limbs, gripping the prisoner's hand in his own, Solovyov helped him to sign his "voluntary confession." His case closed, now Dmitri had to wait for the court hearing. He had no illusions about the outcome of the trial. Having signed an admission of guilt, he knew there were only two options for sentencing him: a long prison term or the death penalty. Considering the weight of his crimes—espionage, terrorism, conspiracy—and the fact that all of his cell mates accused of similar crimes were sentenced to capital punishment, he was convinced that he was also marked for death.

To occupy himself, Dmitri tallied all the bodily traumas he had endured during his interrogation. His toes fully recovered from the damage, but a dull pain persisted in the area of the seventh and eighth ribs. Sometimes when he attempted to turn his torso the pain sharpened, meaning that the ribs were either cracked or broken altogether. This was where they had beaten him using a steel cable with a ball bearing attached to the end of it. His brain function was also impaired by the beatings. From time to time, it was difficult for him to recognize his cell mates or even the cell he was in. He also found that when he became agitated he started stuttering.

His incoherent speech and loss of words especially worried him. It meant that the speech center of his brain hadn't fully restored itself. He tried talking to himself in some of the foreign languages he knew and discovered that his speech defects were even more profound. His vision was also harmed. He had episodes of blurring and flashes, which he took as signs of high blood pressure.

His physical suffering was exacerbated by excruciating loneliness. Most of the time he remained alone in his cell, having no one to share his feelings with. Prisoners had to clean their cells themselves, and one day, while washing the floor, he discovered a small cavity in it.

He poured some tea and crumbs of bread into it and planted a small chunk of an onion with roots in the little pit. Soon the onion yielded its first green sprouts, and Dmitri felt as if he owned a little garden with a living thing, which became his companion. Now he could talk with it as much as he wanted. He recalls this with humor: walking around the cell, he felt proud of his onion sprouts as if he were a plantation owner.

After months of tormenting wait, it was finally Dmitri's turn to be taken from the cell for his court hearing. He was hardly given a chance to utter a word. His last thoughts before sentencing were full of indifference to his fate: "Life? Death? How ridiculously everything ended. Self-sacrifice . . . Heroism . . . Cruelty . . . Everything comes to nothing . . . Life for me was struggle and hard work, a desperate striving toward a heroic feat. And here nothing is left of it. Everything's befouled." On May 8, 1939, nearly eight months after his arrest, he was found guilty of committing crimes that came under the most often invoked statute at that time, Article 58 of the Criminal Code of the Russian Soviet Federative Socialist Republic. He was sentenced under three different items of the article: item 6 (espionage), item 8 (terrorism), and item 11 (taking part in a conspiracy to commit those acts).

Nowhere in his voluminous memoirs does Bystrolyotov address the possibility that in the long run, unbeknown to him, his decision to refuse to sign self-incriminating testimony right away and to submit to torture might have saved his life. On November 25, 1938, when Dmitri had already spent two months in prison, Beria replaced Yezhov as the head of the NKVD, and death sentences became much less frequent. Thus, while during 1937 and 1938, 681,692 prisoners (353,074 and 328,618, respectively) received death sentences (nearly 1,000 per day), there were only 2,552 death sentences in 1939. During his interrogation, after prolonged torture when Dmitri had finally agreed to cooperate with the investigator, he was ready to incriminate himself in whatever he felt they wanted from him. But, when he began to tell how he had wormed his way into "the holiest place of the Soviet state, Soviet intelligence," Solovyov jumped at him and clapped his hand over Dmitri's mouth, saying that he should revise his story. He should say that he was recruited as a student and had conducted anti-Soviet activities in Czechoslovakia only within the Union of Student Citizens of the USSR Living in Czechoslovakia. Thus Dmitri realized that the decision was not to execute him but to banish him to the camps for a long time. He was sentenced to twenty years in prison and five years of deprivation of civil rights, which, among other things, meant internal exile.[3]

Listening to his sentence, Dmitri was disheartened that he wasn't able to feel like a hero in the way that Soviet propaganda portrayed political prisoners of tsarist times. The difference was staggering. Proud of their defiance of the tsarist government, those prisoners "firmly and calmly said farewell to and comforted those close to them. Their heads raised high, they were bound for immortality. Death was a worthy crown for their lives. It was their victory. But that was under the tsar . . . Under Soviet power, I was afraid to think about those close to me. I chased away thoughts of them, because I was ashamed of my doom!" He recalled the inscription "for fearlessness and mercilessness" engraved on the gun presented to him for his successful handling of Oldham. Now it sounded like a mockery. Now he felt that the weapon was presented to a "fearless and merciless man for his *stupidity*." "Am I a hero or a fool?" This question would torment him for the rest of his life.

After sentencing, he was returned to the Butyrka prison, the starting point of his sad journey in captivity. In comparison with what he had been through, now Butyrka seemed like a paradise on earth. The joy of living overwhelmed him. Taken into the inner courtyard for a walk, he marveled at seemingly ordinary things—the greenery of trees, the chirping of sparrows, and the blue sky. "What a pleasure! Mummy, what a pleasure!" he exclaimed.

Soon he was transferred to the special Sukhanovka Prisoner Pre-transport Post. A month and a half later, in early July 1939, along with other prisoners he boarded a heavily guarded train of fifty freight cars, each carrying seventy-five men. A long journey was ahead for all of them. The train's destination, Krasnoyarsk Raspred (Prisoner Distribution Center), was located in the depths of the vast country, in western Siberia.

As might be expected in his situation, on the road Dmitri's mood vacillated. He tried to maintain an appearance of calm, but like the other prisoners, "a raging, sometimes sobbing howl stayed inside [him]." At times, he began thinking of himself again as a hero holding on to his battle post: "The key to immortality is in my chest. I must become worthy of my destiny." As the train moved across the country, passing through large cities and little towns, peeking through the tiny grated window of the railroad car and noticing men frowning and women crying furtively, he came to realize that he and his fellow prisoners weren't alone in their terrible predicament. The whole country was in trouble. "By mid-1939," he sums up, "there was no cultured family left in the country that hadn't had at least one of its members arrested."

On thin pieces of cardboard from his cigarette packs, he wrote three short messages to his mother, along with her address, and dropped them from the car wagon in the hope that someone would pick up and mail at least one of them. (He learned later that all three letters reached his mother. This fact alone restored his belief in people's goodness and sense of justice: if they were caught with a letter from a prisoner, the senders risked their freedom and the well-being of their families.)

After a long cross-country journey the train finally arrived in Krasnoyarsk. Soon after the prisoners had disembarked, been sorted out, and placed in barracks, Dmitri suddenly found himself on the verge of death. Wandering around the courtyard, he spotted an enamel cup on the ground. Rejoicing that now he would drink not from a tin prison cup but from a decent vessel, he reached for it, but instantly a gunshot resounded, and a bullet snatched the cap from his head. The cup happened to be in the "firing zone"—where sentries had the right to shoot without warning anyone who entered. He found it ironic and symbolic that his "fashionable cap from London took a Krasnoyarsk bullet." Like many other new arrivals from prisons, Dmitri was still dressed in the street clothes he was wearing when he was arrested. With his khaki shirt, purchased in Touggourt on the border of the Sahara, he also had an Amsterdam suit, a Swiss jacket, and a Scottish lap robe.

Waiting to be transported farther to the north, he wrote another letter to his mother. He informed her of his sentence and tried to console her with assurances that it was the result of a court error and that his case would be reexamined very shortly. He also wrote to his wife urging her to divorce him and remarry as soon as possible. That was her only chance to survive. First of all, only through marriage, by changing her surname and place of residence, could she avoid being arrested as a "member of the family of the Enemy of the Revolution," according to the NKVD decree of 1937. In addition, after his arrest Iolanta was left with no means of support, and her chances of employment were next to nil, and on top of that, hunger could exacerbate her dormant tuberculosis. Deep in his heart, sentenced to twenty years behind barbed wire, Dmitri believed that he wouldn't come out of the camps alive. But he wanted his wife to survive.[4]

He soon discovered that imprisoned doctors worked in their profession in the camps. His medical doctor diploma from Zurich University had been issued not in his real name but in one of his aliases, most likely that of Enverov (the name his ex–fellow convict Ivanov remembers seeing in his file next to his real surname). However, to function as a medical assistant in the camps he hardly needed a diploma. The acute shortage of medical personnel often forced the authorities to assign any convict who could, after brief training, work in that position under a doctor's supervision. Although no documents in Bystrolyotov's KGB file survived to prove his medical qualifications (which likely existed at the time of his imprisonment; in his memoirs, he indicates that the documents were confiscated), interviewed many years later, his fellow prisoners had only good things to say about him as a medic.[5]

Dmitri was late in applying for a position as medical assistant; there were no more openings. But since prison life was unpredictable and medical personnel often in short supply, he was offered a transfer from the general barracks to the medical unit quarters to stay in reserve. While helping the medics distribute pills in the barracks, Dmitri soon ran into trouble on account of being ignorant of the dramatic difference in relationships between prisoners in the camps and those in jail, where they most often regarded each other as comrades-in-misfortune. In contrast to political prisoners, officially branded as "enemies of the people" (in camp slang, *kontriki*, the shortened form of *kontrrevoliutsionnaia deiatel'nost'*, "counterrevolutionary activity"), the camp authorities regarded common criminals (in slang, *urki*) serving their terms for theft, robbery, rape, or murder, as a "socially close element," that is, as coming from the working class and therefore trustworthy. Thus, the camp administration delegated to these hard-core criminals key positions and assignments. This arrangement gave them a free hand in shortchanging, robbing, and looting other prisoners: "It was a nightmare . . . Encouraged by the camp authorities, harassment, malicious insults, and crimes created the basic background of camp life that oppressed all of us on a par with our awareness of [the] injustice of our incarceration."[6]

He would learn about that in full measure later. But now, awaiting the next leg of his journey in the prisoner distribution center in Krasnoyarsk, his ignorance of the rules of his new life suddenly brought him again to the brink of being murdered. As he was making his rounds with the medicine, one of the *urki* liked the fancy, foreign-made neck scarf that Dmitri's wife had given him shortly before he was taken away from his home. Without hesitation, the criminal snatched it from him. Dmitri attempted to recover it, but the robber threatened him with a knife that he suddenly retrieved from somewhere under his clothes. This encounter awakened Dmitri to the realization that, in the camps, he had entered a new world whose mores were different from those of the prison world.

Finally, counted and documented, all the prisoners of the Krasnoyarsk Raspred (Prisoner Distribution Center) were loaded on a lighter. Pulled by a tugboat, it headed downstream on the Yenisei River toward Port Dudinka, twelve hundred miles north of Krasnoyarsk and a short railroad run from Norilsk. It was a long, tiring journey. On his way to one of the harshest camp sites in the country, Dmitri, as well as many other prisoners, ran the full gamut of feelings. Most of the time, he felt desperate, falling back into a state of shock similar to the kind he had experienced right after his arrest. It was the time of his "first transformation from an active man into an unthinking zombie . . . I considered myself a worthy son of my times. And suddenly, I was removed, crumpled, banished, and thrown out into a wastebasket. [On the day of my arrest] I wasn't just doomed to die slowly. I was also humiliated and morally degraded, which is worse than any physical death. Why? What for? For whose need?"

Sometimes he was able to share his feelings with his travel companion, Stepan Medvedev, a railroad worker and devoted Party member. Since the most difficult thing for them to swallow was an overwhelming sense of injustice, the reasons for which they couldn't comprehend, they had to come up with some explanation that would help to alleviate their pain, at least a little.

Echoing Dmitri's conversation with the Jewish fellow prisoner he had met back in his Butyrka days, now on board the lighter taking them to where they would serve their sentences, Dmitri and Stepan acknowledged to themselves and to each other that they shouldn't consider themselves totally innocent. They too had a hand in what was going on in the country. Due to various circumstances of his life abroad Dmitri hadn't joined the Party, but he considered himself a "non-Party Bolshevik" (*bespartiinyi bol'shevik*), a widely used term to denote a highly conscientious Soviet citizen, especially popular in the 1930s. After all, didn't they close their eyes to arrests and other lawlessness in the country? Along with many other political prisoners, they came up with different explanations for the disaster that shattered their personal lives and life in the country in general. At this point, like a great many other Soviet citizens, they both still believed that Stalin was unaware of the horrific injustices and mass arrests. They were convinced that those acts were the handiwork of "scoundrels and crooks, bureaucrats and fools" who had crawled their way into the Party ranks.[7]

Dmitri also felt that, although he wasn't accused of it by his interrogators, he was now being punished for his own numerous trespasses of moral boundaries while spying for his country in the West. He justified these trespasses with his fight for the grand human ideal he thought he was helping to bring to life: "The main things that accompany struggle of all kinds are filth, cruelty, and heroism . . . If I expose my chest to bullets, I also have the right to shoot somebody else in the chest. For the sake of the great idea of [humanity's] future happiness nothing is to be begrudged. . . . For this future perfection of tomorrow and somebody else's life, I [was] ready to sacrifice myself, joyfully and proudly."

But these conversations and acknowledgments relieved Dmitri's anguish only for a while. Looking around the lighter packed with hundreds of other convicts, he realized that the beloved slogan "Forward only," under which he had operated in his past life, meant nothing now. In fact, as Stepan pointed out, he should have modified it to "forward to the Soviet prison, to a slow death in the Siberian camps."

Stepan said, "You [Soviet spies] did mean and cruel things, and life cruelly laughed at you: you're being punished with the realization that your evil acts were useless. There can be no worse punishment: heroes turned into fools."

Stepan's comments on the inefficiency of Soviet foreign intelligence reflected Dmitri's having confided in him that by the end of his spy career, working behind a desk in one of the Lubyanka offices, he had come to realize that so much of what he had obtained, often at great risk, was mismanaged and utterly wasted. To be fair, it must be pointed out that this was not unique in the history of world espionage, but still, an important element objectively explains Dmitri's frustration. Stalin forbade any analysis of intelligence data, thus rendering the information merely raw material for his own deliberate interpretations. As a result, he was fed only the data deemed in accordance with the dictator's world outlook, usually full of mistrust of the West and suspicions of conspiracy against the USSR from every corner of the world.[8]

On August 20, 1939, at last the lighter reached Port Dudinka. All of the convicts were taken ashore and loaded onto a train, which, along the narrow-gauge railroad line, took them to the place where they would begin serving their terms—the Norilsk camp, Norillag for short. The camp had been organized just a few years earlier, on June 25, 1935, near Norilsk, then a settlement, situated on the Taimyr Peninsula between the Yenisei Bay of the Kara Sea and Khatang Bay of the Laptev Sea, nearly two hundred miles beyond the Arctic Circle. The Norillag, along with two other northern camps in Vorkuta and Kolyma, was one of the harshest places of service. The Taimyr Peninsula, over six hundred miles long, was a place of solid permafrost and fossilized ice. The northern part of the peninsula consisted of Arctic deserts and tundra, an empty space overgrown with moss and lichen. In the south, tundra was interspersed with forests, and mountains were intermingled with stone deserts. The subarctic and sharply continental climate with freezing temperatures held for up to eight months; the short summers of only two months brought clouds of relentless mosquitoes. The wintertime was especially hard to endure: extremely low temperatures, at times reaching minus fifty-six degrees Celsius (minus sixty-nine degrees Fahrenheit), often combined with strong, gusty winds. Snow remained on the ground up to nine months out of the year. Added to this were two months of total darkness during the polar nights and twilight most of the rest of the time, except for the brief summer.

Similar to other harsh places where prisoners served time, this uninviting place wasn't chosen for the sake of punishment alone. The Norilsk camp was organized to provide a workforce to construct and operate facilities for mining and processing the area's copper and nickel deposits, as well as deposits of mica on the Taimyr Peninsula (the Birulinsk deposits). And slave labor was indispensable. Since its creation the Norilsk camp population had grown tenfold, and during Dmitri's term, it had reached nearly twelve thousand.[9]

Upon arrival in the camp Dmitri was assigned work as a medical assistant in the camp dispensary. The position gave him considerable privileges, the most important being excused from the backbreaking outdoor work and having the benefit of sleeping in his own bed in the medical personnel house instead of on plank beds in the barracks.[10]

But soon, highly disturbed at witnessing the death of a mental patient who had run into the "firing zone" and was shot by the guards, Dmitri committed an act of madness himself. At least no one around him—neither his immediate superiors, nor the other prisoners, nor the camp guards—could comprehend why, instead of holding on to his cushy job as medical assistant, he had volunteered to work outdoors in the tundra in freezing temperatures and fierce winds. At the time he reasoned that the impetus for his actions was that he didn't want to miss the opportunity to work at the Norilsk nickel-processing plant construction site because, in the Soviet political parlance of the time, it was designated as the "front line of building Socialism."

Clearly, his impulsive move was a desperate attempt to reconcile the horrific reality of his existence with his long-held ideological beliefs; otherwise, his life would have lost its meaning altogether: "A human being cannot go on in life without feeling the load of duties and ideals to which he's accustomed. But somebody emptied my backpack . . . [It became] immeasurably more difficult for me to go on: my beloved word 'Forward!' [has come to] mean nothing." He had to reconstruct the reality of his life on his own terms. Yes, he told himself, some scoundrels in the state apparatus had snatched him out from active life and thrown him behind barbed wire. But he was still a citizen of his country, wasn't he? And he must see his situation not as a punishment but as an opportunity to serve his country differently than he had served it before. He must remain a Soviet man no matter what. Other considerations were "only for people who lived on this [Soviet] land as strangers." To be anyone else but a "conscious fighter for building Socialism" disheartened him. It meant to be a "philistine oblivious to the grand designs of the Soviet state." In the vocabulary of the time, to be called a philistine was the harshest moral judgment, short of being an "enemy of the people." Anyone looking first and foremost for personal gain in life was dismissed as an individualist, self-seeker, and careerist (*shkurnik*).

This doesn't exclude any possible ulterior motive Dmitri might have had for joining the workforce in the field. As camp rumors had it, there was a downside to working in the camps as a medic. Those who remained in the rear (which included all medical workers) were to serve their full prison terms, unlike those assigned to manual labor, who had a chance for shortened terms for doing good work. He, Stepan, and another prisoner they had befriended on the way from Moscow to Krasnoyarsk decided that, as soon as they reached Norilsk, they would choose manual work, their "passport to freedom." It is not clear, however, whether the prisoners knew that at about this time, in the late 1930s, Stalin had abolished reduced sentences for good work performance. In his view, it "reduced the profitability of the camps."[11]

There was another, deeply personal, psychological dimension of Dmitri's actions at the time. With his early experience of parental neglect and abandonment, the humiliation of imprisonment crushed his fragile ego, which was an even harsher aspect of his Gulag existence than the physical demands of his new life. "Vermin," "filth," and "weeds" that had to be pulled from the healthy Soviet soil, complete with their nasty roots—that was how Stalin referred in official speeches to "enemies of the people," to whom Dmitri now belonged. To lessen the painful effect of this stigma, he had to do something truly outstanding, nothing short of an act of self-sacrifice and heroism.

He wasn't alone in his painful reaction to the excommunication of political prisoners from the body Soviet. After 1937, the guards and other camp personnel no longer referred to the prisoners as "comrades," as they had before, but exclusively as *zeks*, an abbreviation of *zasekrechennye kadry,* "classified cadres." In response to a prisoner addressing his investigator or a guard with the word "comrade," a dismissive proverbial repartee was born: "A Tambov wolf [read: a wild beast] is your comrade" (*Tambovskii volk tebe tovarishch*). During his spy years, Dmitri called all of his colleagues "comrades-in-struggle."[12]

Much later, when a fellow imprisoned doctor asked him why he had volunteered for such backbreaking work, paraphrasing the Butyrka prisoner's judgment, he explained to her that he felt himself "master of [his Soviet] house" who "had helped to build it and [was] responsible for it before [his] conscience." He added that he also felt responsible for the camp system itself: "I'm not a coward and scoundrel, but an honest citizen. I'm one of those who raised his hand in voting [to punish the 'enemies of the people']. The fact that I was mistaken doesn't change a thing. Now I am paying the bill."

But, he was attempting to pay another bill at the same time. Sometime later, another prisoner asked him about volunteering for work in the field: "Did you want to atone for your mistakes with suffering?" He replied, "No. I wanted to know everything, take it all on myself, and throw the responsibility from my shoulders. To free myself internally from the burden. This is the only path to self-cleansing."

Although he said no, it was, in fact, yes. What was this other burden in his life? What else did he feel he had to cleanse himself of if not the trespasses of normal human morality, no matter that Soviet ideology demanded to reject it for the sake of the new, class-based morality? According to that new morality, any vile act that benefits the toiling classes had to be considered good. Yet in all of his writing, Dmitri returns again and again to the immorality of his actions as a Soviet spy. He tries to reconcile these actions with the Soviet moral canon—as perfectly justified by the sublime goal of fighting for the future happiness of humanity. But it turned out not to work for him in the long run. On his own admission, in the camps, he told himself daily, "It serves me right!" (*Tak mne i nado!*).

Many years later, recalling this episode, he attributed his volunteering to do backbreaking work in freezing temperatures to a much more prosaic reason—a severe mental breakdown. "Suffering is the shortest path to loneliness . . . A suffering man is always lonely and self-absorbed; I was such a man." Apparently referring to the bouts of severe depression he had suffered first in Constantinople, then in

Prague, and later again, in Berlin, at the end of his spy career, he writes: "After all, in the past I had already suffered a severe mental illness with a clearly expressed inclination to withdrawal; in fact, I never felt mentally healthy." His personality was split at the time: while his "body [remained] behind barbed wire, [his] head [was] immersed in sweet dreams"; that is, by his own judgment, his mind was in a "schizoid state." (One can only wonder how, writing such things, he still hoped to publish his memoirs during his lifetime, that is, during Soviet times.) Dmitri was not alone in holding on to his Communist beliefs as a way of coping with the nightmarish reality of imprisonment. Anna Larina, the spouse of prominent Soviet leader Nikolai Bukharin, arrested shortly after her husband, also didn't immediately denounce the revolution. Incarcerated, she preserved her allegiance to it and even wrote a poem on the occasion of its anniversary. She later also referred to it as an "act of a lunatic."[13]

But, on the very first day of volunteer work, something unexpected happened. The harsh conditions on the ground triggered his self-preservation instinct and sobered him up for a moment. What was considered the "forefront of building Socialism" turned out to be a desolate and barren terrain with thickets of bushes and puddles of water into which wet snow was falling. He and the other prisoners wound up in icy slush up to their knees. Naturally, everyone, including him, became despondent. Then the construction site chiefs atop their horses came over and announced that they would handpick brigadiers who would not have to do manual work themselves but would select a group of thirty men whose work effort they would direct and whose productivity they would be responsible for. The chiefs handed out pieces of paper and pencils to the newly appointed brigadiers, which they were to use to maintain work records.

Dmitri's first impulse was to find a way to become a brigadier. Luckily, since he had early developed a passion for sketching, wherever he went he always took along pieces of paper and a pencil. Not relying on sheer luck, he inconspicuously took his pencil and paper from his pocket, walked around the mounted bosses, and joined the group of men chosen as brigadiers. "What could be done!" he explains. "After all, for so many years I had been an intelligence operative."[14]

But soon his self-destructive impulse returned. As a brigadier, although he didn't have to toil himself but only direct the efforts of others, he threw his own muscles into the work. He decided to make his brigade one of the most productive on the construction site. The job at hand consisted of using crowbars to pick deep holes in the permafrost where explosives would be placed to move large amounts of ground to make space for the foundation of the future plant. It was an enormously difficult task. After much effort, if you ran into a stone in the ground, you had to start all over again in another place. He worked himself without mercy. During his long, ten-hour shift he would break three or four crowbars. (In his self-denial, he seems to be emulating the highly publicized fictional superhero of Soviet propaganda—Pavel Korchagin—the protagonist of Nikolai Ostrovsky's much popularized novel, *How the Steel Was Tempered.* In the novel, Korchagin, sick with typhus and running a high fever, volunteers to build a railroad line for a local town. Some other man who, after working two weeks in harsh conditions, is quitting and going back to his family evokes contempt and is called a traitor. That was the spirit of the times.)[15]

Now Dmitri stayed in the general barracks with the other prisoners. His bed was located too far from the heating stove, so he had to sleep in his padded jacket and cover himself with his undersized sheepskin coat. Before lying down, he wrapped his head with gauze so his hair wouldn't freeze to the headboard of the bed. Yet, it was still the best place in this barrack: the beds closer to the stove were also closer to the poorly sealed doors. During the frequent snowstorms, snow streamed through them and piled high on those beds. His life impressions shrank to a handful of images and sounds:

> Dispassionate play of the northern lights, and the
> muffled coughing of hundreds of people, and the dull
> striking of crowbars against the permafrost, and the
> hoarse swearing and orders through the raging roar of
> the blizzard, and marching on ice into pitch darkness,
> and shouts of "Mama!" from under the masks, which
> resemble the whining of a hare, when somebody next
> to you is slipping and falling heavily under the feet of
> others, and shots of the guards, and moans, and turbid
> drowsiness, standing next to a bonfire kindled on the
> snow, and snowdrifts, which look like mountains, and

cave-ins, deep as abysses, and then a tiny trail [back to the barracks].[16]

Winter beyond the Arctic Circle was depressing not only because of its subzero temperatures and snowstorms but also because of its long, seemingly eternal nights. The absence of sunlight gradually depleted human strength. Exhaustion of both his body and spirit made Dmitri listless and totally indifferent to anything. He felt he had turned from a human being into an animal with only primitive drives:

> I remembered that I had a mother and a wife. I remembered their names and surnames, but these people had receded into an immeasurably faraway place and melted into it—they became small, superfluous, barely comprehensible, and above all, totally estranged. I rarely thought of them, but when they did come to mind, I thought of them as if they were literary characters to whom I related with total indifference. That was natural. After all, I had to work, eat, and sleep, and there was no strength for anything else.[17]

Every month both his mother and his wife sent parcels and letters, which he scanned without a thought. He knew that their monthly parcels were "proof of their sacred and ardent love." He knew that because of his imprisonment, his wife couldn't find work, and that because she lacked nutrition, her consumption had reactivated. He knew that they were both enduring hunger but sent him the most expensive cigarettes and the best canned food money could buy, spending their last kopecks. But he remained dead inside; both his mother and his wife "remained dead notions, apparitions of the other world."

Before they reached him, most of the contents of his twenty-pound parcels were stolen. Yet, he was forced to sign papers saying he had received them intact. Sometimes, he was lucky to get a can of condensed milk or a pack of cigarettes. But even this was a perishable gift. If he didn't slurp up the milk right then and there, either the guards at the camp entrance would snatch it during a routine body search or the man on duty at his barrack would find it and consume it himself. Dmitri would punch two holes in the can with a nail sticking out from his plank bed and suck the milk out. Often, tired after a long day's work, he would fall asleep while he was doing this and the "precious liquid would leak out onto [his] dirty mattress stuffed with moss."

He admits that during this stage of camp life, he underwent a second transformation—that of a suffering man into a "suffering animal." His whole life turned into "a little piece of bread of his ration, a cracked cup, and a small darned bag dangling on his rope belt."

Eventually, outdoor work under the harsh conditions of the Far North took a toll on him. Having been a sailor in the past, he had good muscle tone, but his heart, weakened by scarlet fever he had as a teenager, soon began to malfunction. His swollen feet made it difficult to take off his felt boots before going to bed; often, he slept without removing them. Yet, he was lucky to have these boots at all: one out of four prisoners didn't.[18]

His face also swelled so much that it interfered with his vision. He barely moved. Helpless and desperate, he felt that he was dying a slow death. He was commissioned to a hospital and given invalid status. The episode of his volunteering to work outdoors made him realize that his attempt at heroism was delusional. He was just a disposable instrument of the authorities who "worked him to the bone." On his own admission, he didn't feel morally bad for failing in his attempt to be at the "front line of building Socialism." He didn't regret leaving the fieldwork, because he was disappointed in the cause. While he had expected that at the "front line" he would join ranks with other highly conscientious political prisoners of Communist persuasion who, like him, had decided to disregard their situation and keep building Socialism, instead he found himself next to common criminals who were oblivious to politics. And they did better work. This group of prisoners consisted mostly of young peasants or blue-collar workers who were accustomed to physical labor and thus much more productive than the intellectuals, mostly aging, who were accustomed to working with their brains, not their muscles.[19]

After recuperating in the camp hospital, Dmitri was returned to his job as a medical assistant. Now he found it much more satisfying. He carried the wounded, frostbitten, and sick prisoners from the construction site to the camp infirmary and felt as if he were a medic on the battlefield. He tried to be where he was most needed, in remote camp units where the shortage of medical help was especially acute.[20]

Still, something was missing that would serve as ultimate proof to him that he should remain fully devoted to the cause of building Socialism. Soon an opportunity to prove it to himself came his way. One day he was returning from one of those remote camp units, several miles away from the base hospital. Escorted by a young and inexperienced guard, he was carrying a sack of canned food. On their way, they had to cross what seemed to be a shallow lake. Dmitri, with his load, easily swam to the other side, but the guard didn't know how to swim and attempted to cross the lake on foot. Soon his feet got stuck in the thick sludge at the bottom of the lake, and he began to drown. Dmitri tried to rescue him by throwing him the end of his belt. The guard grabbed it, but after Dmitri made many attempts to pull him out of the lake, the belt snapped. Frightened, a gun in his hand, the guard shot at Dmitri a few times but only lightly wounded his shoulder.

Soon the guard drowned, and Dmitri found himself in the tundra unescorted and, as far as he could tell, out of anyone's sight. He knew his way back to the hospital. But having been an experienced intelligence operative in the past, he quickly summed up the situation and decided he could make his way to freedom. At nightfall, he would circumvent the city of Norilsk and the railroad station, where they could hide secret guard posts in the surrounding bushes. Then, he would move across the deserted terrain northwest, toward Ust'-Port, at the mouth of the Yenisei River, where he knew he would find foreign ships unloading cargo in the harbor. He estimated that the journey would take him a week or so. He had enough canned food to sustain him for that long. Once he reached the harbor, he would make his way at nightfall to one of the boats flying a foreign flag. The next thing to do was to shout a few words in English, Dutch, or Norwegian to the watchman on board. Something like, "I got drunk, dizzy, and fell overboard. I'm freezing. Get me out!" Once on board, he would demand to see the ship's captain and tell him in confidence that he was a British agent escaping the Soviet police. As a reward for his rescue, he would offer the captain one thousand British pounds at the first foreign port. He was confident that the plan would work. He believed that captains of those foreign cargo ships were poor and often not too bright. He already had visions of himself back in the café Rotunda in Paris or dancing at the Algonquin in New York, which he remembered from his trip to the United States on Bazarov's orders.

It is hard to say to what extent his plan was realistic. It was most likely just a case of wishful thinking. The journey on foot over the vast and uninviting terrain of the Far North could take much more than a week, and he could run out of food long before crossing such a distance. Besides that, although he thought he could elude his pursuers by taking a route different from that of other escapees, they would have plenty of time to redirect their search. After all, it wasn't so hard to spot a person walking across the open terrain. As for the money, it's not quite clear how he planned to get hold of such a substantial sum of hard currency to pay off the captain who took him on board. Nonetheless, in Norilsk at the time, he seemed to believe that his escape plan was viable.

Then something happened that made him change his mind. As he reached one of the hills overlooking the new construction site of the Norilsk plant, he stopped in awe. The majestic picture of the industrial site growing in such a remote part of his country overwhelmed him. He felt proud of his Motherland's enormous efforts. If he left Russia, he would never be able to take part in his country's "peaceful construction and multiplication of its riches." All those working at that site would forever be part of this achievement. In his mind, staying put where he was at the place of such a heroic deed meant getting back on the "path to immortality." And he scrapped all thoughts of escape.

Because this part of his memoirs was written in the Suslovo camp unit of the Siberian Camp Management (Siblag) in 1945 and continued in the special camp at Omsk in 1954, it is tempting to explain them the easy way by saying that his writing about his conscious rejection of an opportunity to escape from a hard labor camp and his accolades to the glory of Soviet man were no more than a ploy, a way to avoid harsh punishment if the camp authorities found his writing, otherwise filled with condemnation of the inhuman treatment of innocent victims of the Soviet penitentiary system. However, from today's historical perspective, it is known that he was hardly alone in his admiration for the scope and achievements of the Socialist constructions of his time. Recalling a visit to the gigantic construction site in Magnitogorsk back in 1931 as a young man, well-known writer Veniamin Kaverin remembered experiencing feelings similar to those of Bystrolyotov. He also felt moral inspiration from "witnessing history in the making that filled him with hope and a powerful sense of progress—his progress, the country's progress." Kaverin, too, overwhelmed by the majesty of the grand scale of the work effort, tried not to see the connection between the human cost of such effort—the suffering of forced labor, the peasant women deported to Magnitogorsk and living in horrifying conditions, often starving and dying.[21]

Like yet another non-Party Bolshevik, one Prokhorov-Pustover, Dmitri also considered work in the camps not "slave labor but labor to the advantage of the Socialist state." The slogan about labor in the USSR being "a matter of honor, of glory, of valor and heroism" was ubiquitous not only in the Soviet cities but also in labor camps. Yet, it wasn't *any* labor that was so highly valued, it was manual labor: after all, on the books the Soviet state was a "state of blue-collar workers and toiling peasants." Therefore, in the Soviet Union, the biblical notion of "earning one's bread by the sweat of one's brow" was not a symbolic expression of honest work but a literal one. Like other "loyalists," as Solzhenitsyn categorizes prisoners of Dmitri's type at that stage of his life, Dmitri also equated Communism with Soviet patriotism, for he felt that, "despite what had happened, . . . Siberia is our Soviet land, on which we are building our Soviet plant. Only you [as a prisoner] do not have to give orders but to work with your own hands. It's hard? Yes. But it's necessary. You shouldn't escape from the camp . . . but remain on the Soviet land as its master."[22]

Bystrolyotov admits that such thoughts may "sound strange and ridiculous coming from a political prisoner, but it's necessary . . . to continue doing the only thing worthy—being master of your own land, to build and adorn your native land, your fatherly home. I voluntarily stay in the camp, voluntarily report to work. I don't care about the guards, I don't need them. I'm a citizen. That's why I'm alive and will remain alive." Elsewhere he repeats the last point: "We are given our Communist ideology. It's our compass; it will bring us out. It is [our] core that will save us from going astray and falling."[23]

In all fairness, Dmitri also wasn't alone in his eagerness to be part of the grand cause of building Socialism, even having experienced—in his case, literally on his own skin—the injustice of the Soviet system. Another ex-prisoner of the Gulag, released after many years of captivity, wanted to join the Communist Party. He insisted that his "unflinching, ineradicable belief in [the] Leninist Party, in its humanist principles" helped him to survive in the camps. In Dmitri's case, his need to belong was exacerbated by the circumstances of his early life. Still under the spell of the Communist ideology, which fit with his early harsh experiences as a hungry and homeless youth, he felt a strong need to belong, which had already served as a powerful factor in his decision to return to Russia. And now, looking out over the plant construction site, he felt that excitement of coming home again: "What happiness to regain your Motherland again! What a joy to feel yourself a citizen again!" And turning back, he headed toward the camp dispensary.[24]

However, he was destined to remain at the Norillag only a few more months. At the beginning of summer, after spending a whole day removing snow and chopping away ice from the roof of the dispensary hut, he fell ill. He was running a high fever, which refused to abate, and he was taken to the camp hospital. There they diagnosed an advanced stage of festering pleurisy, the long-term impact of injuries he had sustained during interrogation. When they had beaten him using the steel cable with a ball bearing attached to the end of it, his two lower ribs were smashed and had traumatized his pleura. Now he would require surgery.

After he recovered from the operation, the doctor proposed that he stay in the main camp hospital as his medical assistant. Dmitri refused and made another attempt at heroism. He asked to be transferred to another camp in Port Dudinka or any other one located farther to the north toward Dixon Island, because as he explains it, "among *zeks*, those places were considered more troublesome and dangerous." But his state of health was hardly adequate for such an ordeal. First, they assigned him to a lighter job as a housepainter. Then he worked for a while as a medical assistant again. Finally, the chief doctor had mercy on him and decided to save him from his own self-destructive impulses. He included him in an invalid group of prisoners to be transported via Krasnoyarsk to Mariinsk Recovery Camp. It was a "lucky transport" that every prisoner dreamed of joining by any means possible, including self-mutilation or by faking insanity.

On August 21, 1940, a year after his arrival in the Far North, the invalid prisoner contingent of Norillag was loaded onto a lighter heading south, upstream on the Yenisei River. At the last moment before boarding, Dmitri made another self-destructive attempt to stay behind. He approached an officer of the guards who was on horseback and told him he wanted to remain in Norilsk to build the plant. It took the officer a whole minute to look him over, head to toe, before whispering into his ear, "Are you out of your mind? They give you life, warmth, and light! Rejoice that you got into this lucky prisoner transport." Then he spurred his horse on and galloped away.

With five hundred other crippled, wounded, and terminally ill prisoners, Dmitri had no choice but to continue his journey through the Gulag Archipelago.

SIXTEEN | The Invalid Camp

The notion "human being" has a proud ring to it.

—MAXIM GORKY

On September 22, 1940, a special invalid transport, a barge pulled by a tugboat, cast off the pier of Port Dudinka. All five hundred prisoners on board were written off in the accompanying documents as "not responding to treatment in the conditions of the Far North." Most of the patients were blind, legless, dying of tuberculosis, or swollen with edema. A separate cell in the hold contained thirty-two mental patients with their own doctor and his medical orderly.[1]

The invalid prisoner barge was the most coveted transport, for it promised the end of a miserable existence in the harshest climate on earth, but at the same time, it was the most dreaded transport. Many of those on board these invalid transport boats thought of it as a "journey into the abyss, sailing across the Styx away from the known world." In many ways, the prisoners' conditions on the boat were even worse than those in the jails or the camps. The transportation of prisoners was a matter of strict secrecy and carried the potential risk that some would attempt to escape by diving from the barge, so they were kept in the hold where they had restricted space and only limited access to fresh air. The hatch between the deck and the hold was locked and sealed, leaving only a small opening for ventilation. The hold was equipped with multistoried plank beds, and tuberculosis patients who couldn't breathe lying down crawled onto the floor, upholstered with steel sheets and flooded with sewage from the three barrels that served as prisoners' close stools.[2]

The food situation was equally dismal, even lower in quality than the camp food, and water was in shorter supply than in the camps. "Imagine the faces and hands of people who couldn't wash for the duration of the trip under such conditions," Dmitri recalls. The prisoners looked like "gray worms swarming about on the dark background of stinking entrails."

The chief doctor and two other female doctors, prisoners themselves, ran the transport dispensary located on the deck, leaving only three doctors to serve the whole contingent of five hundred prisoners in the hold. These three medical workers were chosen not on the basis of their professional qualifications but because all three were considered troublesome; the camp authorities used the sending off of hopelessly sick and handicapped prisoners as an excuse to get rid of these doctors. One suffered from schizophrenia, and another wasn't really a general medicine physician, but a psychiatrist who was addicted to morphine. As for Dmitri, since the time he had volunteered for manual work in the tundra, he had earned a reputation for being strange and restless.

Now he was left practically alone to care for all five hundred patients. He had to climb from one row of plank beds to another, distributing medicine, examining wounds, and changing bandages. He often lifted patients' spirits with a sympathetic word or a joke. Having no soap, he washed his hands with strong tea before making rounds, which lasted eight hours. He had to do his job accompanied by the sounds of the "splashing of fetid swill, hoarse breathing at the crack in the small openings of the frames above, and the incessant murmuring of a schizophrenic patient." [3]

The whole atmosphere prevailing in the hold reminded Dmitri of his trip through the African jungles: "Everybody crawls over the plank beds in the darkness, like monkeys in the wilds of a tropical forest . . . The same gray semidarkness. The same mortal danger, lurking every moment. Finally, the same necessity to move on, that is, to consciously expose myself to the inevitability of attack."

And one day while he was making his rounds, he was attacked, it seemed, out of nowhere. Somebody grabbed him by the throat with an iron grip. As he gasped for air, someone else struck the attacker over the head. The attacker turned out to be a mental patient, a small-postured, frail military engineer, who during a psychotic fit, mistook Dmitri for the interrogator who had tortured him to force his cooperation.

In a half hour, the attack was repeated. Then it came again and again, every time from an unpredictable side. The situation made Dmitri's already intense work extremely difficult. He asked the medical orderly in charge of the mental patients to keep an eye on the mad engineer.

The next morning, Dmitri learned to his horror that the orderly, a common criminal, fixed the madman problem in his own way—by strangling him. The orderly told Dmitri that he had done it as a service to him. Nor did he forget about himself: he expropriated the deceased man's army boots, leather coat, and cap.

It was useless to report the murderer. The authorities didn't trust any political prisoners, the "enemies of the people," and the orderly, as a common criminal, was considered a much more trustworthy, "socially close element," one of their gang.

From time to time, Dmitri was allowed to bring patients upstairs to see the chief doctor on the deck. During one of these visits, the chief doctor's assistant, former director of a military plant, one Zalman Amdur, recognized in Dmitri a cultured man and talked the doctor into allowing him to linger on the deck for a longer time. Needless to say, Dmitri was very appreciative: along with plenty of fresh air, the food was much better, too. Here's how Amdur remembers Dmitri: "He was a very handsome man, with smart blue eyes and a soft smile that revealed dimples on his cheeks. An excellent storyteller with an unhurried quiet voice, clear diction, and the literary and rich vocabulary of a highly cultured person. His stories were full of humor and very subtle sarcasm. He was extremely reserved in showing his emotions."[4]

Now Dmitri could take a break, and as he spent some time on the deck he took stock of his life back in Norilsk. At that first stage of his Gulag experience, he had often suffered from loneliness. There was a dearth of friends in the camp. It was understandable: like him, many prisoners still hadn't been able to overcome the shock of their displacement and the disruption of life as they knew it. As Dmitri notes, "A suffering man is always lonely and immersed in himself." Lost and disoriented in his feelings, he had met a similar forlorn soul, a young woman with whom he unexpectedly had a short-lived but deeply emotional romance.

She was a young Evenk woman, that is, she belonged to one of the indigenous Tungusic peoples of the Far North. Also a prisoner, a nurse at the camp hospital, she approached him first but couldn't communicate with him: her Russian was barely comprehensible. He couldn't even understand what her name was and nicknamed her "Sasha-Masha." The young woman expressed her disposition toward him with smiles and gestures. He responded by jokingly touching her nose and producing a buzzing sound: the tiny nose reminded him of a doorbell button.

Some time later, he saw her stealing and then eating, on the spot, fish from the camp kitchen. As an apparent gesture of gratitude for not reporting her to the authorities, the next day she gave Dmitri a small jar of tangerine preserves sold in the camp shop for prisoners. He responded by exchanging a pair of woolen socks he'd received in one of his parcels for a big fish and giving it to Sasha-Masha: she seemed to enjoy fish more than anything.

They had a few dates in some nooks on the campgrounds where they could find privacy for at least a short while. On one of those dates, a polar snowstorm began. The two-month-long polar night had already started—they lost their way in the darkness and wound up in a woodshed. They began making love, but they inadvertently discovered that they were sitting on a stack of frozen corpses under a pile of snow already accumulated inside the shed. During the winter, the prisoner hospital used the shed as a local morgue.

After Dmitri joined the brigade working in the tundra, he saw Sasha-Masha only sporadically. One day, when they ran into each other accidentally, she took him aside and put his hand on her belly, which was already showing. Dmitri was moved by this unexpected development in his life. He caressed her belly tenderly. After all, the young woman was carrying his baby, as it turned out, the one and only time in his life this was to happen.

But he wasn't destined to become a father. Soon, they found Sasha-Masha with a knife in her back: one of the common criminals confused her with another woman whom he was jealous of. When Dmitri was called in, the baby was still kicking for a short while in the dead woman's body. But it was too late to save either mother or baby.

Now on the deck of the barge, Dmitri was sad as he thought about the tragic fate of this young woman who had become very dear to him. He left behind a nameless grave that he would remember for the rest of his life.

His musings were interrupted by wild shouting coming from the hold. The cause of the mayhem was a fight that erupted in a group of common criminals who, despite numerous body searches before boarding the barge, had managed to smuggle on a deck of cards. One avid card player accused another of cheating. Razor in hand, he chased after the suspect, cutting up several other prisoners who stood in his way.

The wounded were pulled up onto the deck. Dmitri and a female doctor stationed upstairs were called in to take care of them. He and the doctor worked together until the job was done. Then they stepped aside for a break. Standing next to the relatively young and attractive woman, he felt torn between two conflicting feelings: erotic desire and an urge to grab her "graceful little legs" and throw her overboard, into the icy Yenisei water. In his view, this woman, Anna Anatolievna Rosenblum, had played a gruesome part in his life.

He had met her in the camps a year earlier, when he first reported to work as a medical assistant. The minute he stepped into the dispensary office, he recognized her as the very same female doctor who had been present during some of his endless interrogations and torture sessions in Lefortovo prison. When he lost consciousness, she was called in to administer a shot. She did so several times, and every time he regained consciousness, she informed the interrogator that he could go ahead and renew his efforts.

Now in the camp dispensary, she smiled at him, and he stood silently trying to assure himself that the woman was real, not an apparition of his horrific past. Obviously, she didn't recognize him: she had attended to too many tortured men as part of her job at the NKVD. Barely keeping his rage in check, Dmitri didn't show that he recognized her. At the very first opportunity, he told his boss at the dispensary, an imprisoned Dr. Nesterenko, about her. The doctor, an eccentric man, immediately agreed to conspire with Dmitri to murder her. One day when all three of them were in the office, Nesterenko engaged Rosenblum in conversation, while Dmitri stepped out into a little hall and got a thin crowbar used to crush chunks of coal before feeding the stove. His heart racing, his face sweating, he grabbed the crowbar, trying to decide quickly at what part of Rosenblum's body he should direct his blow.

At that moment, through the slightly ajar office door, he overheard the doctor asking Rosenblum whether she had worked in Lefortovo prison. When she nodded, the doctor asked whether, if Bystrolyotov's case were reopened for review, she would be willing to confirm that he had signed his testimony under torture. She replied, "Of course," and Dmitri put aside his crowbar in relief. Now he had a good excuse not to blemish his soul with another sin—murdering this woman. She could be of help to him, at least theoretically: reopening cases of "enemies of the people" was extremely rare.

Unbeknown to her, Rosenblum had escaped an unjust punishment at the hands of one of the innocent victims of terror she had secretly helped. What Dmitri didn't know was that in her capacity as head of the medical unit at Lefortovo prison, this military doctor of the third rank had saved many lives of prisoners who were tortured there. In fact, the prisoners even nicknamed her "the good fairy of Lefortovo." In January 1939, soon after attending to an unconscious Bystrolyotov, she too was arrested and found guilty of keeping records of unlawful means of interrogation. She was accused of exactly those things that she was opposed to—"Fascist methods of interrogation and annihilation of Soviet cadres." During her short, less than two-year (since April 1937) tenure at the prison, she had documented forty-nine cases of prisoners tortured to death. One of her best known testimonies told of severe bodily harm inflicted on one of the most distinguished Soviet generals, a hero of the civil war and Marshal of the Soviet Union, Vasily Blyukher, who was imprisoned in Lefortovo and died after Bystrolyotov had already been arrested. In turn, Rosenblum was also tortured and sentenced to fifteen years in the labor camps. Now on board the barge, on her way to Moscow for a new trial, she was worried that she could be sentenced to capital punishment.[5]

It took the prisoner transport a very long time, a month and a half, to reach Krasnoyarsk, an extremely slow pace: one could have covered the distance on foot. The fact that the barge was barely moving was a source of great worry to the prisoners. As if the unbearable conditions of being locked up in a hold with little fresh air and scarce water and food supply were not enough, it was already late autumn, and the snow had begun early. With this came fears that the river would become icebound anytime now and remain frozen for more than half of the year. If that happened, the authorities would have no choice but to disembark the prisoners and move them to Krasnoyarsk on foot. Considering that the contingent on board consisted exclusively of invalid convicts, this meant that hardly any of them would survive such a trip.

Nevertheless, the barge made many stops at the sheer whim of the guards' wives, who hurried nowhere and couldn't care less about the well-being of the prisoners. The many stops they demanded along the way were for frivolous reasons: now to pick berries, now cedar nuts. Meanwhile, all crew aboard, including the captain and the guards, indulged themselves in heavy drinking around the clock. The captain's wife, also drunk, often took hold of the steering wheel as she necked with one of the intoxicated guards. The prisoners watched in horror as the barge moved from side to side, not forward. It could crash at any moment. The body of the old boat could crack open, and all of them would wind up in the icy water. Things like that weren't unprecedented in the Gulag. With the constant shifting of prisoners from camp to camp, news traveled fast: through the grapevine, rumors spread about a similar accident that had taken place with a prisoner cargo boat that ran into the reefs in the Far East Sea.[6]

When the barge finally reached Krasnoyarsk, a pile of eighteen corpses was stacked on the deck. Because the head of the convoy and the rest of the guards were drunk, there was a danger that others would not know how to handle the rope and cables, causing the tugboat and barge to collide at the pier. Here Dmitri was able to intervene: as a former sailor, he helped to secure both boats correctly.

First, the prisoners were taken on foot to a temporary camp. Soon, through a hole in the fence, enterprising wives of the guards smuggled vodka into the camp and sold it to the prisoners. They set exorbitant prices, robbing the prisoners blind. Sick and tired, worn out by their protracted journey, the prisoners became quickly intoxicated, and a drunken orgy began. They jumped all over the plank beds. It was a sad spectacle; it looked like "the feeble thrashing about of heavy rags hanging on a rope to dry."

After everyone got tired and fell asleep, the common criminals set the barrack on fire.

Dmitri threw himself into saving those inside the barrack who couldn't move. With dark humor, Bystrolyotov admits in his memoirs that, since he was also intoxicated when he rushed to carry out the patients from the fire, at the end of the ordeal, he discovered that he had mixed up the doors of the barracks and carried out eighteen corpses from the morgue, instead of live patients.

The authorities decided to move the prisoner transport farther. But, a series of prisoners' deaths followed. Having held up during a month and a half of dangerous travel, decompressing when they reached Krasnoyarsk, they let their internal defense mechanisms go and began dying, one after another.

Finally, the whole prisoner contingent was loaded onto a train and taken via the Trans-Siberian Railway to Mariinsk, a town in Kemerovo oblast, some one hundred and twenty miles northeast of Kemerovo. Here, they set up the Siberian correctional labor camp of special designation, somewhat an anomaly: a recreational labor camp for invalids and the overexhausted—as Dmitri calls it, a "sanatorium-like camp."[7]

The first few days at the new location were hardly happy for him. First, he was robbed by criminals posing as authorities. Then a gang of common criminals mistook him for somebody else and beat him up. Finally, he managed to go through the bathhouse and reach his plank bed. Falling asleep, he experienced unusual joy: "It seemed to me then that I was like a drowning swimmer who had discovered in himself the strength to find his way out of the ocean depths: he crawled out onto warm stones, closed his eyes, smiled gratefully, and pressed his face against the bosom of Mother Earth."

"Doc, your wife has arrived from Moscow to see you."

This news reached him on the morning of June 22, 1941, when they called him to the headquarters of the camp armed guard (*vakhta*). The camp was located near the village of Suslovo, one of ten camp units (*lagpunkt*) of the Mariinsk division of Siblag. The units were located from fifteen to twenty miles apart. Mariinsk division was its capital, a small provincial town with a prisoner distribution center and the camp headquarters. Five such divisions constituted the Siberian Camp Management (Siblag) with its center in Novosibirsk.[8]

He listened to the news with no emotion. It was too sudden and too confusing. He had already written to Iolanta several times, begging her to cut him out of her life so that she would have a chance to survive. She must dissociate herself from him for her own sake. But she kept sending him expensive parcels containing clothes and canned food. Left without means of sustenance after his arrest, she went hungry herself to send the packages, and he knew it. He begged, even demanded, that she stop wasting her money, at least for the reason that almost everything she sent was stolen by the common criminals employed along the route of parcel deliveries to prisoners. But she continued doing the same things over and over. In her letters, she never complained and wrote very little about herself. As to parcels, she wrote that she sent them not only for him but for her own sake as well. It gave meaning to her life: "I can't live otherwise."

And a few days before they had told him that his good work in the camp had earned him the award of five, three-hour-long dates with his wife. The visitation was to take place in the little back room equipped with a single long, wide bench, on which the guards usually rested between shifts. And now his wife, whom he was sure he would never see again, stood before him. He froze in horror:

> Her cheeks sunken and her nose sharp as that of a
> corpse, her huge eyes glistening brightly on her skull.
> The feverish redness of her cheeks turned scarlet, and
> her disheveled hair stood on end. It was the ugly head
> of a dying woman . . . An unnaturally long neck and
> sticklike hands stuck out from her worn jacket. For a
> moment, her embrace wide open, her arms spread, I
> saw a scarecrow, a regular garden variety scarecrow, but
> a horrific one, for it was alive, painted in various colors
> and smiling. Her huge eyes gleaming, through cough-
> ing and husky breathing, the scarecrow said: "Well,
> now we are together again . . . As we were before . . .
> in Paris and Prague . . . my dear."[9]

She began hurriedly removing packs of expensive cigarettes and small bottles of perfume from her shopping bag, asking him to give them to the guards so that they would allow her to stay longer. He touched her forehead. It was hot and dry. She was running a high fever. She was coughing and wiping her mouth with a handkerchief, already stained with blood. It was clear that she was dying of an extreme flare-up of tuberculosis. She talked and talked nonstop, coughing and gasping for air.

When she intercepted his look of horror at her incredibly thin figure with sunken breasts, she misinterpreted it and smiled: "Do you recognize the dress? It's the same one that I had made in Paris." She named the fashionable atelier on Avenue Paix. "The same one I wore when I was 'Countess Rona Esterhazy.' Why are you silent?"

He sat next to her without daring even to move. The pain of seeing her suffering gradually turned into burning shame for being healthy. At the end of their meeting, at the gate of the camp, she said, "I'm dying, my dear, and I've come to say farewell to you. How wonderful that I could do it, isn't it?"

He remembered that a year before, when he was serving his term in the Far North, he was informed that his wife had made an attempt to see him in the camps. She traveled as far as Krasnoyarsk, but at the last moment before beginning the last leg of the trip to see him in Norilsk, she was informed that her visit was canceled; no explanation was given.

Now when she had finally succeeded, before stepping outside the campsite, she did something strictly forbidden by the rules for visitations: she threw her hands around his neck, saying, "I'm leaving you . . . forever . . ."

The prison guard jumped at them and tore her from Dmitri. She fell on the ground. Blood began oozing from her mouth. Dmitri lost his self-control. Sick to his stomach with guilt and despair, he attacked the guard, beating him until he bled.

He expected severe punishment. In his memoirs, he registers his thoughts upon being called to the *operchast'* (operational state security unit) of the camps: "What had all of those incredible sacrifices been endured for? For the sake of what did we go to battle so bravely? What is this, injustice or retribution? How much suffering we bore and inflicted on others! And now there is just emptiness. Everything is nonsense."

(In the 1960s, looking back at his life in the camps, he resolved that dilemma. While what happened to him in the camps was injustice committed by those who had sent him to fight, he accepted his suffering there as the payoff for the distress caused to others on the other side of the Soviet border. It was why he titled the part of his memoirs devoted to his camp life "Retribution.")

Luckily for him, on that day, June 22, 1941, war broke out with Germany, and in the ensuing commotion, instead of another trial that would undoubtedly add at least ten years to his term, he got away with fifteen days of incarceration in a dark, cold prison cell.

In late 1941, with the front line of the war approaching Moscow, extraordinary measures were taken to remove all especially dangerous political prisoners (those who had been sentenced under Article 58 for grave counterrevolutionary crimes) from any privileged positions in the camps and assign them to hard labor. Dmitri was relieved of his position as a doctor and sent off to another Mariinsk camp unit with orders to be assigned to manual work only. However, because of an acute shortage of qualified medical personnel, the local camp authorities gave him a less visible position—as a doctor assigned to the sick barrack.

A month later, he received a postcard informing him that his wife had died. Some time later, a young woman working in the censor's unit secretly passed a letter to him. She risked punishment for violating strict rules requiring the destruction of letters of the kind she felt compelled to pass on to Dmitri.

The letter was from a stranger who had witnessed Iolanta's last days. She wrote to Dmitri, fulfilling his wife's last wish that he know the truth of what happened to her. On January 1, 1942, in Moscow, they had rounded up a group of "untrustworthy wives" of repressed husbands, Iolanta among them, loaded them onto open platforms, and taken them by rail to Kuibyshev (now Samara), a distance of over five hundred miles. Many became chilled to the bone along the way. They put the arrivals into an empty barrack that lacked even plank beds. As Iolanta lay on the cold floor, her throat bled continuously and copiously. She realized that she was a hindrance to everyone: there was no soap, no hot water. Somehow, she managed to get her hands on a kitchen knife, hid it in the sleeve of her overcoat, and holding on to the walls, crawled into the bathroom, where she cut her throat. They found her dead in the morning. The letter ended with words addressed to Dmitri that Iolanta had asked the woman to pass on: "You must survive. At least as a witness. For your own sake and for the sake of all of us."

He read the letter again and again, walking outside of the barrack until his legs gave in. He fell on the snow, his eyes open, and lay there without moving, oblivious to the fact that if he didn't get up soon he would freeze to death. After a while, by luck, one of the other prisoners passing by recognized him and, with help from others, dragged him to the barrack.

At yet a later date, he received a postcard from his mother's neighbor informing him that, when Iolanta had left for Siberia to see him for the last time, his mother, who had lost her sight from grief, took advantage of her absence and, to stop being a burden to her sick daughter-in-law, ended her own life by taking an overdose of sleeping pills.[10]

All of this hit Dmitri hard. The deaths of both his wife and his mother had a profound effect on him. Never before had he felt such excruciating loneliness. The only physical mementos left of Iolanta were several high-quality photographs taken soon after his return to Moscow from his work abroad. These pictures were his "most sacred personal treasures," almost like icons, representing not only the memory of his perished wife but also his whole stormy life abroad. He kept these "holy little pictures" in the safest place he could think of, under the mattress of his bed. But soon after he learned of Iolanta's death, the photos disappeared. Horrified that someone had torn this "thread that tangibly and visually" connected him with his past, with trembling hands, he frantically searched his cabin and the sick barrack in his charge. But to no avail.

Soon, pieces of the photographs were spotted in one of the camp lavatories. The gruesome symbolism of where his past life had wound up enraged him. It was clear that the pictures had no value for the thief (besides, they could also have become pieces of evidence against him). With the photographs, the thief also stole Dmitri's manuscripts and a package of blank paper, which he had managed to obtain from a young woman working in the office, giving her in exchange a small jar of lipstick he produced by mixing some ambulance paint with a lanolin ointment. Paper was extremely hard to come by in the camps. The thief aimed to make a fortune selling (or bartering for goods) every scrap of these papers. The sheets containing Dmitri's notes were still good for rolling cigarettes, and clean paper was in high demand for writing letters and, even more so, for making playing cards, one of the main entertainments among the hard-core criminals.[11]

Blinded with thirst for revenge, Dmitri lost his usual reserve, resolving to find and kill the perpetrator. There was only one way to do that in the camp: hire one of the "bitches," turncoat thieves who violated even the thieves' law; they were the cruelest of hard-core criminals.[12]

The thief turned out to be a young lad who owed quite a bit to Dmitri, who had recently done everything in his power to save this man's life and health: he kept him in the sick barrack for three months and ensured that he received good nutrition. After Dmitri's superiors demanded that the young man be removed from that sick barrack, he placed him in another one for recuperating patients and kept him there as long as he could. After that, he made the young man, whom he liked for being "affectionate like a calf," a hospital attendant and registration clerk. But after transfer to another place in the camp, the young man robbed his benefactor. The loot was found, revealing that every page of Dmitri's papers had been cut into neat pieces. Everything dear to him had been ruined. For Dmitri, the destruction of Iolanta's pictures, his "little icons," as he called them, was an act of sacrilege. Not to mention the staggering loss of the product of many months of labor—the manuscripts of his notes written under extreme physical and emotional duress, in stolen bits of time at the risk of being caught at any moment, notes that were all but impossible to restore.

He could eventually forgive both crimes. But for him, who had always felt aversion for commerce—let us recall him starving but preferring manual labor rather than selling some goods on the streets of Constantinople during his miserable months as a raw youth—seeing everything sacred to him turned into merchandise stacked up in "neat piles," recounted and carefully priced, specifying both wholesale and retail prices, and marked with precise handwriting was too much. It drove him crazy: he snapped and called on his hired hand to carry out the punishment. The "bitch" took the perpetrator of the crime into a separate room and, with a deliberate blow, permanently ruined his liver. To hide it from the camp authorities, they reported he had accidentally fallen into some pit in the zone. The thief died soon afterward in the camp hospital.

For the next several months, Dmitri went on about his doctor's duties in a state of stupor and total indifference to his fate. That was hardly wise, for he could easily run into trouble on a daily basis. Even for a trifling error, an imprisoned doctor could be stripped of his position and sent to general outdoor work at once.[13]

He had to be on guard at all times and be sure not to miss anything that was expected of him. To have enough time to visit the camp kitchen and taste the food, he had to get up earlier than the general prisoner population. Then he had to rush back to the dispensary and attend to the sick who had fallen ill during the night, as well as those who had been assigned the night before to have their temperatures checked, so that their diagnoses could be finalized. Then he had to show up at the prisoner lineup with a list of those who were excused from work because of sickness. After that, he also had to fulfill the functions of sanitary inspector, that is, to check for potential sources of infection all over the camp site: in the bathrooms, the garbage pits, and the morgue.

If a new prisoner transport was due to arrive, it spelled additional—and quite unpleasant—chores. As a rule, such transports carried a number of corpses of prisoners who had died en route. It was his responsibility to do the paperwork related to accepting the dead and to perform an autopsy on each to determine the cause of death. Then death certificates had to be filled out and signed, and the corpses had to be stored in the hall of the morgue, awaiting others to be buried in a specially dug ditch.[14]

Meanwhile, life in the camps was even tougher than before the war broke out. The camp food supply became even worse than before. Food shortages were the main cause of death for many prisoners. When working in the fields, they stole and ate whatever they could lay their hands on, including raw vegetables and even grass. As a result, they suffered stomach ailments, of which many died. But this didn't seem to bother the camp authorities. They were required to have a thousand prisoners in the camp, and while camp prisoners died daily, sometimes at the rate of ten to fifteen per day, new ones kept arriving, thus keeping their quota in balance. During the year of 1942, the camp "resembled a pot on a hot plate: in exchange for evaporated water, fresh water was poured in, and the level in the pot stayed the same."[15]

Actually, the prisoners died not because of hunger per se but because of kwashiorkor, a disease caused by lack of protein. Swollen or dried up prisoners were brought to special barracks for the dying. Their mental capabilities destabilized, they couldn't move. They covered themselves, putting blankets over their heads, turned toward the wall, and died, one after another—"without moaning, without regrets or grumbling."[16]

Of course, Dmitri was in a much better position than regular convicts, but he, too, was looking for a way to get some more food. For that purpose, he put his artistic talent to use. The town outside the camp had no facility for taking pictures, so he made pencil sketches of the civilian employees of the camp. He also catered his services to the fellow prisoners. Many of them wanted to send pictures home to their families, and they often asked him to embellish their looks. For example, one customer asked him to draw him not the way he looked at the time, emaciated and bald, but the way he remembered himself before his arrest—well fed, with a thick head of hair. One aging man asked Dmitri to draw the hands of a youngster in the camp, for they reminded him of the hands of the young wife he'd left behind. Pleased with Dmitri's work, the prisoner then sewed the portrait into the front of his tunic. In lieu of payment, Dmitri received now a half ration of bread, now a half dozen cigarettes, now some goodies stolen from the kitchen—a couple of onions, a piece of salt pork. At one point the camp chief set up a shop producing children's toys that he sold in the nearest town. He hired Dmitri to paint the toys, sometimes rewarding him with salted fish, sometimes with a few potatoes.[17]

But life remained dreadful. There was also a lack of fuel. Though there was plenty of peat nearby beyond the zone, the camp authorities didn't bother to organize its supply. There was no electricity in the barracks; it was dark and cold. According to the camp rules, Dmitri had to perform autopsies on all prisoners who died without a diagnosis. He had to do dozens, sometimes hundreds, of them with a dull knife and without gloves. After losing both his wife and his mother, being put in charge of the barracks for the dying, and witnessing numerous deaths around him, Dmitri became increasingly depressed. In a state of constant dread, he became withdrawn, self-absorbed, and alienated. He began seeing things: a human hand, with its moving fingers coming toward his eyes, or some ugly faces. He couldn't decide whether these were hallucinations, that is, psychopathological phenomena, or the result of an eye hemorrhage due to increased blood pressure. Occupied all day long with the dead, he saw them in his dreams. The images of life around him and those that came in his dreams were equally horrific.[18]

But, in time, Dmitri saw the truth of Dostoevsky's observation about human nature, as expressed by Raskolnikov in *Crime and Punishment:* "After all, a human being, scoundrel that he is, gets used to everything!" (*Ko vsemu-to podlets chelovek privykaet!*). Dmitri gradually adjusted even to the horrible conditions of the Gulag. Using the perks of his position as a camp dispensary doctor, he not only found a way to write but also, unexpectedly, found himself in a young woman's arms.

There would be no fortune for me,
if misfortune didn't give it a helping hand.

—RUSSIAN PROVERB

My dear one,
Take me along with you.
There, in a faraway land,
Call me your wife.

—FROM A POPULAR RUSSIAN SONG

One early spring day in 1942, late in the evening, as he was making last rounds in the camp, Dmitri was called to one of the women's barracks to take away a body they had found on the floor. Dmitri checked for a pulse but found none. Small-postured and puny, with closely cropped hair and a face smeared with thick dirt, it was hard to tell either the sex or age of the deceased. He loaded the light body onto his back and carried it across the camp all the way to the morgue. It was raining and dark. He put the body down on the floor of the morgue and was about to leave, when he heard a quiet moan. Swearing in every language he knew, he hoisted the skeletal body back onto his back and lugged it to the other side of the camp, to the sick barrack. A few times he fell into the pits and clambered up only to fall again after taking a few more steps.

He carried his load to the barrack, washed it up with warm water, covered it with a blanket, and placed it near the stove. Soon, the man on duty in the barrack called him to report that his load was a teenage girl. Dmitri came to give her a shot of caffeine and camphor. Since she had no papers, when he recorded her in the ledger, he christened her "Liuonga"—the name of a girl he'd known during his time in Africa.[1]

He later found out the girl's real name, Alenka, and that she was almost fifteen. An orphan—her father had been arrested in 1937 as an "enemy of the people," and her mother had died two years later—the girl was adopted by a local collective farm and given a cleaning job at the creamery. One day, as some peasants working in the field passed by, they asked Alenka to give them a small piece of butter. She did. Someone reported her to the police, and as the daughter of an "enemy of the people," she was sentenced to ten years in the camps for "embezzlement of Socialist property." In the camps, she was drawn into the company of hard-core criminals. Then she fell seriously ill. To give her a chance to recuperate, Dmitri assigned her a prolonged stay in the sick barrack and went on about his camp life.[2]

A half year later, late on a summer evening as he lay in his cabin, somebody entered. Always on guard, he was relieved to see that the guest was a beautiful light-haired, blue-eyed teenage girl, whom he recognized as none other than Alenka. She told him she knew that he had saved her life and wanted to show her appreciation. She began mumbling something about being clean, just coming from a bath-house. Still weak from prolonged illness, she cried on his chest as he reproached her for this stupid way of expressing her gratitude.

Another six months passed, and the next winter Alenka called again. During the previous summer, Dmitri had recommended her as a cook's assistant in the slaughterhouse, where prisoners worked preparing pig carcasses for delivery to the military. Always wary that the ever-hungry prisoners would steal pieces of pork by randomly cutting bits from the carcasses, thus spoiling them, the authorities allowed them to have pork scraps, which they could cook for extra nutrition. As a result of working there, Alenka gained so much weight that at first Dmitri had a hard time recognizing her. Now again she came to thank him for both saving her life and giving her the chance to regain her health. She began undressing, and pieces of cooked pork fell out from under her clothes. Dmitri was horrified: if caught, the girl risked another ten-year term for stealing state property.

He again tried to stop her romantic advances. She begged him not to reject her, for not only was it a matter of showing appreciation for what he had done for her, but it was also a way of protecting herself. He knew that she was telling the truth. At any given time in the *lagpunkt* where Dmitri served his term, female prisoners constituted no more than 20 percent of the camp population. Thus, women were always in demand. All of them, with the exception of old women and nuns, had sexual relations with men.[3]

They hardly had much choice. As in other camps, here, too, female prisoners were preyed upon by all males, whether they were the guards or the camp free workers or other prisoners. The pressure to cohabit was unrelenting, often accompanied by threats of physical attack, especially by hard-core criminals, complete with torture and humiliation. Those who resisted would be overwhelmed with back-breaking work, hounded by camp hoodlums, or cheated by the camp cooks of their rightful share of food, thus crushing them with hunger. A female prisoner was therefore forced to pick a sexual partner to save herself from these everyday threats. And no less important than anything else, if prisoners weren't overly exhausted and on the verge of collapse, they were looking for true love; even platonic relationships flourished. As Dmitri remarks, "Despair, fear, and loneliness pushed men and women toward each other"; otherwise, "melancholy would drive them to the grave." As another former camp prisoner, Frid, observed, such relationships "humanized" a prisoner's life. "In that life where, from early morning until bedtime, women heard only obscene language and threats and saw injustice, disorder, high-handedness, and violence," Dmitri recalls, "the only solution was cohabitation. And everyone who could do so took advantage of such an opportunity."[4]

According to the unwritten moral code of the camps, once a woman made her choice, she was left alone and was considered under her partner's protection. As other former camp prisoners testify, despite rampant rape and prostitution in the camps, women who had a camp "husband" were spared. Astonishingly, this unwritten rule was observed in the camps religiously.[5]

Neither he nor Alenka were exceptions. After all, camp life was first and foremost about survival. Responding to Alenka's persistence, Dmitri finally gave in to her pleas. To be on the safe side, she asked him to list her as a syphilis patient, which would save her from men once and for all. To support the legend, she even learned to speak in a hoarse voice, imitating the voice of patients affected by that disease. Of course, it also meant she had to let go of her job at the slaughter-house kitchen. But now strong and healthy, she was ready for it. They transferred her to a brigade working in the fields.

She and Dmitri became lovers. Now fully recovered and matured, Alenka became an eager and passionate lover. However, both she and Dmitri were aware of the temporary nature of their arrangement. As Dmitri explains it, such cohabitation was "rarely the result of calcula-tion or physical need, but always, in all cases without exception, of the need of peace and quiet, for inner balance, for heartfelt kindness and friendship, for familial comfort. But camp liaisons lacked exactly these things. Surely the love of miserable people forbidden by the authorities couldn't give them what they hoped for: embracing each other, both sides thought of those who had been left behind, their loved ones, and the inner closeness didn't take root." Soon, Alenka was sent to another camp. They said farewell to each other wholeheartedly. "Like two migratory birds, we came together for a time and parted forever," Dmitri recalls.

But he was destined to see Alenka again. In December 1947, on his way to Moscow for possible retrial, he was crouched in the snow outside some railway station with a group of prisoners, when, among another group of prisoners sitting in the snow nearby and waiting for a different train, he saw a tall young woman, blue-eyed, with a proud demeanor, and recognized his former camp lover. As he learned from other prisoners in her group, she was now on her way to another camp, having received another five-year term for violating camp rules. She turned around, also recognized him, and shouted, "Doctor! My one and only joy!" But the locomotive whistled, and they parted again. This time, for good.

In the first *lagpunkt* of Suslovo Siblag, Dmitri began writing in ear-nest. Here he had enough comfort to do it. After making rounds in the barrack for the deceased and finishing the required paperwork, he sat down in his small cabin and took to the pen. The thought of keeping a record of his life had occurred to him back aboard the barge going upstream on the Yenisei River on his way to Mariinsk. Shocked by the appalling conditions of the prisoner transport, he kept telling himself, "You should remember this . . . Make sure not to forget that . . ." In the hold among the other prisoners was one dying man, whom Dmitri nicknamed the Librarian. The man told Dmitri that he should make it his duty to the country to record what was going on in the camps, because future generations of Soviet people must know about it. This gave Dmitri a tremendous boost of energy, for it gave his life new purpose and meaning.

He had actually made his first attempts to write about his camp experience back in Norilsk. Quite in the spirit of his resistance to accepting reality and persistence in believing in the eventual victory of Communist ideals, there he composed something of, as he characterized it, a "heroic poem in prose, a hymn to living and fallen fighters." For that purpose, he selected the most interesting prisoners' life stories and added his sketches of them. In time, he compiled fifty of them, giving the manuscripts for safekeeping to a doctor who worked in the camps. But the doctor was transferred to another camp, and with him the writings disappeared without a trace.

Now, in Suslovo, under the impression of Alenka's story, Dmitri began writing about women in the camps. He set himself a daily norm—do four pages in his tiny handwriting. As in many other camps, there was a shortage of both ink and paper. He stole some ink from the desk of the camp chief and mixed it with iodine. He used the backs of discarded medical records. When he ran out of these, he turned to pieces of plywood, scratching on them with a nail.[6]

Though writing in the camps wasn't officially forbidden, describing the horrors of the Soviet camps was certainly a risky undertaking: if caught, he could get a new prison term plus a year of hard labor in the penal camp. Having a heart condition spelled a slow and painful death. But as in his young years, playing with danger still thrilled him. And his deep conviction in the historical value of his eyewitness reports gave him strength.

He mentally planned the forthcoming writing while doing other things, and by the time he had the opportunity to sit at his desk, he worked very quickly. If the writing session went without interruption and he succeeded in recording whatever he had planned, his morale was boosted. First, he reconstructed his notes about the Norilsk camp. Because of their potentially dangerous nature, he mixed these pages with other pages of writings and called the whole collection "Three Virginities." If searched, such a title would give the impression that his writing was no more than some erotic fantasies. He cut out two pieces of material from his long johns and pasted them over the covers of two notebooks, one rough draft and one final draft of the first and second parts of his African travelogue, titled "Telliua, or the Beginning of One Journey" and "Bubu, or the End of One Journey." A prisoner working in the camp carpentry shop supplied him with glue. Dmitri adorned the covers with exotic-looking profiles of a girl and a savage to ensure that the camp censors would give the manuscripts an "OK" stamp.

But he had to be on guard all the time. At one point he panicked when he was called to report to the camp security officer (*oper*, in camp slang, short for *operativnyi upolnomochennyi*, "operative representative" of the security police). He thought that in his absence somebody had snuck into his cabin and denounced him for writing anti-Soviet pamphlets. What must he do now? One voice inside shouted that he must tear his writing into pieces: without hard evidence of the denunciation, he had a good chance of surviving. But it was too painful to destroy the labor of so many hours that was of such importance to him. He decided to wait and see the reason for his summons. Before leaving his cabin, he placed the notebook onto the oven door of the stove pipe so that with little effort he could slip it into the fireplace. And he ordered the man in charge of the stove to keep the fire going. Luckily, they called him in for the usual: to translate letters in foreign languages sent to the prisoners before censoring them.

One sunny day at the beginning of September 1942, a female prisoner patient came to seek his help. Her name was Anna Mikhailovna Ivanova. She had sad gray eyes and, though a light gray strand of hair covered her forehead, a youthful face. Dmitri noticed her beautiful legs, her whole small but elegant figure. Like many other newly arrived prisoners to the camps, she was wearing her own clothing, taken along from her home after her arrest—a ski suit and good shoes with thick socks. That day, with a group of other prisoners, she had been escorted from another camp unit, covering the distance of nearly twenty miles on foot. The trip took a toll on her. She asked the doctor to attend to her sore leg and to give her some medicine for her heart condition.

As he examined her leg, she asked him whether she could leave a can of real coffee in his office so that she could come from time to time to drink it there. That wasn't an unusual request. Due to his reputation as a decent man, some prisoners used the doctor's office as a safe place to keep certain items that would be stolen from their parcels if kept in the barracks for too long: salt pork, cigarettes, canned food. Exhausted after a daylong walk, she fell asleep as he was making the bandage. When he had finished, he discovered that the newly arrived patient had mistaken the dark liquid in a measuring cup on his desk, the mixture of ink and iodine, for her heart medicine and had drunk it. At first this made him angry: now his precious writing material was depleted. Then, looking at her "well-bred but exhausted face," he felt sorry for her. He knew that she had walked all day long "with her belongings on her back and surrounded by bayonets and dogs."

It was dinnertime, so he woke her up and offered a bowl of hot soup. She began eating, her eyes still closed, but soon she came back to life. He offered to take her to a club to attend a concert organized by the Cultural-Educational department of the camp.

As in other camps all over the Gulag system, such a department's officially sanctioned goal was to increase prisoners' labor productivity via propaganda-oriented artistic performances. As one directive had it, "Every performance must educate the prisoners, teaching them greater consciousness of labor." However, in many places, prisoners used these concerts as a means of consuming some culture, as moral support, whether it was a chance to listen to some classical music or attend the performance of a play. Often, out of vanity, the camp authorities tried to outdo their colleagues in other camps with higher-quality concerts. For this purpose, when a new party of prisoners arrived, they would look for the most talented among them. The Mariinsk transit camp was especially known for the artistic activities of its prisoners. Its bosses were the first to pick talented people arriving with the convict flow. Among scientists and scholars, there were also musicians, artists, singers, actors, painters, and ballet dancers. It was easy to remove them from the crowd of other miserable people and put them in the local hospital to rest. Using their talents, the Mariinsk camp bosses organized concerts and festivals of arts.[7]

Dmitri took Anna to one of these concerts. Sitting in the hall next to each other, they imagined being back in Moscow at a Bolshoi concert. To complete the illusion, he told her that some chocolate treat was needed. And he offered her something that, in the camp environment, was a no less exquisite treat—two potatoes baked in coal. He had been able to get a hold of these potatoes by bartering another small jar of lipstick he produced in his cabin for them. During the concert, Dmitri inconspicuously admired Anna's profile. At one point, as they played a tango on an accordion, Dmitri recalled his trip to Valencia, Spain, where, late one evening, he had seen La Argentina, a famous flamenco dancer of her time, dancing right on the city embankment to the delight of sailors and hobos.[8]

By winter 1943, he and Anna became a couple. "We have our meals together. There are two of us. We are not lonely. For us, loneliness has ended" was how, a few months after they met, Dmitri described the fact that he and Anna had become an item. For the always-hungry prisoners, mealtime was a holiday in the camps. And although their meal might consist merely of leaves of decaying cabbage, scraps of turnip, and rotten potatoes swimming in gray, badly smelling liquid, it was still a feast. In the morning, as Dmitri attended to his daily ritual of dispatching work brigades to different tasks, he already knew that back in his cabin Anna was bustling about the hot plate, warming up the soup and baking two slices of bread.

Once Anna was bursting with happiness that she could treat Dmitri to a small piece of salt pork on top of a piece of black bread. They sucked on it as if it were candy. On another occasion, to impress him, she concocted a soup with onion, which she had exchanged with another prisoner for a few zwiebacks. To compliment her, he told her that it reminded him of a fish soup with sterlet they used to serve at the restaurant near the Grand Opera in Paris, run by Russian émigrés.

He tried to reciprocate in any way he could. One day, he brought her a present of the last item remaining from home in his bag: open-worked long underwear made of silk that he had bought at an expensive store in Paris before going to the Sahara. He also gave her a food item considered a delicacy under camp conditions—a fried cat's thigh. He wasn't sure she would eat it, though.

Of course, while he courted Anna, other women vied for the chance to form a relationship with the doctor, considering his many privileges. One of these women walked into his cabin and asked that he see her as a patient. When she undressed beyond what was required for the medical examination, he asked her to put her clothes back on: he had already set his heart on Anna.

Under camp conditions, he and Anna, like all prisoner couples, suffered an acute shortage of privacy. In summertime, well knowing the camp routines, they found short breaks of time to sneak into the thickness of tall weeds close to the "firing zone," a place where it was less likely anyone would approach for fear of being shot at. There, half-buried in the ground, were a few basketlike arrangements woven by prisoners from bush twigs, creating a kind of cocoon big enough to accommodate a couple. They crawled in there to make love and talk of the most intimate things. It was bliss to them, their love behind the barbed wire. "In the vast majority of cases," Dmitri recalls, "under camp conditions where a prisoner experienced degradation at every step, a couple's relationship was reduced to a minimum, to a physical act without spiritual closeness. But we [he and Anna] felt lucky that we had found soul mates in each other."

Bit by bit, during their dates, he learned about Anna. She was born on December 26, 1902, in a southern provincial town of Kherson gubernia. She came from a gentry background. Her grandfather was a landlord and army officer. Her father was a "kind man, a fop, and a talented lazybones." Spoiled by his father's wealth, he behaved irresponsibly, and nobody took him seriously. At one time he even supported the local underground revolutionaries by offering them his apartment as a meeting place. Anna grew up a daredevil. She learned to ride a horse in a man's way, and once out of sheer mischief, she even contemplated blowing up their house, using her grandfather's hunting cartridges.

When World War I broke out, followed by the revolution of February 1917, and then, with the October 1917 Bolshevik takeover of power and the ensuing civil war, Anna's whole family fell apart. When the Red partisans passed through their town, she recognized one of them as a man she had known as a girl. He convinced her to join the Reds. She did and soon became a reconnaissance scout. At one point, she was captured by the Whites and, together with other prisoners, was shot. But she survived the shooting with only a wound. Then she joined the famed First Red Cavalry Army, where she met and married a revolutionary army fighter, Vassily Rybalcheko. She gave birth to their daughter Magdalina.

When the civil war ended, Anna entered a university and graduated as an engineer. Soon afterward, she met another man, Sergei Ivanov, fell in love with him, and left the husband she didn't love. The couple moved to Moscow, where she found work at a military aviation plant as a quality control inspector, signing off new planes into operation.

She was arrested on June 11, 1942, and accused of treason. Quite in the spirit of the time, the arrest was the result of her being denounced to the secret police by one of the girls who worked in the lab she managed. The girl reported that Anna planned to fly away to Persia with a test pilot. She did it out of jealousy: she had a crush on the pilot, who paid her no attention and, though not encouraged, romantically pursued Anna. During the simultaneous questioning of the witness and the defendant, the girl repented and took back her accusation. Nevertheless, Anna was convicted for anti-Soviet propaganda and sentenced to five years in the labor camps.

After she told him her story, Anna reproached him for being tight-lipped. While she had revealed so much about herself, he hadn't reciprocated. Dmitri replied, "I feel uneasy about many things from my past." "Working for the OGPU?" she asked. "After all, you worked abroad, there's none of our blood on you."

"Ah, isn't it all the same whose blood it was? Blood is blood, little Anya," he replied.

He told her the truth about the circumstances of his birth and that, from his mother's side, he had "bad heredity," that is, he was the great-grandson of an "erratic woman," as he put it. "Without knowing this," he added, "it's difficult to understand me and my life," which he characterized as "confused, full of mistakes, yet outstanding." He also told her about his work abroad in general terms, skipping details that might reveal any state secrets related to his operations. Even in the camps he felt bound by allegiance to his oath of secrecy.

In the spring of 1945, the war with Germany in its final stages, the food situation improved, and now for breakfast they had bread that didn't have crushed wormwood mixed into the flour. One day Anna was even able to cook kasha out of wheat, boiled in sweetened water. Assigned to work outside of the camp at a cheese factory, she smuggled a piece of cheese into the camp one morning and offered it to Dmitri. He bit off a piece and began sucking on it as if it were a sweet dessert. It immediately reminded him of the aged Brie he used to order in the Parisian café Royal and the Stilton cheese he had eaten at Stimson's on the Strand in London in the company of Sir Ernest (i.e., his British agent Oldham) and the amber bits of Parmesan cheese he used to eat, washing them down with sips of Chianti when living in Florence.

Dmitri and Anna's union was anything but trouble-free. One bookkeeper, fat and wide shouldered, a middle-aged man with access to extra food, hinted to Anna that he was in a position to improve her food situation. She ignored his overtures toward her, and one day he grabbed her and attempted to molest her. She told Dmitri about the episode, and the next morning he rushed to the headquarters' accounting department and beat up the man. Dmitri was punished with ten days in solitary confinement.

He later regretted acting without thinking of the consequences. The episode gave his female boss—who was also a prisoner but because of her background as the wife of a regional party committee secretary was put in charge of the dispensary—reason to spoil things for him and Anna. She formerly had a camp lover, another prisoner, whom she forced to cohabit with her, but he made a daring escape effort and was caught and shot dead on the spot. Then she turned to Dmitri one morning and told him point-blank: "Shave off your beard, and I'm yours." When he turned her down, out of sheer jealousy because her subordinate Dmitri preferred Anna, she used her ties to the *operchast'* (operational security unit) to make sure that the couple was separated and recommended that each be dispatched to different camp units. That almost killed Anna. At the other *lagpunkt*, she was grossly mistreated by the camp unit chief. They gave her a sleeping place with no bedding on a frozen floor near the barrack entrance. She quickly developed pneumonia. She would have died, but another woman, head of the Suslovo medical unit, saved her by hospitalizing her, thus giving her an opportunity to rest and regain her health.

Other good-hearted people also rescued the camp love of Dmitri and Anna. One Dr. Nosova, a former prisoner herself, who continued working in the same place after serving her term, many times struck Dmitri's and Anna's names from the list of prisoners to be transported to other camps, which would separate them forever. They would lose track of each other: prisoners didn't have the right to correspond with other prisoners; letters with camp addresses were not accepted for delivery.

But their camp life remained full of unpleasant surprises. One day Dmitri received orders to move his medical office into a disciplinary barrack (in Russian, *BUR, barak usilennogo rezhima*) with hard-core criminals and to stay there around the clock. It was a dangerous place to be, for it was hard to control violence between prisoners in that barrack. After a few tension-filled days had passed, he spotted Anna in a new group of prisoners coming into the barrack: she had snuck into the group just to pay him a short visit. He was both very happy to see her and, at the same time, horrified at the very thought of what could happen to her in such a barrack. Dmitri remembered what a group of hard-core criminals in Norilsk had done to a female doctor who entered their barrack unescorted by guards: they gang-raped her savagely (in camp slang, "passed her under a streetcar") until she died, her body torn into pieces.[9]

Soon after Anna left, Dmitri was himself attacked by a group of hard-core criminals in the barrack. He survived the onslaught by barricading the door of his office with furniture and holding out until the guards, usually oblivious to fights between prisoners, mistook the commotion in the barrack for an attempted escape and intervened in time.

One day, Anna told Dmitri she had received a letter from her husband, Sergei, informing her he had set her free of their marriage ties. He was at another camp working as a chief mechanic and cohabiting with an imprisoned nurse; they lived as husband and wife. Besides, they wouldn't see each other anyway, for he was dying slowly of a serious stomach illness. After hearing the news about Sergei, Dmitri considered himself married to Anna.

The years 1946 and 1947 were bad ones for Dmitri. As is typical of war veterans, while stress and the survival instinct kept him going during the most trying years of wartime food shortages, when the war was over and camp life tension was relatively less, a series of health setbacks followed. He suffered from three cases of pneumonia, one after another. Soon, tuberculosis began in his larynx. If not for Anna's care, he would surely have perished. In the summer of 1946, her term to end in a year, Anna received the status of nonescorted prisoner and was transferred to work at the camp headquarters in Suslovo. But she was allowed to travel between camp units. Working as a dishwasher at a diner for the military commanders, she now and then managed to smuggle some food under her skirt for Dmitri. Each time, she risked an additional term if she were caught.[10]

On July 11, 1947, her term ended, and she was freed. She put Dmitri's notebooks under her summer dress. It was risky: she could be rearrested, get a new, ten-year term, be sent on a punitive transport, and then to a punitive camp. But she insisted that it must be done. Before they parted, she swore she would pull him out of the camps for good.

As he learned later, the whole group of women ex-prisoners was stopped en route and searched. But she was lucky: at the last moment, the officer decided not to search her. Together with other freed women, they were placed into a train car transporting quicklime. But that didn't trouble her much: she was free at last.

From the day they parted, Dmitri was tormented with doubts about whether Anna would wait for him as she had sworn she would. She wrote to him, but not too frequently, and her letters were short and businesslike. She wrote that she had arrived in Moscow and received a job assignment at a plant in Siberia, but she didn't say exactly where, as if she didn't want to be found. It seemed to him both strange and suspicious. Under the influence of many prisoner stories about similar relationships that had started in the camps but were quickly forgotten by the other party once freed, Dmitri calmed down and began cohabiting with the camp doctor, Mukhina. He found it reasonable, for as the camp proverb goes, "A free person and a prisoner are not a couple." And he didn't write to Anna out of pride: he couldn't bring himself to remind her about himself obtrusively.

Sometime later, he learned that Anna was working at a military plant in Slavgorod in Altai Region as an engineer. Then, one day, a letter came from her informing him that soon he should expect to be recalled to Moscow for reexamination of his case and released.

While he wanted to believe it, he couldn't. Parting with Anna was a major blow. By that time, his camp experience had already shifted his world outlook further in the direction of a more realistic one. He no longer believed that his arrest and imprisonment were just honest mistakes of the system he had served so selflessly. During the first years, he had duly petitioned for reexamination of his case but was turned down routinely. Later, his name was twice stricken from the list of prisoners to be freed before the end of their terms. In the eyes of those who had put him behind barbed wire he remained an "enemy of the people." As humiliating as it was to one who had given everything he had to the Soviet system, on all major Soviet holidays, May 1, and the day of the anniversary of the October revolution (November 7), as an especially dangerous political criminal, he was habitually shut behind the door of the camp solitary cell.

Now he was deeply convinced that the camp system was a totally corrupt institution that left no room for justice. He saw that, with rare exceptions, the camp chiefs were "cold and calculating" people who "cared above all about their position in the Party that fed them"; it was as impossible to appeal to them as it was "for a sheep to appeal for justice to a wolf that is tearing its body into pieces."

He didn't believe he'd come out alive. One prisoner about to be freed came to say good-bye to him, asking how much of his term was left to be served and when it would be his turn to get out. Dmitri answered, "A lot is left. I'll be here till I die." He began losing faith in his future. One day, working in a children's toy shop and charged with drawing an elephant, he despaired that he forgot what the animal looked like, he who had seen hordes of them during his African trips.

But in November 1947, his fate suddenly took an unexpected turn. He was called to the headquarters in Mariinsk: a special escort consisting of an officer and soldiers came for him.

EIGHTEEN | The High Price of Decency

Suppose you succeed in breaking the wall with your head.
And what, then, will you do in the next cell?

—STANISLAW JERZY LEC

When he was suddenly summoned to Moscow, the news made Dmitri wary. What was it for? During the war, they had twice turned down his appeal for reexamination of his case. In prisoners' slang, he had been given the "full spool" (*na vsiu katushku*)—the maximum term for the crimes of which he was convicted. Did they want to review his case and add more years of imprisonment to the initial term, as was often the practice, or had they now thought of bringing him before a firing squad? For almost ten years of imprisonment, especially harsh during the wartime, his near-starvation existence had weakened him to such a state that he often felt indifferent to whatever would happen to him.[1]

It took over a month and a half to reach Moscow. He managed not to die en route from either hunger, or cold, or beatings, or nervous overexertion, as many prisoners had.[2] When he finally arrived in Moscow, he was considerably weakened by the series of pneumonias he had suffered in Mariinsk: he could neither stand on his own nor move without help. They brought him to Lubyanka and gave him time to recuperate.

Finally, they called him in to be interrogated about the activities of Colonel Norman Borodin.[3] In March 1930, about the same time as Dmitri, Borodin had become an undercover operative of Soviet Foreign Intelligence, working first in Norway, then in Germany. After

Hitler's ascent to power, Borodin was transferred to the Paris illegal *rezidentura*, where, although Dmitri doesn't say it explicitly, their paths crossed. (During the interrogations, Dmitri assumed that Norman had already been arrested, but as is known today, they had just been collecting compromising material in preparation for his arrest, which followed in March 1949.)[4]

Dmitri confirmed his previous, totally unessential, testimony regarding Borodin's days as a spy back in Paris. He wondered why they couldn't take his testimony in the camp, either in Suslovo or in Mariinsk, and had dragged him all the way to Moscow. By now, he knew the system in whose hands he had been for almost ten years too well to expect anything good from it and braced himself for further developments.

After a while, they took him from his cell, bathed him in a bathhouse, shaved him, and dressed him in a brand-new civilian suit. His heart skipped a beat in a premonition of trouble. Then two guards took him under the arms and brought him into a spacious office with two men sitting behind a table. One of them was Major General Viktor Semenovich Abakumov, who, during the war with Germany, had been the head of GURK (Chief Counterintelligence Directorate), better known as SMERSH (the Russian abbreviation of "death to spies"). He had a reputation as a notoriously brutal official who was known to torture prisoners with his own hands. At the time of the meeting, he was Minister of State Security (MGB). The man sitting next to him was head of the investigation department in charge of especially important cases, Colonel A. G. Leonov.[5]

Abakumov ordered the guards to position Dmitri facing the window. "Do you recognize it?" When Dmitri gave the right answer (Lubyanka Square), he was asked another question: "And what's the name of the boulevard that starts to the left of the Grand Opera in Paris?" Dmitri replied correctly. "Good, very good."

Suddenly Abakumov said, "In a half hour you might turn up over there, near the subway station. And in a month, in Paris! Do you hear? Answer!"

Since Dmitri stood silent, Abakumov added, "Well, it's understandable that you're bewildered. I'll explain. I decided to get you through the amnesty campaign. You're a useful person. Already today you can dine in the Metropol Restaurant [in Moscow] and, in a couple of weeks, at the Hotel Ritz in Paris. They'll talk about your work over there later. Do you hear me? Do you?"

Here, Dmitri gathered all his strength and said, "My crimes are invented. There's no proof of any wrongdoing on my part. I'm a suspect whom you can't amnesty. You can only reexamine my case and set me free. Then we can begin talking about work."

The general laughed harshly. He tapped on a window glass. "Do you see the multitude of people on this square? These are ordinary citizens, and all of them are suspects who remain on the other side of the walls of this building so far. On this side, there are no suspects—only convicts. You're arrested, therefore, you're convicted. If it's expedient, we're ready to grant amnesty to you."[6]

Then Abakumov said, "Listen, Dmitri Aleksandrovich, what would you do if you walked out onto the streets right now? On such a sunny day? Tell us, don't be afraid."

Dmitri knew that this was his last chance. His heart beating fast, he replied, "I would come to the very first store window and knock it out."

"Why, Dmitri Aleksandrovich?" The men in the room exchanged knowing glances: the convict's lost his marbles.

"So that I'd be returned to prison as soon as possible," Dmitri replied.

He was led out of the room. It appears that, as had happened many times in his life, always looking for a father figure and role model, at this fateful moment of his life, Dmitri was emulating the behavior of the former Suslovo camp chief Sidorenko. He openly admired the man for his humanity and dedicated many pages of his memoirs to him. Sidorenko was one of those few camp chiefs who exercised restraint in their power and, at times, saved the lives of prisoners under their watch. On the eve of Dmitri's departure for Moscow, wrongly accused by his superiors and given a prison term himself, he had done exactly this—when offered amnesty, he stated his innocence before the law and refused to accept amnesty and demanded a full acquittal.[7]

Dmitri's thoughts went along the same lines. "To release me with a brand on my forehead so that, first, they would use me again, say, in the capacity of provocateur, and then, when I stop being useful, they would bring me back to prison but now with no right to ever claim my innocence . . . No, some time ago I was able to carry out their orders, enthusiastically and voluntarily, but now I must not be a flourishing slave."[8]

As soon as Dmitri returned to his cell, he asked for paper and wrote a letter to Abakumov reiterating what he had said during their meeting—that he refused amnesty and demanded a new investigation of his "crimes," a new trial, and full rehabilitation of his civil rights. He added (rather naively) that what had happened to him "would be unthinkable in any cultured country."[9]

Dmitri received a response to his demands not in words but in deeds. At night, he was told to gather his belongings, and after two hours in a waiting room in the Lubyanka basement, they placed him in a Black Maria and drove across the city for a long time. Finally, they brought him to a prison called a "special object" (*spetsob'ekt*), Sukhanovka. Established by the NKVD in 1938, for "especially dangerous enemies of the people," it was organized on the grounds of the old Ekaterinskaia Pustyn', a monastery built in the time of Catherine the Great, in the village of Vidnoe, outside of Moscow. As Solzhenitsyn notes, the Sukhanovka prison had a reputation as the "most terrible prison" of the Ministry for State Security (MGB). The very threat of being sent there was often used as a way to intimidate prisoners during interrogation. Many Sukhanovka prisoners couldn't survive there, often losing their sanity. After being relieved of his post and subsequently arrested, NKVD head Nikolai Yezhov was imprisoned there on April 10, 1939.[10]

The prison consisted of two buildings, one with a row of cells in which prisoners served their terms and the other with sixty-eight monastic cells, where they were interrogated. For starters, they put Dmitri in a special punishment cell designed to break a prisoner's resistance. Its cement walls dark from filth and dampness, the tiny cell (no more than five by six and a half feet) was barely lit by a small bulb under the entrance door. There was also a small frozen window under the low ceiling. The collapsible berth was locked onto the wall. Beside a minuscule table made of iron, a rail that stuck out from the floor served as a support for the berth at night. It was so cold, his breath produced vapor.

Dmitri was convinced he was living the last day of his life. Then, in full silence, they gave him a cup of tea with sugar and bread and quickly retrieved the cup from him. There was no place to sit and no room to move around. After an hour of shifting from foot to foot in front of the door, he became tired and sat down on the rail, which was first uncomfortable, then even painful. After ten minutes, his back began to ache, and he had to stand up without resting. For variety, he began shifting from foot to foot on the other side of the rail. He lasted only a half an hour, after which he sat down but couldn't remain seated for longer than five minutes.

After two more hours, he found himself incapable of either moving or sitting on the rail. He had no idea how long this torture would continue.

There was mortal silence around him. Unlike in regular prisons where wardens at least shouted "Breakfast!" or "Dinner!" or "Get out for a walk!" here in Sukhanovka not a word was spoken. And there was no walking in the yard, and there were no books to read.

Before nightfall, they entered his cell and unlocked and lowered his berth. But come early morning everything went the same way.

The regime was so unusual that Dmitri decided he was marked for execution for his refusal to accept amnesty. He pondered why they were dragging things out instead of shooting him right away. It would be the end of all his misery. He thought that Anna must be somewhere nearby in Moscow. But it didn't matter now, when they were about to kill him.

But one day followed another, and the torturous treatment of keeping him in a cell, unable to move and in full silence, continued. He felt they had buried him alive, without even telling him why they had changed his punishment. He was at a loss to know why they had jailed him without telling him his term or giving any reason for substituting his camp regime with the regime of a strict prison.

After a month of passivity, he decided to fight his silent jailers with the only weapon a prisoner has in jail—a hunger strike. During morning check, he announced to the chief of guards that he demanded to be told why he was confined in a solitary cell and what the term of this confinement was. The officer shrugged, indicating that he had no inkling about it himself. Dmitri then asked for a piece of paper and a pencil, so he could write a letter to Colonel Leonov, the chief of the investigation department. When he was refused again, the next time they brought him food, he didn't touch it. Soon he heard a loud whisper behind the door of his cell and tramping of guards running in the corridor: a hunger strike in a jail was considered an emergency situation.

Now his silent treatment was broken: his jailers began ordering him to eat. He refused, and from that moment on, he was placed under constant surveillance: the peephole of his cell door remained open at all times.

After the first five days, his sense of hunger subsided. On the sixth day, a gray-haired colonel, head of the Special Object, came in. But neither his threats nor requests changed the prisoner's mind, and Dmitri continued refusing to eat.

In the evening, a warden on duty stepped into his cell, lowered the berth, and pointed at it. Not understanding what he wanted from him, Dmitri sat down on the berth. Immediately, several guards burst into the cell and subdued him, and with the help of a medical assistant, the warden pushed a tube down his nose and force-fed him.

Thus, his hunger strike didn't bring him any results: he received neither a piece of paper nor a pencil. After a while, he resumed his strike, which again failed. He used his hunger strike two more times, demanding books and courtyard walks, which he considered the unalienable right of a prisoner. But he got nothing.

In the autumn of 1948, a half year after they had brought him to Sukhanovka, they moved him into another cell, dry and better lit. He was about to rejoice about this fortunate turn in his life, but as he listened to the sounds around him, he realized he was in the part of the corridor where they placed prisoners who had gone mad. From the cell next to his, some young man shouted one and the same phrase endlessly, day and night: "Mama, tell my little Valya that I'm still alive!"

Finally, the shouting took a toll on Dmitri, and he felt that he was also losing his mind. Desperate, he went on another hunger strike, demanding to be transferred somewhere else.

This time he was successful. They moved him to yet another cell, in a remote corner on the second floor, a cell with a window facing the yard. It was warm, and the room seemed like a hotel lounge to him. These new circumstances changed his mood. He decided that all was not lost yet and that he should be patient. He even composed a short hymn to himself, with the refrain, "I shall fight to the end!"

But the days passed one after the other, and he found that the hardest aspect of his imprisonment was the absence of books and the lack of opportunity to write. He was afraid of losing his mind unless he found a way to occupy it.

The most grueling fact was that he still had no idea how long they would keep him in there. If he knew that he had three years to wait until his release, he would hope to survive the term. But, if they intended to keep him there for another ten years or more, he would do his best to end his life himself. Yet if he did it without knowing the term, while there was a chance that the term was shorter, it would mean that he would pass away prematurely, thus rendering his suicide an act of cowardice.

In despair, he came up with an idea for giving some meaning to his life: he would write a book mentally. The idea of composing a novel without paper and pen came to his mind when he thought of a well-known poet, novelist, and playwright, Bruno Jasieński. Like Dmitri, the writer had also been imprisoned in an NKVD prison. Severely beaten, in order not to go mad, he began writing a new novel in his head.[11] To compensate for the boredom and emptiness of his existence in the cell, Dmitri turned to the period of his life that was most exciting and full of colorful impressions, the time of his travels to Africa. Pressing his back against the wall of his cell, Dmitri began mentally outlining his future book. He decided to base the protagonist of his novel on the biography of Henri Pieck (code-named COOPER), with whom he had worked in Holland and Switzerland on various assignments. He recalled Pieck telling him how, before his own trip to Africa, he had lived with no interest in politics, but observing firsthand the horrors of colonial reality, he decided to fight for justice in the world and joined the Soviet undercover intelligence.

As Dmitri engrossed himself in outlining all the details of his future book, he needed company, someone to talk to about his exciting new way of life. To his joy, he found he was sharing his residence with two spiders. Trying to individualize them, he christened one of them with a Russian surname, Ivanov, and the other with a Jewish one, Tsyperovich. Moreover, he made Ivanov a non-Party member and Tsyperovich a Communist. Ivanov was a lazy bum and couldn't catch enough gnats. Tsyperovich was a "shock-worker," one who overfulfilled his own plans, but the quality of his webs was poor, and gnats easily freed themselves from them. (In defining the characters of the spiders, Dmitri foreshadowed his future critique of the Soviet system.)

He befriended the insects, talked to them all day long, and sometimes, even saw them in his dreams. Now, he began each day in joyful anticipation of creative labor. As soon as he closed his eyes, he would mentally take himself now to the jungles of Congo, now to the dunes of the Sahara, now to the rain forest where the Pygmies lived . . .

It took him two months to learn to do it with his eyes opened. After six months of mental juggling day in and day out, he developed a severe headache, which began upon awakening and lasted the whole day, receding only at night. Another month or two passed, and his life became a hell. Even in his sleep, he stayed in the realm of his recollections. His brain took over, and after months and months of being locked in the past, it refused to work in the present. He immersed himself in the past to such a degree that he could barely function in the present, and that happened only after he was prompted by the guards to do something. Sometimes, he found himself trying to put his pants over his head or forgetting which way his shoes should be put on. One day when the warden ordered him to get ready to go to the restroom, he couldn't understand right away what was expected of him. At one point, he had to force himself to recognize simple items in front of him. He had to tell himself: "A spoon. A spoon, a spoon, spoon, spoon, spoon . . . kasha, kasha, kasha. Here I'm holding the spoon . . ."

There were more health troubles to come, however. One day, he couldn't recognize the warden or understand what the warden wanted from him. Soon, these episodes of agnosia, loss of the ability to recognize things, became regular.

Next he lost the ability to orient himself in space. Mosquitoes coming from the window flew directly at him, and he couldn't find a way to move his hand to catch them midair.

After another six months, he lost any ability to think in concepts and abstracts; he had to visualize whatever he was thinking of at the moment. His brain went out of control, wound up stuck in endlessly going over his African impressions, and refused to get back to the reality at hand.

In yet another six months, after another cell rotation, they brought him to a new cell, but he was oblivious to his surroundings. He had lost the ability to live in the present.

In the spring of 1951, in the third year of solitary confinement, as a result of his brain working nonstop in full swing, one day he found himself in a doctor's office. His eyes ached; he couldn't see much beyond some brown spots floating in front of his eyes. He developed glaucoma, and he could potentially lose both of his eyes by surgery. But the moment the threat of losing his vision came to his consciousness, it served as an emotional whip that brought him out of his lethargy. He knew that a blind prisoner wouldn't survive in the camps for too long. "They'll trample me to death . . . They'll peck me to death. In prison, helplessness is worse than death," he thought at that time.

He began wiping himself down twice a day with cold water and exercising up to ten times a day. When they finally gave him a package of books, he almost kissed them all over. Though with his eyes still aching, he wasn't able to read them, the very sight of them excited him. As he had in Lefortovo after the end of his interrogation, now Dmitri took stock of his state of health. Based on sensations in his body, he presumed that his blood pressure was very high, far above 200. This was likely the cause of his headaches and unstable walking. It also, in part, explained his glaucoma. Not every patient with high blood pressure developed it, but in his case, three additional factors contributed to the illness: the head trauma inflicted on him during his 1938 interrogation, his ten years of imprisonment, and the overtaxing of his brain with his attempts to write mentally.

But, gradually, his health began to return, and one day he was considered fully recovered. They returned him to the first floor of the prison and placed him in another dark and damp cell. Now, in the sixth half-year term of his Sukhanovka life, the term of his current punishment still not known, he was convinced that he would spend the rest of his twenty-year term in a solitary cell.

He decided it was best for him to move around as much as possible in his tiny cell. He found a way to stomp around in small steps for as long as he could, sometimes up to sixteen hours a day. According to the prison regulations, he was always to face the peephole in the door. This made it more difficult to exercise; his neck ached by the end of the day from turning his head all the time as he moved around the cell. They took the books away, and he was afraid to resume writing in his head, for now he knew how it could damage his health.

Soon some other health problems started: he began seeing brown rats on the floor of his cell. He diagnosed himself as having episodes of scotoma, disturbances of the visual field due to the appearance of dark spots before his eyes. He attributed these to spasms of the small blood vessels.

After a month, these symptoms subsided, and he resumed his exercises, twice as many. But at the end of the third year of confinement, when the guards came to take him back to the Lefortovo jail, he again couldn't figure out who had entered his cell and what was wanted of him.

Soon after his arrival at Lefortovo, he lost consciousness because of a spasm of the blood vessels in his brain. He also had a problem with his gallbladder, which prompted an episode of acute jaundice. He was taken to the prison hospital. There he befriended another patient, a Jewish scientist (in his memoirs, mistakenly identified as academician Lev Semenovich Berg, a leading Soviet geographer and biologist who served as president of the Soviet Geographical Society between 1940 and 1950). Dmitri discovered that the man had been jailed for a ridiculous reason. When he was invited to a scientific congress in America, the Soviet authorities refused to let him go, citing the lack of state funds for foreign travel. When the Americans offered to send money for the trip, he was arrested and accused of secret collaboration with the "capitalist warmongers." In those years of virulent anti-Semitic campaigns that took the form of the "struggle with the cosmopolites," the fact that the venerable scientist was a Jew certainly didn't help him. The old man was beaten during interrogations; his heart was failing.

Finally, one day, Dmitri's health having been restored by the intensive treatment of the prison doctors, he was ordered to gather his belongings and go back to the camps. As the train was taking him back to Siberia, he thought of his time in Sukhanovka and smiled with happiness. Now he ironically considered the hellish time spent there as "fierce proof of the steadfastness of his little Anna's love." Trying to understand what prompted the authorities to take him from the camps and bring him to Moscow and offer amnesty, he came up with the following scenario. In Moscow after her release, his Anna, who had sworn to get him out of prison no matter what, to raise money for a good lawyer who would help her to intervene with the authorities on his behalf, sewed dresses at night to sell them privately, a source of income some Soviets with sewing skills turned to at that time. Then the lawyer delivered on his promise: his case was retrieved from the archives and moved for reexamination. The lower-rank authorities took an interest in it and passed it to the higher-ups. Finally, his case evoked the interest of the head of the Investigation Department, Leonov, who reported to his boss, Abakumov. They apparently deemed him, Dmitri Bystrolyotov, useful for some reason and recalled him to Moscow. There, they offered to free him as a repentant criminal and to have him resume his work in foreign intelligence.

But this scenario was hardly more than wishful thinking on his part. Judging by the high positions of the men involved in this process, most likely, he was retrieved from the camps to be used in connection with the case not only of Norman Borodin but also of his father Mikhail Borodin. For a long time (from 1941), the man had served as editor in chief of the most important government information agency (Sovinformbureau). In the course of building up a statewide anti-Semitic campaign in the postwar years, Mikhail Borodin (born Mikhail Gruzenberg) was earmarked for purging from his important position. It was expected that, in exchange for freedom and the renewal of his intelligence work abroad (or, quite likely, merely the promise of both, a carrot dangling before his eyes), Dmitri would give compromising testimony against both men.

Exactly the same ploy had been used when they were building the case against Dmitri himself: the investigators jailed his former colleagues of the Union of Student Citizens of the USSR Living in Czechoslovakia to give testimonies implicating him in sabotage and espionage for the Czechs. Although Dmitri's memoirs do not mention Mikhail Borodin by name or the offer to defame him and his son, there is a hint that this was the case: "For me, [the Sukhanovka term] was retribution for my inner steadfastness, for my refusal to accept freedom: I lost it, but one more time, I confirmed in myself my decency toward people. I saved those whom I could have ruined, and I suffered for their sake." (As is known now, Bystrolyotov's refusal to cooperate with Abakumov didn't save the men he tried to protect. First, Mikhail Borodin was relieved of his post in the Sovinform-bureau, then, in February 1949, arrested, accused of spying for the United States and England, and tortured in Lefortovo prison. He died on May 29, 1951, before his trial, and his son, Norman, was exiled to Karaganda.)[12]

Riding with other prisoners on the train taking him back to Siberia, Dmitri assumed that they would return him to his old camp. But he was mistaken. Despite his protests, they took him farther to the east, to a camp near the town of Taishet; in this camp the prisoners were used to build a railroad to the Angara River. Upon arrival at the camp, cut off from the outside world for three years, Dmitri discovered that, in his absence, the camp system had undergone a major overhaul: male prisoners were separated from female ones, all prisoners had to wear numbers on their clothes, and especially dangerous ones with long terms, regardless of articles of conviction, were gathered in forced labor camps with extremely strict regimes.

Upon arrival he underwent a medical examination, was diagnosed with significant myocardial weakness, and received the status of a "working invalid." He was ordered to sew his number onto his clothes—AD 245 (which he found to be quite prophetic: *ad* in Russian means "hell"). He was assigned to work as a doctor at the camp hospital and dispensary. The first day, still weak from his long and tiring journey, he nearly died of exhaustion, having served hundreds of patients.[13]

As part of his duties he also had to perform autopsies. In many of these operations, he discovered something perplexing: the corpses of prisoners considered shot on attempting to escape had bullet wounds not in their backs, as would be expected, but in front. Sometimes, they had been shot point-blank. He would discover the sinister meaning of those wounds a few months later.

Soon other, no less troubling, discoveries followed. He realized that the camp was a playground of well-organized crime aimed at material gain. Newcomers with gold crowns on their dentures were offered a lighter work assignment in exchange for letting their gold crowns be removed. Sick and dying prisoners, especially foreigners, were robbed blind. Thus, they stole the gold watch of one of the female prisoners, a secretary working in Hitler's chancellery. In time, Dmitri would discover much more horrifying crimes committed by the camp personnel.

For a long time, he received no letters from Anna. He wrote to a former prisoner they had both known in their earlier days to ask about her whereabouts and learned that after working in Pavlodar for a while Anna had gone to Tambov and settled there. But soon her correspondence with Anna also stopped, and the letters came back. Dmitri understood that Anna might have been rearrested. Indeed, he turned out to be right. Anna was in prison again. Dmitri already knew that a series of systematic rearrests of political prisoners had occurred all over the country. But he didn't despair. He decided that she was strong enough to survive her new term, in both body and spirit. He dearly wanted to see himself reunited with her one day and firmly believed in it. To help himself, every morning and evening, he spent a few minutes thinking about her and her only. This helped him to lift himself spiritually, as a prayer would.[14]

Meanwhile, Dmitri's immediate boss, the head of the camp medical department, learned about his artistic talent and made him draw kissing or dancing pairs. She especially liked pictures of young men dressed in tuxedos, with their mustaches and parted pomaded hair, the type of Berlin gigolos of the 1930s Dmitri remembered from his time visiting the German nightclubs as part of his work. That brought back a lot of memories about "Greta" and everything that happened to him then.

In the postwar camps with male and female prisoners now detained separately, Dmitri felt a longing for women. Sometimes he wished one of them would faint in the baths, so he would be called to see her. One day, he was ordered to see a woman in the female zone. Excited, he doused himself with an enormous amount of cologne only to find out that the patient was an old lady suffering from incontinence. He laughed at fate's snub of his erotic imagination.

One day, for refusal to snitch on one of his fellow imprisoned medics, he was sent to the taiga to work in a small, remote point, *lagpunkt* 07, located eleven miles from the town of Novo-Chunka;

he spent nine months there, from March to December 1952. Dmitri's first concern was to ensure that the camp *oper* (state security officer) wouldn't be able to recruit him as a stool pigeon. Well aware that it would spread around the camp quickly, he told one prisoner that before his arrest he had been an intelligence operative. That disqualified him from being recruited by the camp security authorities under pressure as their secret informer, because no prisoner would trust him.

But he ran into trouble here, too. One winter day, when he told the camp chief that since the temperature was minus forty degrees Celsius, which meant, according to the rules, the prisoners couldn't be sent to work outdoors, they threw him into a cold solitary cell.

When summer came to the taiga, swarms of bloodsucking gnats attacked prisoners who worked in the forest, making their lives unbearable. Dmitri tried to determine why the vast majority of men were attacked by the insects, while a handful were mysteriously spared. Rubbing his hand against their bodies, he established that it had something to do with a scent emanating from these people that only insects were capable to discern; their scent served as a powerful repellent. He thought in despair that, if he had the requisite lab equipment at hand, he would be able to come up with a remedy to preserve many prisoners from the merciless insects.

But another, psychological "gnat" eventually brought Dmitri down. Back in Norilsk, one day he and other prisoners had pleaded with the guards not to shoot at a mentally ill patient who had walked into the "firing zone." But the guards shot and killed the man anyway. Dmitri had always wondered why they acted in that manner. Now in Taishet, doing autopsies of bodies of the prisoners who were documented as having been shot down while attempting to escape, he pondered what made the guards so trigger-happy. It turned out that the guards had a very high incentive for shooting dead an escapee: the reward was a bonus of two hundred rubles plus two weeks' vacation. He concluded that the killing took place so easily because the shooters had absorbed the moral climate of lawlessness prevalent in the country at that time. The young eighteen-year-old peasant lads employed as guards were oblivious to one of the most fundamental tenets of morality: "Thou shall not kill." Human life had no value for them, unless they received the authorities' direct instructions regarding the matter.

On one occasion he witnessed the murder of a prisoner for profit. As a doctor attached to a group of prisoners working in the forest, he saw a guard order a prisoner to bring a bunch of branches to kindle a bonfire. When the prisoner approached the guard with the load in his arms, the guard ordered him to turn around and shot him in the back. According to standard procedure, the work zone was demarcated by a chain of little red flags. Unconcerned about doing it in front of other prisoners, the guard calmly pulled up the chain of flags and relocated it in such a way that the body of the man he had shot was now positioned outside the work zone: the position of the prisoner's body made him appear to be an unsuccessful escapee.

The scene shook Dmitri. His psychosomatic reaction to the cold-blooded murder committed right before his eyes overstrained his nervous system, and he found he could barely move his right hand and right leg. It's clear that, to prevent the fatal consequences of his wish to strike the guard (if he would even attempt it, he would undoubtedly be shot on the spot), his self-preservation reflex immobilized his dominant, striking, right hand.

He diagnosed himself as having paresis, a weak form of paralysis. They transferred him to a position as a yard caretaker (*dvornik*). Forcing himself to do physical exercises, Dmitri gradually regained function on the right side of his body.

After a while, he returned to his position as *lagpunkt* senior doctor. But he knew that his health was declining. While shocked by the abuses of the guards, as a doctor, he fought in vain with another killer that took more lives than the mindless shooters did—hypertension. The main cause of high blood pressure was the lack of vitamin C in the prisoners' diet. Dmitri found that many deaths resulted from the lack of elementary medical equipment and the arbitrary rulings of camp authorities.

He now saw the camps as an integral part of the Soviet system in which his disappointment was growing day by day. One day, a "volunteer-compulsory" campaign to raise funds for the state by signing up for state bonds began in the camp. All prisoners were forced to give up a sizable portion of their miserly earnings. Dmitri felt disgusted at the cynicism of the authorities who robbed blind those who weren't in a position to resist them: "I didn't begrudge the sixty rubles [his monthly salary as a doctor], but I . . . was ashamed of my country and the Party, the party in which, some time ago, I had sincerely believed."

One day, out of the blue, he received a parcel from Anna. Her note revealed what had happened to her since the time of their last contact. After working at a military plant in Pavlodar, she returned to the European part of Russia and settled in Tambov. There she was arrested on some trumped-up charges, released, and then rearrested. Realizing that she had to come up with something that would give the authorities a reason to jail her, she "confessed" to stealing a bottle of industrial spirits. She received a sentence of a few years for a common criminal offense and was sent to the construction site of the Volga-Don Canal. Later, as an outstanding worker, she was freed before completing her term and appointed, now as a hired employee, to head an industrial lab. Soon, again thanks to her outstanding work, her criminal record was erased from her personal file.

Looking at the items packed by "dear hands with such love and thoroughness," he couldn't help but feel his eyes well up with tears: "Unseen by anyone, light and warm sun suddenly peeked into the little window of the camp barrack, and I felt that under its rays I wouldn't perish. I had obtained a reason to exist; to perish now would be senseless."

Anna sent him parcel after parcel with items he especially needed: garlic and dry dill to spice up the camp soups, which he found nauseating, as well as paper, pencils, and paints, medical handbooks, and even desserts.

On January 13, 1953, *Pravda* published the infamous article announcing the arrest of Jewish doctors accused of subversive activities directed at Soviet leaders. Dmitri was outraged. He referred to the paper as "having the insolence to call itself *Pravda* [Truth]" and saw the announcement as a "manifestation of the baseness of the anthropomorphous beasts of Stalin's circle, who, with the help of such false accusations published in their court organ, signaled to the country and the whole world the beginning of a new wave of mass destruction of people and the direction in which it planned to snatch its victims. This time, on Hitler's model, a knife was raised over Soviet people of Jewish ethnicity, specifically, over its most educated elite."

At this point in his life, Dmitri still believed in the ideals of the Lenin-led revolution and understood the witch hunt unleashed in the

Kremlin as a new provocation that the system created by Stalin needed. He saw that, in so acting, the dictator was trying to follow as a "faithful pupil" in Hitler's footsteps: "It doesn't matter whether it's Russian blood or Jewish; it's all the same. It's important that it's needed as fuel for Stalin's machine: if there is no blood, the machine would stop, and millions of fooled people would rest and come to their senses . . . And they would bring the executioners to justice. I'm sorry not only for the Jews but for the Party of which I wasn't a member but with which I felt solidarity . . . I had been shoving my head into a noose for that Party, and now it's acutely painful to me that I did it."

His disillusionment with the Soviet system reached an all-time high. At the beginning of his prison life in Norilsk, he had pushed himself to work hard, believing that any labor in the camps benefited his beloved Motherland, but now he found the very name of "corrective labor camps" to be nothing more than a lie: "For seventeen years of Soviet imprisonment, I saw thousands of people exhausted to death by unbearable toil, saw morgues packed with corpses of hard workers (*rabotiagi*), saw deep quarries filled with corpses that resembled skeletons upholstered with skin, but nowhere and never had I seen even a single camp prisoner corrected by labor. And I had never heard of such a case."

The reason for this finally became clear to him: camp labor was nothing but slave labor. "How can you love labor while guard dogs are barking?" he asked himself a reasonable question. "Such a supposition is monstrous in itself!"

He also came to a conclusion that dealt another blow to his long-held Communist belief that called for predominance of the common good over personal interest. He recalled some instances when prisoners had worked well and honestly and admitted to himself that they had done it "not for the idea of labor, not for the Motherland, not for the glory of [Vladimir] Ilyich [Lenin], but for extra food, for a place in a barracks with normal beds instead of plank beds, for better clothing—that is, for one's own gain, for oneself."

He also came to realize that the hypocrisy of the Soviet system was akin to that of Nazi ideology: "No, no, and again no: education by way of labor with a machine gun in hand and a dog is a conscious and base lie! It was for a good reason that the sign 'Labor makes you free!' was displayed on the gates of Hitler's camps." Dmitri found the two systems similar in many other respects and believed that they themselves recognized their mutual kinship "by smell."

Anticipating similar conclusions that Solzhenitsyn would make in his book *The Gulag Archipelago,* Dmitri admitted that "ardent Stalin 'patriots,'" such as the former division commander Pavlov, whom he had met during his time in Norilsk, "came to the camps with a willingness to labor for the glory of the dear Party and its leader, but none of them took a shovel and crowbar in their hands. All this is a vile lie." As if laughing at himself for his naiveté, Dmitri now admitted to himself that, like Pavlov, he had also managed to get a brigadier's position, for it gave him an opportunity to work as much as he wanted himself but to make others do the most work.

His health slowly returning, Dmitri threw himself in many directions, including scientific research on the causes of leptospirosis (also known as Weil's disease), a virus that affected prisoners' brains and led to a quick death. With permission from his boss, Dmitri looked through some twenty thousand patient files and found that the cause of the disease was infection coming from the sewage of toilets located at the top of one of the hills where one group of prisoners worked. It was obvious that to avoid spread of the disease the authorities had to restructure the work zone. The head of medical personnel knew that the authorities would disapprove of such an idea and balked at Dmitri's suggestion.

Dmitri continued his research surreptitiously. He turned for help to one of the prisoners, an ex–field sergeant of the Waffen-SS, who in his prewar civilian life had worked in a Frankfurt laboratory. The man had managed to bring his German-made microscope with a dark camera to the camps. Dmitri found a way to get access to some laboratory dyes, had the German prisoner transferred to his charge, and began his experiments with dyeing specimens of spinal liquid following one of the methods he remembered from medical school. After a number of failures, he learned to find agents of leptospirosis. Dmitri also consulted with an Estonian prisoner from a neighboring *lagpunkt,* a microbiologist by training. Next, using watercolor paints he obtained from the camp Cultural and Educational Department, he made a number of color sketches of those agents. When this part of his research was done, he began statistical analysis of those twenty thousand patient files.

At the last moment, when he found scientific proof of the causes of the disease, he experienced fear. If he approached his medical bosses, who were reluctant to change the ways they worked, as a prisoner he could get himself in trouble. But on that day, a new patient arrived, a cultured man, formerly editor in chief of a big publishing house. He had a brain form of leptospirosis. Dmitri imagined the brain of that thin, smiling man, a prisoner with a number on his chest, who would most likely die in a couple of days, his brain teeming with viruses from the disease, and decided that he couldn't be silent.

Circumventing his medical boss, he submitted his findings to the camp chief. As he expected, the chief disregarded the report, and on the heels of Dmitri's other offense—his protest that prisoner patients under his watch were given rotten meat swarming with worms for dinner—he wound up among the prisoners selected for the next punishment prisoner transport to be dispatched from the camp to another location.

They loaded the prisoners on a train. Dmitri felt indifferent to where fate would take him this time. "I didn't know who would go where, but I did know that I would drift closer to my grave."

In October 1953, in a shipment of three thousand prisoners, he came to Zone 05 of Kamyshlag in the city of Omsk. The new camp was unusually clean, prisoners were well fed, and the camp chief was seriously concerned about their health. But these changes had come after many years of deprivation, and many prisoners had lost the will to live.

Among prisoners passing through the camp temporarily, waiting to be shipped farther on with the next transport, Dmitri met an old acquaintance from his past camp life. He was in poor health, yet joyful. He explained to Dmitri the reason for his good mood: "Death is the only form of true liberation for a Soviet man. Soon I'll say goodbye forever to Marxism-Leninism and Socialist realism and Soviet democracy."

Unlike his fervent rejection of anti-Soviet sentiments expressed by other prisoners during his first years of imprisonment, now Dmitri didn't object to the man's pessimism. He only called on the dying man to hang on, for there was no reason to hurry death.

In postwar times, the conditions of prisoners' lives in the camps improved somewhat, but other problems arose for people like Dmitri.

After the end of the war, the contingent of prisoners dramatically changed. Now it also included prisoners of war from Germany and its allies, as well as Nazi collaborators from the territories occupied by Hitler's troops. Often those who had only recently been adversaries (for instance, Jewish prisoners and former SS officers) were forced to work and rest side by side. For Dmitri, this change that now included sworn enemies of his country among the prisoner population brought about moral torture. Now he had to exist and work shoulder to shoulder with traitors of his Motherland—former Nazi collaborators, who expressed their moral superiority over him. Thus Dmitri felt pain that one such convict served only fifteen years for collaborating with the enemy, while he, Dmitri, guiltless, had been sentenced to twenty years.

In time, his outrage subsided, being gradually replaced with indifference. The long years in prison began taking a toll on him: "How long should all this keep going on? I'm dead tired of all of it."

He understood that he was reaching a threshold when, having always been on his toes when it came to his immediate duties, he grew oblivious to them. Moreover, being in the privileged position of doctor made him feel "burning shame." When entering the gloomy corridors of the camp prison, he knew that in the eyes of other prisoners he was playing the part of an assistant to the administration, which, for him, was a "denigrating and base part." Thus, when he had to force-feed a prisoner on a hunger strike, he found himself in the shoes of those who had done it to him in Sukhanovka. Now doing what his duties as a camp doctor demanded of him, he felt "all wet from sweat and as if bathed in shit." He scorned his fate: "Oh, what a lousy life!"

But, in the topsy-turvy world of the Soviet labor camp, he didn't have much room to choose his own position in life, because his very survival often depended on collaboration with prisoners whom he abhorred otherwise—an assortment of hoodlums and enemies of his Motherland. Since many prisoners demanded a doctor's release from work, which would give them a day of rest, he was often threatened physically—not only with fists and sticks but also with knives or even axes. Therefore, he had to accept protection from three heads of hard-core criminal groups (*pakhans,* in camp slang), all of them ex-colonels fighting on the side of the Nazis during the recent war. One of them had served in the Bandera contingent of Ukrainian nationalists, another in Hitler's Muslim Battalion, and the third had been attached to the headquarters of General Andrei Vlasov, a former Soviet Army general who collaborated with Germany during the war. In exchange for their protection, each of these group representatives expected the doctor to free a few prisoners on their list from work.

Dmitri didn't have a free hand in whom to include in this list: the doctor's diagnoses were subject to check. He was allowed to free from work only bedridden patients after surgery or prisoners with blood pressure higher than 185. (His own blood pressure was higher than that, which made him reel, but he couldn't be relieved of his duties.) At the time, with three thousand prisoners in the zone, every day the line of patients at his office door seemed endless. But he knew that sometimes a truly sick patient's life depended on his diagnosis. He would end his reception hours totally exhausted.

One day, his usual protection arrangement failed. When he refused one of the prisoner's demands for relief from work, he received a strong blow to the chest, so strong that it seemed to break his breast-bone. The second blow landed in the place where, back in Norilsk, they had to saw out his ribs to cure the trauma caused by his being beaten during interrogation. Although his protection squad finally intervened and killed the attacker, the next day Dmitri lost control of his speech, responding to questions with gibberish; he also began sweating profusely. Thus began the second paralysis of the right side of his body. Placed in the prison hospital, he asked for a mirror. He was horrified at what he saw: his eyes were those of a dying man, one of them contorted. When they brought him a newspaper, he couldn't discern the words; he was mortified that he had lost the ability to read. He felt like crying: all his hopes of a future life with Anna were now crushed.

What could he do? After many years of camp life, he knew that he shouldn't expect charity or compassion from anyone. Being inca-pacitated in the camp meant having no hope of survival in a cutthroat situation. And right away, a saving thought came to him on how he could solve the problem: he had to end his life right then and there. Scanning mentally through the pages of his medical books dealing with suicide victims, he came up with a solution: since he was unable to walk, he would do it by making a noose out of his towel and tying it to the headboard of his bed.

But the towel turned out to be too short. Then he thought of using the linen on which he lay. At night, slowly, inch by inch, with only his left hand fully functional, he began pulling out the linen from under his body. But, half paralyzed, the sheet tucked too tightly under the mattress, he made little progress during the night. He almost cried from grief. As a new day started, he rehearsed every move in his head all day long and waited impatiently for the next nightfall.

When nighttime finally arrived, he renewed his efforts, eventually pulling the sheet from under himself. But no matter how hard he tried, after a long time lying on his side and working with only one hand, he still hadn't been able to make the noose.

The hospital personnel noticed his actions. Now they put him under around-the-clock watch. He decided on a new course of action: he would train himself to make the noose at night, and when he had mastered it, he would take the linen to the bathroom and hang himself mounting the noose on a water pipe close to the ceiling. He understood that it might take him a month to carry out his plan. Every time his medical assistant took a smoke break, Dmitri practiced making a noose out of his towel. Bit by bit, he also learned to walk, taking a firm step using one leg and training himself to depend momentarily on the other before taking another step.

His resolve to end his life brought about unexpected results. He calmed down and developed a healthy appetite. To make his right-hand fingers better able to tie the knots on the linen, he frequently massaged them with his healthy hand. All this slowly but surely led to his recovery. One day he even found that his speech capabilities had returned. Yet, he didn't abandon the decision to end his life. Moreover, he felt proud of his stubbornness, willpower, and resolve: "Of course, I am a crippled eagle," he thought to himself. "But I am an eagle nonetheless."

Finally, he felt ready for the final act. At three in the morning, he slowly made his way to the bathroom and was about to slip his head through the noose when a surprising thought crossed his mind: if he had succeeded in making it to the bathroom after a few months of effort, then in a few more months he could reach his office desk. If that was the case, it meant that, contrary to his initial self-diagnosis, he hadn't had a brain hemorrhage, which would have caused permanent brain damage, but only the spasm of a blood vessel in the brain. This is why he had been able to restore some of his faculties.

Encouraged by this discovery, he began training himself to hear properly, then to speak, and eventually to write, which, in time, he could do at least to some extent. The only function that refused to return was the ability to count—he still suffered from acalculia.

With the permission of the head of the medical department, he became the hospital courtyard caretaker. First, he picked up cigarette butts around the building, then he began taking care of the hospital's little garden.

By summertime, he was capable of doing what he had done when he had stepped into the prison medical world in Krasnoyarsk for the first time back in 1939, shortly before entering the gulag: making rounds to distribute pills to the hospital patients.

At the beginning of spring 1954, he was informed that he was included on the list of prisoners considered for release from the camps before serving their full term for reasons of poor health. Before taking his picture, following the instructions, the camp photographer covered the number on the prisoner's padded jacket. For an extra pack of cigarettes, for memory's sake, Dmitri had another picture taken— with the number showing. No longer able to hold a pen firmly in his hand, he dictated a letter to Anna. Thinking about their possible future meeting, he wanted to prepare her for the fact that he was an invalid now. She shouldn't imagine him the way he was in 1947 in Suslovo. Since then he had spent three years in solitary confinement, almost gone insane, and suffered paralysis twice here in the special camp. Now he was an old man, totally unemployable and incurably ill. He saw poorly, thought with difficulty, dragged his right leg, and his right hand hung like a broken branch.

Then he advised her, without any sentimentality, to make a decisive and clean break with him, to stop writing letters and sending money and parcels: "My life is now hard and beastly, little Anna. It's not settled. And therefore our liaison comes to a natural end." He informed her that she shouldn't worry. He had applied for a place in the Omsk Invalid Home as a homeless ex-prisoner, and he'd been accepted.

He remained unmoved by the atmosphere of total joy among prisoners foretasting freedom. He knew all too well that not much joy was in store for him. Having nowhere else to go, he also knew that life at the invalid home would be like a branch of the camp hell where the cutthroats among the criminals would not be controlled by the guards. The jungle law of the survival of the fittest would reign there too.

As he awaited his release indifferently, a letter arrived from Anna protesting his decision in the strongest possible language. She underscored that she had long ago committed herself to support him for as long as he lived and that she had never changed her mind. Since she was still tied to her job in Tambov, she gave her daughter's Moscow address and instructed Dmitri to go straight there the moment he was released.

Reading these lines, he was seized with joy. He felt like jumping and shouting.

But little did he know of what truly awaited him on the other side of the barbed wire.

NINETEEN | Taking On Challenges of Freedom

We'll come out of the camps and mesh into the country's
life as smoothly as cogs of one gear mesh with the cogs of
another.

—PRISONER BYSTROLYOTOV TO ANOTHER PRISONER
ON THE EVE OF RELEASE FROM THE CAMPS

Freedom is not the camps. It'll crush anyone.

—AN EX-PRISONER TO PRISONER BYSTROLYOTOV

In the most current official biography, the description of Bystrolyo-tov's life after his release from the camps would have the uninitiated reader believe it was a life of glory and roses. However, what truly happened to him after he stepped outside the camp gates makes one cringe at the hypocrisy of these official pronouncements. In the prologue of his unpublished typescript devoted to that period, "The Hard Road to Immortality," after describing an enthusiastic crowd at a railroad station warmly welcoming ex-prisoners coming from Siberia, complete with congratulatory posters and bouquets of flowers, Bystrolyotov asks the reader to guess who these men were before being thrown into Siberian camps. And he answers with bitter sarcasm: not innocently persecuted Soviet patriots like himself, but ex-SS officers captured in the course of World War II.[1]

Dmitri was freed from the Omsk camp on October 29, 1954, at 11:00 A.M. When, a month and a half later, he stepped onto the platform at Moscow's Kazan station, dizzy from overwhelming emotions and the exhaustion of a long journey in a cargo car from Siberia to the country's capital, he was anything but ready to begin his new life. His right hand still didn't function well, and he hadn't regained the full use of his right leg. His tongue barely moved, and he was able to open one of his eyes only partially. Especially troublesome was his sporadic loss of memory, including the inability to remember his own name, and episodes of disorientation in time and space. His prisoner's number plucked out from both the front and back of his padded jacket, he exited the railroad car bareheaded, though it was cold outside: while he slept on the train, some other ex-prisoner had stolen his warm hat. Thus, the very first policeman at once recognized him as a former prisoner and ordered him to move quickly out of the railroad premises. The papers in his pocket stated that he had been serving a term as a spy, a terrorist, and a conspirator and was now freed because of poor health. And that he had no lice.

The road to Moscow from Omsk had been long and tiring. At times, surrounded by other ex-prisoners in a car packed to capacity, he felt oblivious to what happened to him next. Only at desperate moments did his will to survive push him to action. Changing trains several times on the way to Moscow, he was forced to wait many hours with the others during each transfer. He was so infirm that he realized if he didn't reach Moscow very soon, he would die. In a desperate upsurge of energy, together with one of his travel companions, he pulled off a scheme, a carbon copy of one of his most daring operations—when he had smuggled samples of new Italian weaponry across the Italian, Swiss, and German borders. Ironically, this time he had to resort to the same ingenuity to survive not on hostile territory but in his own country.

His accomplice was another ex-prisoner, one Rudov, whose life story was bizarre, like that of many ex-prisoners they both had met during their many years in the camps. As a Jew, Rudov was first imprisoned by the Nazis and marked for death in one of the concentration camps. He was kept alive on a temporary basis, from one round of executions to the next, because as a high-class tailor, he was making suits for the SS officers. Eventually, he was freed by the Red Army but soon arrested again, sentenced to twenty-five years in prison "for collaboration with the enemy," and sent to a Siberian camp. Like Dmitri, he was freed many years later because of poor health: he suffered from severe arthritis. To get themselves tickets, Dmitri told Rudov to feign being a mute mental patient, while Dmitri posed as a doctor accompanying him.

When at last Dmitri reached the Moscow apartment of Anna's daughter, Magdalina, as he spent a night on the couch, the numbness of his feelings finally subsided, and he woke up in the middle of the night from euphoria. He was "finally free, free, free!"

But the joy of being free didn't last very long. Soon, considerations of how to find a means of existence took over. He had been freed on the basis of poor health—he hadn't been rehabilitated, which, in the Soviet context, meant that his conviction was not officially recognized as unlawful, and therefore, his civil rights were not restored.[2] He couldn't receive a residency permit to live in Moscow or Leningrad or to obtain a professional job. He also was not eligible to receive a pension or other social benefits. He was still considered a foreign spy and a traitor. Like many political ex-prisoners, he was forbidden to live closer than one hundred kilometers from Moscow. In fact, if visiting, he could stay there no more than a day.

Soon Anna quit her job in Tambov and reunited with him. Although there were plenty of openings for an engineer of her qualifications in Moscow, when she listed Dmitri, a political ex-prisoner, as her dependent in job applications, all doors were closed to her. In desperation, Anna took Dmitri to the KGB headquarters on Lubyanka and begged the head of the Medical Department of the Gulag, Comrade Ustinchenko, formerly a major, now a colonel, whom Dmitri knew from Suslovo camp, to help them get on their feet. But they were both denied assistance of any kind.

In December 1954, they moved to the village of Istie, near Ryazan, where Anna found a job as head of an iron-casting shop at a local metallurgical plant. They gave her a small, half-dark room with a tiny window in a barrack. It was a severe winter, and every day to survive the cold, both suffering from dizziness and weak hearts, they laboriously used a two-person saw to supply themselves with firewood for their stove.

Dmitri's health remained fragile. He continued to experience poor blood circulation. He couldn't think clearly for too long, and his speech was often hard to understand. His other mental capabilities were also still affected. Anna spent many hours at work, and Dmitri cooked for both of them, now confusing salt with sugar, now losing any sense of time.

By the summer of 1955, his health had gradually begun to improve, and most important, his ability to think clearly was largely restored. This encouraged him to renew his efforts to push for rehabilitation and to find work using skills obtained in the West. Of course, his émigré law school diploma from Prague was worthless: in the first place, the training he'd received there was geared toward the old tsarist law. But he could make use of his medical skills. At the beginning of 1955, he wrote to KGB headquarters requesting confirmation that under one of the aliases he used abroad when working for Soviet intelligence in the 1930s, he had completed the full course of the medical faculty at Zurich University. He explained that upon his return to Moscow in December 1936, together with his passport for foreign travel, he had surrendered his medical doctor diploma to the NKVD. Since this document had apparently been lost somewhere in the NKVD archives, he asked them for a certificate stating his medical credentials. His appeal was rejected.

Then he wrote to the camps, asking them to confirm his work as a medic during his imprisonment. This move was partially successful. He received certificates stating that he had worked at a number of camps in various capacities, as a stationary and ambulatory physician and as a prosector. But that was hardly enough to give hope that a political ex-convict would be hired to do any medical work.

Meanwhile, the highly principled Anna couldn't adjust to the work environment at her plant, where bribery and toadyism were part and parcel of the system. They returned to Moscow. The shortage of living quarters, the curse of the Soviet system for its whole duration, was especially acute in the first two decades after World War II. Anna found a taxing job as foreman of a galvanizing shop at a Moscow radio plant. She rented a room from her daughter's mother-in-law. Since Dmitri had to live at least one hundred kilometers outside Moscow, the couple had to part for the time being. Dmitri settled in the small provincial town of Alexandrov, which had a historically interesting past. In the thirteenth century, it was the place of the estate of Alexander Nevsky, the grand prince of Novgorod and Vladimir; in fact, the town had been named after him. Three centuries later, Ivan the Terrible locked himself in the local Kremlin and lived there nearly twenty-five years, guarded by his "death squads," called *oprichniki*. Here, too, there was no place to live. Dmitri rented a bed in a room occupied by a family of three.[3]

He slowly regained his strength and felt the need to do something to lessen Anna's burden of supporting him. As the first step, by law an ex-prisoner had to register at the local police precinct. Looking over his papers, duly instructed in how to deal with released political prisoners, the police ordered him to see the local KGB executive right away.

While the current successor of the KGB would have uninformed people believe that the mistake of prosecuting Bystrolyotov was repaid in the abundance of care he received upon release, his own record of that period testifies to quite the opposite: his denigration and humiliation continued at every step of his existence for many years after his release. For starters, on that first encounter with the KGB upon regaining his freedom, the KGB executive of the town forced him to wait for an hour and a half. As Dmitri entered the premises of the organization, his horrifying memories of pain and suffering overwhelmed him. He was on the verge of fainting. His head splitting with pain, Dmitri realized he was doomed: "The past without fading a bit hung over me like a poisonous fog, and for the first time since leaving the Omsk camp, I suddenly felt I would never ever tear myself away from it, that no matter where I was or what I did, this poisonous fog would be with me to the very last day of my life."

Although he tried talking himself into keeping his chin up and acting assured and calm, he failed. To the KGB officer, who exuded tremendous contempt and coldness, he was just some severely crippled old man. When Dmitri tried to take a seat in front of the desk, the officer stopped him and motioned to a chair at the other end of the office. Then, giving him no opportunity to say anything, he cautioned Dmitri that now he was under his watch and threatened to send him back to the camps if he got involved in any suspicious activity.

Dmitri settled for leading a quiet life, concentrating all his efforts on restoring his health. Soon something happened that gave him a huge burst of hope. The ability so important to him that he had been deprived of for such a long time—the ability to read—slowly but surely began returning to him. The discovery made him so excited that he felt dizzy, and his heart started beating violently. He began learning to read and write anew, using whatever paper he could find, even if it was a piece of wrapping paper.

Now his hope of finding some work was renewed. At the risk of being arrested for violating the prohibition against political ex-prisoners staying in the capital, he made occasional trips to Moscow. There he visited a few local schools, asking for an opportunity to teach any foreign language, whether French, English, or German. But the directors turned him down because his papers indicated that he had served a long prison term as a foreign spy and terrorist. He couldn't even get a job as night guard of a street kiosk.

But he lived to see his luck turn around. On February 25, 1956, Nikita Khrushchev addressed the Twentieth Congress of the Communist Party, in the course of which he publicly admitted for the first time Stalin's part in terror and crimes against humanity. Although it had begun before on a smaller scale, a campaign of rehabilitation of innocent victims of Stalin's terror was announced. This changed the climate in the country as a whole, and in Alexandrov in particular. One night, Dmitri was awakened by a messenger from the very same KGB official who had treated him with disdain not so long ago. Now he asked Dmitri whether he would mind giving foreign-language lessons to his young son.

On April 6, 1956, Dmitri received a telegram informing him of his official rehabilitation. But it would be wrong to assume that his troubles were over once and for all. In his own assessment, the next year, 1957, was one of "strenuous efforts, alarms, humiliations, and tormenting disappointments." To survive, he had to summon all of the qualities that had made him an outstanding intelligence operative in his past life—ingenuity, persistence, and doggedness. But if he had previously used all those qualities to fight real (and imaginary) enemies of his country, now he had another enemy to conquer—Soviet bureaucracy and red tape; the indifference and arrogance of the very same organization he had served selflessly.

Now with his name finally cleared of ignominy—sixteen years after "stepping up on my native scaffold"—he began his fight to receive assistance from the state he had served as an intelligence operative abroad. The welfare office informed him that he was not eligible to receive a pension because of his age (he was a few years short of the required age of sixty), and to qualify for a pension based on disability, he would have to submit medical papers certifying this, together with his employment record.

For that, he had to go back to the KGB. In the reception office at 24 Kuznetsky Most, he was met with nothing but coldness, mistrust, and disdain.

"Bystro . . . who? How are you going to prove that you worked for our intelligence? Do you have any documents?"

"No. But there are people and documents at the INO, the Foreign Intelligence Department, that . . ."

"We don't have time to find things out. It's your business to prove that you worked for us."

Overcome with recurring dizziness, fatigue, and heart problems, he dragged himself from one KGB office to another asking for the needed papers. The problem of his official status as intelligence operative was that he was never given an officer rank.[4] His work record showed only his initial employment with the INO as a translator. As mentioned already, in 1937, after his return to the USSR, his boss, Slutsky, had received Yezhov's permission to start moving the documentation that would have given him the rank of senior lieutenant. But then he was arrested. Now, he had to plead with them that while the paperwork declaring him a cadre worker was missing, for thirteen years, he had nevertheless carried out high-level state orders and risked his life many times for the sake of his Motherland.

Endless red tape ensued as he tried to get a pension from the KGB. To prove that he had worked for the INO, Dmitri had to deal with numerous KGB officials, which proved to be an utterly denigrating and painfully humiliating experience. Their telephones were always busy, and when he arrived for an appointment, he would hear over and over again that his papers weren't ready and that he should come back in yet another two weeks: "It was like spooling my nerves—no, to be exact, my empty intestines—onto the drum of the bureaucratic machine." First, it took months of dragging himself on semiparalyzed legs all over Moscow from one little bureaucratic office window to another to get his papers in order. Then when he applied for a pension, he was advised to call them in a month and a half. Then in two. Then they said that the question was still under examination, and he should wait some more. "They knew how to fight a sick and old man—to stall things for as long as possible." But he didn't want to give up: he was a fighter, and they were his new enemies.[5]

Finally, after two years of fruitless struggle with the KGB officials, a new law on pensions came out, making Dmitri eligible for a pension as a former employee of the Chamber of Commerce. Only then did the KGB phone him and offer their pension. The sum they offered was nearly half of the one he was to receive from the Chamber of Commerce. He hung up in silence. (Now his official biography states that he refused the KGB pension, making it seem as if it were an act of generosity on his part toward the state, while in fact, he felt disgusted by their offer, seeing it as a gesture of insult and ingratitude.)

He also had to fight the KGB tooth and nail to get at least some living space for himself and his ailing wife. At that time, overworked and in poor health, Anna became incapacitated because of high blood pressure. In his memoirs, Dmitri includes a few samples of his correspondence, asking the reader to bear in mind that before and after sending each letter he had to make dozens of phone calls and then go to numerous appointments, where he spent dozens of hours waiting on lines in reception rooms. Dmitri cautions the reader that, even taking all this into consideration, he would hardly be able to fully assess the whole experience of his "technique of breaking with his damaged head the bureaucratic stone wall of Socialism at the stage of its transition to Communism."

Here is a sample from his numerous letters to General Ivan Serov, head of the KGB between 1954 and 1958. "I'm an invalid of the first degree. Until October 1956, I spent nights on a stool in the kitchen of my acquaintances and days sitting [in the rooms of] the Museum of LENIN. [He capitalized Lenin's name, apparently, to shame the minister.] Please inform the head of the Housing Department [of the KGB] about the disastrous situation of your former employee."

At one point he managed to arrange an appointment with the head of the Department of Foreign Intelligence. The man was dressed in civilian clothes, well groomed, and as Dmitri remarks sarcastically, during their conversation, he played with his fingernails, which had been done by a manicurist. "Looking carelessly at their shine, the lord in a splendid suit preached some truisms to me from the height of his somewhat elevated desk and chair: 'All you talk about is money, Comrade Bystrolyotov. We, the Soviet people, should think not about money but about Communism and our Motherland. You served well, and you should be proud of it and satisfied with it.' The lord treated me to a sermon but refused to help."[6]

Living on the verge of starvation, he tried to recover the valuables taken from him when he was arrested. By selling them, he hoped to sustain himself while fighting the red tape of the KGB bureaucratic machine. But he immediately discovered that, besides being confirmed bureaucrats, those "fearless and irreproachable knights" (rytsari bez strakha i upreka), as the KGB men portrayed themselves to the country, were, in fact, nothing but thieves and robbers. For his five suits, each of them custom cut by the best tailors of Paris, Amsterdam, and Berlin, he was remunerated with just a few rubles. When he protested, they showed him the list of his belongings confiscated at the time of his arrest: the suits were described as "work robes," as if they were some auto mechanic's overalls. When he reasoned with them that, working for foreign intelligence undercover as a high society gentleman, he couldn't possibly have worn "work robes," he was brushed off with, "We have no time to go into details. Sign here, take your money, and run."

He also tried to recover the accessories he had bought to fit his image as a Hungarian count or British lord: a gold family ring with a crown and monogram on it, a gold cigarette case with an enamel plate depicting the count's coat of arms, a small pair of gilded scissors to cut cigars. But to his astonishment, the KGB documents listed all those accessories as made of copper. "Next!"[7]

Dmitri tried to address the issue of the gold belongings confiscated during his arrest to the higher-ups: he wrote to the KGB minister himself. It took them three months to reply that an eyewitness testimony was needed. When Dmitri finally secured it, the minister's office took another three months to respond that, actually, they wanted not one but three testimonies. When Dmitri obtained them, they took another four months to inform him that only the testimonies of former INO employees were valid in his case. Dmitri worked on it and sent the papers to the minister, who replied that the papers should not come from just any INO employees but only from those who were currently employed. Dmitri went back to work, but his appeal was rejected again. This time, they let him know that the only

INO employees that could testify on his behalf were those who were present in the room at the time of his arrest and saw with their own eyes that the gold accessories were truly taken from him. Dmitri's patience collapsed, and he gave up.

At that lowest moment of extreme poverty, help came from totally unexpected quarters. Iolanta's sister, Bozhena, found him and wrote to him from Prague. Now she was Bozhena Synkova: she had married eventually, she had a son, and now she was a widow. She had an occasion to send Dmitri some of his and her deceased sister's belongings that had been left behind in Prague: Iolanta's gold watches and astrakhan fur coat and Dmitri's Swiss watches. Later on, Ivanek, Bozhena's son, also helped now with money, now with clothes, and even with a package of Prague hot dogs, a delicacy for any Soviet citizen at that time.

In the middle of his uphill battle with the KGB bureaucracy, with his nerves already stretched to the limit, his emotions received a tremendous jolt. On June 16, 1956, a telephone call from the Central Committee of the Communist Party summoned him to appear the next day at the Party headquarters on Staraya Square, at 10:00 A.M. sharp. As he arrived at the building in a glistening black car with a silent driver, he was full of premonitions that his fate would turn for the worse again. In a desperate move, he tried to reason with the official on duty in the hall of the building that there was some misunderstanding, for he, Dmitri, wasn't even a Party member. But without any discussion, a guardsman walked him along endless corridors. Dmitri's old mental tapes began running, and he anticipated with horror that his dreaded camp past was about to make a comeback any second now. In a fit of paranoia, he imagined that he was about to be arrested again, and that's why he had been lured into the high office. What, what had he done wrong again? (For the rest of his life, he would not be able to shake off his fear of rearrest, and he was hardly unique in that respect.)[8]

They brought him into a large room where a KGB colonel arose from his seat to greet him, and his heart sank. Arrest!

But the colonel exuded cordiality and asked about his health.

Scanning the room, Dmitri immediately recognized at least two people sitting there. Their portraits were ubiquitous in the country at the time, for they had occupied high offices. One was Nikolai Mikhailovich Shvernik, who, in the last seven years of Stalin's rule, had held (nominally, of course) the highest post in the country, that of chairman of the Presidium of the Supreme Soviet of the USSR (or president of the USSR).

The other man was Georgy Maksimilianovich Malenkov, the prime minister of the USSR for the first two years after Stalin's death. In February 1955, he was forced to resign after coming under attack for his close association with Lavrenty Beria (who was executed as a traitor in December 1953). But he remained a member of the Politburo's successor, the Presidium. Also present were two KGB generals and a half dozen old women—old Bolsheviks judging by their demeanor and turn-of-the-century clothes.

As they sat Dmitri down on a sofa, Shvernik stood up and announced the opening of the meeting of the Party Control Committee of the Central Committee of the Communist Party of the USSR. One of the committee members reported that he had recently been charged with investigating a claim made by KGB Colonel Shukshin that at one of the most secret military research and development plants the most valuable workers were, in fact, nothing but American agents. When the accused refused to admit their guilt, Colonel Shukshin tied them to their chairs and began kicking their wives, whom he had arrested for that purpose only.

Now Dmitri saw a hefty middle-aged man with graying hair in whom he barely recognized the young, thin intern of the time of his arrest and interrogation. Shukshin!

Meanwhile, the man calmly denied his personal responsibility in the case described. He hadn't kicked anyone, and he asked them to believe that he had always been an honest worker, observing Soviet law when dealing with persons under investigation, from the very first one to the very last. When asked whether he remembered the first one, he shrugged defiantly: he couldn't possibly remember them all. One of the KGB generals ordered him to look around the room to see whether he could recognize the man. Anticipating that he was in much deeper trouble than he had thought, with great difficulty, Shukshin finally spotted Dmitri and cried out, "I don't know this old man! I've never seen him!"

Dmitri couldn't keep his emotions bottled up any longer. He jumped from the sofa toward Shukshin and pulled up his own shirt: "And do you recognize my intestines that bulged under my skin when you kicked me with the heels of your boots? And do you recall two ribs hammered into my lungs with a steel cable? What about my skull? During the interrogation, you banged on it with a hammer, you reptile, you motherf . . ."

Dmitri grabbed at Shukshin's throat, but other men put their arms around Dmitri and pulled him back to the sofa. Others gave him water. It took him a while to come back to his senses.

Bystrolyotov gives conflicting information on what happened to Shukshin later on. In one place in his memoirs, he writes that the man was arrested and died in prison of heart failure soon after; in another place he writes that he was shot. However, it looks like Dmitri was misled by the KGB, who fed him that information. As is known now, an attempt was made to bring Colonel Fyodor Shukshin to stand trial for "violation of Socialist law" in many other cases as well. In 1951, he arrested a group of Moscow University students (K. P. Bogatyrev, V. D. Latkin, and others) and exhausted the prisoners with all-night interrogations, using threats and blackmail. Besides Bystrolyotov, he also took part in torturing other prisoners, for example, S. M. Matveev and N. Ia. Spivak. Nevertheless, despite Dmitri's testimony to the contrary, the Party Control Committee found that "the verification materials had not established Shukshin's personal participation in beatings of prisoners" and that it was possible to "retain him in the Party with a strict reprimand and a warning for violating the law in his investigative work." Later, Leonid Brezhnev, then a secretary of the Central Committee of the CPSU, after familiarizing himself with Shukshin's case, recommended his expulsion from the Party. At the time, Brezhnev wasn't yet secretary general of the Party, so no further action was taken on the paper with his resolution, and it was later written off and filed in the archives. Many other KGB cadres who violated the law retained their privileged positions, some until the present day.[9]

After that memorable encounter at the Party headquarters, his former employer threw a token perk to Dmitri in the form of a short-term pass to the KGB-run rest home, where he could at least eat well and breathe some fresh air in the adjacent forest. During dinner, looking at Dmitri's emaciated face and infirm body, some colonel guessed he had been a former Gulag prisoner. The man "chewed on a pork cutlet with appetite, then he wiped off his lips with a blindingly white napkin, and from the corner of his mouth, murmured as if into space: 'I can imagine how you hate all of us.'" Although the colonel had guessed right about him, many years of living on the edge, both as an intelligence operative and a Gulag prisoner, made Dmitri do the right thing—he abstained from any response. He doubted the colonel's sincerity and suspected that it was a provocation. The wrong response could get him in trouble again.

His experience in fighting the indifference and red tape of the cumbersome KGB bureaucracy came in handy a few years later, when, in July 1961, his former shipmate and friend Zhenya Kavetsky, with whom he had sailed on board the *St. Trotsky* and shared other adventures, found Dmitri and paid him a visit. Dmitri had involved him in working for Soviet foreign intelligence back in the 1930s. Like Dmitri, he worked selflessly. Yet, under the pretext of receiving an award, he was recalled to Moscow, arrested, maimed during his torture, and subsequently, served two terms. After spending five years in the camps, in the spring of 1951, he was rearrested as a German spy and exiled to the Krasnoyarsk region.[10]

According to Bystrolyotov, Kavetsky was arrested when one of the most distinguished "Great Illegals," Theodor Mally, in an attempt to survive, decided to give his semiliterate interrogator testimonies that could serve as a basis for future appeal. He said that he had recruited Kavetsky to work for a Fascist spy ring while traveling on a steamship from Geneva to Lyon. One look at a map of Europe would be enough to see that this could never have happened.

Like many other Gulag prisoners, including Dmitri himself, Kavetsky was broken not only physically but also mentally. Kavetsky also feared rearrest at any moment, which in his case turned into paranoia. He visited when Dmitri wasn't at home, and when Anna stepped out to the kitchen to boil some water for tea, he jumped up from his chair and attempted to flee. He thought Anna was about to call the police.

Kavetsky didn't have enough strength to fight for his rehabilitation. Dmitri intervened on his behalf. He found Mally's wife, Lidia, and asked her to write what she knew about Kavetsky's service to the country. Securing Lidia's testimony and supplying his own, he took his friend to the KGB reception room, whose bureaucratic tricks he knew all too well by now, and helped him to get at least some pension.

Dmitri also learned about the fate of his friend Kotya Yurevich, whom he had seen in the Butyrka prison for the last time. He was sentenced to eight years in hard labor camps. He survived, was later rehabilitated, and worked as an engineer in his native Odessa. Fate took a different turn for his steadfast assistants in many operations, Erica Weinstein and Joseph Leppin. In 1937, upon recall to the USSR, Erica was arrested, and, though she was pregnant, severely tortured; she died in prison. By some miracle, Leppin was spared. Upon return to the USSR, first he worked as a translator for Dmitri at the Chamber of Commerce (after his transfer there from the NKVD), then he taught languages at a university. He had begun work on his dissertation when the war broke out. He volunteered to go to the front line. A machine gunner, he perished on the battlefield, squashed by a German tank.[11]

In September 1956, Anna's high blood pressure reached a critical mark. Bedridden, she made a will for Dmitri's benefit, at least in terms of freeing him from moral responsibility toward her. In her will, she asked him to forget about her as soon as possible and find himself a "better mate." Dmitri made desperate attempts to find some employment. Since he couldn't be hired as either a doctor or a language teacher, he looked for a place where he could use both his medical knowledge and his language skills. He searched and searched until he found one place of potential freelance work, the Moscow Medical Synopsis Bureau. For starters, his hands trembling, he took a few German journals to make abstracts of its articles. The first one was about narrowing of the male urethra. Highly excited about finally finding an opportunity to use his brain and earn some money, he exclaimed to himself, "May you be blessed, dear urethra!" Overcome with dizziness, almost falling from the chair, he began his work.

In January 1957, he found a true "gold mine," as he calls it, in the form of *Zhurnal nauchnoi i tekhnicheskoi informatsii* (*Journal of Scientific and Technical Information*). (In ten years, the journal served as the impetus for the establishment of the Institute of Scientific and Technical Information.) Here, as he had in his intelligence work, Dmitri benefited from his acquaintance with many languages. He charged headlong into the sudden opportunity. He chose biology and geography as his fields of specialization and took on translation from all of the languages in his command. The list is quite impressive, both in sheer numbers and linguistic variety. Besides English, German, and French, he also translated from Danish, Dutch, Flemish, Norwegian, Afrikaans, Swedish, Portuguese, Spanish, Romanian, French, Italian, Serbo-Croatian, Czech, Slovak, Bulgarian, and Polish. As he began working, he also learned Japanese and Chinese to the extent necessary and refreshed his knowledge of Turkish, to which he had first been exposed by his Turkish nanny during his early years in Anapa and later learned during his émigré life in Constantinople.

Because of the country's long isolation from the civilized world, there was an acute shortage of translators, especially for rare languages, and he had practically no competition. The only problem was that at times his memory gave out on him. Sometimes, the word he needed would come back to him at night as he slept. In November of that year, he was offered the position of chief language editor.

Still taking reserpine, at the time the most advanced medicine for control of hypertension, he worked without pause, resting only during vacations. Among other works, he translated an article from English on Chinese medicine at the time of the Ming dynasty and two books from Czech, both dedicated to the physiology of puberty, male and female. His name became known in the field of medical translation, and he was offered work writing in-house reviews for the State Medical Publishers. In March 1958, after living nearly four years under somebody else's roof, he finally obtained a room for himself and Anna in a communal apartment. He experienced a sense of pride in having a room of his own, rejoicing that from then on, nobody could burst into his quarters shouting, "Get up, you Fascist mug!" as had happened when he was renting a bed in someone else's home in Alexandrov.

Eventually, he was able to earn enough to support Anna, whose high blood pressure made it very hard for her to work. She stayed home and took care of the domestic chores. Dmitri was delighted to return the favor, for he was immensely grateful to her for pulling him from the depths on the eve of his release from the camps. Their marriage was a happy one. They merged into one as a genuine couple.

"Each of us feels like a cutoff half that seems to lack something," he writes. "But together we are a whole." They understood each other with half a word, and many people even thought they bore a close physical resemblance to each other. He often marveled at the irony of fate: that he had found his personal happiness behind barbed wire.[12]

Early mornings before going to work, Dmitri made the rounds of all the stores, bought what was needed for the day, and brought it home to his still sleeping "little Anya" (Anechka), as he lovingly calls her throughout his memoirs.[13] He was happy that despite signs of aging—wrinkles and excess weight—"time hadn't stolen" what he valued the most: "the imprint of high breeding," that is, her gentry origin. Dmitri felt deeply satisfied that even among his cultured and highly educated friends—some old ones, former Gulag political prisoners like himself, whom he had befriended in the camps, some newly acquired while working for the publishing house—Anna stood out with "her regular facial features, the whiteness of her skin, her good gait, and unforced cheerfulness." He liked it that, unlike the vast majority of Soviet people, who, in his judgment, were "accustomed to humiliation," she was "sure of herself and wouldn't allow anyone to offend her."[14]

Now Dmitri earned enough to afford a vacation in the Caucasus and even to travel abroad—to Prague. Understandably, this reminded him of many emotional tribulations during the time he had lived there.

He devoted most of his waking hours to his translations, and whatever time he could steal from his regular hours in the office, he spent writing. In 1960, a number of African states gained independence from colonial rule, and without slowing down his translation work, Dmitri decided to write his African novel, the one he had already outlined in his mind and tried to compose in his head during solitary confinement at the Sukhanovka prison. At the time, it had almost driven him insane. Now he could finally write it down. He saw it as an exercise for his writing muscles, which he wanted to put into full use for writing his Gulag memoirs, his ultimate goal.

It took him a year and a half to finish it. A typescript of his novel in hand, he set out to find a publisher. Apparently, even the camps had failed to give him a full sense of what a totalitarian country was all about. After wandering unsuccessfully from one publishing house to another, he came to the sobering conclusion that, essentially, there was only one publisher in the USSR—the department of literature at the Central Committee: the ultimate censor that decided what the country was going to read. Although his African novel was politically timely, and his description of cruelty toward the indigenous people of Congo was in line with Soviet propaganda of the time, it wasn't deemed suitable for publication for other reasons. Dmitri was obviously unaware of the prudishness of Soviet literature. What was permissible in the camps for prisoners' personal consumption was off-limits when it came to the general public. Not even a hint of sexuality was allowed to appear on the pages of Soviet books. His naiveté about this raised the eyebrows of more than one editor: "You write, 'Her breasts touched my chest.' How can you write things like that?" He tried to reason that native-born women in the Congo forests always walked around naked. The editor shrugged: "Can't you put some bra on her or something else?"[15]

(However, as Dmitri hoped, the editor missed that the author encoded his own life story into the novel by giving its protagonist, a Dutch artist traveling along the African continent, the name of "van Egmont." Dmitri found his own fate quite akin to that of the real-life sixteenth century Flemish warrior Count Egmont, the hero of Goethe's tragedy. Like Egmont, he, Dmitri, also under threat of arrest, refused to run away and give up his ideals of liberty for all mankind, was also imprisoned and, in practical terms of Siberian camps, sentenced to death. Unlike Egmont, he survived by miracle.)

His African novel rejected time and again, Dmitri gave up, deciding that now he had developed the literary skills he needed to undertake the most important writing project of his life—his camp memoirs. He reminded himself that he had promised the dead a thousand times that if he survived the ordeal, he would write about it. He began to spur himself on: "I'm approaching seventy. I mustn't even dare to die without giving my eyewitness testimony to the Soviet people."

He held down only his full-time job at the institute and quit doing all the freelance work that brought him extra income and provided him with little luxuries, of course, in Soviet terms. Now he felt that his reviews of medical books and his painting (which he resumed after reconnecting with the Union of Soviet Artists), all of this, was a betrayal of the dead. He must describe everything that had happened in the camps, not so much for the sake of his own record, but as a moral obligation he felt toward the countless other victims of the Gulag he had met along the way.

He knew that writing his memoirs and getting them in print would be the last major battle of his life. But it was his most important battle now, and he swore to himself that he would spare no effort in fighting it to the end.

You can close your eyes to reality but not to memories.

—STANISLAW JERZY LEC

What is written with a pen cannot be cut out with an axe.

—RUSSIAN PROVERB

Dmitri made an outline of his work. He estimated that he had to write about twenty-five hundred pages broken down into twelve volumes. He planned to finish them by the end of 1965. It was an enormous task for an aged man in failing health. As he wrote his memoirs, he kept asking himself whether he would be able to pull it off: "I'm infirm. My vision is poor. And I'm old. Will I manage? Will I have time?" During a routine checkup, his doctor noted some growths on his body that had to be checked for cancer. For lack of time, he refused to pursue the tests as he had sworn to himself to finish the most important business left for him in life—writing his memoirs: "I must. I must manage!"[1]

His initial approach to writing his memoirs, which he had started in the camps, was as a loyal Soviet citizen. Although he had witnessed many crimes against humanity committed under Stalin, he was still devoted to the Communist cause and praised the Soviet people for their heroism. He saw his memoirs as a record of "cruel, difficult, but splendid times." The main hero of his books would not be him personally, but Soviet man as a collective hero. The title he came up with for his work—"Pir bessmertnykh" (The Feast of Immortals)—was supposed to convey his stand, as he states in his epigraph:

All things living on the earth are afraid of death; only
a human being is capable of consciously conquering his
fear. By overstepping the fear of death, an ideological
man becomes immortal, and in this is his highest and
eternal reward! There are millions of mortals on the
earth, and they disappear without a trace; for them,
the dangers and rigors of life are their damnation, but,
for us [Soviet people], they are joy, pride, and triumph.
Struggle is the feast of immortals.

In the course of the next four years, overcoming his infirmities and
using whatever time was left after working at his main job as a translator and consultant at the All-Union Research Institute of Medical
Information, he did it.

Having gone through all nine circles of Stalin's man-made hell,
he couldn't help but gradually revise his world outlook. His memoirs
somberly record his transformation from an idealistic youth caught
in the cross fire between two opposing ideologies to a selfless fighter
for his country's proclaimed ideals, to a deeply disillusioned man,
whose main preoccupation in the waning years of his life was to leave
at least some trace of it for future generations. During his first years
in the camps he had thought that "the root of the evil [was] not in
people but in the two-faced [Soviet] system—a contradictory mixture of Lenin's sensible humanity with Stalin's beastly inhumanity."
But, after years of tormenting ruminations, he changed his mind.
He was no longer inclined to exonerate either Lenin or the Soviet
people. In his concluding volume, "Trudnyi put' v bessmertie" ("The
Hard Road to Immortality"), he made clear his view that Lenin was
the cause of the country's troubles. After all, through the principle
of Party "democratic centralism," none other than Lenin had implemented the personal power of a dictator, thus making the fate of the
state dependent upon the personality of the ruler. As Dmitri logically
concluded, "Stalin didn't fall from the skies and capture the position
of secretary general by force; he was the logical heir of Lenin."[2]

Dmitri realized that Lenin's fatal "mistake" was the result of the
country's much deeper historical and cultural problems. Russia was
"accustomed to centralism," which was predicated, among other reasons, on the sheer vastness of her territory and the multitude of eth-

nicities living on it. And Russia was a country of "unbelievable cultural backwardness." Before his arrest Dmitri had lived only a short time in the Soviet Union as an adult. It was thus during his camp years, and, to an even greater degree, going though the turmoil of his first years in freedom, that he arrived at a much deeper understanding of his country. When he started his memoirs, he wanted to write "from civic, Soviet, Party, and patriotic perspectives," but his conclusions, full of pain and shame for his country, were eventually hardly pleasing either to Soviet power or the Communist Party. Now, no longer a blind believer in the viability of the Communist idea, he concluded that the camp was "a little world that, on a smaller scale, reflects life outside of it . . . like a little drop of water reflects the huge sun"; that is, the camp was the whole Soviet Union in miniature.[3]

As he saw it, the main problem of the Soviet system was, first and foremost, its lawlessness, the fact that the country's judicial system had long ago been replaced by Party decisions. He also acknowledged to himself what he had refused to see before—that democracy Soviet-style had always been nothing but a sham: neither Stalin, nor Khrushchev, nor any other Soviet leader had come to power as a result of free elections. And despite its claim to be a society of equals, Soviet society was stratified into classes the same way as in capitalist countries, only adjusted by the poverty of the vast majority of people and a lack of culture. He found the two causes interrelated. Living in the showcase of the Socialist capital, the southwestern sector of Moscow, he observed that the people around him, who "presumably [would] step into the Kingdom of Heaven during their lifetime," lived in "hopeless and deadening boredom, dragging themselves to Communism with vodka and foul language." Thus, poverty wasn't the only reason for their miserable existence but also the low cultural habits of the nation in general: "In Germany, such poverty would look different; it would be better and cleaner . . . The tattered and bogged-down Soviet man grows spiritually only on the pages of Soviet newspapers."[4]

Dmitri was also appalled by the thinning moral fabric of the Soviet people. After he returned from the camps, he was shaken by the realization that no one expressed any sense of moral responsibility for the national tragedy of persecution of innocent people that had occurred, as if millions of human lives were meaningless. Life went on as if nothing had happened, as if no one was guilty of bloodshed on such a grand scale.[5]

Now Dmitri totally dismissed the very idea of Communism, which he called "a great mirage" that was "no better or worse than any other religion . . . But we work honestly only for the joy of labor, not for the sake of believing in the possibility of such nonsense as the future satisfaction of all human needs." And he predicted the Soviet Union's eventual downfall, because it lacked a mechanism for economic development due to the system's rigidity, the lack of competition, and absence of personal interest. He was also sure that the Soviet Union would collapse for another reason: the unresolved issue of relationships between the nationalities. (As we know now, all of Dmitri's predictions came true a quarter of a century later.)[6]

During the years of writing his memoirs, Dmitri's hopes of seeing his work in print went up and down. In November 1962, a literary sensation took place in the Soviet Union. Written by a former Gulag prisoner and a non-Party member like Dmitri himself, *One Day in the Life of Ivan Denisovich*, Aleksandr Solzhenitsyn's novel devoted to life in Stalin's camps, was published with the explicit approval of Khrushchev. It was the first major work of Soviet literature since the 1920s that had a politically controversial theme.

As could be expected, Dmitri took Solzhenitsyn's writing to heart. In his "Zapiski iz zhivogo doma" ("Notes from the House of the Living"), one of the camp memoirs he was working on at the time, he disputed Solzhenitsyn's approach to the description of camp life. He found the novel a "boring tale by a boring author about boring aspects of bright life, which he overlooked." He attributed the novel's success only to the fact that it had broken political taboos.[7]

Dmitri also tried to publish at least part of his memoirs, but he didn't succeed. When he gave his manuscripts to the Union of Soviet Writers for review, his work received a strong and unequivocal rejection. Arguably, there were objective shortcomings that Dmitri could easily eliminate with careful and judicious reworking. One of these concerned the genre problem. Although his introduction qualified his writing as pure memoir and "raw material for future historians' analysis," here and there he slipped into the genre of an autobiographical novel, taking poetic license, mostly in rendering the life stories of other prisoners. There were some stylistic glitches for sure. A talented painter, he possessed extraordinary descriptive power when depicting landscapes, such as early morning in the African desert or a spring day in the Far North, but his attempts to render the speech mannerisms of prisoners of lower strata of society were less successful.[8]

But style was not the main reason for the sharp and unequivocal rejection of his work—it was his political stance. Although unable to refute any of Dmitri's observations and conclusions about his camp experience or about the country, using a typical Soviet strategy for dismissing any criticism, the reviewer accused him of ignoring the bigger picture, of "wearing not only blinkers but also special glasses for local vision."

The rejection bruised Dmitri's ego. But the pain was of his own making: he had naively taken the official claims of de-Stalinization of the country at face value. The thaw in Soviet cultural policy, started under Khrushchev, was a cautious and carefully controlled process. Camp memoirs denouncing Stalin's excesses were balanced by ones reaffirming a core belief in the Communist ideology. Dmitri was outraged by the publication of another work on the same topic, Boris Diakov's *Povest' o perezhitom* (*A Tale of Survival*), justly seeing in it the Party's attempt to set an example of how one should write about the controversial topic. In this work, the author chose as the main hero a four-star general and focused his vision on the lives of imprisoned Communists, complete with a Socialist competition for the most productive work efforts and, as Dmitri caustically puts it, "enthusiastic signing up for state bonds, quotations from Lenin's work that produce abundant tears [of admiration] rolling down the cheeks."[9]

As much as Dmitri mocked such writing and felt outrage toward it, his own work reveals an inner struggle. His criticism of the Soviet system and the Communist Party for abuse of power, lawlessness, and crimes against humanity is devastating. To that end, he also takes to task another book on camp life, Dostoevsky's *Notes from the House of the Dead*. Indeed, its author's plight was much easier than his. Dostoevsky was sentenced to four years of hard labor for taking part in an antigovernment circle. Symbolically addressing his famous compatriot, Dmitri writes:

> A hundred times I put my head into a noose for my
> government and received twenty years of imprisonment

and five years of "a muzzle" ["exile," in camp slang], not counting the destruction of my family, my broken ribs, my damaged head, and my battered abdomen. Socialism isn't tsarism, and the secretary general of the Communist Party isn't the tsar, the little father. And you didn't see the true horrors of life, Fyodor Mikhailovich. I was taken from the camps as an invalid, and now they refuse to publish [my camp memoirs] "Notes from the House of the Living," for the invisible camp fence still stands in my way.[10]

Among many examples of the heartless treatment of prisoners in Soviet camps that Dostoevsky couldn't possibly even imagine, Dmitri records one episode that he was unable to forget for the rest of his days. In Norilsk, late in the evening, walking through a blizzard to his cabin, he stumbled upon a naked boy about twelve years old, covered from head to toe with snow. The boy wasn't shivering from the cold: his freezing body had already passed this phase. Dmitri thought the boy had gotten lost and couldn't find his barrack. When he attempted to take him indoors, with whatever life remained in him, the boy uttered his request that he be left alone—he wanted to freeze himself to death. Dmitri picked him up and took him into one of the barracks. He later learned that the boy's father, a prominent Party official in Kiev, had been arrested together with his wife. The father was shot, and the mother got lost somewhere in the camps. Without bothering to conduct at least some semblance of investigation and trial, they sent the teenager to the camps. Totally neglected by the whole world, he lost his will to live.[11]

Meanwhile, times changed for the worse. In October 1964, Khrushchev was ousted from power. The opportunities for any work of literature with anti-Stalinist themes to appear in print were slowly but surely curtailed. The time of Brezhnev began, and with it came the reversal of the thaw. Soviet cultural policy became increasingly conservative and repressive. In his May 1965 speech commemorating the twentieth anniversary of victory over Germany, Brezhnev used Stalin's name positively for the first time. Other alarming signs of freeze came along. In February 1966, the infamous trial of two writers, Andrei Sinyavsky and Yuli Daniel, the first such trial since Stalin's days, took place. Although there was no return to the purges of the 1930s and 1940s, under Yuri Andropov, who became head of the KGB in 1967, the notorious agency regained much of the power it had enjoyed under Stalin.

Yet, all these developments didn't stop Dmitri. On the contrary, now he felt that writing about the camps was an even more urgent matter as the political climate of the country chilled. He believed that eyewitnesses like him could undermine Party efforts to falsify history. "I must become worthy of my fate," he kept telling himself.

He knew quite well that the omnipresent KGB had informers in all layers of the population, and he worried that his memoirs could be confiscated and destroyed. First, he attempted to deposit at least part of his work for safekeeping in the Lenin Library in Moscow, the largest and most prestigious library in the country. When they didn't accept his manuscripts, he took them to Leningrad and deposited them in the Saltykov-Shchedrin State Public Library. First, they put them in a general manuscript vault, but after examination by the KGB censor, they were transferred to a "special" vault, which meant that only those with special clearance would be allowed to read them. Dmitri hoped that his work would survive until better times in that "special" vault. In fact, in the foreword to his manuscripts, he wrote, "Without any hope of being heard in my lifetime, I firmly believe in our future and work for its sake . . . [Meanwhile] I'm writing for my own drawer, but in the deep belief that someday these pages will come into the hands of someone who will use them for their intended purpose—for the common good, for restoration of the truth."[12]

Since his Gulag memoirs had no prospects of finding their way to the press, and knowing that now as an old and sick man, he might not live very long and any trace of his life would vanish along with his body, he felt that at the very least he should somehow make known his service to the country as an intelligence officer. With ingenuity that harked back to his best days of spying in the West, he designed a scheme aimed at attracting the attention of the KGB brass. Using a new format popular in Soviet journals of the time, interviews with celebrities under the heading, "A Conversation with Interesting People," he composed a self-interview, complete with the "journalist's" questions and his own detailed responses. Of course, without giving the actual names of the nations upon whom he had spied in the past, in a very succinct form, Dmitri described his most important operations. To make the interview sound real, he interjected details about his present self, such as "The aged man smiles; his face gets younger" or "Dmitri Aleksandrovich strokes his white beard." Certainly, he omitted from his text any mention of his arrest, torture, and the many years spent behind barbed wire. He sent his self-interview to the popular journal *Ogonyok* (*Little Light*), which had a circulation of several million copies.

Of course, by now he knew quite well that in the Soviet press, tightly controlled by the Party and KGB censors, his text didn't stand a chance of being published. But he was counting on the domino effect, on what would happen after his submission landed on the editor's desk. While all KGB activities constituted state secrets, information about the agency's operations in the West were guarded even more tightly. Duly alerted, the editor rushed the material to the attention of the KGB. As expected, Dmitri's self-interview was banned from publication, but it produced the desired effect. First, the KGB censor, G. A. Sokolov, invited Dmitri for a talk to make sure that the author was a real person and that he hadn't invented all the mind-boggling adventures described in his self-interview. Then, after the censor's report, the KGB bosses examined the agency's archives and found that most of the material about Dmitri's work in the West hadn't survived the thirty-year span. They invited the old-timer over to headquarters and asked him to write everything he remembered about his operations in minute detail. This was how Dmitri's memo, titled "Rukopis' Gansa" ("Hans's Manuscript"), written in one of the KGB offices, came about. (Several decades later, this memo became the main source of writing on Bystrolyotov for KGB officers-cum-writers, such as Oleg Tsarev, Evgeni Primakov, and others.)

Writing the memo produced some good results for Dmitri. Soon, the omnipotent organization made sure that he was given a two-room apartment on Vernadsky Prospect (the same place where I had visited him in September 1973) and money for furniture. The unusual generosity and change of heart on the part of the agency, not known for its good-heartedness, can be explained by the effect of one paragraph that Dmitri added as a postscript to his memo: "The best years of my life were connected with my work in [our] intelligence. I'm proud of them. I'm glad that I returned to the USSR; granted, I did it to my ruin, but I returned consciously, drawn by a patriot's duty. I believe that I've lived a good life and am ready to live it the same way again."[13]

Today's KGB successors widely publicize these lines of Bystrolyotov, now reclaiming him as their hero. In so doing, they suppress from the public the fact that by the time these words were written, the KGB had completely forgotten about him and his selfless service to the country. From what is known today about his real life, it is hard to accept the words of his postscript at face value. As was any Soviet citizen, Dmitri (to even a greater degree) was well familiar with the unlimited power of the KGB over the life and death of any person in the country. He was only too aware that any expression of bitterness about his ruined life would mean falling out of grace with the almighty organization.

It may also be that the last phrase of his postscript ("I believe that I've lived a good life and am ready to live it the same way again") had another, hidden meaning that anyone who knew Dmitri would find quite in line with his defiant nature. The phrase could mean "Up yours! Despite your efforts to destroy me, you didn't succeed. I'm alive and kicking."

Whatever his postscript may suggest, the fact is that Dmitri took a revenge of sorts: he tricked the KGB. Writing what was expected of him in this memo, he knew that classified as "top secret," it would be read only by a handful of KGB officers with the highest clearance.

If the KGB officials possessed more refined literary sensibilities, they may have paid attention to the unusual style of Dmitri's writing in his memo. Instead of the dry reports typical of such documents, his style was novelistic, complete with dialogues and minute details. In fact, many passages of the memo are verbatim reproductions of his memoirs, already completed by that time, the memoirs he hoped would someday be read by the widest public possible. In them, he had made his true thoughts about his life crystal clear. Besides numerous ruminations about the senselessness of the self-sacrifices he had made during his spy career, which are scattered throughout his voluminous writings, he asks himself the same rhetorical question many times: "Am I a hero or a fool?" By that time, he already came to realize that what he had earlier considered heroic deeds for the benefit of the

Motherland turned out to be nothing but "blind diligence" (*slepoe ispolnitel'stvo*). He states very clearly that what pushed him into spy work was his "youth and beautiful illusions," which were "dragged through the mud on the night of September 18, 1937," the night of his arrest.[14] His memoirs clearly show his conscious attempts to understand himself and his own motives in spying, his painful search to find an answer to what circumstances of his life, including that of his birth, made him susceptible to recruitment into spy work. And he makes it absolutely clear that, his life coming to a close, he considers it totally wasted. He sums it up in the concluding part of his memoirs:

> At night, I wake up from burning grief and shame and
> think: for what had we [Soviet spies abroad] endured
> so much torment and committed so many crimes? . . .
> At the time, we appeased ourselves with thoughts of
> sacrifice for the benefit of our Motherland. Morally
> speaking, it was a dubious explanation . . . Now I burn
> from shame after realizing how we were fooled. Our
> belief in the Party and love for the Motherland have
> been dragged through the mud. Everything is fouled.
> As your life comes to a close, it's frightful to be left
> with zilch [*ostat'sia u razbitogo koryta*].[15]

But what the KGB didn't know didn't hurt it. Dmitri was given the green light to produce a screenplay based on his spy exploits. He went to work and, by the end of the year, had prepared a script for a film titled "Shchedrye serdtsem" ("Generous Hearts"). To prove that nothing in the script was a product of his fantasy (in fact, his main task was to preserve from total oblivion his life as an intelligence officer, a life he already qualified in many places in his memoirs as totally wasted), he attached to the script a two-page letter marked "confidential," in which he disclosed the real names of all those involved in the action.

The KGB censors found the screenplay unacceptable for production and rejected it. Indeed, no matter how hard Bystrolyotov tried to scatter Soviet propaganda clichés and obligatory optimism here and there in the script, he couldn't help but violate the canons of Socialist realism, the artistic method proscribed to all Soviet writers: to depict life not as it is but as it should be. The stereotypical Chekist was not only a tireless and self-sacrificing fighter for the cause of Socialism but also one who knew no doubts and operated with "clean hands" only. That is, he never resorted to the seduction, bribery, or blackmail of prospective agents.

Dmitri decided to make at least some of his life known, even if it meant bending his personal standards. After all, something was better than nothing. He went back to work, and by cutting out pieces of the old script, he produced the ideologically acceptable script *Chelovek v shtatskom* (*The Plainclothesman*). This time the screenplay was approved and went into production at the Mosfilm Studios. Although the KGB provided the studios with their own consultants, knowing that they knew next to nothing about the times and mores of his operations, Dmitri visited the set and, an artist in his own right, gradually took over many functions of the production, including the roles of the consultants, the set and costume designers, and at times, even the director. Naturally, he was excited: his life story, which he had thought would fall into oblivion, was making a comeback before his eyes, at least to some degree.

He made every effort to ensure that the director would cast actors who resembled as closely as possible his former comrades-in-arms—Boris Bazarov, Nikolai Samsonov, Theodor Mally, and Abram Slutsky. He also insisted that the actor playing the part of the British agent Ernest Oldham (in the film, his character is a German agent) would resemble the Brit, a blond drunkard. Bystrolyotov even made a cameo appearance in the film, playing the rector of a Western university handing a diploma to a younger self played by handsome Soviet actor Yuozas Budraitis. The only thing he wasn't able to influence was the choice of actress for the part of Doris, the disfigured SS officer he had seduced to gain access to Hitler's plans for the rearmament of Germany. For this role, a star of Soviet film, the beautiful Lyudmila Khityaeva, was chosen, which, of course, did not convey to viewers his self-sacrifice in this episode of his career.

The film premiered in December 1973 to cool critical reception. However, the following year it met financial success when the film drew more than twenty-six million viewers.[16]

The film opened the doors for publication of some of his work. At the beginning of 1974, the journal *Nash sovremennik* (*Our Contempo-*

rary) published in installments his novel *Para Bellum*, which, among other details, reveals his operations in procuring the names of Hitler sympathizers in pre–World War II France to the public for the first (and last) time.

It seemed everything was going well for him at last. But the long years in the camps caused him always to be on guard, attuned to any movement of the outside world that could turn dangerous, even when that danger was only imagined. Toward the end of 1974, he received another call from the dreaded organization that had brought so much grief and destruction in his life—the KGB. The first deputy of the KGB chairman, Semyon K. Tsvigun, met with Dmitri and, apparently having in mind his own ambition to get into the movie business (which he accomplished a few years later), asked him many questions about the basics of filmmaking that Dmitri had acquired on the production set of *The Plainclothesman*.

It is likely that's all Tsvigun was interested in—but distrustful of the KGB, expecting nothing but trouble from any of its functionaries, Dmitri became alarmed. He found the timing of the meeting ominous. The initial green light given to Solzhenitsyn's writing had changed to red. Though approved by the Union of Soviet Writers, Solzhenitsyn's novel *The Cancer Ward* was banned from publication, and soon afterward his other works ceased being printed. As a writer, he became a nonperson, and by 1965, the KGB had seized the manuscript of another of his novels set in the Gulag, *The First Circle*. The KGB also learned he was working on his most subversive book, the now-famous *Gulag Archipelago*. In 1970, when Solzhenitsyn was awarded the Nobel Prize in Literature, he was venomously attacked in the Soviet press. The writer went into hiding in the homes of his friends. In February 1974, he was deported from the Soviet Union to West Germany and stripped of his Soviet citizenship. Writers and other cultural figures, such as poet Yevgeny Yevtushenko and renowned cellist Mstislav Rostropovich, were subjected to reprisals for their support of Solzhenitsyn.[17]

Dmitri decided to take precautionary measures. Despite his occasional attempts to sweeten up his writings about the camps, the overall depiction of Gulag and post-Gulag life in his memoirs was unequivocally damning from a political point of view, especially in his last book, "Trudnyi put' v bessmertie" ("The Hard Road to Immortality"), unmistakably anti-Soviet in its analysis of the sources of evil to which he had been both witness and victim. Only a few people, a small circle of friends who read them, knew about the existence of his memoirs. But he knew all too well that the ubiquitous KGB informers would eventually get their hands on his writings and that those who read his work could also get in trouble. Dmitri decided to outsmart the KGB by staging his own destruction of the manuscripts. He called all of his friends and his stepgrandson, Sergei Milashov, and asked them to return whatever copies of his manuscripts they had. Then, with only his stepgrandson as a future potential witness who would confirm the fact, he threw his papers into the bathtub and set them on fire. (Of course, an experienced spy in his past, he made sure that at least one copy of his voluminous labor was safely hidden away.)

In April 1975, his health took a turn for the worse; the effects of his last stroke reappeared. He lost the ability to read or to speak. He tried to overcome the loss by sheer force of will. One day, when Milashov came to visit, he found his stepgrandfather sitting in front of a mirror, reading a newspaper, and watching whether he was able to move his lips. He uttered words with difficulty.[18]

On May 3, 1975, while trying to move a sofa in his apartment, his heart failed, and he collapsed. He died as he wanted—on his feet, as the ancient Romans did. Anna survived him by eight years, passing away in December 1983.

Dmitri's body was taken to Khovansky Cemetery in Moscow. Besides his close kin, the ceremony was attended by some of the KGB brass and his colleagues at the Institute of Medical Information, where he had worked for the last ten years of his life. After the ceremony was over, one of these colleagues whispered into another's ear, nodding toward the KGB brass: "If you only knew how much he hated them all!"

AFTERWORD

As my research of Bystrolyotov's life progressed, his official image underwent a gradual change as well. The FSB, the successor to the KGB, chose him to play the part of one of its heroes, a man they could be proud of, a "poster boy" whose exemplary life would inspire a new generation of Russian spies. In January 2001, at the former KGB headquarters in the Lubyanka building, a public celebration took place commemorating the centennial of Bystrolyotov's birth. His picture was displayed in the KGB/FSB Hall of Fame at the SVR headquarters in Yasenevo, among other portraits of the leading heroes of foreign intelligence. Within a few years, they transformed a complex and flawed man—an indisputable hero in terms of his accomplishments and bravery, but by the end of his life, a man tormented with self-loathing and remorse for his actions as a spy—into a saint who didn't even mind the devastation of his life that was caused by his employer's actions. In fact, neither of the books written by the ex-KGB officers Evgeni Primakov and Oleg Tsarev (the latter in coauthorship with Nigel West) mention the gruesome torture Bystrolyotov endured at the hands of their agency.

First, his former masters sanitized his memoirs, disencumbering them of the most damning descriptions of the atrocities he had witnessed and experienced. Of eleven volumes he had written, they published only a small portion of them posthumously.

In recent years, Bystrolyotov was chosen as the subject of numerous journalistic articles, a novel based on his life and dedicated to his memory, and three documentary films. The central hero of a new television serial titled *Rodina zhdet* (*The Motherland Is Waiting*), a Russian intelligence officer, now fighting against terrorists, not only carries Bystrolyotov's surname but also possesses several of his personal qualities: good looks, charisma, proficiency in many languages, courage, and of course, sex appeal.[1]

To reshape the real Bystrolyotov into a mythological figure that meets the political demands of the day, five years after the centennial of Bystrolyotov's birth was celebrated in 2001, his biography has been superseded by the new one—ten times longer(!). Surely, his legend has skyrocketed in importance: even poet Alexander Pushkin, the highest Russian cultural deity, has never been feted so frequently, in five-year increments.[2]

I wish that this excessive posthumous generosity toward the memory of one of their own were a way of assuaging the pangs of conscience, to make amends to the hero, horrifically mistreated when he was alive. Alas, this overwhelming veneration of Bystrolyotov has a different reason. The more I read of the last official biography (though *hierography* would be a more appropriate term for it) of the man I had met back in my Moscow days, the more I had an eerie feeling that the system Bystrolyotov and I had dreaded was coming back to life, if it had ever actually died. I was astonished at the unabashed crudeness with which the facts of Bystrolyotov's life are sanitized. Every one of them is airbrushed to remove the pain, embarrassment, and denigration he had endured, not at the hands of his country's enemies, but at those of the one he loved selflessly and in whose name he had sacrificed everything dear to him—at the hands of his Motherland.

As in Stalin-era history books, in the official biography of Bystrolyotov, outright lies are mixed with half-truths; deliberate omissions also abound. To make it seem that the man occupies the desirable political stand of today, the biography tries hard to disassociate him from the Soviet regime. Thus, it claims that he "never received state awards." Contrary to the legend in the West that the KGB/FSB is an impeccably functioning spy machine, sloppiness in covering its tracks is still one of the agency's shortcomings. On the same SVR Web site where the most recent Bystrolyotov biography is posted, it is enough to click on the "Personalities" link, and another write-up about him, commemorating the centennial of his birth, duly states that, in 1932, the OGPU granted him a much-prized award—a personalized handgun bearing the inscription: "For merciless struggle with the counterrevolution." And, at a later time, he was also recommended for a much-sought-after award, the "Honorary Chekist Badge."[3]

To fit the political sensibilities of today, the new biography also claims that Bystrolyotov "didn't take part in actions against the White

Army and Russian monarchists," a laughable statement for anyone familiar with the history of Soviet clandestine operations in the West in the 1920s and 1930s, the height of Bystrolyotov's career as a spy. It's enough to recall his Prague period—his fistfights with White Guardsmen and his penetration of Inostrantsev's school for spies.

While in the 1999 book *KGB v Anglii,* Bystrolyotov's controversial claim of being a descendant of the Tolstoy line is characterized as his fantasy, the new biography states it as an immutable fact. Moreover, he is made to look the direct heir of the intelligence service of the Russian Empire, going back to the time of Peter the Great.

Much is also made about his modesty in serving his Motherland as a "plainclothesman" who "never joined the Bolshevik party" and "even had no military rank." However, the official biographers have goofed again. In the very same text, a few pages before this statement, they carelessly mention that he was about to get the rank of senior lieutenant and become a bona fide Party member, but his arrest and subsequent persecution made it impossible. In his new biography, you also won't find much about the horrific treatment of the hero after his release from the camps. Swallowing his pride, the man had to beg his former employer to recognize his service to his country and give him a decent means of existence, as he describes it in his unpublished memoirs.

And all these attempts at misinformation only scratch the surface . . .

With the current Russian Security Service's choice of Bystrolyotov as one of their role models, by extension he serves as a foil to many KGB brass that now constitute the upper echelons of power in the country, preeminent president-cum-prime minister Vladimir Putin included. But the real Bystrolyotov would hardly suit their political philosophy of relying on autocratic methods of governing the country. The biggest and most devastating personal discovery that the famed Russian spy made at the end of his life was that all of the numerous sacrifices he had made as a spy to serve his country's good amounted to practically nothing. A country ruled by the whim of one person (during his spy career, it was Stalin) is bound to waste the efforts of even its most devout citizens, which Bystrolyotov undoubtedly was. In the long run, any governing system that relies exclusively on the judgment of its supreme leader is bound to hurt the most vital interests of the country. The current Russian politicians prefer to turn a deaf ear to this, perhaps, most important lesson of Bystrolyotov's life.

Today, as I read the official biography of Bystrolyotov and think back on my meeting with him, I begin to suspect that he might have had another, prescient reason for inviting me to his home. As I know it now, the one he gave me—that he needed help with his writing—made no sense. By the time of our meeting, he already had considerable literary experience, of which I had no inkling. He had written (but not yet published) two novels, *Para Bellum* and *V staroi Afrike* (*In Old Africa*), two screenplays (while one of them, "Generous Hearts," already existed in manuscript form, the film based on the other one, *Chelovek v shtatskom* [*The Plainclothesman*], was already in the final production stages), and his voluminous memoirs. The latter, mostly dealing with his Gulag experience, hardly had a chance of being published in his lifetime. Khrushchev's "thaw" had passed, Brezhnev was in power, and prison literature was out. Few could imagine that the Soviet Union would collapse in less than two decades.

So perhaps Bystrolyotov, desperate to make the truth of his life known, wanted to get it out in the world by other means. As an experienced intelligence operative, always looking ahead of events, he might have anticipated something that I myself didn't know at the time—that I would soon be leaving the country. Talking to my father-in-law, he might have found out that I wasn't particularly happy with my life. Although I was published widely, I could write only as a freelancer and only under the Russian-sounding pen name: in the judgment of my editors, my own name was too Jewish-sounding for Russian ears. Bystrolyotov could also have learned that no matter how hard I tried, I wouldn't get a staff position on any of the Moscow newspapers, the very same that were happy to publish me incognito.

He might also have learned from my talkative father-in-law—what tailor doesn't chat with his customer during a fitting session?—that, by the time of our meeting, I was already deeply disillusioned with the Soviet system and not just because of racial discrimination. As a writer and journalist, I'd experienced the system's profound hypocrisy. Not only did the Party ideologists secretly make a mockery of the proclaimed "equality of all Soviet nationalities," but they lied about many other matters as well, especially those that affected my writing. On one hand, they called for "objective criticism" of any official (they termed it *nevziraia na litsa*, "without regard for rank"), which they claimed was designed to help the system perfect itself. On the other hand, it was silently assumed that those who belonged to the *nomenklatura,* the high-ranking appointees of the Party, couldn't be publicly criticized.

I had the misfortune to sin unwittingly against the last secret rule. Two years earlier, in 1971, I had published a scathing review of a vulgar and stupid play in the magazine *Krokodil.* The playwright turned out to be the editor in chief of a major journal on theater—that is, he was part of the *nomenklatura.* After my review appeared, I was attacked in the press, stripped of my journalistic credentials, and blacklisted. During that period, I couldn't publish a single line in those very same publications that had always welcomed my submissions.

It was only shortly before seeing Bystrolyotov that I was finally pardoned and my press card was returned to me. Only then did my writing begin to appear again in the Moscow press.

It was hardly necessary to possess the intellect and insight of an ace spy such as Bystrolyotov to anticipate that, given the opportunity, I would want to leave the country. In September 1973, though still a risky undertaking (any applicant could be refused under a deliberate pretext thus forever ruining his professional career), Jewish emigration from the Soviet Union was already a reality. I may have seemed to him the perfect repository for his life story.

I came to this conclusion when I recalled the story he told me at the end of our meeting. He claimed that he had heard it firsthand from people whom he had gotten to know when working undercover abroad. Here it is as I recorded it in my notes shortly after our meeting:

> An undercover Gestapo agent named Hans came
> to Amsterdam to make a list of Jews who had fled
> Germany. He was young and good-looking. Some
> Jewish women recognized him as a servant they used
> to employ back in Berlin, when they had money. They
> used to admire his good looks, but nobody took him
> seriously. When Hitler was on the rise, Hans joined
> the Nazi Party and, in time, made a career in the Ge-

stapo. Now these Jewish ladies Hans used to work for had lost all their possessions. They no longer had hired housecleaners and laundresses; here, in Amsterdam, they became housecleaners and laundresses themselves.

When they realized that Hans was a Gestapo agent, they decided to act. First, they treated Hans to schnapps. When he got drunk, a beautiful Jewess lured him into a brothel, where he was intoxicated even more. Finally, when he fell asleep, they brought in a rabbi and circumcised him. Before throwing him out into the streets, they stamped his passport with a seal that read, "Circumcised in the Synagogue of Amsterdam," thoroughly ruining his Nazi career.[4]

Bystrolyotov delivered this story masterfully, talking in his soft baritone, wearing a sly smile. The story about an outwitted and disgraced Nazi made me feel especially good, because both of my grandfathers, my aunt, and six cousins, aged two to fifteen, perished at the hands of the Nazis soon after the Germans invaded Russia. In addition, I was a small child during World War II and had experienced the horrors of German bombardments. That perhaps explains why I retold the story to my relatives and friends over the years, without questioning its authenticity.[5]

Only recently, while researching Bystrolyotov's life, did I take another look at the story and began to doubt it. First, there are some technical inaccuracies. A rabbi himself never performs a circumcision; the act is entrusted to a man with special training. Also, it has never been part of the Judaic tradition to certify the act by stamping a passport; the act is considered sacred and personal, part of a man's covenant with God. At the time Bystrolyotov told me the story, I didn't pay attention to these inaccuracies: like the vast majority of Soviet-educated people, I was woefully ignorant of religious matters, as Bystrolyotov, a Soviet citizen, would have known.

Second, it is doubtful that the Gestapo would send its agent to Holland to get a list of specifically German Jews: it is well known that the Nazis hunted down the Jews regardless of their national origin.

Then, when I read his screenplay "Generous Hearts," I encountered an episode that closely resembled the story Bystrolyotov had told me during our meeting. In the cover letter to the KGB censors, which accompanied his screenplay, Bystrolyotov stresses that his descriptions are taken from real life. This episode could not have been relayed to him by one of the prank's participants soon after it took place, as he told me (and as implied in the text). He returned to the USSR at the end of 1936 and, before his arrest, he made his last short trip abroad in the summer of 1937. This makes the presence in Amsterdam of destitute German Jews running from Hitler before that time doubtful. The Nazi expropriation of Jewish property began several years later, after the infamous Kristallnacht in late 1938.[6]

Since in his memoirs of his Gulag years Bystrolyotov mentions meeting some German prisoners of war in the camps, it is possible he heard this story from them, which could have taken place as late as 1940, after the German occupation of Holland.

However, there are two seemingly insignificant differences between the variant of the story Bystrolyotov told me and the way he renders it in the screenplay that he wrote before our meeting: in the screenplay, the name of the Nazi officer who fell victim to the Jewish prank is not Hans, but Stormführer Siegfried Lulke, and there is no mention of his good looks.[7]

As I went over my notes, again and again, about the story as Bystrolyotov had told it to me, these two small discrepancies made me think that, most likely without realizing it, as happens with storytellers, he had unconsciously woven strands of his own life into it. To begin with, both the victim in the story and Bystrolyotov himself have certain things in common: "Hans" was one of Bystrolyotov's code names. Both the Hans of the story and the Hans of the storyteller served in the state secret police, its intelligence branch. Moreover, Bystrolyotov's memoirs show that, by the end of his life, he realized that he had worked for a criminal regime, one that in many respects was not unlike the Nazi regime that Hans served in the story.

And the whole course of the story resembles that of Bystrolyotov's life as he saw it: A gifted and good-looking young man is slighted by virtue of his birth, but by dint of hard work and siding with the dominant power of his country makes a name for himself, overcoming his feeling of inferiority. When he finally rises in rank and proves himself worthy of more respect than he received in his youth, he is betrayed by his conniving masters and subjected to physical pain and disgrace.

Of course, that is not why Bystrolyotov told me the story of Hans. He had a different purpose. He had me over for tea and told the story to win me over. In telling it, he played "the Jewish card." A tale of a Nazi officer's disgrace at the hands of the persecuted Jews could not possibly fail to please me.

Bystrolyotov was a man of clear vision, whose years spent in the Gulag opened his eyes to many things of which he had previously been oblivious. Let us recall that, in his memoirs, written back in 1965, he predicted the fall of the Soviet Union, an event that took place a quarter of a century later.

But apparently he foresaw even further. From today's perspective, it looks as if, back in the fall of 1973 when he talked to me, he knew what is crystal clear today: in his own country, the full truth about his life, something he tried desperately to tell while still alive, might not be revealed even after the collapse of the USSR. And today, I'm struck by how accurate his premonitions have turned out to be.

Although brought about by a different set of circumstances, so many years later, Bystrolyotov's calculations proved to be right after all.

This book is the first biography of Bystrolyotov that has not been doctored by the infamous agency and its current successor. Though extraordinarily dramatic, it is, nevertheless, representative of the fate of the whole first generation of Russians (and non-Russians) who believed in the proclaimed ideals of the Bolshevik revolution and sacrificed everything they had on its altar.

To set the record straight on Bystrolyotov's life is to counter the new dangerous tendency on the rise in Russia—to rewrite Stalin's bloody history by whitewashing the KGB's role in it as his willing executioners. The Bystrolyotov myth being spread in today's Russia is one of the neo-KGB's means to control its own past. Since, as Orwell observed, "who controls the past controls the future," telling the truth about that past is one way to interfere with the comeback of those horrors.

NOTES

Prologue. Tea with a Master Spy

1. The following account of Bystrolyotov's career is reconstructed here from my notes taken immediately after the meeting, September 11, 1973.

2. Recently published sources indicate that Lev Manevich was a Soviet intelligence officer who worked undercover in the West before World War II and was captured in Italy. He later spent some time in German camps. There is no mention of Spain. See http://www.hrono.info/biograf/manevich.html (accessed July 2, 2008).

3. See Snegirev, "Drugaia zhizn' Dmitriia Bystroletova."

4. Corson and Crowley, *New KGB*.

5. Milashov, in preface to Bystrolyotov, *Puteshestvie na krai nochi*.

6. See CSApol.

7. On comparative analysis of Stalin's and Putin's systems, see Olga Pavlova, "Plan Putina" [Putin's Plan], http://www.grani.ru/Politics/Russia/m.126299.html.

One. Sowing the Wind

1. The fateful meeting with Artur Artuzov is described in KGB2, 128–29. When writing it, Bystrolyotov re-created by memory the text he had written three years earlier in his memoirs; see Bystrolyotov, "Pir bessmertnykh," 3:368–69 (hereafter in the notes, this work cited as "Pir"). On Artuzov's career, see "Memorial" International Historical, Educational, and Civil Rights Society, "Rukovodiashchie kadry NKVD" [Senior Cadres of the NKVD], http://www.memo.ru/history/NKVD/kto/biogr/index.htm; go to "Artuzov." See also Mlechin *Istoriia vneshnei razvedki*, 29–50. In his book *Tragedii sovetskoi razvedki* [Tragedies of Soviet Intelligence] (Moscow: Tsentropoligraf, 2000), Vitaly Pavlov erroneously identifies Artuzov as head of the Foreign Intelligence Department of the OGPU at the time of his first meeting with Bystrolyotov (111); the same mistake is repeated in the Russian-language electronic Encyclopedic Dictionary of Russian Special Services (http://rusrazvedka.narod.ru/base/htm/bystr.html [accessed February 11, 2009]). For the text of Dmitri's address to the Congress, see "Privet ot zarubezhnogo studenchestva" (Greetings from Foreign Students), *Pravda*, April 18, 1925, 3. For Artuzov's photo, see http://www.lubyanka.org/personalii/a/artuzov_artur_hristianovich/.

2. KGB2, 128; "Pir," 3:368.

3. On the profound effect of a child's separation from a caregiver during the first years of life, see Jerold J. Kreisman, M.D., and Hal Straus, *I Hate You—Don't*

Leave Me: Understanding the Borderline Personality (New York: Avon Books, 1989), 160.

4. Although the date and place of Bystrolyotov's birth in published sources, and even on his official birth certificate, vary greatly, in this book I follow his handwritten autobiography from his private archive; it was submitted to the exit visa office to seek clearance for foreign travel in 1965. Unless otherwise noted, Bystrolyotov's experiences and quotes from his writings in this chapter refer to "Pir," 2:234–43, 277–92.

5. Andrew and Mitrokhin consider Bystrolyotov's claim of belonging to the Tolstoy line to be his "fantasy" (*The Sword and the Shield,* 44).

6. On the lack of any evidence of Tolstoy's paternity of Dmitri Bystrolyotov, see Razumov, "Rukopis' D. Bystrolyotova 'Pir Bessmertnykh,'" 109. There is no evidence to the claim that his father was "General-Governor of St. Petersburg," as the Russian-language electronic Encyclopedic Dictionary of Russian Special Services does (http://rusrazvedka.narod.ru/base/htm/bystr.html [accessed February 11, 2009]).

7. Milashov, in discussion with the author, July 2003.

8. Milashov, in discussion with the author, July 2003.

9. Milashov, "Kommentarii k glavam 1–3," 1.

10. Apparently, Bystrolyotov misspelled the author's name. It should read "Chelpanov" instead of "Chelpakov." The book he refers to is Chelpanov, *Vvedenie v filosofiiu.*

11. Fyodor Dostoyevsky, *The Brothers Karamazov* (New York: Vintage Books, 1955), 284–85.

12. Ibid., 284; "Pir," 1:436–37.

13. These insights into Bystrolyotov's personality are suggested by psychiatrist K. P. S. Kamath, M.D., in discussion with the author, March 2008.

14. Foreign Intelligence Service of Russia, "Dmitri Bystrolyotov—Razvedchik v shtatskom" (Dmitri Bystrolyotov: A Plainclothes Intelligence Operative), *Novosti razvedki i kontrrazvedki* (Moscow), January 30, 2006, http://svr.gov.ru/smi/2006/novrkr20060130.htm.

15. "Pir," 2:339.

16. Milashov, in discussion with the author, July 2003.

17. Most likely, by leaving the country, Bystrolyotov also escaped being drafted into the advancing Red Army. That's why, in his book *Chekisty rasskazyvaiut,* published in Soviet times, Listov attributes Bystrolyotov's first flight abroad, to Turkey, with such a vague motivation as that of the young man being "carried away by a chance impulse" (216).

Two. A Leaf Torn from a Branch

1. Unless otherwise noted, Bystrolyotov's experience and quotes from his writings in this chapter refer to "Pir," 2:279–80, 291–95, and 303–24.

2. Ibid., 293.

3. This version is also given in Listov, *Chekisty rasskazyvaiut,* 216. Listov mentions that, in the course of a few days, Bystrolyotov was given instructions. Since both my conversation with Bystrolyotov and the publication of Listov's book occurred in the Soviet era, it may well be that Bystrolyotov used this version when

talking to journalists, such as Listov and me, as it was less politically embarrassing for the Cheka, in comparison with the self-serving behavior of the Red commissars during the trip to Bulgaria, which he had already recorded in his memoirs and which couldn't be published at that time.

4. Milashov, in discussion with the author, July 2003.

5. Slobodskoi, *Sredi emigratsii*, 65.

6. "Pir," 2:317–18.

7. Slobodskoi, *Sredi emigratsii*, 112–13.

8. Georgiev's name appears among the list of other gymnasium students graduated in 1921; see Svetozarov, *Russkaia gimnaziia v Moravskoi Trzhebove*, 38.

9. Ibid., 7–9.

10. For the list of gymnasium graduates, see ibid., 38; for Bystrolyotov's Prague Law Faculty personal file, see GARF. His claim that he was accepted into the graduating class of an American college is also doubtful for he had only a high school (Anapa gymnasium) diploma to his credit. It is no wonder that, aside from his proficiency in foreign languages, he doesn't mention having studied any other subjects at that college or the specialization of the "American bachelor degree" he had allegedly earned. The only connection to America the Russian gymnasium in Constantinople had was the patronage of the American Red Cross. The KGB memo of December 18, 1968, also confirms that Bystrolyotov studied in a Russian gymnasium in Turkey, without mentioning that it was run by Russian émigrés (cited in Snegirev, "Drugaia zhizn' Dmitriia Bystroletova," 61).

11. "Pir," 1:395.

12. Ibid.

13. On the Russian émigré plight at that time, see Pivovar et al., *Russkaia emigratsiia v Turtsii*, 51.

14. For secret instructions to Soviet Trade Missions on subversive actions abroad, see CSAinst.

15. Svetozarov, *Russkaia gimnaziia v Moravskoi Trzhebove*, 7–9.

Three. In the Grips of Holy Wrath

1. L. Petrusheva, ed., *Deti russkoi emigratsii* [Children of Russian Emigration] (Moscow: Terra, 1997), 14; see also GARF.

2. Postnikov, *Russkie v Prage*, 83; "II sessiia Soveta Soiuza russkikh akademicheskikh organizatsii za granitsei (4–7 oktiabria 1923 g. v Prage)" [The Second Session of the Council of the Union of Russian Academic Organizations Abroad (October 4–7, 1923 in Prague)], *Studencheskie gody*, nos. 6–7 (Oct.–Nov. 1923): 31.

3. KGB2 [136]; quoted in Tsarev and West, *KGB v Anglii*, 113.

4. "Pir," 2:330.

5. Ibid.; Tsarev and West give the location of the filtration camp (*KGB v Anglii*, 114).

6. "Pir," 2:331.

7. KGB2, quoted in Tsarev and West, *KGB v Anglii*, 114–15.

8. "Pir," 2:332.

9. Ibid., 1:67.

10. Ibid.

11. Bystrolyotov, in conversation with the author, September 11, 1973, Moscow.

12. "Pir," 2:333.

13. Ibid.

14. See CSAinst.

15. Ibid.

16. See CSAmil.

17. KGB2, quoted in Tsarev and West, *KGB v Anglii*, 115.

18. Ibid., 116.

19. Ibid., 119.

20. "Pir," 1:395.

21. Ibid., 393, 395.

22. Pivovar et al., *Russkaia emigratsiia v Turtsii*, 51.

23. "Pir," 1:391, 394.

24. Ibid., 392.

25. Bernice Glatzer Rosenthal, *New Myth, New World: From Nietzsche to Stalinism* (Philadelphia: Pennsylvania State University Press, 2002), 114.

26. N. An-ov, "Prazhskoe zhitie" [Life in Prague], *Studentcheskie gody*, no. 28 (1928): 7; "Pir," 1:411; Tsarev and West, *KGB v Anglii*, 116.

27. See CSAinst.

28. KGB2, 126–27; "Pir," 1:395–96; Tsarev and West, *KGB v Anglii*, 116.

29. See CSApol.

30. "Pir," 1:396.

31. On Mikhail Gorb's career, see Abramov, *Evrei v KGB*, 163–64.

32. "Pir," 3:369; for an entry on Bystrolyotov's hiring, see his official work record (*trudovaia knizhka*) (Milashov's private collection).

Four. Looking for Love in All the Wrong Places

1. Unless otherwise noted, Bystrolyotov's experiences and quotes from his writings in this chapter refer to "Pir," 1:392–430.

2. This is the last stanza of Baudelaire's poem "A celle qui est trop gaie" (To She Who Is Too Gay).

3. "Pir," 1:397.

4. Ibid., 430.

5. Milashov, in discussion with the author, July 2003.

6. "Pir," 1:134.

7. KGB2, 122–23.

8. Milashov, in discussion with the author, July 2003.

9. Translated into English by the author.

10. See appendix to Bystrolyotov, *Puteshestvie na krai nochi*, 585; see also http://www.law-order.ru/reference/ru_s/t64639.html.

11. For Bystrolyotov's study record, see GARF. On the uselessness of the school program for a career as a lawyer in Czechoslovakia, see Andreyev and Savicky, *Russia Abroad*, 113.

12. Harville Hendrix, *Getting the Love You Want: A Guide for Couples* (New York: Holt, 1988), 30.

Five. Marriage and Other Calamities

1. Unless otherwise noted, Bystrolyotov's experiences and quotes from his writings in this chapter refer to "Pir," 1:430–59, 469–86, 503.

2. The name of Marie-Eliane Aucouturier is rendered in Russian in Bystrolyotov's handwritten memo to the KGB (KGB2, 123). This is the source cited in Andrew and Mitrokhin, *The Sword and the Shield*, 578n12. Recruitment of a French Embassy secretary, without mentioning her name, is cited in other sources as well.

3. Although, referring to the KGB Bystrolyotov file, Mitrokhin cites 1898 as Aucouturier's birth year, she was born in 1900; see a copy of her passport in CADN. This mistake is repeated in Degtiarev and Kolpakidi, 65.

4. Aucouturier's birthplace is indicated in her passport. Her family background was given to the author by a consultant who prefers to remain anonymous.

5. For Schiller's description of Count Fiesco in the list of his dramatis personae, see, for example, http://www.gutenberg.org/files/6783/6783-h/6783-h.htm.

6. Gustave Aucouturier's affiliation with the Havas Agency is indicated in his file (CADN). Roman Jakobson is listed as a member of the Soviet Trade Mission staff (as a correspondent) in 1924 (CSAstaff).

7. Quoted in Papchinsky and Tumshis, *Shchit, raskolotyi mechom*, 78.

8. Bystrolyotov erroneously attributes the phrase to King David.

9. "Pir," 1:502.

10. This version of events was suggested by psychiatrist K. P. S. Kamath, M.D., in conversation with the author.

11. Milashov, in discussion with the author, July 2003.

12. "Pir," 1:473.

13. Translated from the Russian by the author. Quoting these lines from Blok's poem "Z. Gippius," Bystrolyotov substitutes the original "Irish rocks" with "treacherous rocks."

14. Bystrolyotov's Prague period code name, "Zh/32," is indicated in Tsarev and West, *KGB v Anglii*, 125.

15. "Pir," 1:542.

16. For the Schiller reference, see *Fiesco* (act 3, scene 8) (http://www.gutenberg.org/files/6783/6783-h/6783-h.htm).

Six. Going Underground

1. KGB2, 142–43.

2. Kolpakidi and Prokhorov, *Vneshniaia razvedka Rossii*, 2:229–31; see also Papchinsky and Tumshis, *Shchit, raskolotyi mechom*, 75–78. For Zhuravlyov's picture, see http://svr.gov.ru/history/zur.html.

3. Papchinsky and Tumshis, *Shchit, raskolotyi mechom*, 78.

4. Primakov, *Ocherki istorii rossiiskoi razvedki*, 2:235; "Shchedrye serdtsem," 289–300.

5. Primakov, *Ocherki istorii rossiiskoi razvedki*, 2:235.

6. On Leppin's background, see Kolpakidi and Prokhorov, *Vneshniaia razvedka Rossii*, 454–55; Hede Massing file, 45. On details of the Russian school operation, see "Shchedrye serdtsem," 320–22.

7. See GARF.

8. Kolpakidi and Prokhorov, *Vneshniaia razvedka Rossii*, 179. The authors erroneously cite Prague University, instead of the émigré Ukrainian Free University. During my interview with him, Milashov also mentioned Bystrolyotov's specialization in law and economics of the world oil trade, but it's not clear when and how he obtained it. On Bystrolyotov's medical education and his thesis title, see Tsarev and West, *KGB v Anglii*, 120.

9. The full text of these reports is in Grigoriev, *Naiti i zaverbovat'*, 52. Parts of the correspondence are also quoted in Snegirev, in *Po dannym razvedki*, 63.

10. Grigoriev, *Naiti i zaverbovat'*, 53–54; Snegirev, in *Po dannym razvedki*, 63.

11. The Škoda engineer is mentioned in Primakov, *Ocherki istorii rossiiskoi razvedki*, 2:235, and Tsarev and West, *Crown Jewels*, 66, and *KGB v Anglii*, 123.

12. The episode is described in detail, including the dialogue, in KGB2, 141–42.

13. Ibid., 142.

14. "Pir," 1:486–87.

15. Ibid., 487.

16. Ibid.

17. KGB2, quoted in Tsarev and West, *KGB v Anglii*, 122–23. Citing this operation, Primakov indicates that it took Bystrolyotov six months to recruit the agent. He doesn't name the French Embassy as the target of the assault, calling it "an embassy of one of the major European countries." Apparently, to conceal the fact that seduction was the main instrument of recruitment, he also doesn't reveal either the name or gender of the recruited agent (*Ocherki istorii rossiiskoi razvedki*, 2:236).

18. "Pir," 1:41, 396.

19. On Mikhail Trilisser's background, see Kolpakidi and Prokhorov, *Vneshniaia razvedka Rossii*, 98–99, and Mlechin, *Istoriia vneshnei razvedki*, 14–26. The meeting of Trilisser and Bystrolyotov in Finland is cited in Listov, *Chekisty rasskazyvaiut*, 216–18.

20. On setbacks of Soviet spies in foreign countries, see Andrew and Mitrokhin, *The Sword and the Shield*, 36–37; Duff, *Time for Spies*, 75; see also Papchinsky and Tumshis, *Shchit, raskolotyi mechom*, 269. On the Politburo decision, see Andrew and Mitrokin, *The Sword and the Shield*, 42; see also http://www.dosye.ru/archiv/vlast1911200-45_2.htm.

21. On romantic motives for Bystrolyotov's involvement with Soviet intelligence, see Tsarev and West, *KGB v Anglii*, 126.

22. KGB2, 130; Orlov, *Handbook of Intelligence*, 93.

23. On Soviet foreign intelligence assumptions about Western counterintelligence treatment of foreign spies caught in the act, see Andrew and Mitrokhin, *The Sword and the Shield*, 47.

24. Orlov, *Handbook of Intelligence*, 79.

25. "Pir," 1:38–39. (Translated from the Russian by the author.)

26. KGB2, 143; Tsarev and West, *KGB v Anglii*, 125; Primakov, *Ocherki istorii rossiiskoi razvedki*, 2:236.

27. KGB2, 144.

28. Ibid., 146–47; see also "Pir," 3:365–88.

29. Bystrolyotov, in conversation with the author, September 11, 1973; see also KGB2, 145.

30. Snegirev, in *Po dannym razvedki*, 66.

31. Ibid., 68; "Pir," 3:376–77.

32. "Pir," 3:376–77; see also Kern, *Walter G. Krivitsky*, 156–57.

33. Snegirev, in *Po dannym razvedki*, 68.

34. "Pir," 3:376–77; Kern, *Walter G. Krivitsky*, 157.

35. Although current sources list Boris Bazarov as ethnically Russian, it may well be that he was Jewish (perhaps baptized). Bystrolyotov indicates that he looked Jewish ("Shchedrye serdtsem," 183); his colleagues called him Lyovushka (Little Leo), and later, with Hitler's ascension to power, his looks became his liability. In 1934, he returned to Moscow and later went to the United States as the head of a network of Soviet spies (Vladimir Sergeev, "Da Vinchi sovetskoi vneshnei razvedki" ["Da Vinci of Soviet Foreign Intelligence"], http://www.chekist .ru/article/1270). For a picture of Bazarov, see http://svr.gov.ru/history/baz.html.

36. The rest of this chapter refers to "Pir," 1:482–84.

Seven. Hunting Down a Man with a Red Nose

1. KGB2, 133–34; quoted in Tsarev and West, *KGB v Anglii*, 133.

2. The details of the visit were later described by the former second secretary of the Soviet Embassy in Paris, Gregori Bessedovsky, during his interrogation by the MI5 in February 1947; see UKNA, 81A. See also Andrew and Mitrokhin, *The Sword and the Shield*, 45; Tsarev and West, *KGB v Anglii*, 127; Primakov, *Ocherki istorii rossiiskoi razvedki*, 2:242.

3. KGB2, 196; Primakov, *Ocherki istorii rossiiskoi razvedki*, 2:242–43.

4. KGB2, ibid.; Primakov, ibid.

5. On the assumption of aristocratic background of Foreign Office employees, see also KGB2, 197, 203. (In British documents, Bystrolyotov's alias is sometimes spelled "Pirelli.") In West, *Historical Dictionary of Sexspionage*, his name is given as "Ladislas" (209), and in KGB2, 143, as "Ladislav."

6. KGB2, 197; Milashov, in discussion with the author, July 2003.

7. "Pir," 3:371–72.

8. Milashov, in discussion with the author, July 2003; Bystrolyotov, in conversation with the author, September 11, 1973.

9. KGB2, 180–81. Parts of the memo are extensively quoted in Primakov, *Ocherki istorii rossiiskoi razvedki*, 2:239–41. In digest form, it appears in Andrew and Mitrokhin, *The Sword and the Shield*, 44–45. Slutsky's career and his photo are posted at http://memo.ru/history/NKVD/kto/biogr/index.htm (go to "Slutskii"); see also Mlechin, *Istoriia vneshnei razvedki*, 50–57.

10. An abridged English translation of the book, originally published in Russian (Paris, 1930), appeared as Gregori Bessedovsky, *Revelations of a Soviet Diplomat* (London: Williams & Norgate, 1931). In his account of the operation, Primakov erroneously identifies the Soviet Embassy as located in Switzerland, not in France (*Ocherki istorii rossiiskoi razvedki*, 2:240).

11. "Pir," 1:482–83; on the identity of Voinovich, see Andrew and Mitrokhin, *The Sword and the Shield*, 578–79nn18–19.

12. "Shchedrye serdtsem," 10; Duff, *Time for Spies*, 82.

13. For a short description of Leppin's and Weinstein's backgrounds, see appendix to Bystrolyotov, *Puteshestvie na krai nochi*, 583. See also Duff, *Time for Spies*, 82; Kolpakidi and Prokhorov, *Vneshniaia razvedka Rossii*, 454–55.

14. On Pieck's background and activities, see Kern, *Death in Washington*, 233–36; Andrew and Mitrokhin, *The Sword and the Shield*, 49; Kolpakidi and Prohkorov, *Vneshniaia razvedka Rossii*, 471.

15. "Shchedrye serdtsem," 278.

16. Ibid., 288.

17. Ibid.

18. On ROSSI's identity, see Andrew and Mitrokhin, *The Sword and the Shield*, 44.

19. This part of the operation is described in minute detail, including dialogues, in Bystrolyotov, "Shchedrye serdtsem," 268–81.

20. KGB2, 186–87; "Pir," 3:384–85.

21. Milashov, in discussion with the author, July 2003.

22. Bystrolyotov, "Shchedrye serdtsem," 279, 283.

23. KGB2, 186.

24. Bystrolyotov, "Shchedrye serdtsem," 279–80, 287.

25. "Pir," 3:385; Andrew and Mitrokhin, *The Sword and the Shield*, 46–47. For a rebuttal by three Italian historians of Ciano's involvement in selling diplomatic ciphers, see http://archiviostorico.corriere.it/1993/gennaio/16/Galeazzo_Ciano_una_spia_tirate_co_0_930116203.shtml.

26. "Pir," 3:386; Andrew and Mitrokhin, *The Sword and the Shield*, 46–47.

27. Primakov, *Ocherki istorii rossiiskoi razvedki*, 2:240–41. In "Pir," 3:384–85, Bystrolyotov gives another version of the circumstances of this encounter. Presumably, ROSSI lured him to go with him from Berlin to his mansion in Zurich, where he promised to introduce him to Mussolini's daughter Edda and his son-in-law Count Ciano. After they drove all night through rain, ROSSI brought Dmitri to a big, dark mansion at Dolder Mountain.

28. Primakov, *Ocherki istorii rossiiskoi razvedki*, 2:240.

29. Ibid., 241.

30. KGB2, 187.

31. On Lemoine's background, see Paul Paillole, *Notre espion chez Hitler* (Paris: Laffont, 1985), 28–29; Bystrolyotov, "Shchedrye serdtsem," 305–6.

32. Andrew and Mitrokhin, *The Sword and the Shield*, 48.

33. On Lemoine, see ibid., 47.

34. On Poretsky, see ibid.; Duff, *Time for Spies*, 58; Kolpakidi and Prokhrov, *KGB*, 307–22; Papchinsky and Tumshis, *Shchit, raskolotyi mechom*, 347.

Eight. Handling "Charlie"

1. Unless otherwise noted, all details in this chapter related to Bystrolyotov's interaction with Oldham are based on KGB2, 197–203. Some material is quoted and cited in Tsarev and West, *KGB v Anglii*, 132–52.

2. Bystrolyotov, "Shchedrye serdtsem," 173.

3. Ibid., 176.

4. Ibid., 187.

5. Writing more than thirty years after the events took place, Bystrolyotov misspells the name of the sanatorium (in Russian) and slightly misplaces it, calling it "Rendellsham Castle, near Ipswich" in Suffolk County. The place that Oldham went to was called "Rendlesham Hall"; a number of leading alcoholism specialists of that time worked there. It was located in the same county but near Woodbridge. Although the building was demolished in the late 1940s, judging by a surviving remnant, its architecture could have made Bystrolyotov think of it as a castle. (For the Rendlesham Hall picture before its demolition, see http://lh.matthewbeckett.com/houses/lh_suffolk_rendleshamhall_gallery.html.) A train ticket to Wickham Market, the closest railway station to Rendelsham, was found in Oldham's possessions (cited by Edward Kershaw in e-mail to the author, November 11, 2009). For the episode in the cinema, see Kern, *Walter G. Krivitsky,* 163.

6. Milashov, in discussion with the author, July 2003.

7. On Lucy's role in the Oldham affair, see Andrew and Mitrokhin, *The Sword and the Shield,* 45–46; on Lucy's background, see the copy of her marriage certificate in UKNA; for her income of six hundred British pounds a year and her inheritance from her deceased husband in the amount of twenty-two thousand British pounds, see UKNA, 38A (pointed out by Edward Kershaw in an e-mail message to the author September 12, 2008).

8. KGB1, 186; a letter from Bazarov (KIN) to the Center of July 27, 1932, is quoted in Tsarev and West, *KGB v Anglii,* 134.

9. Vladimir Mayakovsky, "Stikhi o sovetskom passport" [Verses About the Soviet Passport], in *Stikhotvoreniia. Poemy* [Verses and Narrative Poems] (Moscow: Gosudarstvennoe izdatel'stvo khudozhestvennoi literatury, 1963), 347–50; Tsarev and West, *KGB v Anglii,* 135.

10. Tsarev and West, *Crown Jewels,* 69. In this source, Franz von Papen is wrongly identified as the German foreign minister: from June 1, 1932, he assumed the post of chancellor of Germany. The reference to the "imminent" Lausanne conference is also a factual error: the conference began on June 16 and concluded on July 9, 1932.

11. In Tsarev and West, *Crown Jewels,* 69; the name of the German general is misspelled: instead of "Schleichen" it should read "Schleicher."

12. See also Snegirev, in *Po dannym razvedki,* 71. Andrew and Mitrokhin date the award two months earlier, on September 17 of the same year (*The Sword and the Shield,* 580n37).

13. "Pir," 1:524.

14. See also Andrew and Mitrokhin, *The Sword and the Shield,* 580n38. Both the timing and circumstances of this turn of events are unclear even today. Citing a 1933 Foreign Office list, Andrew and Mitrokhin name September 30, 1932, as the day of Oldham's resignation, in both Tsarev and West, *Crown Jewels* (70), and its Russian version, *KGB v Anglii* (139); citing Bystrolyotov's report to the Center (KGB1, 175), Tsarev and West mention mid-October as the time of Oldham's severance from the Foreign Office.

15. KGB1, 121–25; quoted in Tsarev and West, *KGB v Anglii,* 151–52.

16. KGB1, 176; quoted in Tsarev and West, *KGB v Anglii,* 140.

17. Andrew and Mitrokhin, *The Sword and the Shield,* 46; Thurlow, "Soviet Spies and British Counter-Intelligence in the 1930s," 618.

18. KGB1, 172; quoted in Tsarev and West, *Crown Jewels,* 71–72.

19. Unless otherwise noted, to the end of this chapter the source of material is "Pir," 1:488–92.

20. This typical anxiety of a Soviet illegal operative abroad is described in Orlov, *Handbook of Intelligence,* 83.

21. Ibid., 160–61.

Nine. The End of "Charlie" and Other British Agents

1. KGB1, 145–46; quoted in Tsarev and West, *KGB v Anglii,* 142, and cited in Tsarev and West, *Crown Jewels,* 72.

2. Tsarev and West, *KGB v Anglii,* 142–43; Tsarev and West, *Crown Jewels,* 72.

3. KGB1, 145–46; KGB2, 204.

4. On Bystrolyotov's remark about Lucy, see KGB2, 208; on the OGPU lack of information on ARNO's true function in the Foreign Office, see Tsarev and West, *KGB v Anglii,* 131. The discrepancies between Oldham's statements and the facts not queried by the OGPU are observed by Andrew and Mitrokhin, *The Sword and the Shield,* 46, 48. Although, apparently quoting the KGB source, accessed by Mitrokhin, the authors state that Oldham exaggerated the importance of his position at the Foreign Office (ibid., 46), both Bystrolyotov's memoirs and his KGB files document that the whole purpose of the first phase of dealing with Oldham was to establish his true value, which he downplayed. The conversation between Lucy and Bystrolyotov about Montgomery is described in KGB2, 201. For the KGB account of these events, see Tsarev and West, *KGB v Anglii,* 143–44; Tsarev and West, *Crown Jewels,* 72, 351n20.

5. In both *Crown Jewels* and *KGB v Anglii* (143–44), Tsarev and West skip over this episode and attribute the order as coming after the next episode in Bystrolyotov's operation.

6. KGB1, 145–46; cited in Tsarev and West, *KGB v Anglii,* 144, and Tsarev and West, *Crown Jewels,* 72.

7. Tsarev and West, *KGB v Anglii,* 143–45; Tsarev and West, *Crown Jewels,* 72.

8. Tsarev and West, *KGB v Anglii,* 143–45; Tsarev and West, *Crown Jewels,* 72; Bazarov's report is quoted in Tsarev and West, *KGB v Anglii,* 145; Andrew and Mitrokhin attributed the report to Mally (*The Sword and the Shield,* 48).

9. KGB2, 204–5; quoted in Tsarev and West, *KGB v Anglii,* 145.

10. At the time of the action, the Defense Security Service was renamed as the Security Service, but in the minutes of Oldham's file, it is referred to by its old name.

11. UKNA, 6A. Thurlow, "Soviet Spies and British Counter-Intelligence in the 1930s," 618; Andrew and Mitrokhin, *The Sword and the Shield,* 53.

12. KGB1, 121–25; quoted in *KGB v Anglii,* 152–53, Tsarev and West, *Crown Jewels,* 74–75. Bystrolyotov reports about an event that came down to him not even second- but thirdhand: Lucy relayed to him the incident as described to her by Kemp, who wasn't present at the time. Therefore, in his version, Oldham came in early morning, and the clerk who watched his every move became nervous and the pack of telegrams in his hands scattered all over the floor. While he was picking them up, Oldham got hold of the keys from archival safes and left the room.

13. KGB2, 205.

14. UKNA, 14A.

15. Bystrolyotov writes that the meeting was arranged around suppertime and that he ran into Kemp there by accident, who, according to Lucy, got himself invited to visit her. However, the record of his intercepted phone call to Lucy makes it clear that, on his, "Joe Perelly's," request, Lucy arranged for lunch at 1:15 P.M. (UKNA, 16A). It's possible that, recalling events of over three and a half decades ago, Bystrolyotov could forget these details. The whole of the following scene is described in KGB2, 205–6; quoted in Tsarev and West, *KGB v Anglii*, 146–48.

16. A number of KGB historians mistakenly assume that Bystrolyotov operated in England under his alias "Hans Galleni," based apparently on information obtained during the debriefing of Walter Krivitsky after his defection. However, all transcripts of intercepted phone calls to and from the Oldham house refer to Bystrolyotov only as "Joe Perelly" (sometimes spelled "Pirelli"); see Kern, *Death in Washington*, 257; Costello and Tsarev, *Deadly Illusions*, 204 (spelled "Gallieni"); for transcripts of telephone calls, see, for example, UKNA, Minutes Sheet, Item 45. Bystrolyotov used the "Hans Galleni" passport when operating in the Netherlands during setup of the cover company GADA (see chap. 6), and on other occasions.

17. UKNA, 22A.

18. Ibid., 23.

19. Ibid., 24A.

20. Tsarev and West, *KGB v Anglii*, 148.

21. UKNA, 27A.

22. Extract from a telephone check, Western 4571, UKNA, 21A.

23. Quoted in Tsarev and West, *KGB v Anglii*, 148.

24. Interlaken as the place of the last meeting with Oldham is mentioned in Tsarev and West, *KGB v Anglii*, 154.

25. Compare Bystrolyotov's letter to the Center (KGB1, 121–25), quoted in Tsarev and West, *KGB v Anglii*, 154, and Tsarev and West, *Crown Jewels*, 75, and UKNA, 26A; see also Minutes Sheet, Item 30, and p. 37A.

26. UKNA, 41A; KGB1, 131–32, quoted in Tsarev and West, *KGB v Anglii*, 148, and cited in Tsarev and West, *Crown Jewels*, 73.

27. UKNA, Minutes Sheet, Item 42.

28. KGB1, 121–25; cited in Tsarev and West, *KGB v Anglii*, 153.

29. UKNA, 46A.

30. The surveillance efforts described below are re-created from UKNA, 47–48A (1–5) and 69A.

31. KGB1, 131–32; quoted in Tsarev and West, *KGB v Anglii*, 149, and cited in Tsarev and West, *Crown Jewels*, 73.

32. *Star*, September 29, 1933. (The article clipping is included in UKNA, 74A.)

33. The content of Lucy's letter is disclosed in Tsarev and West, *KGB v Anglii*, 149. For the surveillance report, see UKNA, 74A. The name of the drug is queried there as "feraldehide (?)" (with the question mark added).

34. UKNA, 74A.

35. Bazarov's letter is quoted in Tsarev and West, *KGB v Anglii*, 148.

36. For the Orlov reference, see his *Handbook of Intelligence*, 91. Regarding the threat of exposure applied by the OGPU to Oldham, see the debriefing of Soviet defector Krivitsky; a copy of an extract of it can be found in UKNA, 79A (extract from PF.R.4342, supp. vol. 1.2, serial 55x, 44).

37. "Pir," 3:498 (for censorship reasons, in the text he calls Oldham "German"); Kern, *Death in Washington*, 257; Tsarev and West, *KGB v Anglii*, 149, 155–56.

38. Tsarev and West, *KGB v Anglii*, 149–50. In KGB2, 207, Bystrolyotov cites Vienna as the place of meeting and reports that the meeting took place in a month.

39. Tsarev and West, *KGB v Anglii*, 150; Tsarev and West, *Crown Jewels*, 75.

40. Tsarev and West, *KGB v Anglii*, 151.

41. Ibid.

42. KGB2, 207; Tsarev and West, *KGB v Anglii*, 155; Primakov, *Ocherki istorii rossiiskoi razvedki*, 2:244; Orlov, *Handbook of Intelligence*, 91.

43. KGB1, 128; quoted in Tsarev and West, *KGB v Anglii*, 156.

44. KGB file on Henri Pieck (COOPER), 27135, 1:2–4; quoted in Tsarev and West, *Crown Jewels*, 76–77.

45. Andrew and Gordievsky, *KGB*, 183; Kern, *Death in Washington*, 184.

46. For a detailed description of recruitment and work with SHELLEY and MAG, see Tsarev and West, *Crown Jewels*, 77–88; Tsarev and West, *KGB v Anglii*, 161–205.

47. Primakov, *Ocherki istorii rossiiskoi razvedki*, 2:245, 461. Parallel to Bystrolyotov and Pieck, working through other channels, another Soviet operative, Axelrod, secured a copy of this document (ibid., 245).

48. Tsarev and West, *KGB v Anglii*, 183.

49. Kolpakidi and Prokhorov, *Vneshniaia razvedka Rossii*, 441.

50. Tsarev and West, *KGB v Anglii*, 193.

51. UKNA, 78A–78C, 79A (extract from PF.R.4342, supp. vol. 1.2, serial 55x, 44).

52. UKNA, 84A.

53. *Daily Express*, June 30, 1950 (a copy of the article clipping is included in UKNA, 85A).

54. This fact was brought to the author's attention by Nick Crittenden (e-mail message, May 8, 2009).

Ten. In the Arms of the Fiercest Enemy

1. Primakov, *Ocherki istorii rossiiskoi razvedki*, 2:327.

2. The operation is also briefly mentioned—and also erroneously related to Mussolini himself—in Listov, *Chekisty rasskazyvaiut*, 218. The same misidentification of the parties to the correspondence Bystrolyotov was intercepting during that operation is duly repeated in his current biographies published in Russia; see, for example, http://www.chekist.ru/article/2357.

3. Bystrolyotov, in conversation with the author, September 11, 1973; Brian R. Sullivan, "From Little Brother to Senior Partner: Fascist Italian Perceptions of the Nazis and of Hitler's Regime, 1930–1936," *Intelligence and National Security* 13, no. 1 (Spring 1998): 87.

4. Milashov, in discussion with the author, July 2003; for vital data of Brockdorff-Rantzau, see *Almanach de Gotha*, 103 (1930), 463.

5. The operation is reconstructed from details in Bystrolyotov, *Para Bellum*, 117–26.

6. Other details of this operation are rather murky. Since no KGB files related to it survived, the contents of the secret correspondence between Count Ciano Sr. and Hitler remain unknown. (Although it is not stated clearly in Bystrolyotov's writing, it seems that "Monaldi" carried only letters from Ciano Sr. to Hitler.)

7. Primakov, *Ocherki istorii rossiiskoi razvedki*, 2:328; "Pir," 3:377; Bystrolyotov, "Shchedrye serdtsem," 180–81, *Para Bellum*, 127–30.

8. Bystrolyotov, *Para Bellum*, 130.

9. "Pir," 3:377; Bystrolyotov, "Shchedrye serdtsem," 162. In the Mitrokhin archive, her name is spelled "Mueller" (http://www.linearossage.it/201-248.htm).

10. "Pir," 3:377; Bystrolyotov, *Para Bellum*, 181.

11. Primakov, *Ocherki istorii rossiiskoi razvedki*, 2:241; Bystrolyotov, *Para Bellum*, 127.

12. Bystrolyotov, *Para Bellum*, 127; Bystrolyotov, "Shchedrye serdtsem," 182.

13. Bystrolyotov, *Para Bellum*, 127–28.

14. Ibid., 128.

15. Ibid., 174.

16. Ibid.

17. "Pir," 3:378.

18. Bystrolyotov, "Shchedrye serdtsem," 175.

19. In Bystrolyotov's *Para Bellum* (132–34) and "Shchedrye serdtsem" (169–71), the scheme Bystrolyotov prepared to involve Doris in is rendered in three ways, slightly different in the details. The most plausible scenario, a combination of the elements of all of them, is reconstructed here.

20. On the state of the German stock exchange of that time, see "Reich Arms Firms Show Stock Gains; Conscription Declaration Has Favorable Effect on Few Issues in the Boerse," *New York Times*, March 19, 1935, 3. See also "Market Stronger in Berlin," *New York Times*, April 2, 1935, 34.

21. Bystrolyotov, *Para Bellum*, 133.

22. Ibid.; on his background, see Bystrolyotov, "Shchedrye serdtsem," 7–8; Tsarev and West, *Crown Jewels*, 113–14. For a picture of Theodor Mally, see http://rusrazvedka.narod.ru/base/htm/malli.html.

23. Bystrolyotov, "Shchedrye serdtsem," 244–45.

24. Bystrolyotov, *Para Bellum*, 133.

25. Ibid., 134.

26. Bystrolyotov, "Shchedrye serdtsem," 169–71.

27. Ibid., 172.

28. Ibid., 194.

29. In fact, the real Alexis Putilov lived in Paris, not London (http://hronos .km.ru/biograf/putilov.html [accessed July 15, 2008]).

30. Bystrolyotov, "Shchedrye serdtsem," 211–12.

31. Ibid., 218–19.

32. Ibid., 212.

33. Ibid., 207, 219.

34. Bystrolyotov, *Para Bellum*, 134.

35. "Pir," 3:379; in both *Para Bellum* (132) and "Shchedrye serdtsem" (256), Bystrolyotov has himself dying as the result of a car crash.

36. KGB2, 195; "Pir," 3:379; Bystrolyotov, in conversation with the author, September 11, 1973.

37. Although, in his memoirs, Bystrolyotov recalls that this operation took place in 1933 or 1934, its details (described in "Pir," 3:379–81 and "Shchedrye serdtsem," 114–22) lead one to believe that it took place later.

38. Primakov, *Ocherki istorii rossiiskoi razvedki*, 2:245.

39. Bystrolyotov, "Shchedrye serdtsem," 123.

Eleven. The "Vivaldi" Affair

1. Peter Jackson, *France and the Nazi Menace: Intelligence and Policy Making 1923–1939* (Oxford: Oxford University Press, 2000), 192.

2. The details of this operation are reconstructed from Bystrolyotov's fictionalized account in *Para Bellum*, 126–34.

3. Although in *Para Bellum* Bystrolyotov doesn't give the true name of the man he calls "Rubinstein," in a confidential cover letter that accompanied his unpublished movie script, "Shchderost'," where the same character appears, he discloses Dawidowicz's name; see Kern, *Walter G. Krivitsky*, 156–57.

4. Milashov, in discussion with the author, July 2003; for Bystrolyotov's acknowledgment of substituting the nationality of some of his targets, see "Pir," 1:503–4.

5. Jackson, *France and the Nazi Menace*, 11, 13.

6. Unless otherwise noted, this operation is described in "Pir," 3:495–525.

7. Alexandra Kollontai, *Selected Writings*, trans. Alix Holt (New York: Norton, 1977); the chapter addressed here is available at http://www.marxists.org/archive/kollonta/1921/theses-morality.htm.

8. "Pir," 1:506.

9. Ibid., 507.

10. Ibid., 523.

11. Milashov, in discussion with the author, July 2003; for Bystrolyotov's admission that he has blood on his hands, see "Pir," 2:277.

Twelve. The Last Operations: Africa and Other Gray Areas

1. Unless otherwise noted, the end of the "Vivaldi" operation is reconstructed from "Pir," 1:524–29.

2. Milashov, in discussion with the author, July 2003; citing this episode in Bystrolyotov's career, Grigoriev writes that "they were forced to take care of the man" (*Skandinaviia*, 77), implying that he was killed by the Soviet intelligence agents.

3. Paul Henry Lang, review of *Antonio Vivaldi et la musique instrumentale* [Antonio Vivaldi and Instrumental Music], by Marc Pincherle, *Musical Quarterly* 35, no. 1 (January 1949): 156 (see http://www.jstor.org/pss/739586).

4. Another author, David E. Albright, concurs with Andrew and Mitrokhin: "In sum, Soviet involvement in South Africa during the interwar years can be viewed essentially in terms of wasted opportunities rather than achievements" (*Communism in Africa* [Bloomington: Indiana University Press, 1980], 90).

5. "I firmly knew that he never, not one day, spent time in Africa, and Africa was never a subject of his professional [read: intelligence operative's] interest" (Snegirev, *Pravda*, February 25, 1990).

6. Bystrolyotov, in conversation with the author, September 11, 1973. On his travel to Africa, see, for example, http://rusrazvedka.narod.ru/base/htm/bystr.html.

7. Bystrolyotov, "Shchedrye serdtsem," 353.

8. Unless otherwise noted, travel details are reconstructed based on Bystrolyotov, *V staroi Afrike*, 15, 132–201.

9. Bystrolyotov, "Shchedrye serdtsem," 353–54.

10. Ibid., 354; on an episode of calling Comintern attention to areas other than South Africa, see Andrew and Mitrokhin, *Mitrokhin Archive II,* 423.

11. Bystrolyotov, "Shchedrye serdtsem," 354.

12. In his African book, Bystrolyotov calls them by their Tuareg name, the Hoggar.

13. Bystrolyotov, "Katanga, god 1937," 29.

14. Ibid.

15. Ibid., 30–31. The fact of the unrest in 1931 and 1935 is cited in Phillip D. Curtin, *The World and the West: The European Challenge and the Overseas Response in the Age of Empire* (New York: Cambridge University Press, 2002), 225.

16. The issue referred to, of July 20 through August 17, 1934, is cited in Bystrolyotov's unpublished memoirs, "Tsepi i niti," 3–5. Other sources confirm the drastic reduction of the Congo population of the period; see, for example, findings of Irish diplomat Roger Casement, cited in Adam Hochschild, *King Leopold's Ghost: A Story of Greed, Terror, and Heroism in Colonial Africa* (Boston: Mariner Books, 1999), 226–32.

17. Bystrolyotov, "Tsepi i niti," 41.

18. http://nvo.ng.ru/spforces/2006-10-06/7_bazarov.html (accessed September 11, 2008). On Bazarov's operations in the United States, see Hoover, 42–43.

19. Milashov, in discussion with the author, July 2003.

20. See the Mitrokhin archive, excerpt 204 (http://www.linearossage.it/201-248.htm [accessed August 6, 2009]).

21. For information on Samsonovici, see http://en.wikipedia.org/wiki/List_of_the_Chiefs_of_the_General_Staff_of_Romania (accessed August 25, 2008).

22. Bystrolyotov, "Shchedrye serdtsem," 302.

23. Ibid., 302–3.

24. Ibid., 322, 336; for Samsonovici's birth year, see http://www.indiana.edu/~league/assemblydelegs.htm (accessed August 25, 2008).

25. Orlov, *Handbook of Intelligence,* 97; Bystrolyotov, "Shchedrye serdtsem," 316.

26. Bystrolyotov, "Shchedrye serdtsem," 317.

27. Anna M. Cienciala, review of *Romania and the Great Powers, 1933–1940,* by Dov B. Lungu, *Journal of Modern History* 63, no. 4 (December 1991): 824.

28. Hugh Ragsdale, *The Soviets, the Munich Crisis, and the Coming of World War II* (New York: Cambridge University Press, 2004), 57.

29. Ibid., 58.

30. Ibid.

31. Ibid., 59; see also Larry L. Watts, "Romania as a Military Ally (Part I): Czechoslovakia in 1938," *Romanian Civilization* (Bucharest) 7 (1998): 44.

32. An interception of Antonescu's report is mentioned in Bystrolyotov, "Shchedrye serdtsem," 338.

33. The actor's full name was Fernand Joseph Désiré Contandin (1903–71); Faligot and Krop misread Bystrolyotov's text, to which they were given onetime access, and made an erroneous supposition about Fernandel's involvement with Soviet foreign intelligence (Faligot and Krop, "Du cas Michel Simon à l'affaire Fernandel," 16–17).

34. Bystrolyotov, "Shchedrye serdtsem," 310.

35. Ibid., 333.

Thirteen. The Return

1. Compare the texts of the letter included in Snegirev, "Drugaia zhizn' Dmitriia Bystroletova," 73–74, and at the SVR Web site, http://svr.gov.ru/smi/2006/novrkr20060130.htm.

2. Compare http://svr.gov.ru/history/byst.html and http://svr.gov.ru/smi/2006/novrkr20060130.htm (both accessed October 28, 2008). See also Duff, *Time for Spies*, 113; Primakov, *Ocherki istorii rossiiskoi razvedki*, 2:245.

3. "Pir," 1:41; Bystrolyotov, "Shchedrye serdtsem," 85.

4. Bystrolyotov, "Shchedrye serdtsem," 139, 179.

5. "Pir," 1:41.

6. For the Bystrolyotov quote, see Razumov, "Rukopis' D. Bystrolyotova 'Pir Bessmertnykh,'" 110.

7. Bystrolyotov, "Shchedrye serdtsem," 326.

8. "Pir," 1:502, 532.

9. Ibid.

10. Ibid.

11. Bystrolyotov, "Shchedrye serdtsem," 103.

12. Ibid., 104–5.

13. See Duff, *Time for Spies*, 67.

14. Bystrolyotov, "Shchedrye serdtsem," 105.

15. KGB2; quoted in Tsarev and West, *KGB v Anglii*, 123.

16. Frederick P. Hitz, *The Great Game: The Myth and Reality of Espionage* (New York: Knopf, 2004), 102.

17. "Pir," 3:371.

18. Ibid., 370.

19. Ibid., 1:397. See also Bystrolyotov, *Para Bellum*, 126–27.

20. The episode, based on Bystrolyotov's recollections, is described by his camp mate, Konstantin Ivanov ("Razvedchik, vozvrashchennyi iz nebytiia," 8).

21. On the fatigue of intelligence operatives, see Bystrolyotov, *Para Bellum*, 126–27. The episode with the loss of passport is re-created by William Duff based on his and Dan Mulvenna's interviews with Oleg Tsarev in January and March 1994 (Duff, *Time for Spies*, 72, 201n10). See also John Costello and Oleg Tsarev, *Rokovye illiuzii* [Fateful Illusions] (Moscow: Mezhdunarodnye otnosheniia, 1995), 160.

22. Milashov, in discussion with the author, July 2003.

23. On Soviet spies living abroad and lacking reliable information about their homeland, see Poretskaia, *Nashi*, 113.

24. "Pir," 1:348–49.

25. Poretskaia, *Nashi*, 79–80.

26. Ibid., 97.

27. See, for example, ibid., 81.

28. Philby, *My Silent War*, xx.

29. See *Sbornik zakonodatel'nykh i normativnykh aktov o repressiiakh i reabilitatsii zhertv politicheskikh repressii* [A Collection of Legislative and Normative Decrees About Repressions and Rehabilitation of Victims of Political Repressions] (Moscow: Verkhovnyi sovet rossiiskoi federatsii, 1993), 32–33, 86.

30. Ivanov, "Razvedchik, vozvrashchennyi iz nebytiia," 8. On kidnapping abroad, see Solzhenitsyn, *Gulag Archipelago: Volume 1*, 9. On Mally's fate, see Edward Gazur, *Alexander Orlov, The FBI's KGB General*. (New York: Basic Books, 2002), 160–62; see also Duff, *Time for Spies*, 175.

31. Orlov, *Secret History*, 229.

32. Razumov, "Rukopis' D. Bystrolyotova 'Pir Bessmertnykh,'" 121; Alexander Barmine, *One Who Survived* (Malinowski Press, 2007), 21n3.

33. Snegirev, "Drugaia zhizn' Dmitriia Bystroletova," 74. The last SVR posting erroneously dates the letter as being sent at the end of December 1936 (http://svr .gov.ru/smi/2006/novrkr20060130.htm).

34. "Pir," 1:534; http://svr.gov.ru/smi/2006/novrkr20060130.htm.

35. Snegirev, "Drugaia zhizn' Dmitriia Bystroletova," 74; http://svr.gov.ru/ smi/2006/novrkr20060130.htm. See also Degtiarev and Kolpakidi, 107.

36. "Pir," 1:42, 534. Although, in his memoirs, true to his oath of secrecy about his intelligence work, Bystrolyotov cites working with a German Wehrmacht headquarters "source" as his new assignment, as known now, his true target was Captain King of the British Foreign Office (interview with Milashov, July 2003). Costello and Tsarev (204) identify the target as Donald Maclean of the Cambridge spy ring.

37. "Pir," 1:534. The boy's photograph is included in Tsarev and West, *Crown Jewels*.

38. Snegirev, "Drugaia zhizn' Dmitriia Bystroletova," 4; "Pir," 1:42–43.

39. Orlov, *Secret History*, 223–24.

40. Poretskaia, *Nashi*, 106.

41. Orlov, *Secret History*, 215; Kolpakidi and Prokhorov, *Vneshniaia razvedka Rossii*, 178–79.

42. "Pir," 1:42–43. On Gorb and Artuzov, see http://www.memo.ru/history/ NKVD/kto/biogr/index.htm. On Samsonov, see appendix to Bystrolyotov, *Puteshestvie na krai nochi*, 585.

43. On details of Poretsky's assassination, see Kern, *Death in Washington*, 133–39.

44. Poretskaia, *Nashi*, 94. On the number of recalled officers, see Orlov, *Secret History*, 225. On Slutsky's murder, see also Andrew and Mitrokhin, *The Sword and the Shield*, 80; Pringle, *Historical Dictionary of Russian and Soviet Intelligence*, 242–43. For details of Slutsky's murder, see Abramov, *Evrei v KGB*, 299–300. In his 2008 book, Mlechin doubts the poisoning scenario and thinks that Slutsky, who had a history of heart problems, died of a heart attack (*Istoriia vneshnei razvedki*, 56).

45. Kolpakidi and Prokhorov, *Vneshniaia razvedka Rossii*, 180. The NKVD order to dismiss Bystrolyotov "on the grounds of staff reduction" is dated February 25, 1938. However, his personal work record book shows March 31, 1938, as the day of his dismissal.

46. Ibid., 287; Pringle, *Historical Dictionary of Russian and Soviet Intelligence*, 152–53. Andrew and Mitrokhin, *The Sword and the Shield*, 78; Duff, *Time for Spies*, 183–84; Andrew and Mitrokhin, ibid., 106; Kolpakidi and Prokhorov, *Vneshniaia razvedka Rossii*, 159.

47. "Pir," 3:398–99. The Operative Department of the Chief Directorate of State Security of the NKVD existed from 1934 to 1939; see http://www.memo.ru/history/NKVD/STRU/.

48. "Pir," 1:19; on the advantages of night arrests, see Solzhenitsyn, *Gulag Archipelago: Volume 1*, 6–7.

49. See RGASPI; cited in Degtiarev and Kolpakidi, 104–12, 316–17.

50. "Pir," 1:20.

Fourteen. In Ink and Blood

1. On the background of A. P. Solovyov, see appendix to Bystrolyotov, *Puteshestvie na krai nochi*, 586. Andrew and Mitrokhin misspell his assistant's surname—"Pushkin" (*The Sword and the Shield*, 81).

2. Unless otherwise noted, Bystrolyotov's experience and quotes from his writings in this chapter refer to "Pir," 1:19–100.

3. For more information on Butyrka prison, see http://www.cdi.org/russia/johnson/7209-4.cfm.

4. See appendix to Bystrolyotov, *Puteshestvie na krai nochi*, 586–87.

5. One example of a prisoner consciously cooperating with the interrogation was Alexander Isbakh, a Soviet writer and literary scholar. Arrested on drummed-up charges, beaten half to death, barely making it to his cell, he kept telling his cell mates: "We have to help our interrogartors; that is our Party duty." Cited in Benedikt Sarnov, *Nash sovetskkii novoiaz* [Our Soviet Newspeak] (Moscow: Eksmo, 2005), 450.

6. As is revealed now, these denunciations had been filed on Dec. 7, 1937, over nine months before, and waited their turn to be used as grounds for Bystrolyotov's arrest; see Degtiarev and Kolpakidi, 106.

7. See the GlobalSecurity site http://www.globalsecurity.org/intell/world/russia/lefortovo.htm.

8. "Pir," 1:352.

9. Apparently, at the time Bystrolyotov was tortured, no longer People's Commissar of Internal Affairs (his tenure ended there on November 25, 1938), Yezhov visited Lefortovo in the capacity of a member of the Politburo Commission on Judicious Affairs; he remained in that post until January 19, 1939 (see "Memorial," "Rukovodiashchie kadry NKVD," http://www.memo.ru/history/NKVD/kto/biogr/index.htm). For Yezhov's full biography, see Marc Jansen and Nikita V. Petrov, *Stalin's Loyal Executioner: People's Commissar Nikolai Ezhov, 1895–1940* (Stanford, Calif.: Hoover Institution Press, 2002).

10. "Pir," 1:353.

11. Bystrolyotov, in conversation with the author, September 1973. On his beatings, see also Andrew and Mitrokhin, *The Sword and the Shield*, 81.

12. "Pir," 1:354.

Fifteen. Sentencing and Entering the Gulag

1. Unless otherwise noted, Bystrolyotov's experiences and quotes from his writings in this chapter refer to "Pir," 1:110–295; on Kedrov's background, see appendix to Bystrolyotov, *Puteshestvie na krai nochi*, 582.

2. On Shpigelglas's background, see Sudoplatov and Sudoplatov, *Special Tasks*, 13; Kolpakidi and Prokhorov, *Vneshniaia razvedka Rossii*, 104–5.

3. The episode with Solovyov is cited in "Pir," 1:87; on Beria's career, see http://www.mcmo.ru/history/NKVD/kto/biogr/index.htm; on the death sentence statistics, see http://www.hrono.info/organ/gulag.html. For a description of the widespread practice of applying these articles, see Solzhenitsyn, *Gulag Archipelago: Volume 1*, 60, 63–66.

4. "Pir," 1:314–15; see also Rossi, *Gulag Handbook*, 36, 497; see *Sbornik*, 86–93; see also Solzhenitsyn, *Gulag Archipelago: Volume 2*, 303–4.

5. See Ivanov, "Razvedchik, vozvrashchennyi iz nebytiia," 8; on shortages of medical personnel in the camps, see Applebaum, *Gulag*, 369; on fellow prisoners' opinion of the medical training of Bystrolyotov, see Razumov, "Rukopis' D. Bystrolyotova 'Pir Bessmertnykh,'" 132.

As to Bystrolyotov's formal training in medicine, both his stepgrandson, Sergei Milashov, and many current biographies (most likely having the same source) insist that, in the years 1931 to 1935, under one of his aliases, Bystrolyotov studied medicine at the graduate school of Zurich University, specializing in obstetrics and gynecology. During our conversations, Milashov elaborated on the subject by making a connection between Bystrolyotov's choice of medical field and his mother's specialization as a nurse in later years. Ostensibly recalling a conversation with his stepgrandfather, Milashov pointed out that the profession of gynecologist was chosen for operative purposes: it facilitated an approach to private information, for "a woman fully opens up only to her hairdresser, her lawyer, and her gynecologist." There is no evidence of any operation in which Bystrolyotov utilized this access to any purpose. But, giving him the benefit of the doubt, he could have thought this way.

It is also stated in current Russian publications that, after his graduation, Bystrolyotov practiced in one of the Swiss private clinics and even made the scientific discovery of a means to control the gender of a baby when planning a family. (See, for example, Degtiarev and Kolpakidi, 382.) Moreover, it is stated that Bystrolyotov published an article on the subject in a scientific journal, again under somebody else's name.

The problem with all this information is twofold. First, it's hard to imagine how, extremely busy with his spy work and almost always on the move, Bystrolyotov could attend and successfully fulfill the rigorous requirements of medical school. Second, none of these statements could be verified with documentary evidence. When I paid a visit to the university archive, no records of graduates in the years 1935 and 1936 matched any of Bystrolyotov's known aliases. (Of course it's possible that, when enrolling in the university, he could have used an alias that isn't recorded in the current KGB files.)

All this said and done, in addition to the fellow prisoners who were his former patients, Bystrolyotov's memoirs confirm his solid knowledge in the medical field when he describes physical self-examinations during his many bouts with infirmities or discusses his attempts at scientific research in the camps.

6. See Applebaum *Gulag*, 282–83; Lev Razgon, *True Stories*, trans. John Crowfoot (Dana Point, Calif.: Ardis, 1997), 185.

7. See also Solzhenitsyn, *Gulag Archipelago: Volume 2*, 325.

8. "The work of an agent in the Intelligence Department is on the whole monotonous. A lot of it is uncommonly useless," Somerset Maugham, in the preface to his *Collected Short Stories* (New York: Penguin Classics, 1995), 3:7. On Stalin's order to supply him with raw intelligence data, without analysis, see Orlov, *Handbook of Intelligence*, 10. For details on deliberate misrepresentation of Soviet spies' information, see Andrew and Mitrokhin, *The Sword and the Shield*, 52–55.

9. On the history of Norillag, see http://www.vtalnahe.ru/index.php?option =com_content&task=view&id=648; for other information on the camp, see http:// www.memorial.krsk.ru/lager/Norillag/1.htm.

10. For medical personnel's privilege of sleeping not on the multiple bunks but on their own beds, see Applebaum, *Gulag*, 200; see also Isaac Vogelfanger, *Red Tempest: The Life of a Surgeon in the Gulag* (Montreal: McGill-Queen's University Press, 1996), 67.

11. On Stalin's order to abolish the shortening of sentences for good work, see Applebaum, *Gulag*, 473.

12. Ibid., 102–3; on the effect of the word "comrade," see Rossi, *Gulag Handbook*, 449.

13. "Pir," 1:315; see also Anna Larina, *This I Cannot Forget: The Memoirs of Nikolai Bukharin's Widow*, trans. Gary Kern (New York: Norton, 1994), 159 (quoted in Applebaum, *Gulag*, 304).

14. "Pir," 2:72.

15. See Nikolai Ostrovsky, *How the Steel Was Tempered* (Moscow: Progress, 1964).

16. "Pir," 1:189.

17. Ibid., 191.

18. On the shortage of warm boots and clothes in Norillag, see GARF 8131/37/4547; cited in Applebaum, *Gulag*, 225.

19. "Pir," 1:312–13.

20. Ibid., 314.

21. Cited in Stephen Kotkin, "Stalinism as a Civilization," in *The Stalin Years: A Reader*, ed. Christopher Read (New York: Palgrave Macmillan, 2003), 217–18.

22. "Pir," 1:316; on Prokhorov-Pustover, see Solzhenitsyn, *Gulag Archipelago: Volume 2*, 347; on posters glorifying labor in the camps, see Georgii Zhzhenov, *Sanochki* [Little Sleigh], http://www.russkoekino.ru/books/zhenov/zhenov-0007 .shtml.

23. "Pir," 1:316.

24. See also Nanci Adler, *The Gulag Survivor: Beyond the Soviet System* (New Brunswick, N.J.: Transaction, 2004), xx; on the attractiveness of the Communist idea as an ideology of social cohesiveness, see Catherine Merridale, *Night*

of Stone: Death and Memory in Twentieth-Century Russia (New York: Penguin, 2002), 418.

Sixteen. The Invalid Camp

1. Amdur [letter to *Pravda* editorial office], May 5, 1990, 1–2. Amdur has the number of prisoners aboard raised to six hundred. Unless otherwise noted, Bystrolyotov's experience and quotes from his writings in this chapter refer to "Pir," 1:182–207, 297–387, 536–54.

2. Applebaum, *Gulag,* 169; on similar experiences of prisoner boat transport in the Gulag, see Applebaum, *Gulag,* 169–75.

3. Razumov, "Rukopis' D. Bystrolyotova 'Pir Bessmertnykh,'" 132.

4. Amdur [letter to *Pravda*], 3; my own impression of Dmitri when we met in the fall of 1973, when he was already an old man, is quite close to that of Amdur's.

5. On Anna Rosenblum's background, see Pringle, *Historical Dictionary of Russian and Soviet Intelligence,* 226–27; see also appendix to Bystrolyotov, *Puteshestvie na krai nochi,* 585, and, on the "Russian Genealogical Tree," http://www.r-g-d.ru/R/rozen1.htm. On her testimony about the torture of Vasily Blyukher, see http://militera.lib.ru/research/cheryshev_ns/01.html. For a similar episode of a prisoner in Norilsk attacking (verbally) an unnamed imprisoned doctor who worked in Lefortovo prison (possibly Anna Rosenblum), see Dr. Georgy Popov's memoir, *Opiat' ozhivaet potusknevshee vremia* [Fading Time Comes to Live Again], http://www.memorial.krsk.ru/Public/80/19891230.htm. Bystrolyotov mistakenly says that Rosenblum was sentenced to twenty-five years of labor camps, not fifteen years ("Pir," 1:356). She was freed from imprisonment and fully rehabilitated only in 1955.

6. On prisoner transport by boat, see also Applebaum, *Gulag,* 169–72; Eugenia Ginzburg, *Journey into the Whirlwind,* trans. Paul Stevenson and Max Hayward (New York: Harcourt, Brace & World, 1967), 351–53; Conquest, *Kolyma,* 24.

7. On similar recovery camp units in the Gulag, see Applebaum, *Gulag,* 371–72.

8. "Pir," 2:59–60.

9. Ibid., 1:541.

10. "Pir," 3:7.

11. On card game rituals in the camps, see Applebaum, *Gulag,* 286–90.

12. On criminals called "bitches," see Rossi, *Gulag Handbook,* 126, 441.

13. On imprisoned doctors' perilous situation, see Applebaum, *Gulag,* 373.

14. "Pir," 2:392–93.

15. Ibid., 61; 3:10; Bystrolyotov, in conversation with the author, September 1973.

16. "Pir," 3:9.

17. Ibid., 2:48, 324–25.

18. Ibid., 42, 98; 3:10.

Seventeen. Love Behind Barbed Wire

1. Giving her the name of an African girl was not whimsy but the act of a guilty conscience. During Dmitri's sojourn in the village of Nianga in the western

part of Belgian Congo, he presented the local chief, Assai, with a finely made dagger complete with a decorated sheath. Overwhelmed with joy, Assai sent him in return Liuonga, one of his daughters—a twelve-year-old girl, pretty and graceful as a "terra-cotta statuette." She was puzzled when Dmitri tried to treat her as a child. Playful and coy, she made attempts at seducing him.

In his memoirs, Dmitri admits that, then and there, during the "humid, hot, and relaxing" African nights saturated with the "intoxicating aroma of poisonous flowers," he found himself disturbingly attracted to the girl and was fighting off temptation tooth and nail.

It's not clear whether he eventually succumbed to Liuonga's charms, but, when the time came for him to return to Europe, she ignored his farewell words and, on the morning of his departure, appeared in his tent fully equipped to follow him. She considered it her joyful duty to accompany her husband, and she was devastated by his refusal to take her along. Her face turned gray and he realized that, by the cultural standards of her milieu, she considered herself an abandoned wife.

He left alone. In Europe, he resumed the life of a spy. But he couldn't help feeling guilty that he had inadvertently crushed the African girl's life. His parcel addressed to her, containing the best perfumes and jewelry that money could buy in fashionable Parisian stores, came back with a note from a local postman that it couldn't be delivered because of . . . the death of the addressee. Between her father's untimely demise while lion hunting and Dmitri's leaving, she lost her will to live.

Thus, by giving the anonymous Russian girl he saved in the Gulag the name of the African girl he had abandoned, Dmitri attempted to at least symbolically bring her back to life. (For his detailed description of this episode, see "Pir bessmertnykh," 2:366–73, 387–92, 406–11.)

2. Unless otherwise noted, Bystrolyotov's life in the camps is reconstructed in this chapter based on details in "Pir," 2:32–164, 204–301, 341–82.

3. According to the official statistics of the year when the action takes place (1942), 13 percent of the Gulag prisoners were women (cited in Applebaum, *Gulag*, 311).

4. On women's plight in the Gulag, see ibid., 311–17.

5. Ibid., 315.

6. On shortages of writing paper in the camps, see ibid., 249–50.

7. The directive is quoted ibid., 234; on the functions of the cultural-educational departments in the camps, see ibid., 231–34; on cultural activities at Mariinsk, see the memoirs of E. Sydakova, *Krutye stupeni* [Steep Steps], 32, http://lib.ru/MEMUARY/sudakowa.txt.

8. La Argentina was the stage name of Antonia Mercé (1888–1936), also known as "The Flamenco Pavlova" and "The Queen of the Castanets." For her short biography, see http://tarotcanada.tripod.com/LaArgentina.html.

9. On disciplinary barracks, see Rossi, *Gulag Handbook*, 37.

10. "Pir," 3:92.

Eighteen. The High Price of Decency

1. "Pir," 3:92.
2. Ibid., 108.

3. Ibid., 2:433. On Norman Borodin's background, see http://www.hrono.ru/biograf/bio_b/borodin_nm.html.

4. Later, in 1951, Norman Borodin was exiled to Karaganda, where, from 1952 to 1953, he worked as a department head of the *Sotsialisticheskaia Karaganda* [Socialist Karaganda] newspaper. At the end of 1953, he returned to Moscow and, in 1954, was fully rehabilitated. In 1955, he was reinstated at the KGB; see http://www.hrono.info/biograf/bio_b/borodin_nm.html.

5. At the time of the meeting with Bystrolyotov, Abakumov's rank was higher; he had held the rank of colonel general since July 9, 1945. On May 4, 1946, he was made minister of state security (MGB), and he remained in that position until July 4, 1951. He was arrested a few days after his dismissal and, after spending three years in jail, convicted of high treason. He was shot on December 19, 1954. For more information and Abakumov's photo, see http://www.memo.ru/history/NKVD/kto/biogr/index.htm.

6. "Pir," 3:109.

7. On recollections of camp chiefs treating prisoners humanely, see Applebaum, *Gulag,* 271–72. For an excerpt from a memoir written by one such camp chief, see Fyodor Mochulsky, "Citizen Boss: A Gulag Memoir," trans. Deborah Kaple, *Nassau Literary Review,* Winter 2008–9, 36–45.

8. "Pir," 3:110.

9. Unless otherwise noted, the details of the Sukhanovka episode of Bystrolyotov's solitary confinement are reconstructed in this chapter based on details in "Pir," 2:434–82.

10. Solzhenitsyn, *Gulag Archipelago: Volume 1,* 181.

11. Writing about this episode, Bystrolyotov made an error, stating that he met Jasieński in Butyrka prison personally. That couldn't possibly have happened because, after being arrested on July 31, 1937, Bruno was sentenced to death by the Military Collegium of the USSR Supreme Court and shot on the same day, September 17, 1938, one day before Bystrolyotov was arrested; see http://lists.memo.ru/d38/f436.htm and http://mos.memo.ru/shot-22.htm. Most likely, Bystrolyotov learned about Jasieński's attempts at composing a novel in his head from other prisoners.

12. On Mikhail Borodin's biography, see G. V. Kostyrchenko, *Tainaia politika Stalina. Vlast' i antisemitizm* [Stalin's Secret Policy: State Power and Anti-Semitism] (Moscow: Mezhdunarodnye otnosheniya, 2001), 329–30; see also http://www.hrono.info/biograf/gruzenberg.html.

13. Unless otherwise noted, in the rest of this chapter the details of the last period of Bystrolytov's life in the camps are reconstructed based on details in "Pir," 2:502–663.

14. On rearrests in that period, see Applebaum, *Gulag,* 463–64.

Nineteen. Taking On Challenges of Freedom

Chapter epigraphs are from "Pir," 3:124.

1. For the 2006 SVR biography of Bystrolyotov, see http://svr.gov.ru/smi/2006/novrkr20060130.htm. Unless otherwise noted, Bystrolyotov's life after the camps is reconstructed in this chapter based on details in "Pir," 3:133–69, 181–94, 212–34.

2. For details of the hardships of the rehabilitation process, see also N. Adler, *Trudnoe vozvrashchenie: Sud'by sovetskikh politzakliuchennykh v 1950–1990-e gody* [The Arduous Return: The Fates of Soviet Political Prisoners in the 1950s–1990s] (Moscow: Zven'ia, 2005); A. G. Petrov, *Reabilitatsiia zhertv politicheskikh repressii: Opyt istoricheskogo analiza* [Rehabilitation of Victims of Political Repressions: An Attempt at Historical Analysis] (Moscow: INION RAN, 2005). By January 1, 2002, more than 4 million former political prisoners had been rehabilitated. A special commission on rehabilitation attached to the Russian president's office is still hearing rehabilitation cases today.

3. On similar struggles to get living space, see Thomas Sgovio, *Dear America! Why I Turned Against Communism* (Kenmore, N.Y.: Partners' Press, 1979), 283.

4. Andrew and Mitrokhin, *The Sword and the Shield*, 578n14; Milashov, in discussion with the author, July 2003.

5. On troubles other ex-prisoners experienced receiving their pensions, see Aleksandr Morozov, *Deviat' stupenei v nebytie* [Nine Steps into Oblivion] (Saratov, 1991), 381–82. For other cases when many years of imprisonment were compensated with just one or two months' salary, see Applebaum, *Gulag*, 514.

6. In his memoirs, Bystrolyotov doesn't give the name of the official, but, most likely, it was Aleksandr Sakharovsky, the head of the First Chief Directorate (Foreign Intelligence) of the KGB from 1956 to 1971.

7. On the situation of returnees from the Gulag regarding their homes and belongings, see Applebaum, *Gulag*, 513.

8. On the fear of being rearrested, see Kathleen Smith, *Remembering Stalin's Victims* (Ithaca, N.Y.: Cornell University Press, 1996), 133.

9. On Shukshin being shot, see "Pir," 1:102; on his dying of heart failure, see ibid., 3:194. On Shukshin's true fate, see Evgenii Zhernov, "Purely Chekist Purge," *Kommersant,* September 28, 2006, http://www.cripo.com.ua/index.php?sect_id=9&aid=24493.

10. See appendix to Bystrolyotov, *Puteshestvie na krai nochi*, 582.

11. On Erica Weinstein's fate, see "Pir," 1:315; see also appendix to Bystrolyotov, *Puteshestvie na krai nochi*, 583, 587. Russian sources do not indicate the exact date of both Leppin's and Erica's return, but it must have been after September 4, 1937, the day Soviet defector Ignace Reiss was murdered in Switzerland. Both Soviet operatives were suspected of taking part in the operation; see FNA, 102–5.

12. "Pir," 3:285, 323.

13. Ibid., 285.

14. Ibid., 291.

15. Under the title *V staroi Afrike*, the novel appeared posthumously, in 1976; with the author out of the picture, the editors had a free hand in substantial cuts and rewritings (Milashov, in discussion with the author, July 2003).

Twenty. Fighting to the End, Now a Different Enemy

1. Unless otherwise noted, Bystrolyotov's life after the camps is reconstructed in this chapter based on the details in "Pir," 3:234–323.

2. Ibid., 2:396; 3:404–6.

3. Ibid., 3:406.

4. Ibid., 2:95, 299.

5. Ibid., 3:132.

6. Ibid., 415.

7. Ibid., 2:489.

8. On stylistic shortcomings of "Pir," see Razumov, "Rukopis' D. Bystrolyotova 'Pir Bessmertnykh,'" 113–18.

9. "Pir," 2:491.

10. "Pir," 2:487.

11. Ibid., 1:290. On the fate of children in the Gulag, see Applebaum, *Gulag*, 317–33.

12. Milashov, in "Slovo o Dmitrii Aleksandroviche Bystrolyotove (Tolstom)," in Bystrolyotov, *Puteshestvie na krai nochi*, 3; "Pir," 1:12–13.

13. KGB2, 144 (1970 pagination); quoted in G. A. Sokolov, in afterword to Bystrolyotov, *Puteshestvie na krai nochi*, 554.

14. "Pir," 3:315; 1:555.

15. Ibid., 3:390.

16. See http://www.kinoexpert.ru/index.asp?comm=4&num=1774.

17. On Tsvigun's background, see http://novodevichye.narod.ru/cvigun-sk.html.

18. Milashov, in "Slovo o Dmitrii Aleksandroviche Bystrolyotove (Tolstom)," in Bystrolyotov, *Puteshestvie na krai nochi*, 7.

Afterword

1. Grigoriev, *Naiti i zaverbovat';* TV documentaries: *Razvedka, o kotoroi znali nemnogie. Dmitrii Bystrolyotov, Okhota za shiframi* [Foreign Intelligence Not Known to Many: Dmitri Bystrolyotov, Hunting for Ciphers], 2003; *Serebrianaia roza* [A Silver Rose], 2006; *Maski nelegala* [An Illegal's Masks], 2008; TV serial titled *Rodina zhdet* [The Motherland Is Waiting], produced by Russian "Central Partnership" firm, 2003.

2. Compare the earlier Bystrolyotov-related posting at http://svr.gov.ru/history/byst.html with the new one at http://svr.gov.ru/smi/2006/novrkr20060130.htm.

3. See http://svr.gov.ru/history/byst.html.

4. Bystrolyotov, in conversation with the author, September 1973.

5. See Emil Draitser, *Shush! Growing Up Jewish Under Stalin: A Memoir* (Berkeley: University of California Press, 2008), 33–45, 221–35, 246–49.

6. Bystrolyotov, "Shchedrye serdtsem," 78.

7. Ibid.

SELECTED BIBLIOGRAPHY

Primary Sources (Archival Holdings)
Russia

GARF   State Archive of the Russian Federation. Bystrolyotov's personal file. Inventory description no. 2, item no. 92; fund R-5765. *Russkii iuridicheskii fakul'tet v Prage. Russkii zagranichnyi arkhiv* [Russian Law Faculty in Prague. The Russian Foreign Archive]. Moscow.

KGB1   KGB Archive. Bystrolyotov file. Record of Service no. 12351. Archive no. 9529. Vol. 1. Reports related to Bystrolyotov's activities. Moscow.

KGB2   KGB Archive. Vol. 2. "Rukopis' Gansa" [Hans's Manuscript]. Bystrolyotov's handwritten memo, signed October 28, 1968 [repaginated a few times]. Moscow.

RGASPI   Russia's State Archive of Social and Political History. Fund 17, register 100, case #247610, pp. 25–31.

Outside Russia

PRAGUE, CZECH REPUBLIC

CSAinst   Czech State Archive. "Secret Instructions to USSR Trade Missions Abroad" (in Czech). File no. 225-215-3.

CSAmil   Czech State Archive. "Confidential Military Information to Soviet Mission in Prague" (in French). October 18, 1924. File no. 225-216-4.

CSApol   Czech State Archive. Police reports on the Union of Student Citizens of the USSR Living in Czechoslovakia, press clippings, and other documents related to Bystrolyotov. File no. 225-98-9-12.

CSAstaff   Czech State Archive. Soviet Trade Mission payroll. File no. 225-214-3,4.

FRANCE

CADN   Centre des Archives diplomatiques de Nantes, Nantes. Documents of Bystrolyotov's agent Marie-Eliane Aucouturier, passport no. 1148, issued on October 15, 1927, and her birth certificate. Doc. no. 371/AR/N.

FNA   Archives Nationales, Paris. File "I. Reiss, P. Ducomet, Ch. Martignat." BB18 3149, dossier 797-A-38.

UKNA   National Archives. MI5 file on Bystrolyotov's agent Ernest Holloway
        Oldham. Public Record Office, KV2/808, no. 224891. Kew, Rich-
        mond, Surrey.

Hoover Hoover Institution Archives. Hede Massing file, Box 2. Stanford,
        Calif.

Bystrolyotov's Writings

"Privet ot zarubezhnogo studenchestva" [Greetings from the Foreign Student
    Body]. *Pravda,* April 18, 1925, 3.
"Po sledam odnogo puteshestviia" [Tracking One Journey]. *Aziia i Afrika segodnia*
    (1963), no. 3:38–41; no. 4:41–45; no. 5:39–41; no. 6:40–43; no. 7:38–
    40; no. 8:42–44.
"Katanga, god 1937" [Katanga, 1937]. *Aziia i Afrika segodnia,* no. 1, 11 (1963).
"Shchedrye serdtsem" [Generous Hearts]. Typescript of a screenplay (ca. 1965).
    The National Library of Russia (formerly Saltykov-Shchedrin Library),
    St. Petersburg.
"Tsepi i niti" [Chains and Threads]. Typescript of a memoir (ca. 1968). Sergei
    Milashov's private archive, Moscow.
With V. Zhuravlyov. "Chelovek v shatskom" [The Plainclothesman]. *Vechernii
    Dnepr,* January–February 1973.
Para Bellum [Prepare for War]. *Nash sovremennik* (1974), no. 3:104–34; no.
    4:117–38; no. 5:123–32.
V staroi Afrike [In Old Africa]. Moscow: Sovetskaia Rossiia, 1976.
"Pir bessmertnykh" [Feast of the Immortals]. Galleys of unpublished book in
    three volumes (1993). Washington, D.C.: U.S. Library of Congress.
Pir bessmertnykh [Feast of the Immortals]. Moscow: Granitsa, 1993 [excerpts,
    1 vol.].
Puteshestvie na krai nochi [Journey to the Edge of Night]. Moscow: Sovremen-
    nik, 1996.

Bystrolyotov's Translations

Li, Tao. "Kitaiskaia meditsina v period pravleniia dinastii Min' (1368–1644)"
    [Chinese Medicine During Ming Dynasty Rule]. In *Trudy instituta
    organov zdravookhraneniia i istorii meditsiny* [Works of the Health-
    Care Organs Institute and History of Medicine], no. 6 (1959): 51–56
    [abridged translation from English].
Peter, R., V. Šebek, and I. Gyne. *Devushka prevrashchaetsia v zhenshchinu* [A
    Girl Turns into a Woman]. Translated from Czech. Moscow: Medgiz,
    1960.
Gyne, I. *Iunosha prevrashchaetsia v muzhchinu* [A Youth Turns into a Man]. Trans-
    lated from Czech. Moscow: Medgiz, 1960; repr., Tashkent: Ukituvchi,
    1970.

Secondary Sources in Russian

Books and Articles

Abramov, Vadim. *Evrei v KGB: Palachi i zhertvy* [Jews in the KGB: Executioners and Victims]. Moscow: Eksmo, 2005.

An-ov, N. "Prazhskaia zhizn'" [Life in Prague]. *Studencheskie gody*, no. 6 (1928): 28.

Appendix to Dmitri Bystrolyotov, *Puteshestvie na krai nochi* [Journey to the Edge of Night]. Moscow: Sovremennik, 1996.

Chelpanov, G. *Vvedenie v filosofiiu* [Introduction to Philosophy]. Kiev, 1907.

Chertoprud, S. "Prikazano vliubit'sia v grafiniu" [Ordered to Fall in Love with a Countess]. *Novosti razvedki i kontrrazvedki*, no. 7 (1997).

Degtiarev, Klim, and Aleksandr Kolpakidi. *Vneshniaia razvedka SSSR* [Foreign Intelligence of the USSR]. Moscow: Iauza-Eksmo, 2009.

Grigoriev, Boris. *Naiti i zaverbovat'* [To Find and Recruit]. Moscow: OLMA-Press, 2003.

———. *Skandinaviia s chernogo khoda* [Scandinavia from the Back Door]. Moscow: Tsentropoligraf, 2002.

Ivanov, K. "Razvedchik, vozvrashchennyi iz nebytiia" [An Intelligence Officer Recovered from Oblivion]. *Leningradskii universitet*, April 26, 1991, 8.

Kolpakidi, A., and D. Prokhorov. *KGB. Prikazano likvidirovat'* [KGB: It Is Ordered to Liquidate]. Moscow: Iauza-Eksmo, 2004.

———. *Vneshniaia razvedka Rossii* [Foreign Intelligence of Russia]. St. Petersburg: "Neva"; Moscow: OLMA-Press, 2001.

Krivitsky, V. *Ia byl agentom Stalina* [I Was Stalin's Agent]. Moscow: Sovremennik, 1991.

Listov, V. "Mikhail Trilisser." In *Chekisty rasskazyvaiut* [The Cheka Members Are Telling Things]. Moscow: Sovetskaia Rossiia, 1987, 216-18.

Milashov, S. S. "Predislovie" [Foreword], "Kommentarii k glavam 1–3" [Comments to Chapters 1–3], and "Posleslovie" [Afterword]. In Dmitri Bystrolyotov, "Fragmenty biografii razvedchika pervogo pokoleniia" [Fragments of a Biography of an Intelligence Operative of the First Generation]. Unpublished texts, Moscow, 2000, 3–6; 594–99.

———. "Slovo o Dmitrii Bystrolyotove." Preface to *Puteshestvie na krai nochi* [Journey to the Edge of Night], by Dmitri Bystrolyotov. Moscow: Sovremennik, 1996.

Mlechin, Leonid. *Istoriia vneshnei razvedki: Kar'ery i sud'by* [History of Foreign Intelligence: Careers and Fates]. Moscow: Tsentrpoligraf, 2008.

Papchinsky, A. A., and M. A. Tumshis. *Shchit, raskolotyi mechom. NKVD protiv VChK* [A Shield Cracked by a Sword: The NKVD Against the VChK]. Moscow: Sovremennik, 2001.

Pivovar, E., et al. *Russkaia emigratsiia v Turtsii, iugo-vostochnoi i tsentral'noi Evrope (grazhdanskie bezhentsy, armiia i obrazovatel'nye uchrezhdeniia)* [Russian Emigration in Turkey, Southeastern and Central Europe (Civilian Refugees, Army, and Educational Institutions)]. Moscow: State Historical and Archival Institute, 1994.

Poretskaia, E. K. *Nashi. Vospominaniia ob Ignatii Raisse i ego tovarishchakh* [Our Own People: A Memoir of Ignace Reiss and His Friends]. Moscow: Voenno-diplomaticheskaia akademiia, 1992.

Postnikov, S. P., comp. *Russkie v Prage: 1918–1928* [The Russians in Prague: 1918–1928]. Prague: Postnikov, 1930.

Primakov, E., ed. *Ocherki istorii rossiiskoi razvedki* [Essays on the History of Russian Foreign Intelligence]. Vols. 2, 3. Moscow: Mezhdunarodnye otnosheniia, 1997.

Razumov, A. Ya. "Rukopis' D. Bystrolyotova 'Pir Bessmertnykh'" [Bystrolyotov's Manuscript "Feast of the Immortals"]. In *Istochnikovedcheskoe izuchenie pamiatnikov pis'mennoi kul'tury* [Study of the Original Sources of Memorials of Written Culture], comp. L. I. Buchina and Iu. M. Liubimova, ed. N. A. Efimova and I. G. Kravtsova. St. Petersburg, 1994, 109–37.

Russkaia voennaia emigratsiia dvadtsatykh–sorokovykh godov: Dokumenty i materially [Russian Military Emigration in the 1920s Through 1940s: Documents and Materials]. Moscow: Geya, 1998.

Slobodskoi, A. *Sredi emigratsii: Moi vospominaniia: Kiev i Konstantinopl', 1918–1920.* [In the Midst of Emigration: My Recollections; Kiev and Constantinople, 1918–1920]. Kharkov: Proletarii, 1925.

Snegirev, V. "Drugaia zhizn' Dmitriia Bystroletova" [The Other Life of Dmitri Bystrolyotov]. *Pravda*, February 25 and March 4, 1990. Also published in *Po dannym razvedki* [According to Intelligence Service Data]. Moscow: Sovremennik, 1991.

Stavitsky, V., ed. *Spetssluzhby i chelovecheskie sud'by* [Special Services and Human Fates]. Moscow: OLMA-Press, 2000.

———. *Tainye stranitsy istorii* [Secret Pages of History]. Moscow: ZAO "LG Informeishn grup," 2000.

Svetozarov, E. *Russkaia gimnaziia v Moravskoi Trzhebove* [Russian Gymnasium in Moravska Trebova]. Prague, 1930.

Tsarev, Oleg, and Nigel West. *KGB v Anglii* [The KGB in England]. Moscow: Tsentrpoligraf, 1999.

Filmography

Chelovek v shtatskom [The Plainclothesman]. Directed by V. Zhuravlyov. Mosfilm, 1973. 103 min.

Razvedka, o kotoroi znali nemnogie. Dmitrii Bystrolyotov: Okhota za shiframi [Foreign Intelligence Not Known to Many: Dmitri Bystrolyotov; Hunting for Ciphers] (TV channel Kul'tura). Directed by Aleksei Gorovatsky, produced by Gold Medium, 2001.

Serebrianaia roza [A Silver Rose]. Directed by Aleksei Pankov, produced by TVTs, 2006. 42 min.

Maski nelegala [An Illegal's Masks]. Produced by TVTs, 2008. 35 min.

Secondary Sources in English and Other Languages

Andrew, Christopher, and Oleg Gordievsky. *KGB: The Inside Story of Its Foreign Operations from Lenin to Gorbachev.* London: Sceptre, 1991.

Andrew, Christopher, and Vassili Mitrokhin. *Mitrokhin Archive II: The KGB and the World.* London: Lane, 2005.

———. *The Sword and the Shield: The Mitrokhin Archive and the Secret History of the KGB.* New York: Basic Books, 1999.

Andreyev, Catherine, and Ivan Savicky. *Russia Abroad: Prague and the Russian Diaspora, 1918–1938.* New Haven, Conn.: Yale University Press, 2004.

Applebaum, Anne. *Gulag: A History.* New York: Doubleday, 2003.

Bessedovsky, Gregori. *Revelations of a Soviet Diplomat.* London: Williams & Norgate, 1931 [abridged English translation of the Russian edition *Na putiakh k Termidoru* (On the Way to Thermidor) (Paris, 1930)].

Brook-Shepherd, Gordon. *The Storm Petrels: The Flight of the First Soviet Defectors.* New York: Ballantine Books, 1977.

Conquest, Robert. *The Great Terror: A Reassessment.* New York: Oxford University Press, 1990.

———. *The Harvest of Sorrow: Soviet Collectivization and the Terror-Famine.* New York: Oxford University Press, 1986.

———. *Inside Stalin's Secret Police: NKVD Politics 1936–39.* Stanford, Calif.: Hoover Press, 1985.

———. *Kolyma: The Arctic Death Camps.* New York: Oxford University Press, 1980.

Cornelissen, Igor. *De GPOe op de Overtoom: Spionnen voor Moscou 1920–1940* [The GPU on the Overtoom: Spies for Moscow, 1920–1940]. Amsterdam: Van Gennep, 1989.

Corson, William, and Robert P. Crowley. *The New KGB: Engine of Soviet Power.* New York: Morrow, 1986.

Costello, John, and Oleg Tsarev. *Deadly Illusions.* New York: Crown, 1993.

Crossman, John, ed. *The God That Failed.* New York: Bantam, 1952.

Duff, William. *A Time for Spies: Theodore Stephanovich Mally and the Era of the Great Illegals.* Nashville, Tenn.: Vanderbilt University Press, 1999.

Dziak, John J. *Chekisty: A History of the KGB.* Lexington, Mass.: Heath, 1988.

Faligot, R., and P. Krop. "Du cas Michel Simon à l'affaire Fernandel" [The Case of Michel Simon in the Fernandel Affair]. *L'Evénement du jeudi,* January 28–February 3, 1993, 16–17.

Jansen, Marc, and Nikita Petrov. *Stalin's Loyal Executioner: People's Commissar Nikolai Ezhov, 1895–1940.* Stanford, Calif.: Hoover Press, 2002.

Kern, Gary. *A Death in Washington: Walter G. Krivitsky and the Stalin Terror.* New York: Enigma, 2003.

———, ed. *Walter G. Krivitsky: MI5 Debriefing and Other Documents on Soviet Intelligence.* Riverside, Calif.: Xenos Books, 2004.

Orlov, Alexander. *Handbook of Intelligence and Guerrilla Warfare.* Ann Arbor: University of Michigan Press, 1963.

———. *The Secret History of Stalin's Crimes.* New York: Random House, 1953.

Philby, Kim. *My Silent War.* New York: Ballantine Books, 1983.

Poretsky, Elizabeth K. *Our Own People: A Memoir of "Ignace Reiss" and His Friends.* Ann Arbor: University of Michigan Press, 1970.

Pringle, Robert W., ed. *Historical Dictionary of Russian and Soviet Intelligence.* Lanham, Md.: Scarecrow Press, 2006.

Rossi, Jacques. *The Gulag Handbook.* New York: Paragon House, 1989.

Solow, Herbert. "Stalin's Passport Mill." *American Mercury,* July 1939, 302–9.

Solzhenitsyn, Aleksandr. *The Gulag Archipelago: Volume 1.* New York: Harper & Row, 1973.

———. *The Gulag Archipelago: Volume 2.* New York: Harper & Row, 1974.

Sudoplatov, Pavel, and Anatoli Sudoplatov, with Jerrold L. and Leona P. Schecter. *Special Tasks: The Memoirs of an Unwanted Witness; A Soviet Spymaster.* New York: Little, Brown, 1994.

Thurlow, Richard C. "Soviet Spies and British Counter-Intelligence in the 1930s: Espionage in the Woolwich Arsenal and the Foreign Office Communications Department." *Intelligence and National Security* 19, no. 4 (December 2004): 610–31.

Weinstein, Allen, and Alexander Vassiliev. *The Haunted Wood: Soviet Espionage in America; The Stalin Era.* New York: Random House, 1999.

West, Nigel. *Historical Dictionary of Sexspionage.* Lanham, Md.: Scarecrow Press, 2009.

———. *MI5: British Security Service Operations, 1909–1945.* New York: Stein and Day, 1982.

West, Nigel, and Oleg Tsarev. *The Crown Jewels: The British Secrets at the Heart of the KGB Archives.* New Haven, Conn.: Yale University Press, 1999.

Index

Emil Draitser is an award-winning author of fiction and nonfiction. Originally a freelance journalist in the Soviet Union, where his work appeared in the leading periodicals *Izvestiya, Youth, Literary Gazette,* and *Crocodile* under the pen name "Emil Abramov," he was blacklisted for a satirical article. In 1974, he immigrated to the United States, where he has been a professor of Russian at Hunter College in New York City since 1986. In addition to his twelve previous books, Draitser has published essays and short stories in the *Los Angeles Times, Partisan Review, North American Review, Prism International,* and many other American and Canadian periodicals. His fiction has also appeared in Russian, Polish, Ukrainian, Belarusian, and Israeli journals. His most recent book is *Shush! Growing Up Jewish Under Stalin: A Memoir.*

Gary Kern has published numerous articles and books on Russian literature and history, including *A Death in Washington: Walter G. Krivitsky and the Stalin Terror* and *The Kravchenko Case: One Man's War on Stalin.*